CREATING
NEW VENTURES

HOW TO SHAPE CONCEPTS
INTO ACHIEVEMENT

CREATING
NEW VENTURES

HOW TO SHAPE CONCEPTS
INTO ACHIEVEMENT

WRITTEN BY
156 Amazing Members of the
CSUF Entrepreneurship Community

PRODUCED BY
Michael D. Ames

DIRECTED BY
John Bradley Jackson

EDITED BY
Linda L. Ames

Pathways to Success Press
Newport Beach, California

Published by
Pathways to Success Press
1 Rue Cannes
Newport Beach, California
(949) 689-0275

ISBN 978-0-692-07223-3

Preface

We are all very fortunate to live in the United States of America. This country, with all its faults, remains the best place in the world to start and own a business. Nearly every major company we all know and depend on in our daily lives was started, here, in the USA by creative, bold, energetic, enthusiastic ENTREPRENEURS. It is the spirit of entrepreneurship that drives us all, inspiring us to believe that we can build the next mega business and change the world!

The Center for Entrepreneurship at California State College Fullerton has been, is, and will be the portal for thousands of students with a dream to become business owners and make those dreams real. At CSUF we learn, practice, experiment, test, and present our ideas to whomever will listen. We are urged to dream and create without limitation. There are no bad ideas, only ideas that have never had the chance to be heard.

As entrepreneurs it is our common mission to promote and encourage creativity and productivity to those around us, especially the next generation of students on their way to college. We must set the right example for them to follow and give them something to aspire to. As you read this,

ask yourself "What inspired me to attend college, who encouraged me and showed me the way?" I am certain that your answer included "a special person in my life", or "I was told I could do anything I could imagine", or "I want to be just like him/her."

Let's continue the legacy of our school, our families, and our nation and CREATE NEW VENTURES. It is our purpose, it is why we are in America, it is what we are meant to do, and nobody does it better than the Titans!

Bill Taormina

William C. "Bill" Taormina
CEO and Founder
Clean City, Inc.
Anaheim, California

Bill Taormina has been an Anaheim stakeholder and community activist for over sixty years. He is a major property owner in Anaheim. He went to high school in Anaheim at Katella High School where he was student body president in 1969. After attending college out of state and earning his MBA, he returned to Anaheim.

Bill was the cofounder of Anaheim Disposal and CVT Recycling Center. He is the founder of the Anaheim Union High School Foundation. He is also a charter participant in the Anaheim PACE Academy and a charter member of the Anaheim Police Chief's Advisory Board.

Bill and his entrepreneurial family members have been CSUF student consulting clients many times. Their strong support has launched several CSUF Entrepreneurship graduates.

Acknowledgments

Starting a project like this is tough. At first, all one has is a worthwhile concept. There are no list of authors, no example letters and no endorsements. Special thanks must go to the five pioneers who responded to our first request for letters: Fritz von Coelln, Bob Godlasky, Oli Thordarson, Michael Sawitz, Nicole Washington and Deborah Ferber.

CSUF Entrepreneurship is a collection of high impact classes and outreach programs that advance free enterprise. It relies on many qualified volunteers who have "been at the sharp end" and have "seen the elephant." They tackle tasks ranging from guest speaking to coaching, mentoring and becoming an entrepreneur in residence.

In our early years (in the late1970's and early 1980's) we did not realize the enormous value of volunteers. They add much to a college entrepreneurship program. Their full worth far exceeds the benefits that students receive from occasional guest speakers.

W. Todd McKnight gave us our wake-up call. He had sold his consumer electronics company. Todd was wealthy enough to retire and under age thirty. One day he rolled his wheel chair into our office and volunteered to be an "entrepreneur in residence." He explained what he meant and we tried his idea. Todd helped us hammer out the essential details of how to effectively use volunteers in high impact entrepreneurship programs. Thanks Todd.

Since Todd's first visit, many hundreds of volunteers have helped guide our students and serve the community. Looking back, one volunteer organization stands out as a stellar source of volunteers.

The SCORE Association's Orange County chapter. It is one of the largest and most productive chapters in the national SCORE Association. It has over 100 volunteer members who are business mentors. All are seasoned business people. Bill Moreland, from the Orange County chapter, wrote a letter for this book. He is Western Regional Vice President of SCORE covering the states of Arizona, Nevada, Utah, California and Hawaii. Mike Edwards also wrote for this book. He is the current chair of the chapter.

Read their Letters to learn more about one of the best SCORE chapters in the nation. Many other past and present SCORE members wrote letters for this book.

One pivotal example of SCORE's support of CSUF Entrepreneurship dates to 2002 when we launched the new entrepreneurship major and minor. We had a big spike in our need for classroom mentors and we asked SCORE for help. Fifteen SCORE members signed up.

Thank you SCORE, and thank you to the fifteen. They are Jim Chamberlain, Bonnie Copeland, Bob Cryer, Bill Gobbell, Howard Hawkins, John "Jack" James, Stan Lewczyk, Angela Liu, Alan Mannason (in this book), Jack McSunas, Bill Moreland (in this book), Chuck Perry, Byron Romig, Barbara Samara and Fred Stern.

Lastly, we thank our Advisory Board, and the many student consulting clients, donors and friends who help us advance. CSUF Entrepreneurship strives to be self-sufficient as we serve more students and increase community outreach. Our Advisory Board members deserve special recognition. They provide both wisdom and finance to help us advance free enterprise. The next page lists our board members.

Entrepreneurship Advisory Board

Current Members

Dr. Michael Ames, Chair, Mihaylo College
Dan Black '67, Entrepreneur & Philanthropist
Andrew Carroll '06, CFO Andrew
Karl Freels '17, Black Family Foundation
Ken Guchereau '74, Guchereau Company
Robert Jechart, RJE International
Raj Manek '94, Vesuki Inc.
David Morris, Royal Business Bank
Jeffrey S. Van Harte '80, Jackson Square Partners

Member Emeriti

Wally Hicks, Affluent Target Marketing Inc.
Kristen Llorente, Llorente SIU
Alan Mannason, SCORE
Laurie Resnick, '77, Associated Group
Michael Sawitz, FastStart.studio
Ron Stein, PTS Staffing Solutions
Art P. Villa, Breakthrough Business Solutions, Inc.

Table of Contents

Introduction

This timely book offers you insights about creating new ventures. We have designed this book to be a gift. That is what its one hundred and fifty-six co-creators had in mind when they wrote to you as a future founder. This design, this express intent, is what gives the book its power. The words from these special people will make a difference in your life. They are the words of people who care about your future and know what you must go through to move ahead. They offer you respect, understanding, inspiration and guidance.

California State University Fullerton's vibrant community of entrepreneurs connects all the co-creators in some way. They are founders, executives and advisors who know what really counts when it comes to launching new ventures. They identify and explain factors, values and qualities that will be most important to your effectiveness as a founder. None of their one-page letters is a scholarly thesis or a sermon. All articulate what works for the writer and provides practical examples.

The one hundred and fifty-six co-creators of this book are your "connections." Their letters radiate positive energy and give you advice that will help you succeed. We challenge you to tap this energy and use the advice to improve your new ventures.

The goal, topic and layout of this book

You will find that the letters in this book stay on point. Each writer in this book received a contributor's guide. It set the goal and the topic. Specifically, "Your **goal** is to create a relevant business letter about creating new ventures for aspiring founders. The best letter will be read often and will provide

inspiration and guidance. The wording will be simple. It will be candid and will cause new founders to think about what really counts when it comes to launching their ventures. The letter will not be a scholarly thesis or a sermon. It will articulate what you know works for you. **Topic:** Identify and explain up to three factors, values, or qualities' most important to your effectiveness as a founder, executive or advisor. Include practical examples (very helpful)."

Similarly, each author received specific **layout** instructions. The contributions in Creating New Ventures will be laid out on two pages in a simple face-to-face format. For each two-page set, the author's one-page letter is the star of the show. It appears on the right. It will be accompanied (on the left) by the author's photograph, a short biographical sketch and a brief description of his/her venture(s)' accomplishments.

In brief, each co-creator's two-page set is a complete story. You can browse through the book in any order you wish. No matter where you open the book, you can explore the writer's insights and read about the writer's background.

The book presents the co-creator's letters in alphabetical order by their last name. The table of contents gives both the writer's name and the title of their facing page. By in large the title is descriptive. You can browse for an interesting title and then turn directly to the page number given to read the two-page set.

Enjoy exploring the book!

The Letters

Rose and Friends

Rose Agracewicz founded Rose & Friends. It is a private, housecall dog grooming service that offers one-on-one grooming in the comfort of each pet's home.

In many ways, Rose's work history is typical of California State University Fullerton students. They are not strangers to hard work. She began working at age 16 as a restaurant hostess and cashier. She soon moved on to assisting the owner of Lane Storage Products where she maintained financial records and receipts, trained the owner how to use computer programs and managed accounts receivable, accounts payable. At the same time, she began her studies at California State University Fullerton. Soon Rose added a second, front end supervision job to her plate while continuing her college course work. As she advanced toward her upper division college classes, she became a server at The Old Spaghetti Factory. Rose received the Governor's Scholarship and Steve Keller Memorial Scholarship and graduated with Dean's List status in 2010. By the time she graduated with her BBA in Entrepreneurship, Rose also had an established work ethic.

After graduation, Rose gained broad experience including restaurant operations, golf course management, event coordination, and more. In 2015, she began thinking about founding a business she could be passionate about. Rose is a lifelong animal lover, growing up with dogs and horses. She decided to follow her passion and take a position as a mobile pet groomer. She quickly saw opportunity.

Her entrepreneurial vision -- more pets, fewer people. In 2016 she launched her first entrepreneurial endeavor -- Rose & Friends In-Home Pet Care. It focuses on minimizing fear, building trust, and providing full transparency for the owners. It uniquely caters to senior dogs and anxious pets who struggle in traditional shop or vet atmospheres. It is currently in its second year of business, has exceeded capacity for clientele and is booming with opportunity for future growth. It has fully employed its owner, earned the organic growth of a 5-star Yelp page, acquired a year-long product sponsorship by a top industry company, and received numerous inquiries for employment opportunities. Mission accomplished.

Rose and Friend -- The Mary S. Roberts Pet Adoption Center in Riverside asked Rose if she would groom some of their shelter dogs. This is Scarlet the Husky right after her bath and deshedding treatment, feeling amazing and ready to find her forever home. She was rescued by MSRPAC from another local kill-shelter, so her age and background are unknown, but as you can see she was just waiting to give her love to someone and was adopted soon after this photo was taken.

Rose & Friends
in♥home pet grooming

Dear Founder,

My challenge for you is to consider happiness as valuable as income. Lack of passion is debilitating for people like us... Passion in what you do is the self-ignited flame that will make the journey worth the work. We are wired for so much more than money.

If you are reading this, I do not doubt that you will find success. You are already on your way by choosing to be here. I do not doubt the knowledge and experience you will acquire during your time studying, or that you will achieve status, pursue greatness, and earn a proud income. I do however, doubt that will be enough.

When I graduated from the California State University, Fullerton Business Administration Entrepreneurship program, I found myself with a fire lit inside. I was confident, and I was excited. I built an impressive resume. I held a variety of positions. I gained more knowledge, titles, experience, pride, and money. I achieved. And my flame dimmed to a bitter flicker.

My mistake was choosing work because I was good at it, and not because it was good for me.

I chose to slow down and regroup, and when I found the courage to pursue passion, I grew. When I didn't settle and began to imagine more, I happened upon the opportunity that has become my new life. When my excitement returned and my fire became self-fueled, I found true success.

Simon Sinek: "Working hard for something we don't care about is called stress. Working hard for something we love is called passion."
Vera Wang: "When you have a passion for something then you tend not only to be better at it, but you work harder at it too."
Bob Dylan: "What's money? A man is a success if he gets up in the morning and goes to bed at night and in between does what he wants to do."
Steve Jobs: "The only way to do great work is to love what you do. If you haven't found it yet, keep looking and don't settle."

I challenge you to consider happiness as valuable as income. Place a price on your spirit and never discount its worth. It is expected that we will achieve, strive, and earn... but you must want more.

Wise Meme: "Do what you love and you will never have a problem with Mondays."
That's what it is all about.

Now go hug your dog and have a good day.

Rose Agracewicz

THRIVE

Karla Amador is a serial entrepreneur and the CEO of THRIVE. THRIVE is a cloud based bookkeeping and consulting firm that specializes in Quickbooks. It manages accounting duties for small to large businesses and wealthy individuals. (www.thrivefinancials.com)

While working on her own ventures, and doing some consulting work, Karla found that many business owners had little time to run their business and keep their accounting in order. Thus THRIVE was born.

Karla loves educating business owners on the importance of having their finances in order. She especially enjoys consulting, setting clients up on QuickBooks, and looking for ways to maximize profits.

Karla holds a BA from California State University Fullerton in Communications and a minor in Business. Karla has been named "30 under 40: Future Leaders in Special Events" by Special Events Magazine and has been quoted in "MSN Money" and "She Knows." She has pitched at the "California Women's Conference, Dolphin Tank," and "Tech Cocktails." She has spoken at "Startup Weekend," "Women 2.0" and the "National Association for Female Executives (NAFE)."

When she's not working on books you can find her climbing the local mountains, volunteering, traveling, cooking or spending time with her family and friends.

Karla is passionate about helping others achieve their dreams. She is committed to both her clients and and her community. THRIVE sets aside a portion of sales for a scholarship for a deserving individual. The "THRIVE Financial & Bookkeeping Services Entrepreneurial Scholarship" is offered to students at California State University Fullerton.

Karla co-founded the 52 Hike Challenge ("52"). It is a global movement empowering thousands of people around the world to get outdoors to gain the physical, mental and spiritual benefits gained through hiking. Since 52's launch in December of 2014, thousands have joined the challenge and changed their own lives. Together, with their community, 52 has created a culture of support for each other. Over 400,000 images have been shared under their hashtags on Instagram alone. (#52HikeChallenge and #52HikeChallenge2016/2017/2018)

THRIVE
Financial & Bookkeeping Services

Dear Aspiring Founder,

My name is Karla Amador. I have started five companies now, two have been successful.
I've always known I was an entrepreneur at heart because I did not want to work for anyone else.
Below are some of the lessons I have learned that have allowed me to get to where I am today.
Remember there is no right or wrong way to be an entrepreneur as long as you keep getting back
up when you fall down (or you think you've failed.) Here are some keys to success that have
helped me along the way:

1. The first phase is planning and executing. It is my belief that in order to be successful,
   you must create goals / milestones with deadlines then work your way through them. You
   should check on your progress weekly, and no less than monthly. For example, if it is
   your goal to write a book, you should start with an outline, then topics to be discussed
   with due dates by each section and a final due date for the entire project. Check on your
   progress weekly to keep you accountable and on track.

2. Next, you must create processes and procedures so you can delegate and grow your
   business. Create systems that help you. In my case I use online applications that help me
   track employee time and allow me to bill clients for their work quickly. You also want to
   have an idea of how long tasks should take, so you can measure employee performance.

3. Be a person of your word and follow through. Do your best work, as your clients become
   your referrers. Solve problems quickly, follow your gut, and don't forget to hire people
   who are experts at what you are not.

4. Lastly, be passionate about your work – after all you will most likely spend many more
   hours than a traditional 9 to 5.

Sincerely,

Karla Amador

Karla Amador

Passionate About Free Enterprise

Michael "Mike" Ames founded the multidisciplinary entrepreneurship programs in the Mihaylo College of Business and Economics. He is Professor of Management Emeritus. Since retirement, Mike has served as the volunteer Chairman of the Board for Mihaylo's Center for Entrepreneurship. He is an active volunteer for CSUF Entrepreneurship projects.

Mike is a member of the Angel Capital Association. He is one of the founders of Titan Angeles LLC, a seed-stage investment fund. While unaffiliated with CSUF, the founders of the fund have ties with CSUF. The fund seeks to invest in startups connected to CSUF.

Mike's personal mission is to advance free enterprise. A strong advocate of principled entrepreneurship and a pipeline approach to startup development, he has helped thousands of business school faculty, students and entrepreneurs to develop their leadership potential, serve their community, build successful enterprises, and become the best that they are capable of becoming. The Freedoms Foundation at Valley Forge awarded Mike the Leavey Award for Excellence in Private Enterprise Education. The Small Business Institute Directors Association named Mike a Fellow in 2000 in recognition of his demonstrated commitment to service for the small businesses of America.

During Mike's tenure, he and faculty experts supervised thousands of undergraduate and MBA students who provided in-depth consulting to over eleven hundred business owners. Coached by seasoned entrepreneurs, rxperienced business people and alumni, hundreds of students enrolled in entrepreneurship classes, created new ventures, found funding, and launched their start-ups. To this day, the programs he founded continue to flourish. Mike says, "CSUF is the perfect place for high impact programs like student consulting. Student consulting teams learn the realities of entrepreneurship by applying what they learn in class to help small business clients succeed. The regional economic impact is tremendous."

Mike swims for exercise and enjoys the chatter at the pool (aka, "the village well"). He is passionate about learning more about the world around him. He observes and synthesizes, often exploring new concepts in his writing and poetry.

Mike is a husband to his high school sweetheart Linda, father to Regina and "Papa" to his two grandsons, Jameson and Solomon. Linda and Mike are members of the CSUF branch of the Osher Life Long Learning Institute ("OLLI").

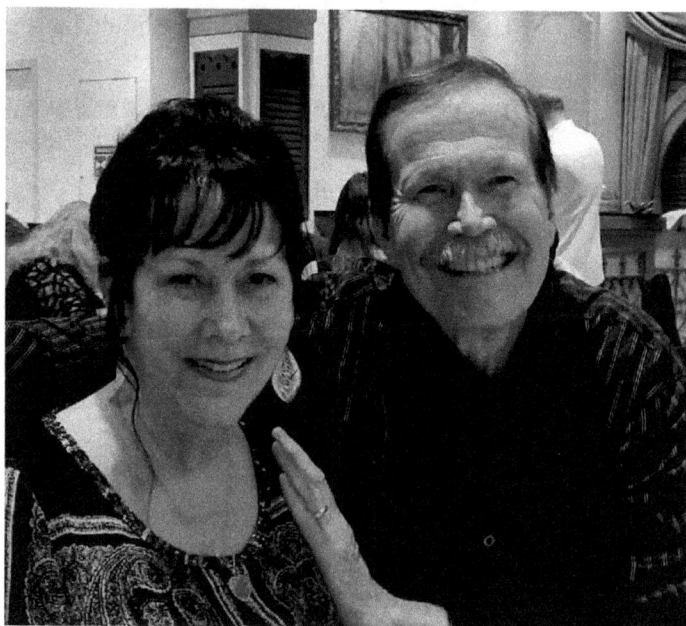

Linda and Mike celebrating their 51st anniversary on a cruise with their family

Michael D. Ames
Newport Beach, CA. 92660

Dear Founder,

I am the founder of the Entrepreneurship program at CSUF. My passion is advancing free enterprise. My core belief is that new venture creation by entrepreneurs is how our land of opportunity opens its doors. It is how our economic growth pedal hits the metal. When I join a cause, I educate. If you go where I educate, you will see three posters hanging on the wall. You may view them on the walls of the CSUF Startup Incubator. The three posters depict three success building blocks that I consider most important.

For me, every success story has three ingredients. The first is the passion that drives you forward. The second is a framework that channels energy and guides it toward your goal. The third factor is doing what you have to do to make good things happen.

1. Passion makes success possible. In my view, success is a mix of three ingredients: a sense of achievement, self respect about how you did it and the respect of others. Understand one thing. Only you will ever know if you are successful. If you do not wholeheartedly pursue your passion, deep down inside you will never consider yourself successful. The first poster on the wall describes the fifteen guiding principles of CSUF Entrepreneurship. It speaks to what makes success possible.

2. Build a framework that channels (and conserves) energy. Classic board games like Chess, Go, and Monopoly are frameworks. They provide simple rules and inject elements of chance. Winning is not easy. Play is challenging and it focuses the energy of players and spectators on the field of play. Even master players will lose if something distracts them or they lose the will to win. Business models, budgets, and flow charts are frameworks. They channel the energy of stakeholders in fruitful directions and reduce waste. The second poster on the wall is a flow chart. It depicts how CSUF Entrepreneurship works.

3. Do what you have to do to make good things happen. As founder, you must quickly climb a tall, rickety ladder of authority and responsibility. Initially, you call all the shots and are responsible for success or failure. Your job is to master your game. However, very soon growth will stall unless you build a team and serve as team captain. Players have the authority to play their assigned roles. You will remain responsible for success or failure. Ultimately, and sooner than you think, you will be challenged to build a championship team. You will have to become a head coach, rather than a player or a team captain. You will remain responsible for success or failure. My hero in this regard is John Wooden. His pyramid of success is the third poster on the wall. It depicts what you must instill in your organization to build a championship team.

Success is a choice. If you want it, make it happen.

Michael D. Ames

Michael D. Ames, Founder
CSUF Entrepreneurship

CSuite Financial Partners

Kelly Anderson is a California Certified Public Accountant. She is a partner in CSuite Financial Partners ("CFP"). CFP is a rapidly growing national, financial executive services firm. It provides financial management leadership to companies in every industry, regardless of size, throughout the United States.

Kelly began her career in public accounting performing audit work for closely-held companies. She soon transitioned into industry where she took on leadership roles in the controllership of private and public companies. She picked up crucial experience in SEC reporting, acquisition accounting, and merger integrations. This preparation set her up for further success in her Chief Financial and Accounting roles to come.

As Kelly's career progressed, she rose to take on senior executive and c-level positions in accounting and finance. Her CFO and CAO positions allowed her the opportunity to have game-changing impact on those companies. Examples of Kelly's accomplishments include, successfully completing SEC registration statements, completing and integrating hundreds of mergers, and raising capital through debt and equity financing deals.

Kelly's expertise has helped her to consistently increase shareholder value and liquidity. Throughout Kelly's career she has held leadership roles with responsibility for revenues ranging from $5M to $8B.

Today, Kelly is part of a strong team at CFP. Her Partners and executive-level resources are CPAs and MBAs who have served on the front lines. On average, they possess twenty-five years of senior-level strategic and operational experience. The team works closely with their clients to develop plans to address their specific needs.

One of CFP's strengths is the flexibility to engage its CFOs and financial professionals on an interim, project or search basis. This flexibility allows CFP to meet its clients' demands in the most efficient way possible.

As a CFP Financial Partner, Kelly continues to deliver extraordinary results. Leading clients through a myriad of engagements, she helps clients drastically improve their operations and maximize value in their organizations. Kelly has held many board positions, including audit, compensation, nomination and governance chair positions.

Kelly is a 1989 graduate of CSUF. She has routinely served as a mentor for CSUF entrepreneurship.

CSUITE

Dear Founder,

Hindsight is 20/20 – what most entrepreneur's wish they would have done differently.

Being an entrepreneur requires many diverse skills. The most successful entrepreneur's understand their strengths and weaknesses and are continually looking to partner with experts to help them with their success. The most successful entrepreneurs do what they do best and not only bring in trusted experts to support them, but empower them to make the decisions needed to support the entrepreneur.

It is critical you understand the importance of partnering with a financial expert from the beginning of your venture. Many entrepreneurs make the mistake of viewing financial expertise as a luxury cost center that brings little or no value. This is the fundamental mistake that most entrepreneurs make.

A strong financial partner will help you mold and shape your business, further, they can be the strongest partner you have, as they are one of the few disciplines that understand an entire business process. By leveraging your financial power, you will be free to do what you do best, develop, innovate and run your business.

A financial partner can be an asset when procuring financing, including both debt and equity. In both instances, your banker and investors will feel more confident in investing in you and your vision when it's clear that there is financial discipline and accountability. Further, your financial partner brings creditability to your projections, market research and cost structure.

Your financial partner can also be very helpful in identifying economies of scale and assist you with your ROI and breakeven analysis. By having a true understanding of your investments and costs, including accurate budgeting and forecasting, you can confidently manage the resources required to grow and run your business. You will have the trust that you have a partner managing the most important aspect of your business – Capital!!

Finally, your financial partner is a great resource to help you with compliance. As we know, there are many different compliance areas that an entrepreneur needs to address, from business license, taxes, payroll, HR, supply chain agreement/negotiations, facilities and finally, investor and banking covenant compliance.

I have worked with numerous entrepreneurs and have continually found that the ones that invest in the financial partnership (both monetarily and philosophically) are some of the most successful entrepreneurs. They prove over and over again to their bankers and investors, that they have the plan and oversight to manage their assets and further, have the trusted partner to help negotiate when times are tough.

As you move into your venture, I wish you the best of luck in working with your expert partners, your venture can be very rewarding and fun when it all comes together, however, rarely does it happen without determination.

Sincerely,

Kelly Anderson
Partner, CSuite Financial Partners.

Revolution Farm

Chad Armstrong is the founder of Revolution Farm. The company's mission is food independence. Not off-the-grid independence but the confidence that anyone, urban or rural, homeowner or apartment dweller, can grow some of their own food. The mission of Revolution Farms reflects Chad's background and beliefs.

Chad proudly served 9 years in the Marine Corps and did 3 tours in Iraq. Chad advanced to the rank of Sargent. He earned 17 ribbons, medals, and commendations including a Navy Unit Commendation and a Navy and Marine Corps Achievement Medal. He recalls, "I was in boot camp on 9/11. I didn't know what the Marine Corps was when I was a kid but from the moment the barracks in Beirut were bombed, the Corps has represented the best of America. To me, honor, courage, and commitment aren't slogans, they're the standards I judge myself against."

Chad met his wife just prior to his last deployment. She is a probation officer for Orange County. When his contract was up, he moved to California and they were married. Then he began Saddleback Community College and set up Brain Bucket Marketing, an affiliate marketing company ("Brain bucket" is a Marine Corps term for a helmet.) To earn additional income he worked at Consumer Credit Counseling Service of Orange County and H&R Block.

After Chad earned his AA degree, he transferred to California State University Fullerton. He concentrated in Marketing and completed several Entrepreneurship courses. At CSUF he tutored at the University Learning Center and was involved in the Entrepreneur Society, Student Alumni Ambassadors, Committee for Environmental Sustainability, Beta Gamma Sigma and Phi Kappa Phi. While in college Chad volunteered for the United Way as a volunteer income tax preparer for low income families. He also volunteered at the Coast to Coast Foundation a homeless outreach organization based in Fullerton. In his spare time, Chad also took up regenerative farming as a hobby. He says, "CSUF was challenging. With the support of my family and friends, I rose to the challenge, I'm proud of my school and my work there. Why am I proud of Cal State Fullerton? To me, CSUF represents the American Dream. It doesn't matter who you are or where you came from, if you work hard and give it your all, you can create a better life for yourself here. Our campus is diverse and mostly first-generation college students. I could have chosen any school in Orange County, I'm grateful I chose CSUF."

In 2017, Chad graduated Magna Cum Laude from CSUF. Upon graduation, he pivoted Brain Bucket Marketing. It now helps other small business owners. Recently his wife and he purchased an acre of land in Jurupa Valley, CA. They are turning it into the home base for Revolution Farm.

Dear Founder,

Take action. It's the most effective thing you can do.

It's not always easy.

Entrepreneurs are resource constrained. Never enough time. Never enough money.

It's intimidating to spend scarce resources on a mistake. Yet, mistakes are necessary. Mistakes move us forward.

There are different kinds of mistakes. Mistakes that allow us to fight another day are acceptable. Fatal mistakes are not.

Take action, even an action that is probably going to be a mistake, even an action you KNOW is going to be a mistake. It will move you forward and teach you something you didn't know. Often, our real problems (and opportunities) lie hidden from us. Taking action moves us to a place where we can see them.

Creating a business means creating something new. There is no map. Prepare as best you can but keep moving forward.

You don't know what you don't know. You must take action to find out.

This is where resources come into play. What are you going to do? Who are you going to call? What do you have in reserve when your plan doesn't go as planned?

A university education is a valuable resource. It introduces us to future partners, mentors, and best of all, to parts of ourselves we didn't know existed.

But a formal education alone doesn't make an entrepreneur. Resources must be continually developed throughout your journey.

Resources won't protect you, they only increase the stakes. The more resources you accumulate, the bigger the mistakes you will make. That's a good thing. It shows that you're growing.

Welcome and encourage less-than-fatal mistakes. There will never be enough resources. Take action. Keep moving forward.

Sincerely,

Chad Armstrong

March Capital

Jim Armstrong is the Managing Director of March Capital Partners in Santa Monica, California. March Capital Partners is a venture capital firm. It has one of the largest funds in Southern California. Founded by industry veterans with over 50 years of investing experience, March Capital is unique in the Southern California market with its active investments in both early and late stage companies in mobile, enterprise, infrastructure, gaming and other growth industries.

Jim 's a successful and experienced early stage venture investor across a variety of enterprise and consumer facing technology companies. He has established himself as a leading investor based in Southern California.

Jim co-founded March Capital Partners in 2014. He has applied his experience and industry contacts to help companies deliver a strong record of venture performance.

Jim invests nationwide and focuses on information technology investments. His particular interests are consumer Internet, application software, and Internet enabled market places. On several occasions, Forbes Magazine has recognized Jim on its "Midas List" as one of the top Venture Capitalists in the United States.

In addition to co-founding March Capital Partners, Jim is Managing Director at Clearstone Venture Partners. He has been with the firm since 1998. He worked with Idealab, the incubator, in the late 90s and started his career at Austin Ventures in 1995.

Jim led Clearstone Venture Partners' current investments in SupplyFrame, Vast, and UserTesting and is on the board of two incubators -The Hive (big data) and The Fabric (cloud networking). He actively represented several of Clearstone Venture Partners' early stage, "pre-revenue," investments in former portfolio companies. Eight major examples include: PayPal (acquired by eBay as a public company), United Online (NASDAQ: UNTD), Internet Brands (NASDAQ:INET before being taken private), Integrien (acquired by VMWare), Jump Networks (acquired by Microsoft), Comet Systems (acquired by Miva), TriVida (acquired by BeFree) and Composite Software (acquired by Cisco). You can follow Jim's thoughts on market trends, investing, and venture capital on his blog www.jimarmstrong.vc, on his video series www.clearstone.com/jim and on twitter.

Jim earned an MBA in Entrepreneurship and IT from the University of Texas at Austin in 1996. He earned his B.A. degree in Economics from UCLA. He notes, " I worked 16 different jobs while an undergraduate student. Tiling houses, to fueling planes at the airport, to flipping burgers to selling formica kitchens on weekends, I would not trade that 'education' for anything."

Dear Founder,

After working in venture capital for more than two decades, I have noticed a few patterns and attributes among the founders I have had the privilege of working alongside. The first is that founders are special. Taking risk is the first step, and believing in yourself to make the effort is an exercise in self awareness and self confidence. There is honor and excitement in the creation of a new venture. The learning curve is vertical, and creates value all on its own. Here are some of the patterns I have noticed and pass along.

Good product matters and that should be the focus. Too often the lore of the startup ends up being the misdirection that misleads entrepreneurs. Yes, there is excitement around the launch of a company that is 'yours', the hiring of employees and the creation of a new brand. However, the quality and differentiation of the product must demand your focus always. Unfortunately, I see energetic and talented people toiling away for great lengths of time selling an undifferentiated product into a crowded market. If selling is very hard, you are doing it wrong. Peter Thiel is known for saying "competition is for losers." I was the first venture investor into Paypal, and when he and I worked together, we made many mistakes on the corporate level. However, despite all the mistakes we made, the product kept growing and finding a value proposition with users. It was easier to use and more secure than the other options available to early online sellers and buyers. This product growth gave the company options.

Check your ego and train yourself to become self aware. The minute you take any capital from outside investors or recruit anyone else's valuable career time to your effort, it is not about you any longer. It is about the Company and about the shareholder. Recruit the best people you can, when you can, to your effort – even at the CEO position. When I meet an entrepreneur raising capital in a first meeting, this is the trait I look for first and foremost, because without the ability to be objective about your company and focused on the shareholder, I don't believe you can create real value.

Be relentless on progress and culture. Progress because every week counts in the life of a startup and in the life of a person. Startups never go in a straight line, but they always keep moving and asking the tough questions. Sometimes progress is backing up. Progress is always about authentic conversations, and this must sometimes include the recognition that what you are doing or building is "not good enough." My experience has taught me that for a startup there is ALWAYS a way through to success if you can be honest and figure out the right questions to ask. Culture counts because honesty has to be part of the culture, as does professionalism, fun, camaraderie, debate and honest disagreement. Great cultures attract and retain talented people who ask honest questions and have a desire to win. I will invest on that every time.

Best of luck,

Jim Armstrong
Managing Director

An Entrepreneur at Heart

Richard Aronson, Entrepreneurship class of 2010, began his entrepreneurial journey in the halls of the Mihaylo College of Business and Economics. Enrolling in 2007, he learned the fundamentals of starting and running a business. Always enamored with the notion of bringing an idea to life, business models and concepts that have the potential to change the world fascinate Richard.

He feels fortunate to have gained entrepreneurial experience from the role of co-founder, consultant, and investor. In 2013, after working in the finance sector, a fellow entrepreneur approached him to start an online marketing business they coined, Sequoia SEO. It specialized in concentrated marketing campaigns using Search Engine Optimization. This relatively successful and modest venture led Richard to change course, return to school, and pursue other interests.

After attaining an MBA in 2015 and then a brief consultation with the global accelerator Echoing Green, he began

working as an Opportunity Analyst for Ryanna Capital (RC), a new private equity cleantech investment firm based in Washington State. Established in 2016, RC is an impact investment firm. The company's mission is to invest in the next generation of entrepreneurs. RC seeks to help them build great companies that make money, and a positive difference to our world. For early stage companies, RC seeks a proven product that customers are purchasing with verifiable revenue growth. Revenues typically range from $300K to $3 million, depending on the industry. Initially, RC will assess market opportunities with early stage ventures in the Pacific Northwest. It has plans for eventual expansion to Canada, the United Kingdom, Europe, and Australia.

At RC, Richard often works as the facilitator between investor and entrepreneur. His process often begins with the assessment of market trends related to the introduction of new technology that aligns with angel investor interests. Using this macro approach, he then assesses individual companies for their individual merit and potential in the marketplace.

RC offers more than capital to entre-preneurs. It offers decades of C-level, first-hand expertise in sales. Many companies face significant challenges with an inefficient sales process at different stages of growth greatly impacting the cash burn rate of invested capital.

Guiding and enabling other entrepreneurs to be successful in their own ventures has unfolded to be Richard's most rewarding pursuit yet. He derives enormous satisfaction helping others succeed while at the same time enhancing his own entrepreneurial skills.

Dear Founder,

When you look at the quotes and advice from many of the worlds' most renown entrepreneurs, certain themes emerge, such as: take risks, follow your passions, and don't be afraid to fail. While this is inspirational advice, it does not mean to be cavalier in making decisions. Nor does it mean you may ignore the obstacles you must overcome to succeed.

Quite the contrary, it means to succeed you must have a realistic appreciation of the obstacles in your path. In fact, studies show the entrepreneurs that succeed are more risk averse than their counterparts. At the outset, be sure to understand the common risks and hurdles of all start-up companies, particularly in your market at different stages of growth. Identify which ones apply most to you. Assess these hurdles, focus on how and why you can overcome them, and then strategically move with your best foot forward.

My job often is to act as facilitator between investor and entrepreneur. In my experience, building a successful enterprise comes down to two fundamental principles: understanding the customer's needs and understanding your organizations capabilities to fulfill those needs.

Know thyself, but know your customer better. While this may be taken out of context, it brings home the point that all companies must be obsessed with learning how to anticipate and satisfy customers' needs. Your most unhappy customers are your greatest source of learning and improvement.

Compare an in-depth competency gap analysis of your own organization with the needs of your target market. This does not require you to overanalyze your weaknesses, but rather to identify and monitor your strengths while making sure there is nothing within your organization that is debilitating enough to hinder you from doing what you do best. All this obsession and effort may go in vain if the organizations neglect the importance of goal setting, metrics, and tracking data. Without numbers, it is very difficult to confirm or dismiss assumptions you make about your customers, the competition, and your own company.

I always remind myself to operate where practicality and passion intertwine. The numbers need to make sense and it must resonate internally. Many aspiring entrepreneurs are dreamers (myself included), but the successful ones operate as pragmatic idealists. This requires emotional intelligence. It is where the heart and the mind meet.

Wishing You Success and Fulfillment,

x _____

Richard Aronson
Opportunity Analyst

Die-Hard Entrepreneur

Vas Arora did not start as an entrepreneur. He was a mechanical engineering graduate from the University of Wyoming. After university, he worked in Oil production and exploration with two large firms.

However, Vas felt that he had entrepreneurial instincts. They needed polishing. He used his industry experience to prepare himself for ownership responsibilities. As he recalls, being an assistant sales and service manager proved indispensable to his future success. Another plus was learning to work with and establishing domestic and international representatives.

Before he bought his first business, a plastic recycling business, Vas understood what he didn't know. He missed the marketing skills in the industry. Vas worked with the company for a year to learn more. After the purchase, he focused half his time on developing a good, sound purchasing network.

Vas also understood what he didn't have, sufficient capital to buy the company outright. He negotiated an exit strategy with the seller and closed the deal with a down payment and an agreement to make three installments. Vas recalls, "Yes, it was a risk. Nevertheless, it was also a negotiated strategy. It was clear what must be done. My motivation was at full strength and NO turning back was a fact."

In his letter, Vas does not write about reversals. He had his share. Medical reasons forced him to sell his booming plastic recycling business. Vas' gas station and food mart was one of his best investments. However, he was a

Franchisee and the oil company was the Franchiser. The oil company elected to shut the location down. Persevering, Vas pushed forward into real estate investments.

In retirement Vas volunteers, promoting entrepreneurship and sharing his entrepreneurial acumen. He is a member of the Service Corps of Retired Executives (SCORE). He represents Rotary in many activities, including a two-year term as a board member for his chapter.

At CSUF, Vas mentors for the Center for Entrepreneurship. He is a self described "die-hard entrepreneur." Vas' passion and skill enrich the program.

Vas Arora
Orange County , California

Dear Founder,

Entrepreneurism is not necessarily in one's DNA; however it can be taught and developed. That was the case for me. As a mechanical engineering graduate I was trained for a corporate career. I worked for two large corporations. Still, I had the instinct for entrepreneurship and I have always kept it burning within me. I proudly recommend it to every young person. Regardless of financial burdens, your entrepreneurial instinct, proper foresight and practical business ideas will see you through. Burning dedication and hard work are the keys to success.

I learned many useful business skills from my corporate career. The experience improved my entrepreneurial instincts. I aspired to control my own destiny and achieve financial independence. Soon, I ventured out on my own. Here I am today, after separating myself from a stable job and taking the risks so many other entrepreneurs face. I do not have a single regret.

My entrepreneurial journey started by purchasing an existing plastic recycling business. I worked with them for a year to learn the tools of the trade and decided to purchase the company. Yes, it was a risk, but my aspirations propelled me forward to challenge myself and pursue my dream of being a business owner.

As a business owner, in order to make my company successful I had to master three management roles: sales and marketing manager, accountant, and procurement manager. In addition, I had to devote half of my 12-hour days to collecting the scrap plastic and other materials needed to make my company grow. One thing you learn quickly as an entrepreneur is that you have to get your hands dirty; you don't sit around and wait for the connections to be made...YOU make the connections!

Within one year the business grew by 300% and I later sold it for ten times what I paid. Next I purchased a gas station with Food Mart and managed it for thirteen years to assure profitability. Then I turned my sights to the real estate industry. Eventually I accumulated a portfolio of residential and commercial properties. Finally, I consolidated my holdings by making full use of 1031 exchange tax regulations to acquire one long term commercial investment that will provide triple net income during my retirement.

Distilling my entrepreneurial journey, I offer you three tips:
1. Passion is a must, and, especially in real estate, long-term planning can save you in the future.
2. Be prepared to work hard to develop your working concept and don't shy away from taking risks.
3. Move slowly and carefully, plan to reinvest for the first few years.

Good luck,

Vas Arora

Be Willing to Move

Joel Backaler is Managing Director of international marketing and corporate development for Frontier Strategy Group (FSG), a global business advisory serving more than 5,000 executives. Joel joined FSG in 2009 as Interim Head of Asia Pacific Operations and Regional Account Manager. FSG promoted him three times to his current position.

Joel brings a diverse, cross-industry perspective to his position. He has worked with many of the world's top global brands, including: Johnson & Johnson, Philips, Cisco, HP, and Danone. He has also advised companies from emerging markets on their globalization efforts.

He is a frequent contributor to media outlets such as the Financial Times, The New York Times, Bloomberg and the Harvard Business Review. He is a Forbes columnist and a member of the National Committee on United States-China Relations. Joel is a sought after public speaker. His previous engagements include the University of Chicago, London School of Economics, Princeton University, the Hamburg Summit, the Emerging Markets Summit, the U.S. Department of Commerce and many other venues.

Joel is the author of China Goes West: Everything You Need to Know About Chinese Companies Going Global (Palgrave Macmillan). The book examines how Chinese companies can build brands and sell products in international markets. The book received an Axiom Business Book award and broke Amazon's Top 10 in the International Business book category.

Joel is a graduate of Connecticut College with a major in East Asia Studies, and a former Fulbright Scholar. He has done post graduate work at Georgetown University in International Business and at Tsinghua University in Advanced Business Chinese. He is a member of the National Committee on United States-China Relations.

Joel is a friend of CSUF Entrepreneurship and had been a guest speaker in the Entrepreneurial Marketing class. He currently lives in Los Angeles, California with his wife Qian.

FSG
FRONTIER STRATEGY GROUP

Dear Founder,

As I think back to the defining moments in my career, the greatest piece of advice I can offer is don't be afraid to move with little notice to take a new opportunity. When I started my career, I spent two years living and working in China. My job was OK, but it was niche because I was focused on consulting for large Chinese multinational companies expanding internationally.

As I began to assess potential opportunities, I reached out to a friend who worked for an American company based in DC that was focused on international business. I met with their management team during a trip back home, and found out that they were in the final stages of building an initial team to open their Asia Pacific headquarters in Singapore.

A few days later their head of HR sent me an offer to join their Asia Pacific founding team. It was a difficult decision to make - I already had a decent job in Beijing with a strong local network and my fiancé had just started a new job herself in China.

Despite the professional and personal risk, I signed on and flew from Beijing to Singapore two weeks later. I had never been to Singapore previously, nor did I realize how much higher the standard of living was there compared to China. All I knew was I had an incredible opportunity to lead a start-up within a start-up in one of the most dynamic parts of the world.

The job wasn't easy - there was no blueprint for success. Late nights/early mornings were spent on conference calls with US headquarters to set expectations and maintain an open line of communication. My small team hit the phones securing sales visits as an unknown entity in the region, signing on new clients, and ultimately managing multinational corporate accounts.

It was trial by fire from the outset, but by being willing to make the move at the opportune moment when my company was expanding into Asia led to an incredible opportunity. I gained professional development, executive interaction and skill-building that I never would have achieved had I simply stayed in China or left Asia all together to start fresh in the US.

There are times when you wish you could have all the information (or at least a little more information) to make an important decision. Just because the organization or individuals you're dealing with do not have all the answers you may want under ideal circumstances, doesn't mean you should write off the opportunity.

In fact, if you're proactive and entrepreneurial, operating amidst ambiguity is an ideal environment to experiment, take calculated risks and grow your skill set. I've found this to be the case time and time again with my career. I hope you find the same when it comes to yours.

All the best,

Joel Backaler
Managing Director, Marketing & Corporate Development

InkSafari.com

Andrew Baker is a 2007 Entrepreneur-ship alumnus of California State University Fullerton. He is the founder of InkSafari.com.

Andrew Baker sold candy at a premium to his 6th grade classmates when his parents refused to give him spending money. He cut back on his candy consumption but remained focused on finding a successful sales niche. His first job at the local grocery store gave him enough money to buy his first car so he could get a higher paying job at CompUSA and then as a rep for Hewlett-Packard at age 18 while still in high school.

Andrew graduated college during the Great Recession in 2007. Rather than give up, he bought inventory from companies that were going out of business, waiting, and then reselling items when prices came back up.

After connecting with a Canadian printing supply start up, Andrew began assisting the owner in sales. Soon, Andrew found an opportunity to open his own printing supply business using the capital he had saved from his previous jobs and humble lifestyle. All those years living low to the ground (driving an old car and on a tight budget) paid off.

10 years later, at age 33, he remains the founder and CEO of Ink Safari, Inc. The business has evolved and changed, but remains a success with over 25,000 items sold annually which gives him the financial freedom to work a relaxed schedule on his own terms. Andrew lives in Orange County and enjoys traveling with his wife Katie and their son Scott.

Dear Founder:

It's been over a decade since graduating from CSUF Entrepreneurship program and starting my own business so I thought it was appropriate to share 10 lessons I've learned along the way.

1. Take more calculated risks when you are young. A wrong decision is better than inaction, and the lessons you learn from failure will be important when you're older and the stakes are higher.

2. Write down your goals, check off your accomplishments and dream big.

3. Don't expect to have a completely balanced life or make a profit the first year (or more) of starting your small business. Long days are par for the course, but don't forget to give yourself a day off.

4. Change is good. What you are doing today will dramatically change 1000 days from now and closing doors will open other opportunities.

5. Work more on your business and less in your business. Set up systems that simplify responsibilities and make you and your employees more efficient.

6. Your time is valuable so don't do minimum wage work. Leave simple tasks that take up time to the employees so you can grow the business. Small tasks quickly add up so it's important to delegate responsibilities.

7. Pay good employees well so they stick around. People you trust and work hard are difficult to come by.

8. Expand slowly and naturally. The more things you own, the more things own you. The more employees you have, the bigger the office space you rent, the less freedom you have.

9. Find a mentor to coach you.

10. Take profits and invest in ways to generate passive income for your future.

Please realize there are exceptions to every rule, so chart your own course with an open mind and prove us all wrong.

Sincerely,

Andrew Baker

Bassman-Blaine, Inc.,

Ken Bassman is a serial entrepreneur. He has founded eleven different businesses and has sold three. Seven of these businesses have been home-furnishings related and four were in various other industries.

Ken graduated from college in 1984 and moved to Newport Beach to begin a career as a manufacturer's representative in the wholesale home furnishings industry. Today, Bassman Blaine, Inc. (BB) is a multi-faceted home furnishings company. BB International & Domestic Sales Management and Marketing manages all sales and marketing efforts for two companies and contracts with over 100 sales representatives throughout North America. Sales management responsibilities also include product development, cataloging, showroom merchandising, pricing, overseas sourcing, financial analysis and general operations consulting.

In 2007, Ken started another division specializing in full service interior design. BB Interior Design (BB Home) has become a multi-million-dollar venture having completed over 400 turn-key residential and commercial design projects from the Hawaiian Islands to Connecticut.

BB's corporate offices are in Costa Mesa. BB currently operates trade showrooms at the LA Mart in Los Angeles and the Laguna Design Center in Laguna Niguel. Looking back, Ken is proud that he has collectively employed over 1,000 people.

Throughout his adult life, Ken has taken on leadership roles in his community. He was High School Student Body President. At UCSB, he was President of Phi Sigma Kappa Fraternity (where he received the national outstanding leadership award).

Also, he received UCSB's outstanding community service award. Ken served two years on The Board of Directors of Kids Konnected, a national non-profit organization. He served four years on The Board of Directors of The Orange County Child Abuse Prevention Center. Ken is a founding member on the Board of Directors of The Orange County Jewish Community Center. Currently, Ken chairs the $11 Million Capital Campaign for his synagogue, Shir Ha Ma'alot. Ken has been a head coach for many seasons for AYSO, NJB and Junior All American Football. He is a mentor at The Applied Innovation Center at UCI.

At California State University Fullerton, Ken mentors for CSUF Entrepreneurship. His focus is on start-up ventures.

Ken is married and lives in Newport Beach with his wife and their three daughters. Ken has trained in various martial arts for over 25 years and holds a second-degree black belt. He is a past California State Bench Press Champion and a private pilot.

Bassman Blaine

Dear Founder,

As I reflect a bit on my life and more specifically my career, the cliché "I wish I knew then what I know now" comes to mind. Having founded eleven businesses and in the final stages of launching number twelve, I think that I have learned the most through the mistakes that I have made; and no doubt, there have been many. However, I try hard and it has become very top of my mind not to repeat a mistake and for the most part, this has served me well. Having served as a Mentor for the past couple of years makes me wish that this had been available to me as I began my own entrepreneurial endeavors. As I have shared with the students that I have had the pleasure to work with, I am here to help you avoid the mistakes that I've made and emulate some of the better decisions as well.

Passion & Enthusiasm: To pursue a venture or start a business that I was not extremely passionate about and did not have a tremendous amount of enthusiasm for would quite simply not be for me. I emphatically suggest that you build your business around a product and/or service that you are excited about. To launch a business is a lot of work, but the fun that you will have, if you love what you do, will make it worthwhile. Additionally, passion and enthusiasm are contagious as well as infectious and others are much more apt to want to work with you, for you, or buy from you if they feel your excitement. "The earth has music for those who listen." - Shakespeare

Fearlessness & Confidence: If you will be building a team, seeking an investment, or trying to sell your product or service, your sales ability (and hopefully not a lack thereof) will come into play. Much like passion and enthusiasm, you just will not be able to fake it so if these are not inherent to you or part of your natural skill set, take the time to get the training and build the skills that are necessary to help you succeed. From Toastmasters (one of the best things that I have done), a Dale Carnegie workshop or seminar to leadership training, any (or all) of these will be well worth the investment of time and money and will pay big dividends over time. I often say that I would take a top rate salesperson with a second-rate product or service over a second-rate salesperson with a top tier product or service all day – every day. Being fearless will help you stay the course when the no's come your way and having confidence will help turn the no's into yes's and get the people that you want to join your team. "Optimism is the faith that leads to achievement. Nothing can be done without hope and confidence." – Helen Keller

Integrity: In a world too often filled with deceit and dishonesty, I believe that this should be a non-negotiable for you and your new venture. For all that I hear about my reputation and that of my companies, nothing makes me prouder than when we are described as honest, loyal, caring, and having integrity. I believe that small business is the backbone of our economy and that we owe it to ourselves as well as our family, friends, and community to go about building our businesses with integrity, a spirit of giving and doing the right thing as priority A#1. "The future belongs to those who believe in the beauty of their dreams." – Eleanor Roosevelt

Wishing you success – keep on striving,

Ken Bassman

bassmanblaine.com bassmanblainehome.com

Emerging Language Entrepreneur

Joey Beim is a 2011 alumnus of California State University Fullerton's Mihaylo College of Business and Economics. He concentrated in Entrepreneurship and Economics. He is currently developing an on-line language learning platform that he has designed for intermediate and advanced language learners.

Joey was born in Kansas and was eager to see the world. While in college, Joey studied abroad for a year at SRH Hochschule Heidelberg, Germany. After graduation, lack of initial success in his job search led him to two sales positions.

Joey first worked for Eagle Graphics, a communications agency that provides comprehensive/integrated print, brand and marketing merchandise solutions. Next, he worked as a sales representative for Auto Insurance Associates. As he states

in his letter Joey realized that he was not passionate about selling graphics or insurance, but he gained experience and learned important business lessons.

He turned to his dream of teaching English abroad. He became a native English teacher in Hong Kong for Monkey Tree International Group. He moved on to teach English at Ciudad Itagui Colegio in Columbia. His goal in Columbia was to be an English teacher who was also fluent in the students' native language.

Joey, found his passion for education, languages, and culture. He is now building a business model that revolves around his passion. He is focused on acquiring the skills he needs in order to make his on-line language learning platform succeed. Joey will begin a master's program in 2018 in second language acquisition.

Joey Beim
Keokuk, Iowa

Dear Founder,

I studied entrepreneurship at CSUF, but I I have not yet become a true entrepreneur. This may turn you away from reading this letter. However I wish to share valuable business/real world lessons that I have learned since my graduation. If I had told what follows to my senior-in-college self, there is no way that he would have believed a word. You may not believe it either, but you should.

I am writing this letter from my third home outside of the United States since graduating. My business education prepared me for what was to follow in my jobs after I finished my bachelor's degree studies. However, the jobs I landed were not the jobs I imagined. I did not obtain my first few job choices. A mentor from a class consulting project helped me to get my first job after college where I gained experience and learned important lessons day after day. It was a sales job. I did my best, but I soon moved on to a sales job at another company. After giving my best for nineteen months, I realized that I was not a salesmen and moved on again.

I moved closer to my family. Of course they were the first to grill me when I arrived on what was my next move. I applied for more corporate jobs where I would have answered more phones, and taken more orders, without joy or fulfillment. If I had continued my search, I would have moved on to serving more customers just as I was accustomed to doing before.

I began teaching as a substitute teacher to earn money in between jobs. I realized that I loved teaching certain subjects. I had always thought about teaching English abroad to see the world and gain the unique experience it entails. I did it. While teaching in Hong Kong I learned of my passion not only for teaching, but also for traveling, culture, and languages. I finished my contract in Asia and went to Medellin, Colombia where I wanted to both continue teaching English and become fluent in the Spanish language.

Only after realizing my passion for languages and gaining the knowledge to teach/learn a foreign language did my entrepreneurial studies come into action. Now that I have dedicated the time and effort to do something better than most, I have the confidence to put forth an on-line language learning platform and provide a service better than most. Finding your passion is not easy, and in all reality it has to find you. My passion has found me, my entrepreneurial spirit is energized. I am fully alive. My CSUF entrepreneurship classes are more applicable than ever.

I hope your passion finds you and that when it does you are able to recognize it. When you discover it, don't be afraid to put in the time to master it better than most. Then do it. Create a business made possible through your passion.

Sincerely,

Joey Beim

Connected Women of Influence

Michelle Bergquist is a nationally recognized author, award-winning entrepreneur, lively moderator and engaging, professional speaker.

Currently, Michelle is the CEO and Co-Founder (with Jaimee Pittman in 2008) of Connected Women of Influence. It is a Southern California association of professional women leading people, projects, teams and companies.

Michelle is also the Co-Founder of SUE Talks™. SUE Talks™ presenters offer bold, passionate talks and viewpoints. They center around business and success. Presenters are successful, unstoppable, and empowering women who are changing the face of business.

In 2015, Michelle became a founding partner of Women Lead Publishing, the go-to-source for aspiring women authors and existing female authors. She is the Founder & Publisher of Women Lead Magazine. It is a leadership publication providing ideas, inspiration and insights for female leaders and those who champion the advancement of women in business.

Michelle is a passionate advocate of advancing women in business. She designs platforms, programs, connections and collaborative opportunities that result in more women leading people, projects, teams, and companies. The National Association of Women Business Owners has recognized Michelle as the Women's Advocate of the Year. The San Diego Metro Magazine named her one of the Women Who Impact San Diego. Michelle is passionate about 'giving back' in business. Her philanthropic efforts have resulted in over $150,000 in contributions for local nonprofit organizations that support women and young girls.

Michelle's corporate background includes thirteen years in commercial banking and over twenty-five years as an entrepreneur and business owner. Michelle is the author of two books: How Women Sabotage Their Success in Business…According to Men and How to Build a Million Dollar Database. Michelle's professional background includes over twenty years' expertise in helping organizations develop winning business plans, obtain funding, increase sales, improve business performance and succeed.

Michelle is a graduate of the University of Nebraska-Lincoln (Go Big Red!). She is a past board member of the National Association of Women Business Owners, the Fountain Valley Chamber of Commerce, the YWCA of San Diego and the American Institute of Banking. Michelle is a past CSUF student consulting case sponsor.

Dear Founder: I have been a small business owner for the last 25 years and here are a few candid and practical pieces of advice that I share with you as you venture into your own business.

You never have enough money or time: No matter if you achieve financing through traditional sources or raise capital through investors, there is never enough money or time. As you grow you need more money. As an owner, I would pay close attention to knowing what's in your numbers and how money is made and spent in your enterprise.

As you grow you cannot add more time to the day, so it's wise to be very efficient in where you spend your time and who you spend your time with. In addition, growing a business requires you, as the founder, to maximize your time with other people's time. I wish I would have learned earlier how important my time was to the success of our business. Once we started adding employees to the company, my time was spent in managing and less in doing. It has been an incredible experience in adding team members to the mix and seeing them flourish and thrive in our business.

Begin with the end in mind: As you launch your enterprise, be thinking of how your business will end. Are you looking to sell the business at a future point or leave your business as a legacy to others? There are many, many options in how a business "ends." When you think of the end-point and how you see the end of your business, it forces you to build your business with that focus. I am currently building our business venture with the intention of selling our company in the future to others. Every decision and initiative and goal we make and do is focused on how this will move us forward to be attractive to outside purchasers in the future. It gives you clarity of focus and purpose like no other.

Always listen to your customers: No matter what business you are in, you must pay close attention to your customers and listen to what they want. While this sounds so basic, our company has come up with new services and initiatives and revenue sources by interacting frequently with our clients (members) and learning what else they are looking for from their experience in doing business with us (and being a member of our association). I reach out frequently to our members and sponsors and have conversations and discussion that gives me insight into what else we should be offering. This information has been one of the most incredible pieces of intelligence we have had in offering new programs and initiatives that have resulted in additional revenue and happy, long-term members and sponsors.

There is SO much more I could share and so many things to pay close attention to in starting and building a business empire! Suffice it to say that your business venture is an "evolution," not a "revolution," and success doesn't come overnight. Success comes from the practical, systematic actions you make day in and day out that build a phenomenal business enterprise. Success also comes from keeping the mindset that things will never be perfect and you are never done. Every day is another day to test new things, try new initiatives, change things up and act on decisions that will bring you the most success.

Wishing you the best of success with your new venture!

Michelle Bergquist
CEO & -Co-Founder

Professor, Coach and Scholar

Lorenzo Bizzi is Assistant Professor of Management at California State University Fullerton's Mihaylo College of Business and Economics. He teaches the undergraduate capstone course in strategic management and the MBA capstone course. Lorenzo supervises student consulting projects. In 2016, a project prepared by one of his MBA student consulting teams won second place in the Small Business Institute's national project competition.

Lorenzo studied at Bocconi University in Italy. He earned his doctorate from the École des hautes études commerciales de Montréal (HEC Montreal) in Canada. He had the opportunity to teach while at Bocconi University and at McGill University in Canada before joining the faculty at California State University, Fullerton.

Supervision of student consulting projects at CSUF has enriched Lorzenzo's profound understanding of strategic management. His student consulting teams have served dozens of companies in multiple industries. Clients learn how to expand their business, understand their markets, improve their operations and analyze the attractiveness of different strategic options.

Lorenzo does research in strategic management, organizational behavior and human resource management. His work focuses on three areas: social capital of employees inside the organization, on the relationship between the company's strategy and the employees' performance, and on inter-organizational relations among businesses.

Lorenzo has published in several prestigious journals. They include the *Journal of Management, Human Relations, Human Resource Management,* and *Strategic Organization*.

He won numerous awards for excellence in teaching, including, among others, the All-Time Outstanding Professor of the Mihaylo Business Honors Program. Mihaylo honor students give this award to the best professor they had in their academic career. He won this award the last three times in a row.

Besides helping companies, researching and teaching, Lorenzo is actively involved in professional service for academic journals. He serves on the Editorial Board of the *Journal of Organizational Behavior* and regularly presents the findings of his works in conferences around the world.

Dear Founder,

As you read this letter, you may be considering embarking on a grand entrepreneurial adventure. It is a marvelous adventure, full of emotions, enthusiasm and personal growth. Yet, it is also a perilous adventure, full of deadly traps. It is my intention to write this letter with the goal of warning you against one of the deadliest traps you could find on your journey.

Depending on industry sectors, the failure rate of startups can reach 90%. My personal experience, combined with cumulative evidence from research, suggests that a major cause for startup failure can be attributed to one deadly trap: overestimation of customer value. Simply put, when you ask entrepreneurs the value they think their product adds to customers and then you ask the same question to customers, you'll probably see entrepreneurs giving a much more positive answer than customers. This trap becomes fatal whenever entrepreneurs spend money to launch products that end up not creating sufficient value to justify their price, thus dooming a company's sustainability.

What is the cause for the overestimation of customer value? Many causes can be found, but one is particularly worthy of attention. Entrepreneurs are often passionate about their business and the product they offer. Passion is indeed the reason for their success. Yet, paradoxically, passion is also dangerous because emotionally charged thoughts tend to lead to confirmatory bias, which is the tendency to see only what one wants to see. Entrepreneurs can be so passionate about their products, that they tend to pay more attention and remember all positive information that confirms their established positive views, while they discount the importance of or forget all negative information that disconfirms them. When you are passionate, you may tend to give more relevance to those who praise your product than to those who hate it. As a result, entrepreneurs' judgment can be distorted and they may risk seeing their products as better than what customers think.

What are the solutions to avoid this deadly trap? First, simply be aware of its existence. When I talk to entrepreneurs, they often tend to consider this issue as rather trivial. Perhaps you may be reading this letter and think the same. Nonetheless, remember that overestimation of customer value is a proven major cause of failure in startups and too often entrepreneurs are unwary of this trap. Before you put all your money and effort into something, you must ensure that your passion is not distorting your thoughts. Second, analyze as much market and industry data as possible from multiple sources to ensure that your judgments are not based on speculations but are solidly grounded and minimally biased. As I have been consulting for several years, I am aware of how data transforms wishful thinking into reliable judgment. Third, benefit as much as possible from the judgment of mentors, friends, and other entrepreneurs in your network. Don't discount their opinion. I often hear that entrepreneurs rebut friends' judgments, claiming that they are limited because friends don't know the product as well as they do. It is as true for friends as it is for customers. Your friends' judgement could actually be closer to that of customers than it is to yours.

To conclude, let your heart energize your adventure but don't let it obfuscate your sight.

I wish you the best of success in your entrepreneurial endeavors!

Lorenzo Bizzi

Titan, Entrepreneur & Philanthropist

Dan Black has been a leader in business for over forty years. Throughout this time, he founded four different companies related to improving the healthcare industry.

The first was in 1973 with the creation of Trace Analysis Laboratory. This company used innovative X-ray Florescence technology to measure low levels of trace elements. After observing an emerging market in human hair analysis, Dan founded his second company a year later, MineraLab.

While experiencing success in running companies focused on measuring trace elements, Black remained open to new business ventures. When a medical doctor approached him with the design of a high potency Vitamin-Mineral supplement, he saw an opportunity to create an entirely new market in the healthcare industry. This vision culminated in the founding of Advanced Medical Nutrition, Inc. (AMNI).

After growing both MineraLab and AMNI into successful businesses, Dan decided it was time to move in a different direction. He sold MineraLab in 1989. AMNI was sold in 1998.

Although he thought his time in the healthcare industry was over after the sale of AMNI, Dan elected to found another supplement business in 2001 with two of his former partners called ProThera Inc. This company experienced enormous success and was sold in 2013.

During his time in business, Dan maintained that his experience at California State University, Fullerton enabled him to achieve success. Due to this, Dan made the decision to start giving back to the University philanthropically. He made his first donation to the College of Natural Science and Mathematics in 1999 and created the Dan Black Program in Physics and Business a year later. In 2006, the CSUF laboratory building was named in his honor as Dan Black Hall.

While Dan's primary focus has been in the College of NSM, he has supported other Colleges throughout his time at CSUF. Examples include contributions to the Center for Oral and Public History and the support of various College of Education programs aimed at creating and supporting diversity in the educational system.

Dan works closely with the Center for Entrepreneurship through his involvement on the Advisory Board and support of the Titan Fast Pitch and Business Plan competitions. He also funds scholarships for select Start-up Incubator residents.

Dan Black
Reno, Nevada

Dear Founder,

As I approached graduation in 1967 with a degree in Physics from California State University, Fullerton, I was uncertain on whether I should seek employment in a research or industry based profession.

I discovered the answer during a required Physics Lab meeting where a sales representative of EG&G's Nuclear Instrumentation Division showcased innovative equipment that could be purchased for use in the lab. I knew halfway through his presentation that I wanted to become a technical salesman myself. At the end of the meeting, I approached the representative and made my intent known. Within two weeks, I had traveled to Boston for an interview and been offered a job as a sales representative for the eleven western states.

I quickly advanced through the ranks and was promoted to Marketing Manager within three years. It was during this time that I realized I was interested in starting my own company. Due to this realization, I chose to resign from my position and made the decision to move back to California. While working for a company called Nuclear Data, I ran into a former customer from my time at EG&G. He had developed a system for measuring trace elements in water at a much lower cost than was available at the time. I ended up partnering with him to form my first company in 1973 - Trace Analysis Laboratories. During the course of the following thirty years, I had founded three other successful companies: MineraLab, Advanced Medical Nutrition, and ProThera.

My career in the military, at California State University, Fullerton, and in the professional workforce taught me that it is essential to treat your fellow colleagues with respect and to develop a strong work ethic. Looking back on the four companies I founded, I have tried to follow what I call "Dan's Pearls of Wisdom".

(1) **Remember your limitations:** Don't try to do everything yourself. Hire workers that address your own deficiencies and let them complete tasks that they are proficient in.
(2) **Share your success:** "Pigs get fat, hogs get slaughtered."
(3) **You can't stay on top forever:** Every foot you step on the way up belongs to someone, and you can be sure you'll meet that person on the way down.
(4) **Trust your instincts:** If it feels correct, the chances for success are far greater.

A common question I am asked is "With all the pitfalls I encountered, would I do it all again?" My answer: "In a heartbeat".

Dan Black

Second Generation In Real Estate

James Bobbett and his mother Martina are partners in Bobbett and Associates. He is cofounder snd Broker of Record for Reliance Real Estate Services.

James "grew up in real estate." He started working for his Mom at age 12. He began his real estate career in January 2000 as a senior in high school. He then worked in real estate while earning his BA in marketing from California State University Fullerton.

As described in his letter, James worked at Modern Realty Company from 2008 to 2012 during the great recession. He specialized in foreclosures. He then pivoted back to the mainstream real estate market as a Broker Associate at Prudential California Realty in Brea from 2012-2015.

In 2015, James partnered with his Mom to form Bobbett and Associates and they affiliated with the newly formed Reliance Real Estate Services(RRES). James became the broker of record for RRES.

RRES is built on the foundation of highly experienced award-winning, hyper-local real estate professionals seeking to provide an advanced level of service to their clients. RRES custom tailors marketing plans specific to the needs of each individual client.

James and his mother bring a wealth of knowledge, experience and teamwork to every real estate transaction. They have familiarity working with the special needs of sellers, seniors, move-up and first time home buyers and investors. Each type of client gets the benefit and strengths of both James and his mother. They have established themselves as trusted advisors for their clients.

Martina's skilled experience in the home staging and interior design industries make her a valuable asset to her clients. She is able to advise buyers on how to see the potential of a home and create the lifestyle they desire. When preparing a home for the market, Martina works to stage the home in order to bring more buyers through the door and receive top dollar for the property. She has been recognized consistently for the highest levels of performance in real estate sales. Her awards and success represent her well established reputation for getting the job done and getting it done right.

James uses extensive, industry-leading marketing tools to make sure each client's home gets the maximum exposure possible. Together, Martina and James dedicate themselves to making the home buying and selling process is an enjoyable one.

Dear Business Founder,

Graduating from Cal State Fullerton (Go Titans!) in 2007 with my Bachelor's degree in Marketing was an important enhancement to my already established Real Estate career. In 2000 I obtained my real estate license, as a senior in high school, and went to work as an associate agent at Century 21 Discovery in Fullerton. In 2007, I obtained my broker's license knowing one day I wanted to head up a brokerage with agents working for me. When the market showed signs of a decline in 2008, I positioned myself to be ready for the cataclysmic shift in the market that was predicted.

I moved my sales license to Modern Realty in Cerritos. That brokerage specialized exclusively in homes that had fallen into foreclosure. My years at that brokerage brought an experience to me of a completely different genre of real estate.

The next step in my career path was to get back into the main stream of the real estate market and to this end I placed my license with Prudential California Realty in Brea. After a short 2 years there, I became broker of record at Reliance Real Estate Services, an independent real estate brokerage started by a core group of agents who wanted the autonomy to create their own brands within a brand. Within this company I continued to expand the branding efforts of, Bobbett & Associates. Together with my Mother and Partner, Martina, we personally rank among the top 10 agents in Fullerton in sales volume.

My path forward is two-pronged in that the group of founders who started Reliance Real Estate want to continue to grow the company organically in both agent count and sales volume. This task will continue to be completed as a group effort, by recruiting local experienced agents on a one on one basis. The increase in sales volume will come with the increase in quality agents hired into the company. Currently Reliance Real Estate Services is the number one residential real estate brokerage in Fullerton, after only 2 years in operation, and in the top 3 across all of North Orange County, with strategic growth we are confident that we will be in the number one position in the next year or two.

The most simplistic advice I can provide to a new business founder is to be yourself, people will always trust a person who is genuinely themselves and also shows a sincere passion for what they do. It doesn't hurt to be tenacious and a go-getter, combine that passion with sincerity and you should find the secret to longevity in the business world.

With greatest regards,

James Bobbett

Alumni, Co-Founder and Marketer

Daniela Bolzmann is an alumni of Mihaylo College of Business and Economics (2009). She studied Entrepreneurship.

As her CSUF graduation day approached, Daniela entered the exciting world of startups. She had the honor to be one of 10 companies to pitch at Google's first demo day in Palo Alto, has worked in edtech, logistics, real estate, and on-demand technologies, and has received investments from notable investors Steve Case (AOL) and Joe Mansueto (Morningstar).

Daniela's first venture, SocialSkoop was a digital marketing agency. It consulted for 200 plus restaurants and retailers in Orange County.

Shortly after, she was recruited to lead Product Marketing for edtech startup, Symbaloo. She helped them launch in the US market where she was able to grow their community to over two hundred thousand engaged educators worldwide.

In 2012, Daniela moved to Chicago and Co-Founded a logistics venture called WeDeliver. Headquartered in Chicago, WeDeliver was a local delivery provider servicing 200 top tier Chicago brands. WeDeliver grew into a 21 employee operation before being acquired by industry leader Deliv in 2015 after graduating from the TechStars accelerator program.

Daniela went on to help Real Estate technology startup, Breather, break into the Chicago market. She is their Senior Marketing and Business Development Manager.

Daniela currently serves on the advisory council for Ms.Tech, a group dedicated to helping women entrepreneurs gain access to the resources they need most. She is an active member of the Chicago Leadership Alliance, a community for Chicago's most ambitious, benevolent and well-connected young leaders.

In 2009, Daniela teamed with an entrepreneurship classmate, Matthew Gallizzi, to present Mihaylo College's Commencement address. In her part of the address she said,
Mathew and I met by working together in group consulting projects. We really pushed each other and although we couldn't be more different in our individual personalities we did grow a solid bond. One thing that we learned and we have in common is that each of us is the first to graduate college in our families. When I realized that, by the time I graduated I was going to be 25 years old I was kind of embarrassed because a lot of my friends from high school graduated when they were 21 or 22. I didn't let this get to me. Instead, I created a personal mantra that carried me through – It doesn't matter how slow I go, as long as I get there.
Daniela would agree with Matt that destiny is not something you wait for , it is something to be achieved.

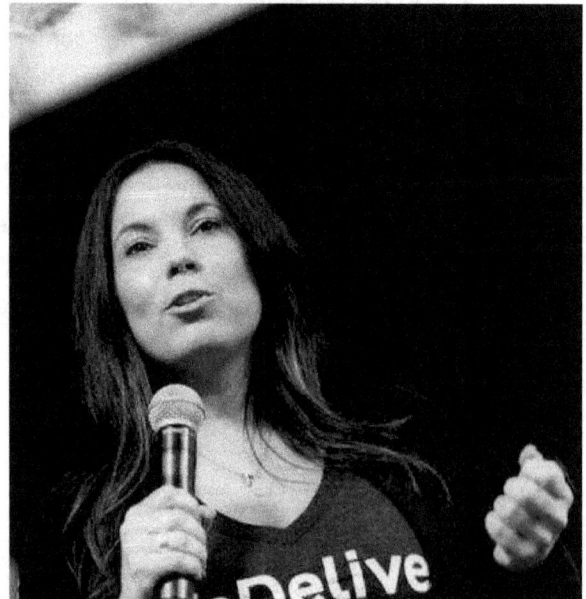

DANIELA BOLZMANN

Dear Founder,

From the outside looking in, it appears that I've accomplished quite a bit, but if I'm being honest with you I still feel that I'm just beginning to scratch the surface. I'm proud of my accomplishments, but have very high expectations for my own success. This is the fuel that keeps me growing as an entrepreneur.

These are the lessons that have impacted me the most:

PERCEPTION. Your perception of success and achievement will change over time. Define yours today and then redefine over time. Success to me used to be raising a Series B or C round for a VC backed business, scaling fast and exiting with a return to my investors. After seeing that I was not happy with this path I redefined my own success metrics. Success to me no longer means a huge exit, stock options, or high salaries. Success is a sustainable company that makes an impact in the world and allows me to enjoy my life with purpose. What is success to you?

TIME. Give yourself a chance to achieve success by investing in your long game. I've started a few businesses and looking back I can see that I quit too soon. Many of the most successful people I have come to admire have built incredibly successful businesses over time, not overnight. One friend bootstrapped for 10 years and just raised her first round of funding, a $500 million investment which valued the company at over 5 billion dollars. Another friend started with $10,000 and grew her business over 10 years to a $50 million dollar enterprise. The common thread is that each of these Founders started small and kept at it, through the long haul to create their own empires over time.

FITNESS. Success is more than touting your latest venture or lifestyle, it's health and wealth fitness. I felt very successful running my own company and hiring a team around me and again when working for a high growth startup making a great salary but I was always missing something. How could I be making more money than ever and still be living paycheck to paycheck? That left me feeling very unsuccessful until I took ownership of my bad habits and started treating my personal finances like a business. I've since adopted the principles of restraint and minimalism which helped me become debt and payment free. A bonus was the effect these principles had when I applied them to my wellness and nutrition, I've lost 18 inches and 15 pounds.

LOVE. Enjoy the ride. Live in the moment, love every moment and remember to be kind to yourself. People often tell me that I'm the happiest person they know. My secret, is that I've learned to love the journey and embrace all the moments. I'm not afraid of taking risks, I enjoy solving problems, and when I fail I remind myself that I am human. A new venture will challenge you day after day. Learn to love those moments because you asked for them when you decided to become a Founder.

There is no blue print for success, it is what you want it to be. If success is running your own business and never hiring an employee but also being able to run your business while traveling the world, then do that. If success means scaling to multiple countries and hiring 500 employees, then do that. I don't have it all figured out, but these lessons have kept me grounded and will hopefully help you define success for your life and venture.

Best,

Daniela

Licensing Consulting Group

Rand Brenner is CEO of Licensing Consulting Group (LCG), an intellectual property management and licensing company. He founded the company in 1996. It specializes in helping companies in strategically managing and leveraging their intellectual property assets. LCG handles many types of IP technologies. Recent client projects include a fried food cooking process, an oral health care device, a non medical treatment sound therapy, branded consumer products and location-based entertainment.

Rand has over 30 years IP management and licensing experience in diverse industries. For example, the list includes consumer products, food, entertainment, software, health technology, medical devices and digital media. He has led international licensing programs as both licensee and licensor. His consulting projects focus on strategy and outbound / inbound licensing initiatives. Rand has developed and managed licensing deals with Fortune 1000 companies. They include Universal Studios, Fox Interactive, Sony Pictures, Dow, Cargill, SmithKline Glaxo, Ranir, Coca Cola, Kellogg's, Hasbro, Mattel, Random House, Harper Collins and Pillsbury.

Before founding LCG, Rand was Vice President of Licensing at Saban Entertainment, where he managed a 100 million-dollar licensing division. He was responsible for developing the licensing initiatives in the US, Canada and Mexico for the multibillion dollar Mighty Morphin Power Rangers TV show. (A worldwide licensing phenomenon that grossed over $3 billion in worldwide retail merchandise sales.) He also developed licensing for two Power Rangers Movies (produced with 20th Century Fox Film Corp.).

Before Saban, Rand was a licensing executive at Warner Brothers Consumer Products. There he licensed out many high profile theatrical, television and publishing properties. They included Batman (which generated over $500 million in box office revenues) and Batman II movies, the animation classic Looney Tunes (i.e., Bugs Bunny).

Rand is a published writer and public speaker. His articles have appeared in respected journals in his industry. He has been a featured speaker at numerous business and investment conferences. He is also a regular speaker on IP and licensing at the ICFO Capital Conferences in Orange County, CA and Los Angeles.

Rand earned his undergraduate degree in Advertising from California State University San Jose and his MBA from Pepperdine University. He lives in Orange County and volunteers as a Judge for CSUF Entrepreneurship's business plan and new venture launch presentations.

Dear Founder,

The best advice I can share with you is "change your thinking."

Before I tell you why, let me share a quick story about my own experience. When I began my professional career in licensing, I knew nothing about it. I was given an office and a phone, and was directed to go out and find companies to license a movie based on a comic book character that hadn't been seen for over 20 years.

Licensing was not a big business for the studios in those days. If fact, there were few people who'd even had experience in licensing. The only companies willing to take the risk on licensing this movie were small entrepreneurial and startup companies. When the movie took off, many of these startups went from zero to hero overnight. That opened my eyes to the money making power of licensing intellectual property and why it's such a great strategy for building a new venture.

Today, the world is in a new type of economy, where innovation and intellectual property are the fuel that's building new ventures. And for you, the future venture builder, using this fuel requires a different kind of thinking. Here's why. Your traditional thinking of "building a business" is limiting you to the tangible side of your IP. You think in terms of starting a business to make products and sell them to grow your business.

But there's a better way. As a new venture, you're really an innovator. Innovation and new products are the lifeblood of every business. Companies worldwide are scrambling to find new ventures with innovative IP to meet their market demand. They can't develop new products fast enough. Rapidly changing technology, customer demand, legal regulations, and a score of other things are constantly changing the marketplace demand for new innovation.

That is why licensing is such an ideal strategy for your new venture. It lets you strike while the iron is hot, and take advantage of the growing demand for innovation. Rather than you working to sell a small piece of the market, licensing puts your intellectual property to work making money from the entire market.

Wishing you all the success in your future venture.

Rand Brenner
CEO, Licensing Consulting Group

World Class HR Solutions

Victor ("Vic") Bullara is the founder and CEO of World Class HR Consulting. The company is located in Lake Forest, California and has been helping organizations, boards and senior leaders achieve breakthrough results since 2009.

World Class HR provides executive assessment, development and coaching as well as succession planning services. With a focus on metrics driven services, the company has documented an average return on investment of 5.9 to 1.

Vic has 34 years' experience in the Human Resources profession and has focused his career on aligning HR programs and processes with the strategic business (operational) plans of his clients and employers. Vic's experience includes 19 years as an HR Practice Leader for Ernst & Young and Development Dimensions International. He implemented HR "best practices" for several major corporations, including PepsiCo, Merck, Lilly, Boeing, Johnson &Johnson, Toyota, and Chrysler.

Before starting World Class HR, Vic was the Chief HR Officer for two high growth technology companies including one publicly traded, $300 Million firm. He was also the Director of HR for a $1 Billion engineering services firm.

Vic worked for Evercore, a $350 million venture fund, instrumental in funding companies with transformative technologies with an aggregate valuation of $4 billion. At Evercore, Vic provided five technology start-up companies with HR infrastructure development. Four of the five startups had successful exits.

As an employee and Chief HR Officer, Vic helped one tech company grow from 7employees to 400 in four years and advance from Angel financing to an IPO.

For IXOS, a CMS software company, he worked with the U.S. based CEO to establish the company's presence in the United States. He recruited the U.S. sales team in sixty days and developed a sales incentive plan and onboarding assistance to reduce "time to quota" by more than 60 days achieving a $75 million sales goal.

Victor is a master certified executive coach and a certified, Winslow Research Institute Consultant. He is a mentor to Executive MBA students at the Paul Merage Graduate School of Business at UC Irvine. Today, he advises CEO's of start-up companies on human capital strategies at a local business incubator. He is on the board of directors of a virtual reality content developer with clients like Disney, Lucas Films and William Grant & Sons. World Class HR has a dedicated team of very experienced professionals helping individuals, organizations and boards achieve breakthrough results. Vic has been married for 20 years and lives and works in Southern California.

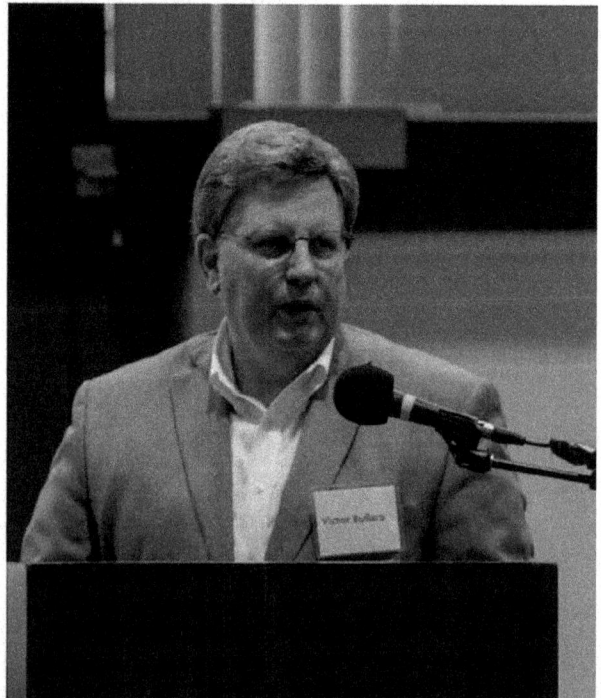

Dear Founder:

I have realized through trial and error that it is better to have an excellent team with an average idea than an average team with an excellent idea. Building an excellent team, however, is not easy and the trial and error method could sink your business. My advice to you is based on hiring more than 2,000 individuals in my career and training 1,500 hiring managers in behavioral interviewing. If you research *behavioral interviewing* you will find more than 1 million resources. Candidates actually have more practice and have done more research than most hiring managers. They know many of our "tricks" and even have access to questions we may have asked previous candidates. Consequently, it is important to acknowledge that interviewing is not just about asking questions. Hiring that excellent team is about knowing *what* to ask, knowing *how* to ask it and knowing *who* is the right fit when you find them.

Knowing *what* to ask starts from the job description you create and provides you with information to develop *competencies* (which skills, knowledge and abilities that lead to superior performance). If, for instance, you are looking for a salesperson, then you are looking for individuals who can sell. Other competencies include but are not limited to persuasiveness, ability to overcome (even anticipate) objections, having passion for the product or service, being resilient (continuing to perform effectively when faced with time pressures, adversity, disappointment, or opposition), possessing good communication skills (including asking questions and listening closely).

Now that you know what you are looking for, you have to develop the *how* using a three step, behavioral interviewing approach. If you start every question with "tell me about a time when...." you are one-third of the way there. Asking for specific examples from their past focuses on what they have done not what they could do or what theoretical knowledge they have. If it is about resilience, you can ask "tell me about a time when you encountered a group who was very negative towards your product (or service) and expressed several objections." If you are looking for experienced sales professionals who can quickly get to a commitment you might ask for them to tell you about a time when they "asked questions that allowed them to discover what the customer's true needs were."

The second part involves pinning the candidate down to specific actions they took. Listen for whether they start by saying "I" or "we" – if the latter, quickly redirect them to what <u>they</u> did. If you hear them say things like "*usually I would,*" ask them for a specific example. Many candidates prepare in advance and have a story ready for you. Asking for a <u>second</u> or <u>third</u> example around critical competencies may help you get past the phony, over rehearsed façade. Plan out your questions in advance. If you try to develop them in real time, you won't be listening carefully enough. Similarly, the interview is for data collection purposes only. You are not trying to screen candidates out at this point.

The third part is a focus on results. Make sure every question you ask probes for the results they achieved. While it is easy to make up stories it is harder for candidates to create results (impact of their actions) on the fly. You can ask follow up questions like "so how did that turn out" or "what was the end result" or "what happened in the end?"

I can confidently say that this approach has helped me sort the high performers from everyone else. Why not invest the time to increase your odds for success in hiring your next employees?

Your partner and supporter,

Victor Bullara

39

Anatomy of Yes

Joseph G. Burke is national award-winning marketing expert. He is the founder of Anatomy of YES (anatomyofyes.com), a creative ad agency that, "gets companies more "Yes."

Joe is known for driving revenues through national campaigns. Seven examples of his work include: "Shop with the Mouse®" (DisneyStore.com), "Get Gifted®" (Wetseal), "Cox Crushes the Competition™" (Cox Communications), "Big Sky Days™"(Three Dots), "Catch the Sun™" (Victory Surf), "Find the Good®" (Goodwill), and the upcoming 2017 "Bring Us your Dreams™" campaign for a major financial institution.

What is the key to the effectiveness of Joe's Ad campaigns? "I am a firm believer in mission over ego and that people and collective mojo build brand equity and shareholder value."

Joe is a former national Brand Director at Disney, Wet Seal, and VP at Goodwill. He actively creates and executes projects as a business strategist, Ad man, startup consultant, producer, public speaker, and former actor in 20+ tv shows & films. He speaks on archetypal patterns in business strategy. He has been a presenter and panelist in over 100 public forums. His keynote speech engagements include Boeing, USC, Marshall School of Business, and NG CX Summit.

Joe gives shares his expertise with Orange county non profits. He has served on Tech Coast Venture Network's board of directors and executive committee. Presently he is on the board of directors of Team Kids.

At CSUF, Joe has been a mentor for students in entrepreneurial marketing classes for several years. He has also been a MBA student consulting case sponsor. The students conducted a comprehensive review of Joe's companies. Joe says, "one key to my success is what I have learned through my years of mentoring college students."

Joe is author of an upcoming book, The Anatomy of Yes: How People Get What They Want. He is the inventor of OLLYBALL, a toy for kids ages 4-13 years. Also, Victory, his new sports training and patent-pending ball system will launch in 2018.

Joe is husband to one amazing woman who teaches in the Department of Special Education at Cal State Fullerton. They have three children. The family lives in Yorba Linda California.

ANATOMY OF YES
Serve More. Se More.

VICTURY Sports
Tra n W thout L m ts.

OLLYBALL
H t t Hard. Break Noth ng.

Founder,

The world is unfair. Business is even more unfair. If you can accept these truths you are well on your way to success as a Founder.

Damaged people damage people. Empowered people empower people. If you can live these truths, you are well on your way to success as a Founder.

Serve More. Sell More. This does not mean serve your customers first, it means serve your team first. Your role as a founder is to serve your team, they will serve your customers and your organization will sell more. The more you serve, the more you sell.

If you have the courage of a founder, you will identify the risks, threats and barriers to making your business succeed. You will see true fear and will do it anyway. Champions are made in the lonely hours, keep yourself disciplined in mind and body.

You hold a 100% chance of success if you do two simple commitments:

#1. Write down your organization's goal and what you want out of it:

Take a picture of this and post it on FB, IG, TW and LI with the #CreatingNewVentures.

#2. Commit to the point that you would rather die than see your businesses fail.

Joe Burke, Founder

LapWorks

Jose Calero founded LapWorks at age 55. Initially LapWorks produced and sold his invention, the Laptop Desk. Success came from becoming a virtual, multi product company that sources and imports products from China. Today, LapWorks' annual online business has grown from $0 in 2000 to $2 million today. LapWorks offers over 60 products for sale on Amazon. It adds two to four new products every year. It has offices in Rancho Cucamonga, Arizona, and Shenzhen, China.

What led to Jose's success? His "Dear Founder" letter only tells part of the story. He might say experience taught him how to see and adapt to new opportunities.

Jose didn't initially see opportunity in High School. He enlisted in the Army before graduating and went to Vietnam. After the Army, age 21, he earned a H.S. diploma.

Jose went into sales. A small Medical Electronics company that sold to doctors and hospitals in the Los Angeles area then recruited him. Jose used this model to start his own medical electronics firm. Jose eventually sold the business.

Jose's first invention was an organizing product for outside sales agents called the OrganizerPak. He sought and received an SBA loan to manufacture and market the product. He was woefully unprepared for this challenge. The business closed after just one year.

Next, Jose used the hard lessons he experienced to work as a consultant for small business owners and serve his community. He got involved in the Los Angeles Hispanic business community. He became President of the Latin Businessmen's Association (LBA), and served on boards, task forces, and committees for L.A. City and County.

Jose discovered how to see and adapt to new opportunities during his years of consulting, volunteerism and his twenty years as a commissioned sales agent. His accumulated experience served him well when he founded LapWorks. As Jose says in his letter, he had to adapt his business model to new opportunities. He pivoted to serve mobile professionals and produce the Autodesk at a lower cost in China.

The need to produce offshore presented new opportunities. After many visits to China, Jose mastered the many fine points of sourcing and importing products from China. He took what he learned and presented it to trade groups in Las Vegas - specifically the ASD conference. Jose became a regular speaker at SCO - a semiannual conference in Seattle for Amazon resellers. These relationships led to expansion of his e-commerce business.

Jose served eleven years as an Entrepreneur in Residence for CSUF. He coached many students about how to see and adapt to new opportunities.

LAP WORKS® When it comes to Mobile Computing . . . We've got your Lap!

Dear Founder –

When one door closes – another opens. Here's my proof!

On March 31, 2000, I retired after a 20 year career as a commissioned salesman in the packaging industry and the next day I launched LapWorks, Inc. The business was started on a product I invented called the Auto Desk. It was a flat work surface in my car where I could set my notepad and calculator and write customer orders. It started out as a shaped piece of triple-wall corrugated that spanned the space between my arm rest and gear shift knob. Over the years, it morphed as I added a capture for the gear shift knob and grips for the arm rest. Eventually I customized it to my car and upholstered it in the same fabric and color as my 1992 Infiniti Q45. It looked like it belonged in the car.

For the two years prior to retiring from packaging sales, I studied most everything I could find on business launches, Internet marketing and product launches. However, I failed to learn the critical step that leads up to launching a new product. I neglected to determine my product's marketability.

Only after I retired did I commission a market feasibility study for my auto desk by a student team at Cal State San Bernardino. The results were that the upholstered auto desk version would cater only to a smaller, upscale market while a plastic, more versatile version would sell in the after-market auto parts stores. Overall, the market opportunity was smaller than expected.

After receiving this disappointing information, I continued to search the Internet for opportunities and discovered a category of mobile worker called "Mobile Professionals". These were individuals who used notebook computers outside of their offices at least one day a week. Among their chief complaints were no flat surface to rest their notebook onto and that the notebooks got so hot they could only stand the heat for a short while.

One night after learning more details about Mobile Professionals, it occurred to me to just lay the auto desk across my lap. Suddenly I saw the potential for a portable lap desk for these Mobile Professionals. There was nothing like it on the market at the time. I knew enough about the Mobile Professional market to know that the lap desk needed to span the average man's lap; it needed to fold in half to fit in a back pack or computer bag; it needed to be very light weight and it needed to deflect the heat being generated by these notebook computers.

By this time, (year 2,000), I had learned those critical steps that led up to launching a new product. I quickly produced a working, low cost prototype and took it along with an 18-question survey to a Gartner Symposium in San Diego that summer. After receiving numerous threats to cease and desist interviewing their customers, Gartner's security staff finally threw me out of the exhibit hall. But not until I collected 28 survey responses from show attendees (all were Mobile Professionals) who were enthusiastically positive and receptive to a portable lap desk. I returned from this show with absolute confidence that I had a winner.

It took us two and a half years and hundreds of thousands of dollars to gain enough attention to put us over the tipping point. One day in March, 2003 we received a call from a prominent technology accessories retail brand that wanted to sell our Laptop Desk. Within six months we were selling over 20,000 units per month and that sales volume continued for six straight years. In 16-years we've sold over 2.5 million units and the Laptop Desk is still a popular item.

Here are the takeaways from our experience; (1) before you go and bet the farm on a single, stand-alone product, you had better vet the product idea thoroughly before making any serious investments. (2) Make an inexpensive prototype of your product for show and tell. (3) Prepare a 20 or 30-second elevator speech about your product's features & benefits. (4) Stand in front of a retail store that would likely sell products in your category and present it to anyone who exits or enters the store. Simply ask "Have you seen this before?" (5) If you receive a sufficient-number of positive responses, consider producing a small number of working "models" – not manufactured units – to send as sales samples to large retailers and brand holders who would be interested in your new and exciting product. Good Luck, founder, opportunities abound everywhere.

Never give up,

José Calero
President & Chief Product Architect

OCTANe

Bill Carpou is the current chief executive officer of OCTANe. He is also a partner in Visionary Ventures.

Prior to joining OCTANe as CEO, Bill was the Managing Partner for TheGreyGroup which he founded. He focused the company on revenue growth and operational improvement for early stage companies.

From February 2010 through September 2014, Mr. Carpou served in an operating partner role at the Blackstone Group LP ("BG"). BG is an American multinational private equity, alternative asset management and financial services firm. Whille at BG, Bill's responsibilities cluded leading a key portfolio company, RGIS. Mr. Carpou was recruited to this position by BG and was responsible for all aspects of revenue including sales, marketing, channel expansion, strategic alliances, acquisitions and customer service.

Mr. Carpou's prior experience includes three years as a partner at Profit Recovery Partners ("PRP"). PRP is a professional services firm that develops, implements and manages cost-reduction solutions for FORTUNE 1000 companies, law firms, private equity firms and private companies throughout North America. Bill was responsible for the firm's revenue growth initiatives as well as their solutions management practice area.

Before joining PRP, Bill served in a variety of senior executive positions at IKON Office Solutions for 18 years. There he led revenue and Mergers and Acquisitions activities for a variety of key areas within IKON's global operations IKON has since been acquired by Ricoh Corporation.

Bill has had diverse experiences. They include full Profit and Loss responsibility in excess of $1Billion; acquisition responsibility as part of the company's growth strategy; extensive vendor relationships and negotiations with global suppliers; and leading sales organizations of all sizes to achieve their performance goals.

Bill has a bachelor's degree in marketing from Villanova University. He has served on the board of the Barclay Theatre, and serves on the Dean's Advisory Board at the Villanova School of Business.

Bill is a member of the Chief Executive Round-table at the University of California, Irvine. He resides in Laguna Niguel, California.

Dear Founder,

It is exciting to start a business, it brings optimism and creativity to the entrepreneur. It generally energizes you at the same time. My perspective comes from years leading Mergers and Acquisitions efforts for a large public company, as an operating partner at one of the world's leading Private Equity firms and as the CEO of OCTANe. At OCTANe we specifically work with early stage companies that are seeking to raise capital. Let me start with some key success factors that are critical, and also must be in place prior to being admitted to the OCTANe accelerator, LaunchPad SBDC.

Start with the problem you are trying to solve. What exactly is it and how large is the market, who will be the customer? Don't fall in love with technology and make certain the idea has a large addressable market and is not just a niche or cool idea. Anything less than this can be a lifestyle company but the opportunity to grow, add employees and eventually be acquired is limited from day one. Think big!

Formalize your idea, build a business plan. If you need help, seek advise and utilize the many incubators that exist or mentor networks to help build a strong business plan. Don't ever give equity for this work, in fact you should not even have to pay for it. As you build the plan provide realistic projections and **assure you have a path to growth**. How will you fund the company, what will your team look like and what is the timeline to market? **Most entrepreneurs underestimate the time it will take to generate revenue and underestimate the costs to achieve revenue**. This is a deadly combination that leads to many company failures, simply because they did not plan accordingly. **In many instances, entrepreneurs underestimate their own limitations, do not understand what the numbers are saying and strive for perfection when 'good' will do**. Remember, the company and products will evolve over time, waiting for perfection early on is simply a delay to revenue and cause for many failures.

Get the best possible advice. Once the business plan is created be sure you **get the best possible advice from both a legal and financial perspective**. If you are in an area such as Medical Technology do not go cheap on Intellectual Property. Hire the best, it will cost you less in the long run. The same applies to how you want to establish the business legally and what financial structure makes the most sense.

After you have successfully addressed the key success factors I describe above, you will be ready to move on to raising money, which is what OCTANe LaunchPad provides. I invite you to go to the link below for my list of fourteen "must haves" for a company to successfully raise money for the long term, not just one event with one investor. This list is a very high level view that encompasses my past experiences and the process we currently use at OCTANe.

Wishing you success,

Bill Carpou
CEO

For in depth discussion of these topics by the author, please go to https://bit.ly/creatingnewventures

65 Enterprise, Suite 330, Aliso Viejo, California 92656

eCommerce Marketing Consultant

Kevin Carr is an eCommerce Marketing Consultant. After graduating from California State University Fullerton in 1998, Kevin turned his hobby into something that makes money. He helps companies pursue their dreams.

For Kevin it all started as a hobby. He played and researched on the Internet in the early 1990's. This was before search engines were available, and when bulletin boards were still common. The "Internet" consisted of connecting to universities mostly for research -- eCommerce as we know it today did not exist.

Kevin started his professional career as an eMarketer in the late 1990's. Those were the days when email marketing, web analytics, and search engine management were just starting. Alta Vista, Lycos, Excite, and Infoseek were the popular search engines at the time. Users paid by the hour to connect using dial-up modems. It was the Wild West.

During his early years Kevin also worked as a programmer and International Webmaster for companies like Fidelity National Financial and Quiksilver. After Kevin found that programming wasn't that much fun, he focused strictly on eMarketing. He helped companies related to mortgage, apparel, and electronics.

Kevin notes that something that has helped him become a better marketer is working on political campaigns. "Working with an online marketing department is easy and predictable. By contrast, when I work on a political campaign, anything can happen, and it happens in a short period of time. Responding well sharpens my skills."

In the past few years Kevin has been working on a startup which takes up most of his free time. He attends startup events around the Orange and LA Counties for inspiration while working on his dream. He is a graduate of the CSUF Start Up Incubator, Y Combinator (start up school), and the Founder Institute (accelerator).

Kevin lives and works in Orange County. In his spare time he volunteers by helping on issues affecting his city and local area.

Kevin Carr
Stanton, California

Dear Founder,

Congratulations on taking steps towards making your dream a reality. I know for myself, working on my idea hasn't been easy but it has been rewarding. The best advice I can give to anyone thinking about creating a startup is to seek plenty of help and to implement your idea quickly.

Luckily, in the Orange County area there are a lot of free resources to help you with your idea. There are startup programs at a few colleges, a couple of Small Business Administration related agencies that offer help, and startup events are happening just about every day. And for those that are not in the area, or aren't able to drive around easily, there are online seminars, YouTube videos, startup groups on social media, and online classes. So, there is no shortage of free help.

Something that works for me is to use a service like an idea incubator to help guide me through the process. This helps me to stay focused and accountable. Incubators aren't free and can range from paying money for help or giving up equity for help. Something else to consider is hiring a coach or mentor to help you through your idea. Also, don't be afraid to share your idea with others. When I share my idea I always receive valuable input. And if you are really concerned with your idea being stolen then don't talk about the patentability or give up the secret sauce. Besides, at the end of the day when it's time to launch there might be a similar offering or competition out there with more money and a faster team and that is who you should really be worried about so share and learn all you can now.

Some would say that having a good idea is important, but execution is key so move your idea forward quickly with a no-frills version of it. If you are going to fail then why not fail fast? I mean, if your idea doesn't work isn't it better to find out now rather than later? For example, in my case I was creating a process where you get paid for each unwanted email you receive. Sounds great, right? I mean, how would you like to get paid every time you received an unwanted email from those that aren't on your safe-sender list? Anyway, I put a lot of work into the project but at the end of the day my prototype failed. You see, the way you would get paid was based on the sender of the email viewing advertisements online before the email would go through. More importantly, the sender had to click on an ad once is a while. Well, my live prototype had almost nobody click on the ads so the financials didn't work out the way I expected so I was unable to make a profit. I could have started my project with a prototype like one of my mentors suggested which would have saved me lots of time and trouble.

So, get moving on your idea, get help, get all the feedback you can, and launch quickly. You can either work on your dream or someone else's. Why not give your dream a chance?

Kevin Carr

Kevin Carr

SCORE Volunteer

Terri Carr began her 30-year professional career with IBM 6 days after graduating with a degree in math from the University of New Mexico. Her IBM career would take her from Albuquerque, to positions in Dallas, Austin, Atlanta, Los Angeles and Orange County, California.

Terri's first position was as a Systems Engineer. Her responsibilities included working with a wide variety of businesses across New Mexico. Terri's clients included an Indian jewelry manufacturer, a dairy, a gravel company, a school district, the largest banks in the state and on and on. Among other activities, she would write computer programs for this wide variety of businesses.

When IBM promoted Terri from Albuquerque to Dallas, she introduced the first IBM portable computer. After that, she became the first female Systems Engineering Manager in a seven-state area and worked in Austin.

Several years later when she came to the Orange County area, she managed Systems Engineers and later IBM Business Partners. She was also the Manager of the completion of the tallest building in Orange County as they were building it.

A few years later, Terri spent five years with Vision Solutions, an international software company in Irvine that was an IBM Business Partner. She was the Director of Strategic Alliances and responsible for a global marketing program for the company.

Terri is currently involved in SCORE as a small business mentor, and has held several different positions with SCORE. Terri served as Secretary of the organization for six years and was the

Success Story Chair for eleven years. She was also a member of the board for nine years. SCORE awarded Terri its Platinum award for her activities.

Terri has worked with a wide variety of SCORE clients usually helping with marketing ideas. Two national SCORE videos have featured Terri and one of her longtime clients.

Terri has been involved in several other non profits in the area. They include the Junior League, The Volunteer Center and ARCS (Achievements Rewards for College Scientists) where she was President.

Terri Carr
Anaheim, California

Dear Founder

Best wishes for your new business!

What to do to be successful in your business?

*I believe that you have to be passionate about what you want to do to be successful. Study hard and work hard! Don't underestimate how hard you will have to work. I faced many struggles and challenges when I started working. Sometimes I would work all night to make sure I would meet the deadlines.

*Networking is a key component in and out of the company. Always be prepared to have a business discussion anywhere you go ...parties, on planes, meetings, etc. Do make sure you always have business cards with you. Be interested in learning all you can about your customers.

I had an opportunity for a chance meeting with an IBM executive who was traveling with his son on a plane trip and that single meeting helped me throughout my career.

*Do take advantage of any opportunity that comes your way. In my position at the time, I had an opportunity to advance the status of women across the nation. In many cases, I was the first woman or the first person to do the job I was being asked to do.

Best wishes for your success.

Terri Carr

www.AndrewCarroll.co

Andrew Carroll is a CPA and consultant based in Orange County, California. He is a 2006 alum of CSUF with a BA in Accounting and Finance. Andrew has been advising people on their financial lives for over ten years.

While he attended college, Andrew worked at NCH Tax and Wealth Advisors (NCH) in Fullerton. He discovered he was a "numbers guy." After he completed his college degree and earned his CPA, CGMA, and PFS designations, he continued with NCH for ten years. During his tenure at NCH Andrew advanced to General Manager.

In 2016, Andrew left NCH to found his own practice. As he describes, "My passion is building businesses. A great product is nothing without one! I am a big believer in my local community and in doing our part to always make things better."

Like many founders before him, Andrew seeks ways to focus his strengths on market opportunities. He recalls, "I have helped in more places and ways that I can count: taxes, investments, insurance, business strategy, operations, mergers, acquisitions and accounting." The question is where to focus. Andrew is systematically exploring answers. Following his own advice in his "Dear Founder "letter, Andrew has several "Plan Bs." He technically has four companies that he runs: Kingstone Family Enterprises, Kingstone Financial, Accrual Empire, and CFO Andrew, Inc. His "home base" is www.andrewcarroll.co. It has links to all of them.

Andrew believes that he must build his practice from scratch. He says three precepts underpin his planning,

"(1) Love what you do, do what you love. I really like working with my clients. I like knowing about them, I love learning about different industries, I love the new problems they bring me. (2) Building a financial relationship. Good advice, the core of my business, is about a good, in-depth and ongoing relationship. I must understand the unique situation that people and businesses are in. Delivering this custom and all-inclusive advice is my pleasure and my skill. (3) Building on principles. I looked at the current, flawed industry and where it is going, and what the customers of the next ten years will be demanding. Then I tried to jump ahead to build something for the future. I wanted to build on principles that my customers and I believe in."

Andrew links to the community include support of Crittenton Services for Families and Children. Crittenton is a non-profit child welfare and behavioral health agency with a fifty-year track record. Andrew serves on their board of directors. The North Orange County YWCA named him Man of the Year. Andrew is a cofounder of Titan Angels.

Andrew works with CSUF to support their main fundraiser, Concert Under the Stars. He also serves on the Advisory Board for the Center for Entrepreneurship.

Andrew Carroll

Dear Founder,

First off let me say congratulations on your new venture. Starting a company, of any size and shape, is an accomplishment that so many people (far too many) are afraid to do. Although most of us that have started companies will you tell you that the ones who do it are the ones too stupid to be afraid. Who knows?

I, for many years, had a small wooden sign in my office that said:

"The most successful people are those who are good at Plan B."

It is unattributed, so if someone famous said that, it is news to me. But I've come back to the sign over and over again over the years. It is probably the best piece of advice that a new business owner can hear. It seems like a simple idea – be ready to move onto another plan if something doesn't work.

And this is a pretty simple idea. Most people get it. And most business people (or students of business) will even tend to nod sagely and say "oh yes, you must be ready to pivot!" Which isn't untrue but to me is only the most surface-level understanding of the phrase. It is easy to say "this business is failing, time to see what else we can do." Any idiot can do that. The real business people know that it is never that black and white. The shades of gray are where the millions are made. The morass of maybes that any business owner exists in never gives a clear indication of when it is time to pivot. And if you do decide to pivot, how far? Are you tweaking the model slightly just to monetize in a different way? Or are you going to address an entirely new market segment? Most of these cases are never "we are failing, try something else." The real boldness comes when you can say "we are successful, but not successful enough – time to try something different."

If you have made those decisions successfully in business, then you are smarter than many other business owners. And these might seem like great big changes. Fundamentally changing the way your company operates. But if we drill down, even more, we get another level of understanding: "What if this just isn't for me?" Maybe the entire business needs to shut down. Maybe you need to find a day job. Maybe the entire staff you worked to hire, and train is going to be laid off. And maybe, just maybe out of the weekends of that day job, and the ashes of the last project, a new thing emerges – Success!

And if you have made THOSE decisions, you are in about the top 10% of business owners. Smarter than average and with more tenacity. But we still don't have the entire picture of what it means. To me, the real, true understanding comes from the grit inherent in the idea. It isn't about the business model. It is about how you approach every task, every day. Do you send an email and say "OK, done my part on that, just waiting on that message and THEN I'll move." Or are you the one that sends the email, follows up and figures out how to get the task done regardless of getting what you supposedly need. That is the true secret.

Success comes to those people who get it done anyway. There is always another way. You just have to be ready to find it. Pull out Plan B!

All the Best,

Andrew Carroll

Mihaylo Entrepreneurship Volunteer

Jim Cenname and his wife Ellen co-founded Birdsong Care, Inc. in 2012. The company ran Nightingale Senior Care a service business that provides for the in-home care of older adults and disabled persons. After three years of effective management, Jim and Ellen sold the company and retired.

Jim's professional life started after graduating Penn State University with a Bachelor's degree in Mechanical Engineering. He worked for a short time as an engineer, he then attended Boston University earning a Master's degree in engineering with a business emphasis. Jim recalls, "I realized early that there was more fun and opportunity to grow by running a business than by being a professional engineer."

Before founding his own business Jim ran other people's businesses. Starting as a supervisor, then a department manager, manager, vice president operations and lastly executive vice president running an international manufacturing business for International Aluminum Corporation. Jim's positions spanned seven different companies. Jim recalls, "Variety is the spice of life, and in business it provided me exposure to many ways to find solutions to problems"
.

During the great recession Jim and his spouse Ellen founded Birdsong Care in Orange County, CA. Their compli-mentary skills were the basis of the partnership. Research indicated there was a growing need for the service. They invested $70,000 of their money into startup cost and working capital, rolled up their sleeves built a profitable operation from scratch.

The business had positive cash flow after three months and was profitable after six

months. After three years in business Jim and Ellen had grown the business to an annualized revenue of $750,000. It had quarter over quarter growth for almost all of those twelve quarters.

To prepare the business for sale Jim hired a manager capable of doing almost all of the founders' responsibilities. This enabled the buyer of the business to be an industry outsider with only a part-time need to participate in the operations.

The sale closed in 2015 enabling Jim and Ellen to retire early (at age 57 and 52 respectively). In retirement, Jim continues to enjoy the business world vicariously by mentoring Entrepreneurship students at Mihaylo College of Business and Economics. He is also on the Board of Trustees for California State University, Fullerton's Osher Lifelong Learning Institute. For three years, Jim served as the Vice Chair of the North Orange County Senior Collaborative. He was chair of the membership committee for the Brea Chamber of Commerce. Jim and Ellen live in Brea, California.

Jim Cenname
Brea, California

Dear Founder,

To be a happy and successful founder please consider these three principles:

Follow the golden rule, "Do unto others as you would have them do unto you."
Be honest with and fair to your employees, vendors, business partners, customers and spouse or life-partner. Use caution when you say: "I will do whatever it takes to..." someday "whatever it takes" may be unethical, immoral or dishonest and that is the proverbial slippery slope from which it is hard to recover. Most importantly, be honest with yourself. Do not justify to yourself why it is okay to be dishonest, not even "just this once." If you use the phrase "To be honest with you..." others will believe there are times you are not honest with them. Any statement to an employee, customer or vendor should not need to be qualified as being "honest."

Accept responsibility for yourself.
When your business succeeds or fails, it will be your decisions and your actions that made that happen. Every business needs employees, customers and vendors. You, as founder will hire the staff, choose the customers, make the decisions and establish the policies and procedures your team uses to do what you incentivize them to do. When you fail in business take the experience to heart and use it to grow and be a better business person.

Know what is important in life.
Founders will work a lot in the first years of their start-up. Be aware of how you balance work and the other important parts of your life; your family and friends. I believe that few dying people say "I should have spent more time at the office". Death can sneak up on us at any age, ask someone losing a battle with cancer or a hospital emergency room worker, don't put off the really important stuff.

Most dictionary-definitions of "successful" do not have the words "money" or "power" in them. May you truly know what you want. May you be successful in getting it.

Jim Cenname

Cognitive Impact

Curtis Chan is President and CEO/Founder and Managing Partner of two high technology Brand Marketing and Public Relations companies, CHAN & ASSOCIATES and COGNITIVE IMPACT, whose clients range from the Global Fortune 500 to venture capital funded startups.

His agencies' services, for over a quarter century, have helped garner early stage and growth companies significant brand exposure, resulting in either acquisition or IPO, with a total valuation of over $2 Billion.

Mr. Chan is a serial entrepreneur, philanthropist, author and angel investor. He played key executive roles early on in helping to pioneer and usher in both professional digital audio and digital video technologies for the recording, broadcast, cinematic and post production industries. He also played key executive roles in helping to develop and market data storage technologies. His expansive background spans four decades in ever increasing executive roles in operations, business development, engineering and sales/marketing in the information technology, media & entertainment, storage and networking, and other related high technology industries.

He is an active mentor and senior advisor to many established and start-up companies, a market/technology analyst, and has three decades of experience in brand development, management consulting, company turnarounds, creative advertising and public relations.

A graduate of California Polytechnic State University (Cal Poly), San Luis Obispo; Mr. Chan is celebrating his 10th year as a Board of Director for the Fullerton College Foundation and recipient of the 2017

President's Award for Outstanding Service in Business; 16th year as an Entrepreneur-in-Residence and mentor for the Small Business Institute at California State University Fullerton and incubators. Additionally, he is a volunteer member of DECA (Delta Epsilon Chi and Distributive Education Clubs of America); an advisor to the College of Engineering's Global Waste Research Institute, Cal Poly, San Luis Obispo and a member of the President's Green and Gold Society. Passionate about hospice care, he was the past Board President for the Healing Hearts Association; and is a regularly featured speaker at many MBA and Doctorate level lectures around the country. He has presented and published over 30 papers worldwide, is a book co-author, an Editorial Board Member for the Society of Motion Picture and Television Engineers, Senior Editor for Broadcast Beat Magazine, past Senior Editor for Computer Technology Review, and is a regularly featured Contributing Editor to many US and international trade publications for over 30 years.

Dear Founder,

Congratulations on the launch of your venture. Mark Twain said that "The two most important days in your life are the day you are born and the day you find out why." I hope that the start of your business is part of the 'why'. It will be the beginning of one of the greatest adventures and self-reflection of your life. One area that will help you reach your vision is to master the art of being a leader. Here's some takeaways from my four decades as an executive and serial entrepreneur.

Creative Curiosity: Be passionate, relentless and infectiously fascinated in everything around you. Great leaders use all their senses to hone their creative vision by observing, questioning, interacting and applying what's around them. Remember that the true sign of intelligence is not knowledge but imagination.

Market Guru: Ask questions, conduct research and learn your market inside and out, including the key suppliers, distributors, competitors and customer base. Take input from all applicable sources to understand your future customer to help create an on-target, go-to-market strategy and rollout plan.

Numbers Wizard: Successful leaders learn to understand all aspects of their financial model – from optimizing their financial condition, to planning for profitability and contingencies, to utilizing every dollar in the most efficient way while minimizing cash-outs.

Calculated Risk Taking: Leaders take informed calculated risks, seek competitive opportunities and are proactive in being a positive force – leveraging their capex and opex resources for the betterment of their people and company.

Warrior Mentality: Leaders deal with and overcome adversity and setbacks head on. Every failure adds to your learning experience and leadership toolset. Learn from mistakes and move on.

Coach and Mentor: Great leaders learn to understand what drives their people, noting everyone's uniqueness, and provides inspiration, encouragement, mentorship, direction, example, compassion and empathy to help their people be all that they can be.

Great Communicator: Leaders are great communicators. They are able to take a complex task, situation or vision and concisely, simplistically and clearly convey it. Great communication has the side benefit of influencing opinion and creating positive change.

Life Long Engagement: Successful leaders find ways to support and continue to engage in stimulating exchanges with their people, long after they leave the company.

Moral, Ethical and Spiritual Integrity: Leaders understand that the two things they leave behind to their heirs and company culture are their integrity and the minimization of prejudices that they may have learned along the way. Keep the first intact and eliminate the latter. The question you should ask yourself everyday is "Would you follow you?"

Philanthropy and Giving Back: Always find ways to give back and 'pay it forward'. You will be remembered for what you did to give back to society, not necessarily for your successes.

Very best regards,

Curtis Chan

Curtis Chan
President & CEO, CHAN & ASSOCIATES, INC.
Founder & Managing Partner, COGNITIVE IMPACT

College Web Media

Rudy Chavarria Jr. is the founder and CEO of College Web Media. His work in the entertainment industry goes back to the 1980's, when he worked in and around Hollywood, most notably as a runner for A&M Records.

Rudy started his first company, Rude Records, in 1993, signing and promoting independent bands on his company's label. He promoted mostly and successfully to the college demographic.

Rudy eventually focused exclusively on promotions and marketing in the college demographic. He started Rude College Promotions, which came to be called American AMP (Advertising, Marketing & Promotions), expanding his scope of services to include promoting film as well as music.

Since then, Rudy has gone on to promote many highly-acclaimed films and recordings. Films include The Passion of the Christ, Rocky Balboa, The Chronicles of Narnia, United 93, The Puffy Chair, OLDBOY, Hidden Figures, Big Hero 6, War for the Planet of the Apes and many others. Recordings include works by Bob Marley and Jaco Pastorius.

In 2007, Rudy started College Web Magazine, an audio/video based website. Part news magazine, part social network. In 2010, Chavarria filmed a college band going through its paces and posted it to the CWM website, calling it, Breaking the College Band. Soon, CWM became college web productions, which produces entertainment and educational programming and continues the magazine's tradition of interviews and event coverage.

In 2017, Rudy shut the doors of American AMP and decided to run full force with College Web Media as a college marketing and media company. He is now working on a new venture called College Web Mentor. It is a company that helps college students make wise education and career decisions. The company has raised seed investment and is currently building a strong team.

Rudy has a long-time connection with CSUF Entrepreneurship. Since 2014, he has been a mentor for student consulting teams enrolled in Management 464, Entrepreneurial Leadership.

In his spare time, Rudy enjoys going to the gym, skateboarding, song writing and reading. He is married and lives in Southern California.

Dear Founder.

Problem solving is at the top of my important list. Problem-solving is a term that is used in elementary school. However, in my 25+ years of experience as an entrepreneur, problem solving stands out. Granted, there is a time for persistence, discipline, negotiation, creativity, and so on. However, nothing else matters if you do not have the ability to problem solve, the agility to do so as the snap of your fingers, and the grit to stand by your solution. To demonstrate, I will tell you a story. Imagine that you want to get into the entertainment business. You don't have a degree in entertainment or know anyone in the business to help you. What do you do? How are you going to problem solve to overcome this obstacle? Start with the basics. If you don't know anyone in the industry you are trying to break into, start at the very bottom.

That is exactly what I did. I was 21 years old and working at Home Depot. I wasn't in college because I had no idea what type of education I wanted. College seemed like a waste of time. I wasn't sure if I wanted to be a singer, songwriter, talent scout or a worker in the recording studio. I just knew I wanted in. One afternoon, I happened to be at lunch with a co-worker from Home Depot and she said to me, "If you really want to be in the entertainment business, what are you doing working at Home Depot? She was right.

I needed to figure out how I could get into Entertainment. I knew working a nine to five job at Home Depot was not going to leave me time to look for work in the industry. I quit Home Depot. I took a job at Chili's as a food server and worked nights. During the day I looked for a job in Hollywood. It was much easier back then to find work. I was able to walk in all the major studios and record companies. I asked for work and filled out applications right on the spot. However I didn't have any connections, I didn't know anyone to refer me to the right person.

After my night shifts at Chili's, I would drive to Hollywood and hang out at every studio security gate and chat with the security guards. I needed a connection. I honed in on the famous A&M Records recording studio in Hollywood off La Brea Boulevard and Sunset Boulevard. Every weekend for almost three months, I would get off work at 1:30AM and drive from the City of Industry Chili's to A&M. The first weekend I visited A&M, the security guards came to the gate and asked, "Can I help you?" Mind you, at the time I looked more like 15 years old then 21. I meekly said, "Well, I want to get into the business but don't really know anyone." The guard just looked at me and nodded and said, "Well you can't hang around here." In less than 40 seconds, I slowly walked away. The following weekend I showed up again. I drove 45 minutes to A&M at 1:30 in the morning. I had a 40 second conversation with a security guard who thought I was just a crazy kid. Still, I knew I stood by my solution. I was going to make something come of it. On that fateful second trip, as I left A&M I noticed all the security guards had one simple thing in common. They all had a cup of coffee in their hand. A" light bulb" went on in my head. I had an idea. The following weekend I showed up with coffee and a box of donuts for ALL of the security guards. The guards looked at me like I was crazy, but they accepted the gifts through the gate and all I said was, "I thought you guys could use this?" They all said thank you and were elated. I immediately excused myself and said, "You guys have a good night." I did this purposely, so they didn't feel like they owed me anything. They had confused looks on their faces, as I left swiftly. I decided to do the same thing the following weekend.

When I went a week later, there was a new guard on duty that came to the gate, and very sternly said, "Can I help you?" All the other guards yelled out, "Let him in, he's cool!" After about six weeks of doing this every weekend, one of the guards, (Henry) said to me, "Rudy, you still interested in working here?" I was in! All my hard work had paid off. Henry gave me a number and a name and told me what day and time to call. I got the job and began my career in the entertainment business.

I have seen many entrepreneurs eyes open up after I tell this story. Their "light bulb" go on in their head. It's different for every one of them, but they get it. I had to problem solve. It took everything in the book to make it work, but the bottom line was that I had a major problem to solve and I did.

Best of luck to you,

Rudy Chavarria, Jr.
Founder, CEO

Synova Life Sciences

John Chi is the Founder and CEO of Synova Life Sciences, a regenerative medicine company. It is currently bringing a medical device to market that can extract a person's own stem cells from their fat. Synova is currently working with orthopedists to give patients their own stem cells for joint regeneration. John is the inventor of the technology and has coauthored two recent patents on it.

John has been a lead developer at Novica, an e-commerce startup; an expert IT analyst at the College of Natural Sciences and Mathematics at California State University Fullerton (CSUF); CTO and Co-Founder of Digital Quest, a visual effects and post-production company, and a lead developer at Magellan Software, a data-warehousing company. He consults in software and web development. One summer, he worked at the Aerospace Corporation, a defense contractor, and quickly realized that world wasn't for him.

John received a BS in Electrical Engineering from Stanford University. It took him five years because he didn't know what he wanted to do, coming in as a French major. He started a Master's program in Electrical Engineering at UC Irvine in Machine Vision, but paused to co-found Digital Quest, and never went back. Later, he completed a Master's in Biotechnology from CSUF with Cal Poly Pomona and Cal State LA. He almost didn't finish because he paused for three years in the middle of it to start Synova. He returned just in time to finish by stretching a two-year program out to its maximum five-year limit.

Besides Synova, John currently advises several early stage startups and mentors several entrepreneurs. He sits on the Advisory Board of STEM-Inc. It is a National Science Foundation funded after-school program between CSUF and the Anaheim Union High School District to advance STEM (Science Technology Engineering and Mathematics) learning with an entrepreneurial focus among underrepresented junior high students. John serves on the Advisory Board of ProgressWorks, a nonprofit venture fund for job creation and retention. He is the head screener for BioPacific Investors, a cross-border angel group with a focus on life sciences and Asian markets.

John won the CSUF Business Plan Competition. He is a frequent guest speaker on campus. He enjoys chess, basketball, volleyball, cycling, and plays guitar and piano. John speaks French and Mandarin. After studying Kung Fu for 14 years, he earned the title of Kung Fu Master and continues to train.

SYNOVA
LIFE SCIENCES

Dear Founder,

You're about to start down a road that will be a wild ride full of ups and downs, and twists and turns. Exciting and exhilarating, frustrating and exhausting, energizing and fun, depressing and lonely, all of these and so much more. The best and the worst feelings in the world will all be there. The intense pressure will create relationship bonds that will be unbreakable, and others that will be totally blown into dust. There is no journey like it. I'd like to share with you three actions that were keys to my success. Ask. Persist. Love.

Ask. I used to have a lot of difficulty asking for what I needed, but this is one of the critical skills I learned for success in being a founder. Being a founder is going to be a roller-coaster ride, and you're going to need a lot of things along the way, so don't hesitate to ask. You'll need mentors. Find people that you trust and respect. Ask them for help and advice. Building a great team isn't easy, but when you find the right people, ask them to join you. You'll need to make sure your product has a market. And that means you'll need to ask a lot of customers a lot of questions. You're probably going to need money, and there are all kinds of ways to get it so you'll need to learn how to ask for money: pitching is a learned skill, as is grant writing. No one comes into the world knowing how to do either. Even more importantly, ask people how you can help them, how they feel, what they need, who they are – and remember to ask yourself the same things. Ask and be grateful, and it will come.

Persist. This is not so much an action as it is a state of mind. When you're a founder, you're going to have to weather many storms and overcome many obstacles. You will be pushed out of your comfort zone in a million different ways. You'll be stretched to your limits and will grow, learn, and do things you never thought you ever would, could, or even wanted to do. You'll win and lose, and will make mistakes, some big, some small. Sometimes things will seem impossible or insurmountable. Don't give up. Some people will doubt you. Some will tell you that what you're trying to do can't be done. Don't believe it. The more you keep going, the more you will prove them wrong. Sometimes when the goal seems impossibly far away, just look at the very next thing that you need to do, and then the next, and the next. Just continue to put one foot in front of the other. Before you know it, you'll have miles of footprints behind you, and your goal will be right there in front of you. You will have arrived.

Love. Make sure you love what you do, and love why you do it. Some people call it passion, some call it enthusiasm. It will be the fuel you need to execute on your idea to make it real. It's why you're the only one still awake working on a problem after everyone else has gone to bed. That passion, that love for what you're doing will keep you on it until you find a solution. It's what will give you the energy to practice your pitch one more time, to talk to one more customer, to run one more experiment, to pitch one more time, to respond to one more email, to make one more edit, and to stay up just one more hour to finish just one more thing. When all else is exhausted, that love will keep you going. It will get you through the hard times, and fill the good times with meaning and gratitude. Love what you do, love the people in your life, and love yourself. If you do these things, you will always be successful!

Wishing you all the best and success in your new venture!

John Chi

Grit, Determination and Optimism

Jerome Chiaro is a 2006 graduate of the CSUF Entrepreneurship Program. While at CSUF, he founded Restaurant Management University ("RMU"), an online community with 50,000 restauranteur members. He still consults for RMU. His current projects are clinical site operations for StudyKiK a network of patient communities, and volunteer work for SCORE and other community non-profits.

Jerome dabbled in entrepreneurship at age nine selling donuts, wrapping Christmas trees, really doing anything he could in the community . He began working at his family's restaurant bussing tables and eventually managed the restaurant. Then he launched a restaurant with a fast-casual Mexican concept from the ground up.

RMU was a natural outgrowth of his restaurant experience, enriched by his college classes. It offers webinars, videos and live training for restaurant owners on marketing and operations skillsets. RMU includes a Restaurant Consultant Agency. The agency's consultants have ownership and management experience in QSRs, Full-Service, and Fine Dining restaurants.

StudyKIK, is an online health community. Its mission is to enable anyone who wants to volunteer for a clinical trial to easily search, find and participate in clinical studies. Clinical trials help bring new cures, medicines and treatments to market.

StudyKIK uses social media as a platform for discussion and

innovation. It builds patient communities on Facebook, Instagram, Pinterest, Twitter and Snapchat to educate and create awareness about large and rare population diseases and to connect patients and caregivers to doctors. StudyKIK started in 2014. Today it has over a million patients in it's network and is connected to over 1200 doctors across North America, Europe and Asian-Pacific.

Jerome serves as VP of Clinical Site Operations of StudyKIK. He makes good use of his specialties in patient advocacy, social media communities, search engine optimization, restaurant consulting and small business mentoring

Volunteer work is a big part of Jerome's life. He is currently a mentor and workshop presenter for SCORE Orange County, helping small businesses grow. He also volunteers at local community projects dedicated to helping Veteran's hospitals, women's shelters, and the homeless.

Jerome is not, "all work and no play." Growing up in the restaurant industry, he has a passion for food, wine and travel.

Jerome Chiaro
Costa Mesa, CA

Dear Founder:

I was told that most successful entrepreneurs come from state colleges and it is true (no I don't have stats on this one but just go with it). I've talked to many a Harvard/ Stanford MBA graduate (and not knocking the program) but these guys and gals typically don't have the *entrepreneurial grit* to bootstrap a startup venture. According to a Mercury News survey, "Two-thirds of the CEOs of the (Silicon) valley's 150 largest public companies who earned their undergraduate degrees in the United States attended taxpayer-funded public universities, state colleges and regional schools. About one out of six studied overseas."

And this is just the largest 150 public companies, imagine the smaller more agile private companies that are disrupting the technology world right now... do you think they are ran by Ivy League grads? The startup world is a completely different animal and I hope you can take something away from the following three tips, if not just the confidence that you can create something amazing in the world no matter what your background is, who you know, how much you think you know, or how much money you have.

Tip one: Ask for Help -- The biggest mistake I made was doing things alone. Entrepreneurs are at times lone wolves (because hey, who else is going to stay up at midnight talking to a team in India about Golang vs. Node.js). We pontificate and pine, searching for the perfect answer to problems and roadblocks. The answer is simple, yet juxtaposeingly difficult for our giant (necessarily), fragile egos. Ask for help!!! Use SCORE in Orange County (I now volunteer for them), they offer a wealth of free business knowledge via mentors (115 in Orange County alone) and workshops. Join a Forum or Meetup.com group, better yet form a weekly Mastermind with likeminded people. (Read Napolean Hill's Think and Grow Rich if you are unfamiliar with this concept.) Use Fiverr.com or Upwork.com to find freelancers to help you with design/ coding/ writing/ heck send your boyfriend a birthday tune (yes that is really a job on Fiverr). Asking for help includes your customers. I am customer obsessed, I ask them how I can improve my product, sales pitch, business model, customer service. They tell me exactly what to build, how to build it and how to deliver it to them. My job is simply to do what they tell me and sell it to them!

Tip two: Don't Reinvent the Wheel -- Pablo Picasso once said, "good artists borrow, great artists steal." Now, I'm not advocating breaking into your competitor's shop to take his or her blueprints. But if someone has already been successful at something in my industry there must be a reason why. I find out, rinse and repeat. I don't let my ego drive me to "create something that no one has done before." In fact, I like to re-create something that everyone has done before (just make it better/faster/cheaper). 99% of product ideas have already been thought of, 99% of business problems have already been addressed and overcome. If I am struggling with anything I go back to step 1 (ask for help) and I don't make stuff up! Find out what others did and repeat it, chances are it's already been done. Entrepreneurship is *straight hustle,* not smartness, intellect or brilliance. Entrepreneurship is breaking down barriers that others are afraid to break down or unwilling to put the effort into breaking down.

Tip three: Leadership is EVERYTHING. Leadership starts with leading myself.... What are *My* Standards? Do I show up to meetings/ life on time? Do I return phone calls in a timely manner? The number one reason why businesses fail is not the product, customer, website and so on, it is the management team (in our case, the founders of the business). And it is usually due to low standards, lack of care/purpose and poor leadership. I've been on both ends of this spectrum. The last company I started, I showed up early and was NEVER late. Guess what. Everyone was ALWAYS on time and we never have had "write ups," "talks," or any other silly corporate "management tactics." If I expect my employees to show up on time and stay late, I better show up before them and leave after they do. If I expect my customers to buy a lot from me, I better give a lot to them. If I expect to find investors, I better invest in myself and my business first.

According to Janet Yellen, the world's most famous money maven, "There is an unfortunate myth that success is mainly determined by something called 'ability'," Anyone can do the above. They are easy to do, and easy not to do. It all comes down to grit, determination, and unyielding unwavering optimism.

Yours Truly,

Jerome Chiaro

Intrapreneurial Spirit

Eleni [Mantalozi] Christianson is Vice President-Business Development for Kana Pipeline, Inc. (KP). KP is a leading wet utility pipeline construction company. It installs new water, sewer and storm drainage pipeline infrastructure. KP serves public works, private residential, commercial, industrial and institutional developments throughout Southern California. It had $60 million in sales in 2016.

KP created Eleni's current position in January 2010. She was the first to hold it. Before that, Eleni served in three other "new" intrapreneurial roles for the Company: first Executive Assistant to the Founder, President and CEO, first Project Coordinator and first female Project Manager. She joined KP Pipeline April 2003, during her Senior year at CSUF. She concentrated in Entrepreneurial Management.

During her time at KP, Eleni meticulously handled over $10 million in construction contracts as Coordinator. She stream-lined key internal operations for better efficiency. She later managed over $25 million in projects, under budget and within schedule. She spearheaded the company's marketing efforts and serves as KP's spokesperson in public relations.

Eleni held several jobs before joining KP. They awakened her intrapreneurial spirit. Her experiences include retail and restaurant, partner in a nonprofit educational and recycling company, sales rep for Vector Marketing Corporation (selling Cutco brand knives) and warehouse clerk for a wholesale beauty supply distributor. Between these jobs she did some acting for television, and freelance work as a Production Assistant for both national and internationally featured television commercials starring several world famous movie stars.

Eleni attributes her success at KP to more than her entrepreneurial management degree. "When I joined KP I was already a serial intrapreneur and an avid networker of value-driven relationships with both external and internal customers." Her motto is, "Persist and you *will* succeed!"

Eleni is active in several philanthropic, civic and cultural organizations in Southern California. She currently serves on several committees within the Building Industry Association of Southern California. She has championed many charitable events through KP such as Donate Life CA/Run-Walk, 2nd Harvest Food Bank. Most recently, she serves on Norco College's President's Advisory Board.

Eleni was born in southern Greece. She lived in Mexico for a time. Since the age of six she has resided in California. English is her third language. She attended Hollywood Performing Arts. The school named her best female musician of her graduating class.

Kana Pipeline, Inc.

Dear Founder:

Every single day you have a choice on how to behave, act and react to your environment and events that happen all around you in both personal and business matters. It is my hope that you will be fair in all your business dealings; that you won't, "trip on your power cord." Don't fear failure and don't be afraid to change course.

While I have not "found" my own company as an entrepreneur (yet), I have treated every business I work in as if it was my own, and doing so allowed me to grow these firms and myself, personally, in the *intra*preneurial spirit.

You will find value in allowing the *intra*preneurial spirit to flourish in your workforce. Allow ideas and suggestions to flow. Allow your team the opportunity to challenge the norm and think outside the box and actually put their skills to use.

Learn to appreciate the value you receive from others. Some of the best lessons I've learned, was from a 4 year old's curious question on life and a 79 year old housekeeper's life experience and her always asking me, "What did you learn?" Take your daily experiences, and ask yourselves, "What did you gain from the experience?"…"How will it propel you forward in other ways?" …"How will it move you to change your behavior in the future?"

The only thing constant is change and you will be a changed person 1,5,10, or 20 years from now, whether you like it or not, and hopefully for the better, so embrace change!

Also, it's not *who* you know anymore; it's how do you know them? Get to know your team. Get to know people. Make the time. Engage in conversation and remember to express gratitude and appreciation for those qualities you admire in others. The phrase, "Love people and use things - and not the other way around," comes to mind.

Find time to read on worthy subjects that intrigue you. Leaders are readers; readers are learners and learners are listeners. Then, share what you've learned and exchange ideas.

Last, but not least, don't be hard on yourself for mistakes along the way. Mistakes will happen. So instead, take it all in as a *learning experience*. There are no problems, only learnings.

We are meant to grow so we have something to give, right? So let the world be a better place because you're in it! Cheers to your growth and much success in your new venture ahead!

Sincerely and Humbly Yours,

Eleni M. Christianson

Bottom Line Remodel

Mark Collins founded Bottom Line Remodel in 2008. It provides business coaching and digital marketing services to contractors and entrepreneurial businesses.

Mark earned his BS in business and accounting at Northern Illinois University where he played varsity baseball. He spent the early years of his career as a consultant with CPA firms Price Waterhouse, and then McGladrey. Mark worked with entrepreneurial clients on financial, operational and computer systems projects. He worked in the Chicago and Los Angeles offices of PW, and the Chicago, Orange County and San Diego offices of McGladrey.

He then accepted a position as Vice President of Finance with a client company, the Grand Prix Association of Long Beach, a special event promoter. Besides his financial duties, Mark was involved with merchandising, souvenir program sales and a celebrity charity golf tournament sponsored by Toyota.

Mark's consulting experience with a variety of entrepreneurial companies, and his hands-on experience with the Long Beach Grand Prix provided the impetus for entrepreneurship.

Mark decided to become a franchisee for a home improvement contractor. A franchise offered him corporate training and support, but provided autonomy for all operations, including sales, marketing, customer service, and management. Mark steadily grew the business over a 12-year period. It eventually became a leading franchisee in overall revenue growth and individual sales metrics.

After selling his business, Mark worked in sales and management for several home improvement companies, both large and small. He learned and gained valuable experience, especially regarding lead generation and the sales process. The fundamentals of success were very similar in all the companies. The fundamentals held true whether the monthly marketing budget was $1,000 or $100,000, or the sales staff consisted of two reps or twenty reps.

Mark's current venture, Bottom Line Remodel, provides business coaching and digital marketing services to contractors and entrepreneurial businesses. Mark's goal is to help his independent clients compete with larger companies and franchisees of established franchise organizations. His firm helps clients with lead generation, sales processes, performance metrics and marketing automation.

Mark mentors for the Center for Entrepreneurship at CSUF's Mihaylo College of Business and Economics. He lives in Tustin, California.

Dear Founder:

What Is An Entrepreneur?

The college graduates of my time were seeking jobs with large corporations that offered a salary, benefits, and security. My first job out of college was in technology, and I had to decide between offers from Burroughs Corporation (the #2 computer company behind IBM at that time) and Sears, who used to be a prominent retailer. So much for security.

The word "entrepreneur" was mentioned very little in my business school, and its meaning wasn't clear. For me, I thought it meant an innovator or inventor, someone like Apple's Steve Jobs or Microsoft's Bill Gates whose products were unique and life changing.

Over the next several years, I was a consultant for two CPA firms, and had the opportunity to work with many different types of clients. Some were large corporations, but most were smaller businesses with individual owners. I learned the true definition of an entrepreneur – a person who starts and runs a business, and took a risk to do so. The type of business is irrelevant. I've known many successful entrepreneurs who did not invent the Mac or Windows. One company repaired industrial fans. Another company manufactured closet organizers that doubled the storage space in a closet. An unemployed sales rep learned how to use Google AdWords for his startup business back when AdWords first came out. He started teaching others how to use AdWords, and now has a leading training and consulting firm.

Entrepreneurs run many different types of businesses, and most didn't require an invention, a patent, or the world's greatest idea. It is about innovation and risk-taking. But the innovation could involve customer service (think Zappos). Or convenience (think GrubHub). Or maybe a new business model (Uber & Lyft). Shoes, food, and ride-hailing are not new ideas or inventions, but innovative companies changed the market.

Entrepreneurship is a mindset. It can be rewarding. It can be frustrating. But it can be worth it. Maybe you will invent a new product, or an app that everyone downloads. Or, maybe you just give new life to an old product, with innovation and differentiation. Whatever you do, make sure it is all about your customer or client. Givers gain. Enjoy the journey.

To Your Success,

Mark Collins

SIATT Insurance Corporation

Jerry Conrey is the CEO of SIATT Insurance Corporation. SIATT is the corporate parent of Conrey Insurance Brokers and Risk Managers, and related consulting operations. He is both the agency principal and the principal consultant.

Although most people call insurance brokers looking for a quote, you'll never "just get a quote" from Jerry's insurance operation. It does insurance differently. Jerry positions his agents as primarily risk managers. His focus is on providing proper protection, not just shopping around for the lowest price. This is why the firm's starting point with new clients is always a detailed risk assessment. Only after this diagnosis is complete, does the firm prescribe the appropriate protection to mitigate or transfer those risks.

When Jerry acquired SIATT in 2002, he immediately started putting his 14 years of insurance industry experience to work. He focused on client acquisition and relationships, and hired an outstanding team to manage the people and processes. Jerry grew the business nearly fourfold, from $4 million to $15 million in annual sales. Nearly all insurers the firm represents recognize it as among the top 1 percent of producers. In June 2016 it was named the Agency of the Month by Rough Notes, a top industry publication.

Jerry is an alumnus of CSUF. Giving back has always been one of his top priorities. For the past 14 years he has volunteered with the Small Business Institute at CSUF's Mihaylo College of Business and Economics. He serves as a mentor to small groups of students as they work to solve real-life problems for participating businesses. He has also mentored for the New Venture Creation and New Venture Launch classes. For many years Jerry

has been a scholarship sponsor, positively affecting the lives of many students. Presently, he is the Executive Vice President of Sigma Alpha Mu Fraternity, an international collegiate fraternity. He joined as an undergraduate at CSUF.

Jerry has served in many volunteer roles. They include, member of the board of directors of the American Agent's Alliance, Chief Financial Officer of the Alliance, 20 year member of his church and Elder for his church. Jerry currently serves as the Elder for Business Administration and Staff Relations.

For the past two decades Jerry has been happily married to his wonderful wife, Victoria Shook Conrey, MD. They live in North Tustin, CA. Jerry's recreational passions include golf, poker, wine tasting, wine collecting and watching Broadway-style musicals. He rocks out as the lead singer in the "Big Boy Band."

Dear Founder,

After nearly three decades in the insurance industry I realize that there are three things I have done that have had the greatest impact on my business' success. As you prepare to launch your own venture, I highly recommend that you do these things, too:

1. **Differentiate your business –** If you want your business to succeed, make sure it doesn't look and sound just like everyone else in your industry.

   There are countless ways that you can accomplish this. For example, you can offer value-added services that a prospective client would perceive as making your offering significantly more valuable than competitive offerings. You can differentiate your business based on your knowledge, the way you communicate and the format in which you present solutions. While these are all things that I do, they are not the only options.

   However you choose to make it happen, you *must* bring a unique perspective and approach to your marketplace. Give people a reason to do business with *you* instead of someone else.

2. **Properly invest in your business –** I cannot overstate the degree to which people are absolutely key. Hire the best people and empower them to add to the synergy of the organization.

   Make sure that your business always has the best technology. Among other things, your technology should make it pleasant for your people to do their jobs and for your customers to do business with you.

   Don't expect the sign on your door to generate business. Invest in a great marketing program. Plus, be aware that marketing is a discipline that requires a consistent, perpetuated effort. Many business owners slow their marketing efforts when business is booming (because they don't have time) or when times are tough (because they don't have money). Both are critical errors that can hinder the success of your business.

3. **Identify and manage your KPIs –** Over the years I have relied on the ability to track my business' key performance indicators (KPIs), and I strongly recommend that you do the same. Why? Because, as Peter Drucker famously said, "If you can't measure it, you can't improve it."

   Determine exactly what the unique KPIs are for your business and industry, and then put a process in place to track and measure them. Your KPIs might be opportunities to sales, average sale, customer satisfaction, output, waste, or a variety of other things. Whatever they might be, learning early which things indicate whether or not your business is running well is critical to your success.

Finally, remember that if you're constantly working *in* your business you can't be working *on* it. Every time you can outsource a task or responsibility to someone else, whether through a direct hire, vendor or subcontractor, you're freeing up time that you can (and should) use to get back to honoring the vision and strategy you have as an entrepreneur.

Wishing you a great deal of success in your endeavors,

Jerry Conrey

Opportunity is a Path One Creates

Jim Cooper is cofounder and CTO of Braid Theory ("BT") in San Pedro California. BT weaves together entrepreneurs, industry influencers and corporate partners to accelerate adoption of transformative technology, drive market growth and create profitable collaborations. It is a strategic advisory company, which also supplies incubation resources for early stage technology startups.

Jim is founder and Principal of Conscientia Research. It is a full-service market research business. Its goals are to make businesses successful and competitive by employing research to understand markets. Its intent is to assure that its clients do not have to rely on assumptions about how a market works.

Currently, Jim advises twelve companies, including one in New Zealand, one in Australia, and another in the United Arab Emirates ("UAE"). Their products range from robotics to genetics. He has fifteen years of experience in commercialization and concentrates on bringing to market novel early-stage technology startups in emerging market segments. Jim specializes in customer and market validation, competitive analysis, business modeling and go-to-market strategy. He is an adherent of evidence-based entrepreneurship, and uses the lean startup methodology, design-thinking, and other more traditional approaches to business modeling. He is passionate about providing a pedagogy for startups to coalesce around and create meaningful benchmarks, way points, and milestones.

Jim was educated in both Australia and the United States concentrating in economics and the life sciences. He has experience in both the public and private sectors, which positions him to help companies in the deep science and engineering fields, including Agriculture and Food Tech, Biotech, Aerospace, Advanced Manufacturing, Transportation, Marine and Maritime.

Prior to Braid Theory, Jim was Entrepreneur-in-Residence at PortTech Los Angeles. PortTech is an incubator in the South Bay. He also was Principal Advisor at the LARTA Institute.

.

Jim is currently an Entrepreneur in Residence in the Global Advisory Program, at UAE University (El Ein). He is on the board of advisors for the Center for Innovation at CSULA. Jim serves on the industry panel in agriculture at Cal Poly Pomona. He is an industry mentor and advisor for NSF i-Corps in the CSUPERB program across all twenty three campuses of the California State University system.

Jim serves as an Ambassador and mentor for the Center for Entrepreneurship at California State University Fullerton. When not advising, consulting with, or incubating startups, he enjoys playing soccer as a goalkeeper, eating ice cream and playing drums in a punk band

Dear Founder,

Opportunity is a path one creates. Those of us who take a hard-right turn into entrepreneurship, are often in a position where we are slogging it out with our own ventures. We struggle to pay ourselves or pay bills. We look for cost savings and still operate at a loss. In my case, the temptation was there to seek employment elsewhere, but I wouldn't have ever considered giving up. The feelings that drove me were both negative and positive. On the one hand, fear that no one would employ me. On the other hand, my desire to create something and leave behind a legacy.

Etched into my mind was my ideal vision of the spirit of the entrepreneur. Its hallmarks are resourcefulness and tenacity. A kind of grit is invaluable when beginning a new enterprise.

I believe it is best to show initiative. It is better to decide, even if wrong, than to make no decision at all. Still charging ahead blindly has no advantage to thinking all avenues through. Sometimes being strategic requires you to stay the course, rather than pivoting too frequently. I find plans indispensable and a business plan is the best of all. A business plan should be a living document. The universe has some twists and turns, which can confound us. Remain vigilant and steadfast. Success will come.

Due to the small size of their domestic market, I like the global perspective the New Zealanders have: day one they start a business, and day two, they go global. That kind of nimbleness is great to cultivate!

Stay mindful. Listen to others. Show empathy. Generate the kind of indispensable nature that we desire in politicians. Cultivate a personality that we find attractive in actors and film stars. Channel your inner general, but not your inner generalissimo. Know the difference between power and money, and where each needs to be applied. Use soft power wherever possible.

Read Seneca or Ovid, maybe the occasional Shakespearian tragedy. These are timeless. Save your money and read lavishly from the shelves of the second-hand book store. You'll need the cash for business.

Finally, always look your best. Make sure your clothes fit, they are neat, tidy and dry-cleaned. I think there is an appropriate time to dress up to represent your business, so put your best foot forward, and be aware of what your appearance may look like to others. Impressions are sometimes, everything

Bon chance!

Jim Cooper

HypeLife Brands

Curt Cuscino is Founder and CEO of HypeLife Brands (HypeLife). Founded in 2001, the company is a progressive brand development+marketing agency that helps lifestyle brands engage the Millennial Generation. It is headquartered in downtown Oceanside, California.

Curt launched HypeLife while in college. He earned his BA in Computer Science and minored in Animation at the University of Missouri-Columbia. For over 17 years Curt has managed teams to build companies that are fundable and produce ROI. He believes in implementing disciplined capital deployment for marketing. He advocates strategic, well-tuned, future-forward marketing practices.

Curt reflects,
"I've helped everything from B2C startups to large B2B companies. I often served as a right-hand man, team manager and Project Manager to Startup Founders, CEOs, and VPs of Marketing. I've helped them define a new vision and position, or reposition, their companies for long-term growth and ROI. HypeLife focuses on helping B2C brands position themselves to harness the power of the Millennial Generation, which is quite literally the future of everything."

Originally from Kansas City, Missouri, Curt is a bonafide child of the 80s. He is a whole-brain, systems thinker who grew up on the early trajectory of technology. He began at a very young age toying with single-color monitors and Compuserve. Curt observes,
"I've always had an undying love for the always-moving crossroads of tech, business, art, commerce, and culture. My passion is to see things yet unseen, and take a vision forward, bringing it to life from little more than a blank page. You can create anything, if you put your mind to it."

Before he was 10, Curt started a fledgling greeting card business (built from cheesy templates, printed on an early dot-matrix printer, and sold mostly to his parents, grandparents and family friends). Later he started a mowing business, a record label & music promotions company, and HypeLife, all before graduating college. After graduation, he started a profitable custom snowboard design company. Today Curt is also the producer & host of a nationally syndicated weekly radio show called FutureSound with CUSCINO. He started the show from nothing more than the seed of an idea.

Curt is a speaker, thought leader, author, DJ, music producer, husband, father, music+ film fanatic. He is an advisor to startups at California State University -Fullerton's Irvine Incubator.

Curt lived and worked for seven years in Los Angeles, and met his wife there. Recently, they moved with their two little boys to live, work, and play in the booming beach city of Oceanside, California.

Dear Founder,

Here are four key highlights from my entrepreneurial journey. I hope that they will help you.

1. The Journey will not always be easy. When I was 22 and starting my business in 2001 I had no idea that I'd be faced with the challenges that come from growth, navigating an economic recession, a housing market crash, and everything in-between. Those challenges were all substantial in their own ways, and many of them are cyclical: meaning we'll most likely see another recession at some point in our lifetimes again, especially during the course of your new business.

Would knowing the challenges have made me NOT start a business and forge out on my own? Not necessarily. But before setting out on your own journey, know that being an entrepreneur is not for the faint of heart. Running a startup is an all in, or not at all, venture.

Know that the road is not always smooth or easy. Entrepreneurship is a long, winding, twisty journey with lots of tricky terrain and challenges to navigate, no matter the industry.

Be nimble and adaptable, able to pivot, and always have your eye on the future no matter what today's challenges. Coupling this agility with the following considerations will help you drive through these challenges, and provide a **purpose** to the temporary "pain" that can come your way when you're manning your own ship.

2. Know your why. Why you do what you do? Why you are dedicated to solving the problems you're solving for your customers?Why you and your business exist? Know your "why" before you start your entrepreneurial journey. Your "why" will be your ultimate guiding light as you navigate all the challenges and problems that can come your way as a founder. If you remain connected to your "why" throughout it all, you will survive. (One caveat, if your "why" is simply to make money, the path forward will be more taxing and soul-crushing (to say the least.)

3. Follow your passion. Knowing your "why" should be inherently tied to your passion. Again, this must be above simply "making money" or "getting rich." Knowing your passion and what fuels you must be much more. You could call it your "higher calling" or your "purpose," but whatever you call it, knowing it will drive you through adversity to "success" as *you* define it.

4. Success Is relative. Understand that "success" is often defined in arbitrary terms by the world at large ("she's successful, I'm sure she's rich"), but in the end, it is my belief that success *should* be defined in terms of the future *you* want to create that ties in with your passion, and your "why." Your business should not define you or be the end of you. It is a vehicle to your next destination in life.

Finding success as *you* define it is an adventure, and entrepreneurship is a journey. At the end of the day "business" is a series of experiments, and some experiments will inevitably fail. If you're trying to have a perfect batting average, it won't happen that way. There will be wins, and there will be losses. Each one will influence your next steps from there tor the next plateau to reach, or valley to cross. If you understand that success is indeed relative to *you*, it is my belief that the rest will fall in line, as has been my experience. And yes, even if you fail and try again, the same is true.

I can sum it all up with one quotation, "Adventure may hurt you, but monotony will kill you." I'll take the adventure any day. Fifteen years later, my adventure continues to be never-ending, challenging, and rewarding all at the same time.

Onward and upward!

Curt Cuscino Founder & CEO HypeLife Brands

Salyra

Zack Dafaallah is a Sudanese-American Entrepreneur. His latest start-up is Salyra. Using cutting edge technology, Salyra helps keep images of cherished memories alive as personalized pieces of art that fill the space where you live.

Zack relates that being an entrepreneur often means taking risks -- in business and sometimes in life. Soon after receiving a BS degree with Honors in Architecture from the prestigious University of Khartoum in Sudan in 1985, Zack decided to immigrate to the USA.. He arrived with with less than 100 dollars in his pocket and a dream to realize. Life would never be the same. Like many immigrants before him, Zack had a humble start. His first job was as a gas station attendant.

Zack soon landed a job as a city planner – a job seemingly more aligned with his undergraduate studies. However, his entrepreneurial nature led him to make start-up attempts. In 1998, Zack started the first all-digital reprographics company in Orange County. To date, Pacific Coast Graphics continues to compete with the largest rival in the industry.

Zack has appeared on the Los Angeles KTLA Channel 5's "Making It!" show featuring business success stories of minority entrepreneurs. He has been featured on the cover of Entrepreneur Magazine, and Modern Reprographics Magazine. Zack, has been nominated multiple times for the Ernest and Young's "Entrepreneur of the Year Award", and the Orange County Business Journal's "Excellence in Entrepreneurship Award."

He founded the Sudanese-American National Affairs and Development Foundation, an eleven year old non-profit aiming to bridge cultural understanding between Sudanese children and their parents. Tt fosters children's pride and knowledge about their culture, while also providing adults with opportunities for civic engagement and citizenship development.

At California State University Fullerton, Zack has served as an entrepreneur in residence and has been a student consulting case sponsor. He mentors CSUF entrepreneurs at every stage of development, from undergraduate to graduate.

Since earning his CSUF MBA in Entrepreneurship in 2009, he teaches entrepreneurship classes part-time. Zack says he enjoys teaching about how "theory and practice merge to culminate in the launching of new businesses."

Zack has now been a Southern California resident for 30 years. He lives in South Orange County. His wife, Marisol Rexach, Ph.D. is a school district administrator and a college lecturer in educational studies. Their son attends UC Santa Barbara.

SHAYA GRILL
SUDANESE FUSION CUISINE

Dear Founder,

As you read this, I hope you are well on your way to realizing your dream of owning a small business. I was in your place over 20 years ago, and writing this letter brings back a flood of memories. I contemplate what is most important to share and believe the following ideas have been guiding forces in my own journey:

1. **Integrity:** In general, we do business with people. Internally "these people" are your employees, your partners, and externally, they are other stakeholders; vendors, clients, representatives of government agencies, etc. Trust is the one single most important element, in relationship building, you can develop with "these people" in the process of building your business. Trust is also the natural outcome of integrity and honesty; both start with you.

2. **Creativity:** Develop your ability to "see" positive links between problems and unsatisfied needs. Ask yourself "Is there a better way of doing "this"? And in your quest to answer the question DO NOT be afraid to step outside your comfort zone because that's where creativity "hangs out".

3. **Resourcefulness:** Where I came from they have a saying that translates something like this -- "You can make a refreshing drink from rotten fish". Developing the skill of being able to utilize what's available to create what's needed is extremely crucial in bootstrapping a venture and beyond.

Like you I had a vision of owning my own business-- creating something that aligned with my passion. As I cobble these words together, I am reminded that my vision began long before my business did; so much prepared me for owning and operating my business. Why is this important? Because long-term success can only be achieved by combining each of your experiences, no matter how seemingly mundane or inconsequential they may seem. These experiences provide you with an opportunity to learn something that will strengthen your business and gain you respect. After all, it's pretty difficult to guide employees at all levels of your organization if you have not had firsthand experience. My career trajectory has provided me deep learning that has supported my business.

Zack Dafaallah
Founder and CEO

Three Generations of Partnerships

Three generations of partnerships underpin **Valerie Goodwin Danzig's** real estate career.

Her grandparents were the first generation. They worked hard, would do business on a handshake, honored their word, and expected the same respect. They moved to San Diego to find work during the great depression. Their tiny chicken ranch start-up attracted loyal customers and built their reputation. As the ranch grew, a series of partnerships with community leaders allowed land acquisition for the business. The first generation eventually branched out, managing partnership investments in land and apartments. Valerie still exchanges holiday cards with descendants of early partners.

The second generation was Valerie's mother. She practiced the same values. During World War II, a teenager, she took on management responsibilities while her three older brothers went off to war. The ranch expanded and so did real estate partnerships and investments. At age 21 in 1945, Valerie's mom earned her real estate broker's license. She continued building her successful real estate career while her brothers moved onto other endeavors.

Valerie was an only child. Her mother made four things clear: Valerie would adhere to family values, graduate from college, go into real estate, and build a third generation of partnerships for her future family.

Valerie earned her college degree in finance. She obtained her real estate broker's license at age 21. She worked first in real estate lending, then title insurance, and finally went into selling real estate. She did very, very well in each. During a slow period in the real estate market she went back to school to study law and earned a law degree. She sold real estate part-time during academic breaks, and proudly recalls how clients that she had worked with before would wait for her breaks. They knew they could trust her to put them first and help them find the best property.

The third generation launched in earnest when Valerie married and had two children. According to Valerie, her husband is her partner in life and business. Presently the third generation's business focus is on buying and holding retail commercial property.

Valerie is a member of the Commercial Real Estate Women's Network. As part of her community mentoring outreach, she served as an Entrepreneur in Residence at California State University, Fullerton.

Valerie Danzig
Newport Beach, California

Dear Founder,

I would like to take this opportunity to share with you three things that have served me best in life and in business.

1. I've been very lucky and/or blessed. I define luck as preparation meeting opportunity. Understand that luck is not enough, you must be willing and able to utilize each opportunity and/or challenge. One needs to research, to be well informed, be willing and able to walk away, so you can seize the appropriate positioning for your business.

2. The second concept that needs to be emphasized is RESPECT. So you might ask, respect what?
Time - yours and others, don't be late!!
People - in all walks of life - who possess an excellent work ethic, experience, knowledge, expertise, skills and abilities, who are dependable, and have integrity.
Money - the 3 S's - Spend, Save and Share. The wise business person knows how to prioritize and allocate under different circumstances.

3. Delegate - When, how and to whom? Surround yourself with those you can trust, that have strengths where you may have weaknesses. One must provide clear directions and leadership for those that will do the work. This is done by example.

And don't forget to be grateful and appreciative.

Wishing you health, success and satisfaction on your journey.

Valerie Goodwin Danzig

Valerie Danzig

Kneadle

Christopher DeCaro has been working in the design industry for over twenty years. In 2003, He founded Kneadle, an award winning creative agency in Orange County. Since its founding, Kneadle has launched more than 500 web sites and completed thousands of print and identity design projects. Industry-leading publications have recognized it. Kneadle has won many design awards including five 2017 American Web Design Awards from GD USA.

Chris started Kneadle while attending classes at CSUF in Graphics Design and Communications. Before venturing into his new business full-time, Chris was both a designer and developer. His range of creative skills allowed him to work and learn alongside clients like Abercrombie, Microsoft, and Danaher. Through these experiences, he built a wide-ranging skill set and knowledge base that allowed him to transition into his own endeavors. Chris was fortunate enough to grow up in a family where entrepreneurship was encouraged. He began several business ventures as a young adult – a trend that has continued throughout his life as a serial entrepreneur. Along with being the driving force behind Kneadle he leads Tegra Labs, a full-service creative agency that builds brands and promotes brand growth. Tegra's services include the identification of creative, social, and technology strategies.

Chris also dedicates time to his professional community. He is active with AIGA and the North Orange County Chamber of Commerce, and guest teaches at AIGA/Chapman University design events. He serves on several advisory boards for educational institutions, and mentors both design students and CSUF entrepreneurship students. He is a frequent guest speaker at CSUF including Comm Week, Entrepreneurship, Business Career Expo, and the Center for Entrepreneurship's Fast Pitch event. As an angel investor and consultant, Christopher is continually involved in helping new ventures. He is one of the founders of Titan Angels. Chris and his family reside in Fullerton.

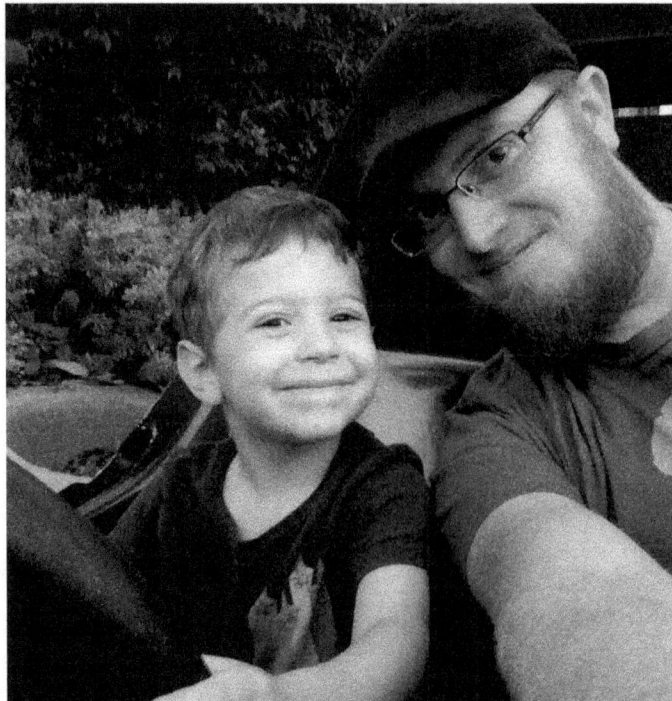

kneadle

Dear founder,

Stop immediately. Wisdom would be to stop and to choose something far easier. Wisdom would be to choose something that will not consume you; to choose something that will allow you a chance at the fabled work-life balance; to choose something that will provide a guarantee for your future; or to choose something that will provide you a fair trade for your time, your efforts, and your life. However, if you cannot be swayed to choose an easier path than leading a new venture into being, I can offer you three humble points of advice as you proceed down this long and often difficult path.

Keep lean. In whatever form it may take – time, money, attention, or effort – capital is the life blood of any venture. Without a lively flow, a venture will not survive. Remind yourself continually, you are not only a champion of your venture's vision; you are also a custodian of its assets, relationships, and health. The allure of "going big" and taking extra risk is ever present; aim for a sustainable stability.

Seek conflict. Intentionally, surround yourself with those that disagree with you; the practice of defending your position, thoughts, and beliefs will strengthen you. Seek council from both ends of a spectrum, identify a possible balance, and make your choices from this widened perspective. If you find yourself surrounded by those that blindly agree with you, seek diversity.

Do right. As a founder, you are on the frontlines of making big decisions; always choose what is right, not what is easy. This will often be the harder and longer road, but it is the one that will allow you to peacefully sleep at night. Your mind needs to be filled with possibility, rather than regret. Think from the perspective of the future looking back; doing what is right will not always feel good at the time.

Enjoy the journey,

Christopher De Caro

A Female Business Pioneer

Suzanne DeRossett is the founder and President of Empire Building Services (EBS). Established in 1982, EBS began as a family-run commercial janitorial business servicing the Santa Ana area.

Today, Suzanne DeRossett, and her Vice President and son John DeRossett, have Made EBS one of the finest commercial service contractors in seven Southern California counties.

EBS service offerings span four categories served by three corporations. They are, maintenance with 24 hour emergency response, construction cleanup (est. 2008), janitorial services and day porter services and EBS construction services that builds out tenant improvements (est. 2011). Examples of clients include out-patient surgical centers, manufacturers, malls, apartment/condo associations and commercial office buildings.

Suzanne recalls how she came to launch her venture,
"I think Baby Boomers are a special lot. Hope for a good future was prevalent everywhere. Self-expression busted out old confines. Folk music, protests about anything, burning bras, flower power and rock & roll kept progress churning in new and different paths. College, higher education, vocational schools were available to all and most were jumping on that opportunity. We could be anything we could dream.

Then, I had to get past my 20's and all those open opportunities and I hit 30 where it all 'got real.' What to do with all that ambition? My son John was born. Two weeks after that life changing event, realization hit (WHOA!). I needed to plan a great future for my little one.

I had studied Spanish for four years and helped out when my parents purchased a restaurant with a new concept ("Mexican Food"). I learned a few new Spanish words that I have never used again, and I met many honest, hard working people.

After my WHOA realization, I saw a need for a Commercial janitorial serve. I got my cleaners together, bought a vacuum, some ajax and started calling around for cleaning contracts.

A woman running this kind of company was a brand new thing in Orange County and it went well. After a few months I got a call from a big OC developer that asked us to do final clean up on buildings being built around our little OC airport.

I was unique walking job sites, providing labor, getting millions of square feet ready for occupancy... and the years passed.
In 2008 I added EBS Clean UP to provide additional services in the same field.
(Maintenance & Repair). In 2011 I made the final leap to a general contractor forming Empire Construction. Today my family legacy continues through my son, John, who's birth started it all!'

Suzanne has served as a classroom mentor for CSUF Entrepreneurship for eight years. She is mother of two and grandmother of eleven. Suzanne is an avid boater, jet skier, off roader, camper, Bible teacher and student of life.

Dear Founder,

I've noticed after several semesters of mentoring students at CSUF, you can "SPOT THEM".

Those are the students that want to exercise independence from the start of their careers.

They sense a passion and courage inside them to step out on their own and feed that hungry beast called AMBITION. The "norm" is OK, but they have unending ideas how to make things "a bit better".

Bravo!

Finding the "right" idea is first. It can be something you love, or something society needs, or just a way to make money for yourself and having a flexible schedule. That is what happened for me.

A single mom, I wanted a savings account for my son. I speak Spanish and all my ideas married into a commercial janitorial company. Clients gave me work and helped get my company off the ground for a lot of reasons I couldn't have imagined. In my case, it was 1982 and a female in this industry was unheard of, so irresistible to my clients.

It doesn't take much more than:

Faithfulness to your cause: This could take the form of unexpected setbacks (the check didn't arrive in the mail) or an injustice (promise of a job only to lose it at the last minute). Make the choice to endure.

Loyalty: this develops as you stay focused as your business grows. Loyalty and respect to what it is is important. Give your business the time it will require..if you "feel" like it or not... Devote your talent and instinct to it.

Your "word": Your biggest asset ....it is the character your company will have. The stronger your "word" the stronger the backbone of your company. Your "word" being your bond, builds your reputation

Creating a solid foundation for you both. Getting a job and starting it is one thing.

Following through to the end with your reputation intact, is another.

TAKE THE LEAP! YOUR FUTURE AWAITS!!

Project Engineer to Founder

Soheil Divani received his MS degree in Civil Engineering from CSUF in 2014. During his studies, Soheil earned a patent for an "adjustable volume preservation system." Upon graduation he founded O2Free and formed a founding team to explore how to commercialize his patent.

In 2014, Soheil had ten years of experience as a project engineer and construction manager. His resume includes cost estimating, preparing bid packages and proposals, and managing varied construction projects. Soheil had directed and supervised construction workers and subcontractors. He prepared technical reports, developed baseline time schedules, allocated budgets and resources. Soheil did construction administration and observation, engineering analysis, health & safety promotion and implementation.

Soheil was an experienced manager. The O2Free team was hard working and technically competent. However, Soheil knew his team and he had much to learn about consumer product design, marketing and sales.

02Free became a resident of the CSUF Start-up Incubator. Like most residents of the Incubator, the 02Free founders continued their daytime careers. Soheil was employed full time as a project engineer at Innovative Construction Solutions.

As described in his Dear Founder letter, the 02Free team invested over two years in developing their product. Results were disappointing and they shelved it.

However, the team gained a great deal from their start-up adventure. With more insight, they moved on to new ventures.

In 2017, Soheil became a senior project engineer with Cobalt Construction Company. Headquartered in Simi Valley, Cobalt specializes in senior, student and multi-family housing, mixed use construction and full service heavy engineering.

Soheil Shakori Divani
Encino, California

Dear Founder,

Get ready for an exciting adventure with lots of ups and downs. You will be challenged, pushed to your limits, fall and rise again, and learn a great deal. It is a game that you are going to win. You are already a success story if you are embarking on the journey to be an entrepreneur. Remember those who change the world are among those who take the leap of faith and try. World needs more of you. Continue to dream and change the world.

Team up with the right people who you can trust and work with. Your team is the key to your success. Great team members contribute to your success and lift you up. Bad team members drain your energy and drag you down. Your success depends on your team; so, choose wisely. Set the expectations from the get go and make sure everybody is on the same page, and everybody knows what they are responsible for and what they get in exchange.

When it comes to making a prototype, try to do it yourself before hiring others to do it for you. That is going to save you lots of money and energy down the road. We hired a design company, spent thousands of dollars on prototyping and wasted almost a year just to learn the company we have chosen was not capable of making our working prototype. Then we went back and tried to do it ourselves. We spent less than a thousand dollars and tried making it ourselves, and in two months we had our proof of concept and a few working prototypes. So, remember to give it a try to make it yourself before you hire others and spend lots of time and money.

Last but not least, when you have an idea study your market, gather as much information as you can, and understand the business you are getting into as much as possible. Study your target market and interview potential clients. Make sure there is a need or a problem and people are willing to accept your product as a solution and pay money to buy it. As a person who comes from an engineering background I always thought if you make a product that works the best people are going to buy your product. My team and I spent more than two years of our time and thousands of dollars and developed a few prototypes and had them tested and made sure they work perfectly. We made the best wine preserver decanter in the market that could save the wine better than any other product in the market for the price, and we were sure it is going to fly off the shelves and wine lovers are going to buy it like crazy. But, unfortunately, when we started going to fairs to showcase our product and interview the wine enthusiasts they showed little to no interest in buying our product for two main reasons. One, they kept asking us where the pop is. They wanted to hear the sound of the popping cork when they open their wine bottle, and our decanter was not making that sound. Second, they were not willing to decant their wine into a secondary bottle that did not have their wine label on it. They asked us, how they can brag about their expensive wine if the label is not on the bottle when they are serving the wine. We assumed that luxury wine consumers could tell the difference and recognize the expensive wines from the cheap ones just by tasting. Well, that was not the case and the wine label was the main identifying item for them.

Our product was working fine; but, it was missing the two main elements that our target market cared about the most, the pop sound and the label. We had a good working product; but, we were not familiar with the wine market and the wine consumer's culture. Had we done our homework in the beginning and studied our target market earlier we could have saved ourselves a great deal of time and money, and we could have had a much higher chance of succeeding in that market. To avoid making a product that nobody wants, remember to do your market research, get to know your audience and their culture, and get proof of market before moving forward with your idea. That will help you to navigate your way to success much more effectively and efficiently.

Our team members learned a great deal from our first adventure. We moved on to new ventures with much more experience. The journey showed us who we are and helped us with new roles in other projects. It is a game that you are going to win. You either succeed or you learn; either way you will be a winner.

Soheil Shakoori Divani

PureFit, Inc.

Robb Dorf is the Founder and CEO of PureFit Inc. PureFit is the maker of the first gluten-free high protein nutrition bar. His vison, since 2001, has been to revolutionize the nutrition bar industry. PureFit now has a complete line of NON-GMO, high protein, gluten-free, vegan, and kosher nutrition bars that pack 18 grams of protein. He is responsible for overseeing sales and marketing, and focuses on growing the PureFit brand. Robb has expanded PureFit's line into 20 countries. Now, PureFit bars are among the top selling gluten-free nutrition bars.

Robb graduated from Arizona State University in 1991. He earned his bachelor's degree in exercise physiology. Robb ran both cross country and track all four years in college.

In his Dear Founder letter Robb gives five tips that he believes contributed to his success. His PureFit product line and his approach to retailers reflect his beliefs. Concerning his products, he says, "Not all nutrition bars are created equal. The premise behind PureFit has always been to offer the finest quality ingredients available. That is why we only use 100% non-GMO ingredients, including US grown non-GMO soy protein. Why? Because the industry is dominated by candy bars dressed up to look nutritious. Despite what you may think, the nutrition industry is unregulated. Cheap, genetically modified ingredients are a staple in the nutrition industry. They are not a staple in our kitchen. Never have been, never will."

PureFit's approach to retailers reveals Robb's business side. His website reads, "Since 2001, positive reviews and recom-mendations of our bars have appeared in 100's of magazines read by your shoppers. To this day, We actively pursue earned-media placements that drive shoppers into stores just like yours. Each month, we introduce PureFit Bars to consumers at marathons and fitness expos all across the country. We have a MAP policy that affords all PureFit retailers with an opportunity to sell through 100% of the inventory 100% of the time. Besides upholding our commitment to quality, we are consistently giving back to the community. We've donated more than 30,000 bars to celiac support groups and conferences, and over 20,000 bars to U.S. troops. When you offer PureFit Nutrition Bars to your customers, you offer them a nutritious, great-tasting bar they can feel good about. And you can feel good about offering a product from a company that is committed to quality, service and supporting its retailers."

Robb is a proud supporter of animal rescue. The PureFit PureFido program encourages you to consider rescuing your next dog or cat.

Robb is a past SBI student consulting client and a friend of CSUF Entre-preneurship. He is still very active today and races both mountain bikes and road bikes. He also practices yoga weekly.

AWARD-WINNING PureFit™

Dear Founder,

That PureFit is still in business more than sixteen years after its inception still mystifies me. The business world is brutal. It doesn't care who you are, what your product is, or even if you have started a successful business in the past. Business changes daily and you have to be flexible in your approach. I have always been able to change PureFit's direction if I felt it was going to save the company. I have made two major changes already, successfully keeping the company alive.

I did not start PureFit until I was in my early 30's. You have the opportunity to start your first company at a much younger age, although I do not necessarily recommend that. In my case I had only one chance to make it work. I didn't have money to lose, and I surely didn't have a bottomless well to go back to every time I made a mistake. It didn't take long to blow through $100,000 and really have nothing to show for it.

The biggest reason it took me 10 years after graduating college to start PureFit was "passion." I did not have a product or service that I was passionate about. Sixteen plus years later I am still very passionate about making the best protein bars possible. Without passion, your business will probably fail. That passion comes from you. Not your employees. It has to come from the owners. Employees come and go.

Regarding owners, I am not a fan of business partners. My advice is to try to do it on your own. Business divorces are all too common and destroy many great companies and products.

It is impossible to discuss every contingency here but I will do my best to point out the most important tips that I believe have contributed to my success:

1. Be passionate about your product or service.

2. Make sure your product or service is the best. Never allow your competition to provide a better product. Customers have unprecedented access to reviews. Make sure you are number one.

3. Be 100% committed to becoming successful. Being a successful entrepreneur is all about hard work.

4. You will make lots of mistakes. Avoid the big ones. The big ones can be devastating.

5. Always do the right thing. Don't cut corners. Have morals in all aspects of your business.

Wishing you continued success as you pursue your dreams.

Robb Dorf

Founder and CEO

Mr. MEWA

William Dyer is the founder of Healthcare Plus Insurances, dba HCP National Insurance Services, Inc.(HCP) It is one of the few brokers in the country who have placed over $500 Million of Stop Loss Reinsurance Premiums.

Bill attended the University of San Diego on a full academic scholarship. He graduated with a BA in English and a minor in Theology.

Bill started his first company called Management's Choice at age 22. Without enough capital, it failed in 6 months. One of his clients was a medical insurance company who offered him a job as their inside sales supervisor. From there, he went to a Canadian insurance company, Confederation Life, where he learned to underwrite self-insured health insurance and other coverages.

At age 26, Bill began a career working as a commercial insurance broker specializing in healthcare. He built a book of clients, and soon became a top producer.

At age 29, Bill launched his own brokerage, HCP. It insures and reinsures the whole spectrum of healthcare: the providers, hospitals, and payers. Its niche is providing complex reinsurance, to health insurance, to medical malpractice, to Cyber Breach et al. HCP provides it all with one team. In contrast, the industry norm is multiple brokerages handling the insurance coverages, No one knows what the other is doing. HCP's mission is to serve its clients first, and itself second.

In the industry, Bill is known as Mr. MEWA. MEWA stands for Multiple Employer Welfare Arrangement. A single plan that covers the employees of two or more employers who are members of the same association. HCP is the leading MEWA stop loss broker in the country, based on written premiums. Few insurance brokers understand MEWAs the way HCP National does.

HCP offers everything associations need to launch a successful MEWA. It has assembled a team of MEWA veterans it can refer clients to. These outside professionals lead clients through the planning process of launching and forming their MEWA. Then once the client's MEWA is formed HCP can provide the Stop Loss and Liability insurance. Bill is the volunteer Vice President and Trustee of the MEWA Association of America.

Bill is a friend of CSUF Entrepreneurship. He has sponsored multiple student consulting teams to assist with his marketing. His joys are his wife and five children, ranging in age from toddlers to adults.

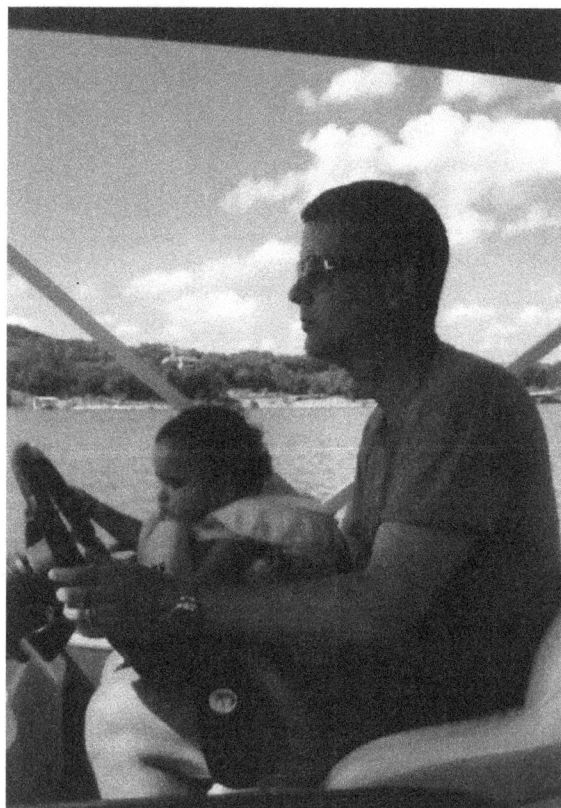

Bill with co pilot Julia

84

HCPNational

Dear Founder,

Buckle up, because you are in for a ride. My advice is pray and workout every day. To own your own business is to be obsessed 24/7, so you need to take care of your body and spirit. When you have the lows or highs, you need to be able to control your emotions. Your business's and your life's successes will be in direct correlation with how you handle stress and anxiety. Here are twelve quips, quotes and other ideas that may help you on the way. Some I credit to the original owners, though others I have likely pirated and I think they are my own.

1. "Tough times never last, but tough people do." (R. Schuller)
2. Your feelings are not real, only facts are facts ... Business is based on facts.
3. Your employees cannot be your friends ever, ever, ever ... Want to test it? Tell them you cannot pay them.
4. A new employee is at their best during their first month. If they do not impress, fire them quickly. They won't get better.
5. Equity are your children ... Only give them up when it is warranted .
6. You are the chief sales person for your company ... If you cannot sell, take classes... If that fails get a partner who can sell.
7. If you have a partner(s), have a separation agreement drawn up before you launch the business... It's a very valuable tool if you should need it.
8. No debt, no partners, if at all possible.
9. Cash flow is your blood, clients are flesh, and employees are bones. You can survive with lacerations, bruises, and a few broken bones ... You cannot without blood. Be obsessed with cash flow or your business will die.
10. Never delegate your financial decisions to anyone, if possible... You sign off on all purchases, checks, payroll, review all canceled checks/bank statements (online or paper), and you review all insurance with your insurance broker ... If you delegate these things and there is a mistake, it's your company and you that will suffer ... The employee who makes the mistake goes onto another job.
11. "If it's going to be, it's up to me" (R. Schuller) ... If your business is failing, it is only one person's fault: : yours.
12. Be confident that you are a child of God, but be humble... You do not own anything; it's all an illusion. You are not that important; you will be forgotten in two generations assuming you have kids and grandkids.

You obviously are an eccentric, as all business owners are . If not, why would you gamble all you have on a proposition where 90% of businesses fail in the first 5 years and then 90% of that remainder fail? You do this because you have something to prove to yourself or others. But please remember to take care of yourself, get a hobby where you are outside, and make sure your family is your life, not the business (very tough to remember). Eat right, stay slim and pray .... " Go forth and conquer as of old" (A. Tennyson).

All the best,

William D. Dyer

For in depth discussion of these topics by the author, please go to https://bit.ly/creatingnewventures

SCORE Volunteer

Mike Edwards' professional career began after graduating from Ryerson University in Toronto Canada. Mike's 45-year career began in Engineering, first at Olivetti and then Lennox Inc, a major HVAC manufacturer.

While at Lennox Mike progressed through engineering management positions to becoming the Factory Manger creating a world class factory. He then moved from engineering into sales management and then Director of Sales and Marketing for the Canadian operation.

Later, the company acquired two private manufacturing companies in Southern California. Mike was asked to move there to consolidate operations and integrate them into a single entity.

While in California Mike was recruited to take an equity position in a troubled company to turn it around. The company had a great product but no structure or financial controls.

As President and CEO, Mike spent the next 14 years to revive and grow the enterprise value of the company. After executing a turn-around the company was sold at a premium and the major investor not only recovered his loses but enjoyed a handsome return.

Mike took an equity position with the new owners and continued to build the company. By introducing numerous product innovations and expanding the sales base this company became an international business with a strong brand and a reputation for innovation and quality.

In 2015 the company was offered for sale and it attracted several Fortune 500 companies. It was ultimately sold to a strategic buyer at an attractive multiple.

Mike has been a volunteer at SCORE since the sale of the company. He is an active mentor, a moderator for the CEO Forum and the workshop chair. SCORE conducts over 375 workshops in Orange County each year. Most recently Mike has accepted the Chapter Chair Position for Orange County SCORE (SCORE Chapter 114).

SCORE///

FOR THE LIFE OF YOUR BUSINESS

SCORE Orange County
5 Hutton Centre Dr., Suite 900
Santa Ana, 92707
(714) 813-8423

Dear Founder,

Whether you are at the pre-startup phase of your business or working at building it, here are a few life lessons I would like to share with you.

I have many clients who come to me with great ideas, their heads are swimming with thoughts, but they struggle with where to start. Using the Business Model Canvas and concentrating on the Value Proposition and Customer Segments helps to create a sense of clarity and understanding. In my own business life, I learned that creating a tight focus on what you want to do will help you to execute. Many of us have a lot of great ideas and want to work on them all. We usually end up achieving little. Keep a focus, develop the idea, test it with your customers and then pivot, if necessary. Don't try to do everything at once and stay focused on your mission.

A second attribute to consider is to maintain a broad view of your business while having the ability to dive in to details, when necessary. This ensures you are 'in-touch' with your business. I have worked with people who 'fly at 30,000 feet' and never grasp the nuances of their business. Others become bogged down in the minutia and lose direction. The most effective entrepreneur I worked with had the ability to watch over the big picture yet when circumstances required, he could get briefly involved and help problem solve. This way he was able to guide the overall direction of the company, knew the details and could contribute on solving specific problems when they demanded his attention.

Finally, in my career, I always stayed in touch with my customers and my employees. When I was in the office I would walk the shop floor several times a day. This gave me interaction with my employees and always gave me a visual of what was going on and alerted me to pending issues. Likewise, I always made it a habit of travelling with my sales people at least one week per month. This provided visibility to my customers and more importantly allowed me to hear their ideas, issues and concerns. These are comments you will not hear if you rely on them being filtered up through your organization. Similarly, the best high-value opportunities were the 'windshield time' with my sales people to hear their frustrations and concerns. Remember, they are alone in the field with limited resources, yet they are the face of your company to your customers.

In summary, create a focus, remain true to your purpose, manage your company with broad oversight yet be ready to dive in to details when they dictate and be sure to interact with your customers and employees and make sure you are visible to both.

Mike Edwards
Chapter Chair, SCORE Orange County

An Inventor Since Birth

Micha Eizen (MS.ME) is the cofounder and CTO of Kimandia, Inc. Founded in 2009 his firm is a technical consulting company.

Kimandia, Inc. offers full R&D and consulting services in many technical fields. They include battery/energy technologies, consumer/industrial products, advanced production technologies, food, beverage, cosmetics, mass production, brainstorming and new idea generation.

Micha's experience spans thirty five years in many technical fields and industries. At age 12, he started to work at his father's metal products' company during his summer vacations. His track record includes many patents in battery technology and consumer products. He combines multi-disciplinary knowledge and hands-on experience to provide unique technical solutions and leadership ideas to diverse industries.

Micha says, "I have always dared to try new things. I have been an inventor since birth, an entrepreneur in my soul." He has developed unique ways of thinking about and analyzing technical matters, which open new ways of resolving issues and finding unique solutions. He often can come up with solutions that others may not. He likes to help his clients to "Do it right the first time."

While working with Power Paper battery company, Micha's solution cut the production costs of two different battery configurations by 50 percent. Using his solution, Power Paper won a 10-Million-battery contract from Estee Lauder company.

At GSI Technologies, Micha designed a complex repair project for a broken mass production line. His solution saved a ten million-dollar investment. He did similar work for Power Paper, Boston Power & Enevate Corporation.

Micha was very instrumental in developing a complete line of remotely controlled battery operated body warmers for the Schawbel Corporation. They are currently selling.

Presently, Micha wants to support start-ups and inventors. He hopes to help them to get to market quicker, to do so at lower cost, and to get a bigger market share.

Micha has been a guest speaker at the CSUF Startup Incubator and for CSUF Entrepreneurship's New Venture Creation class. He finds joy in music, inventing, R&D of new products and thinking outside the box. Micha's mantra is, "Do the best you can to make life better for all while taking care of mother Earth."

Kimandia Inc
Engineering Excellence

Dear founder,

You are probably reading this letter because you are brave enough to plunge ahead on your unique private journey, hopefully to create better lives, and take care of our home planet. If you do so, you will embark on an exciting journey, a personal growth journey, during which you will discover many things about yourself. You will come across deep waters and hard rocks that you will have to cross during your journey. You will have to become "start-up strong" to get to the finish line. I would like to share with you what makes me, and many entrepreneurs I know, start-up strong as we travel along the highways and byways of our creation journeys.

Put The "why" before the "how."

There will be times when things go well, times that are fun and easy to handle. However, there will be times when things do not go well. These are the challenging times. They will demand all of your mental and emotional strength, and commitment. You must muster the courage not to give up when everything seems to fall apart.

The challenging times will be your own private tests, in which you will have to face your fears, and prove to yourself and the world, that you can reinvent yourself, become a better you, quickly get yourself back on track and carry on. This is what I mean by start-up strong. It is an attitude, one that will be your main support along the way. You have to prepare. Do so by asking yourself two intimate questions:

Why am I doing this? Why do I want to do it?

Your answer to the "**why**" must come first. It must be completely clear to you, before you tackle "how." Figure out how to do it later. The best supporting answers to the "**why**" will connect you to the origins of your deep desire to do, and keep on doing, what you are doing. Here are some answers to ponder:

I want to make peoples' lives better. (You can imagine the happy people using your product).
I want to support our planet and make it a better place to live.
I see my mission as a service to humanity. (Service is the highest call and the best motive.)
I am connected with all of my heart to this enterprise.
I feel that I have to do it, that I am on a mission to bring it to the world.
I really love to do it. I am willing to pay to be able to do it.
I feel passionate about doing it.
I want to realize my full potentials, skills and growth opportunities through this endeavor.
I know that this is the right thing to do.

As an entrepreneur, you are a leader. As a leader, you always have to see your goal clearly, and know why you want to get there. Not only for yourself. You have to become a beacon of light for all of your team. Your team will also ask themselves at times, why are we doing it? Why are we helping you? Your clear and deep "**why**" will help them to overcome many hurdles.

A strong "**why**" is your most stable foundation. You can count on it and build on it. A strong "**why**" will help you endure the obstacles and challenging times that you will meet on your journey. Understand that start-up strong is a warrior mindset. Be a peaceful warrior, for the benefit of all.

My last advice to you, for now, is put people (whoever they are) before profits. This will give you the ultimate in strength and support from your team, suppliers, and customers!

To your best success,

Micha Eizen- Co-Founder & CTO

A COO Who Thinks Like an Owner

Matt Erickson is the CXO (Chief Experience Officer) for Sandler Training in Irvine California. He works with companies on how to have more honest and open conversations with prospects and clients,

Matt is an alumnus of California State University Fullerton. He earned his BA degree in Business-Entrepreneurship. When he started at CSUF, Matt brought experience with him.

Growing up, Matt was a World Champion BMX racer in his elementary school years. Later, he was a High School standout in basketball and went on to play NCAA basket ball for Whittier College.

In 2000 Matt joined Kore Partners as part of a small team that reported to the CFO and oversaw the firm's final Chapter 7 bankruptcy. He learned invaluable lessons about managing cash flow.

Matt became the first employee of Ivysport.com in 2002. He led the growth of the startup e-commerce venture from a garage in Aliso Viejo, CA to multiple millions in sales and 12 employees within five years. Matt was responsible for all day-to-day operations of the company including Accounting, Customer Service, Web Development, Procurement, and Marketing. He secured an exclusive licensing contract for the Ivy League.

In an entrepreneurship class at CSUF Matt worked on a student consulting project for Cobra Systems, Inc. ("CSI"). Matt impressed the CEO with his performance and the CEO hired Matt as CSI's general manager. Matt became CSI's COO in 2013. Matt recalls, "My greatest attributes were the ability to inspire teams, to take ownership and to tackle difficult problems passionately."

After moving to Cobra Systems, Inc. in 2007, Matt developed several product lines though innovation, multiple patents, and dedicated go-to-market strategies. As COO he successfully restructured the sales department. He developed a culture of continuous improvement. Matt used business intelligence and automation tools, standard work, sharing of best practices, and eliminated non value-added activities in the business. Matt also led the launch of Chimboo.com, an online inventory tracking solution that simplified asset tracking for thousands of companies worldwide.

Matt describes himself as an "experienced executive who thinks and acts like an owner." His "Why" is, "to make a difference by inspiring people to love their work and enjoy seeing the results from their efforts. My goal is to project a positive can-do attitude that is infectious within organizations and instrumental in creating a great company culture."

Matt Erickson
Irvine, California

Dear Founder,

I believe it is important that I write this letter to help you understand that the core principles of starting a business are simple, but incredibly difficult to execute. I have found that the three main principles in starting up a new venture are: Deliberate Company Culture, Creative Strategy, and Disciplined Execution.

Deliberate Company Culture – Focus on creating a Deliberate Company Culture. If you get the culture right, a lot of the hard stuff seems to fall into place. A company culture is up to you to define, but should touch on making customers loyal, being part of something bigger than yourself, being someone that others want to work with, be an advocate for accountability, and achieving success. One of the most powerful things I did was clearly defining Cobra System's company culture and building a set of values that simplified the hiring and firing decision making process. The ones who bought-in flourished and did amazing things. The ones who didn't buy in found somewhere else to work and hopefully they were more happy there. People who work for you talk. They probably talk a lot. They post things online and talk about work with their friends. What do you want them to say, "Work sucked today" or "I love where I work"? When you start to grow and are trying to attract great talent - which employee testimonial do you want to pitch to this new recruit? The answer is obvious and it starts with a Deliberate Company Culture.

Creative Strategy – I've found that Creative Strategy has become harder to truly achieve. Where brainstorming sessions and think tanks often utilize the creative side of our brains, I've found that taking a processed approached has lead to some very creative ideas. An example of this would be when I worked for Ivysport, Inc. We had grown outside of the garage and were looking at new products to drive new revenue. As a clothing company selling $18 t-shirts to the eight Ivy League Schools, we naturally assumed we were a t-shirt company and that Harvard t-shirts were the highest selling item. I was diving deep into excel at the time and built a data table that would show our profitability per product per school. I was astonished to find that even though we sold more t-shirts to Harvard than to any other school, we also sold quite a lot of Yale sweatshirts. At $60 per sweatshirt, we had greater yearly gross profits from Yale sweatshirts than we did from the Harvard t-shirts. We really enjoyed making a lot of creative sweatshirt designs in the following years and grew the company considerably.

Disciplined Execution – Disciplined Execution is tough and boring. Many people find it unsustainable. That may be why many companies don't make it past the two year point. When starting a new venture, you need to show that there is a demand which usually comes from people wanting to buy it. If people want to buy it, then someone needs to sell it. Sales is tough, but if you're focused on identifying the things that generate sales and doing them for no less than four hours per day - you will be successful. The average sales person spends 45 minutes per day performing sales-related tasks. When I co-invented a sign and label printing device, I spent day after day calling every number of every company I could find and asking them if they had a need for my product. This product has gone on to be the flagship product line for Cobra Systems, Inc. and is used by many of the America's largest and most popular companies.

I'd like to conclude by stating that the principles of Deliberate Company Culture, Creative Strategy, and Disciplined Execution are not just for founders but for everyone within an organization who is inspired to create positive change and growth. At the top, we call them Entrepreneurs, but internally they're called Intrapreneurs. No founder can do it entirely on their own - so build a great team, trust them, and use them to the fullest of their abilities.

Best regards,

Matt Erickson

For in depth discussion of these topics by the author, please go to https://bit.ly/creatingnewventures

91

Brian Evans Photography

Brian Evans founded Brian Evans Photography in 2005. He began his entrepreneurial journey as a 13-year-old skateboarder in Cathedral City, California.

The 18-year-old owner of Epidemic Skateboard Shop gave him his first job. It didn't matter that the payment was stickers and skateboards, because skateboards, the one thing he loved more than anything, surrounded him.

As a young businessperson, the owner of the shop made every mistake in the book. Brian was there to learn the hard lessons right along with him. Brian's interest in high school sports and even skateboarding itself quickly faded as his passion for photography and running a business grew. As a senior in high school, Brian won the Purchase Prize in an art contest hosted by the Palm Springs Museum of Fine Art. It was the first time a digital photograph had won the award and his images are still part of the museum's permanent collection.

Brian moved on from Epidemic after moving away for college. He took many hard lessons with him as he started pursuing Brian Evans Photography.

At California State University Fullerton, Brian was a player, team president and photographer for Titan Ice Hockey in 2008-2009. He earned his degree in Business-Entrepreneurship in 2010. After graduating from the Entrepreneurship program, Brian made the leap to full-time photographer and never looked back. As a freelance photographer, he had the opportunity to travel the United States photographing everything from weddings to commercial real estate to casinos.

Since then, Brian has returned to his high school multiple times to speak with students in the Digital Arts and Technology Academy. He was a part of the program in its first year.

Brian observes that, "I believe that mastery of the technical side of photography is essential. However, I always speak about the importance of being a business person who understands the basics of running a business and investing in people."

In 2017, Brian chose to transition into his wife's family business, restaurant franchises. The company employs 400+ employees in six restaurants. He is currently learning the business and hopes his wife Jessica and he will eventually earn ownership of the company.

Dear Founder,

When I first started Brian Evans Photography I thought I needed the newest and greatest technology to be successful, whether it was cameras, lighting, software or websites - you name it, I wanted it. Unfortunately, there seemed to be a disconnect. I had all the pieces of the puzzle in place, but my business was not going where I envisioned.

It was not until I finally realized the truth and wisdom behind my father's words that things began to change for myself and my business. Weekly conversations with my dad would inevitably turn into "motivational talks," where he often spoke about the importance of investing in people. He would end every discussion by saying, "…well that's enough of your dad's motivational speech." He may have said it over a hundred ways, but the point he tried to emphasize was always about people. It seems simple, but it took a long time for me to really understand it.

I was a one man band. The idea of investing in people seemed to lend itself to a business with actual employees. It eventually clicked that my dad was also referring to investing in mentors, business contacts and clients. These people may not have worked directly for me, but they had more to do with the growth of my business than I could have ever imagined.

The first strategic partner I sought was a wedding planner in Palm Springs known for working on high end weddings in some of the most exclusive venues. I spent an entire year emailing and calling her monthly requesting a meeting. Over the months, the no responses from her turned into minor curiosity, and finally ended in her agreeing to meet with me in person. In her words, she was "sick of my emails." She agreed to give me a shot and booked me for one wedding. Fast forward a couple of years and she is responsible for 70% of my weddings each year.

Though I am still passionate about photography and continue to take on select projects each year, my priorities have shifted. With a young family at home, I did not want to travel for work as I once had. At the start of 2017 I transitioned into my wife's family business, restaurant franchising. I have never worked in the food industry, and to say I am getting a crash course would be a major understatement. I have gone from running a one man show to working in a company that employs over 400 people. I personally oversee 70 employees in the restaurant I manage. The business may be new, the employees may have multiplied, but the idea of investing in people is more relevant than ever.

It is easy to get distracted by the ever changing business world and the technology that comes with it, but at the end of the day it's the people who grow a business. Take time to build relationships, both inside and outside of your business. Pass on your knowledge and be open to anything someone may be able to pass on to you. The most important lesson I've learned in business came from weekly "motivational talks" with my father. Relationship building and investing in people are what makes the difference.

Sincerely,

Brian Evans

Avalanche Consulting

Brent Evans founded Avalanche Consulting in 2004. Avalanche's goal is to enable its clients to visualize and realize their future. Brent brings a solid track record of driving revenue and profit growth to his consulting practice.

Prior to Avalanche, he was involved in the successful sale of Unit Instruments, a publicly-traded semiconductor equipment company where he served as VP, Global Sales and Marketing. Brent was Chief Operating Officer with Syagen Technology, a venture backed start-up developing instrumentation for the Homeland Security market.

Brent has held other senior management positions with publicly traded corporations and private venture backed firms. Successful in both start-up and growth situations, he is recognized as an innovative leader and has demonstrated his skill in international business, marketing, business development and operations. Strategically focused, Brent has been highly effective in developing emerging global markets. He has expertise in commercializing technologies and deploying them globally.

Avalanche's clients represent a diverse range in the technology, manufacturing, professional services and non-profit sectors.

Brent is an authority on business strategy and international trade issues and is a dynamic and forceful speaker. He has taught marketing in the MBA program at the University of La Verne, international marketing at Chapman University, and is a current member of the faculty at California State University, Fullerton, where he has taught entrepreneurship, consulting and strategic management.

Commissioned as a Regular Army officer in the field artillery, Brent served 27 years on active and reserve duty. A respected leader, he was selected for three sequential senior level command assignments and received numerous awards and decorations before retiring as a Colonel.

As a scholarship student, Brent earned his Bachelor of Arts degree from Arizona State University. He attended Oxford University, England, received a Master's in Business Administration from Pepperdine University, and is a graduate of the U.S. Army War College.

Brent has served as a member of a ESOP board of directors, an advisor for several profit and nonprofit organizations and a mentor at the University of California, Irvine Paul Merage School of Business.

An avid outdoorsman, Brent hunts, fishes, sails, and is an American Kennel Club Judge. He recently completed backpacking the 212-mile John Muir Trail in the Sierras of California.

Avalanche Consulting

Dear Founder:

What does it take for your business to succeed? The list every business deals with is indeed long. Based on my experience working with large corporations and startup companies alike, three things stand out. Each take extensive time to develop and yet they rarely get the necessary attention.

First, I can't understate the importance of reputation. Whatever you do reflects either positively or negatively on your business and yourself. A quick internet search will lead you to "best companies to work for" as well as one business scandal after another. A good reputation will bring you customers, employees, investors, board members and service providers of every type. A good reputation also helps attract the best in each category. One additional suggestion, only work with those who share you vision and are willing to fully commit to it. The world is filled with people who say something can't be done, but the world has been changed by those who say it can and then are fully committed to make it happen.

Second, relationship building aka "networking" is extremely important. A business is never built by a solo effort. I regularly ask founders how can I help them. Often there is a muddled response. If you don't let the world know what your business is about and where you want to take it, why would someone help you? Relationships aren't built overnight but are critical to your success. For instance, could you tell me where to find a good intellectual property attorney? An electrical engineer with design skills? Where to get a good pizza in Rome? Someone you know, knows someone who does have the answer. Take the time to get engaged in your community and start building your contacts.

Third, capital raising is an often-dreaded experience. It may be hard to figure capital needs when you don't even have a product in the market, but it will almost always be considerably more than you think. One of the things you will never see in a textbook is how long it takes to bring in funding. In my experience, those companies that actively and continuously seek out capital even before it is needed, fair better than others. It is almost a full-time job but one that often takes a back seat to getting to market. The result is a potentially fatal cash crunch. Take time to get to know bankers, angels and other investors. Considerable free education comes in building these relationships along the way, so that when the time comes you will be positioned to get the best deal for your business.

Give as much attention to these three ideas as you do to your product or service, and you are well on your way to success!

Best regards,

Brent Evans

Brent Evans

Venture Funder & Business Educator

Dr. Deborah Ferber ("Dr. Deb") is a former CEO of several startups, angel investor for companies she believes in and instructor in entrepreneurship, manage-ment and economics.

Dr. Deb's professional career has spanned twenty plus years in the paper industry, technology and education. Her degrees in management and counseling include the following; P.P.S , A.A., B.S., M.S. and D.B.A.

Over the last 20 years, Dr. Deb held several leadership positions, Instructor, Assistant Professor, Associate Dean, Manager, Director, Vice President, Chief Financial Officer, President, and Chief Executive Officer.

She has worked with and learned from the following organizations; Kelly Paper, Deutsche Bank, KPMG, US Navy, 20th Century Fox, Warner Brothers, Allstate, Xerox, Ingram Micro, IBM and Microsoft.

Dr. Deb coaches business leaders on "Best Practice Benchmarking" in sales, marketing and human resource recruitment and retention. She sits on many boards and presents on business topics to international trade organizations.

Dr Deb coaches students at Brandman University, Chapman University, and California State University Fullerton. She has funded several student startups and is looking for ways to help students grow their career,

In addition Dr. Deb sits on the board of Directors at Chapman University's, Leathery School of Entrepreneurship. Furthermore she helps raise funding and mentors the incubator teams, for Angel and VC Funding.

She has been recognized by the following: Who's Who in Universities and Colleges, Spirited   Entrepreneur Orange County Register, Woman of the Year, Melvone Jones Fellowship, Who's Who in Business, Mayor of Santa Ana, California State Assembly Award, and Rosa Parks Human Rights Wall of Tolerance.

Dr. Deb's mantra --
I create
I take risks
I live my passion
I am an Entrepreneur

Dr. Deborah Ferber
Monarch Beach, California

Dear Founder,

Entrepreneurship is like skydiving-

Much like learning to skydive, you must first be taught to become self –reliant and proficient in using tools necessary to respond quickly to the many variables. Procedures will be practiced until they can physically and verbally be demonstrated and executed and with full confidence.

It is not about the invention or service you are creating or where you are launching it, it is about how well you listened to the people around you and asked what they needed. How you tell the story of who you are and how your product or service can help your potential customers will take on a life of its own. Learn to do these things well.

Coming up with and idea is just the first step. It will take research, planning and development strategies that can be implemented and duplicated to provide superior customer relations and operational excellence.

The successful entrepreneur will try to land and hit the target, with the first priority being a good landing from a straight line approach and know when to pivot when necessary, be on the lookout for cross winds, and be prepared for competitive turbulence, and assume a bumpy and hard landing.

These are the steps to create a safe landing and hitting your Entrepreneurial "**TARGET**".

- **T**arget. Outline your target and objectives with intention to hit your designated mark on the first pass, by creating an excellent business plan.
- **A**ctions. Learn to take actions. Follow through with your vision. Persuade and direct others to follow through with their vision as well.
- **R**espect. If you learn to respect your competition and your own limitations, you will discover how to improve your creations and keep it viable.
- **G**rowth. Have the constant foresight to grow your idea, concept, funding and team.
- **E**nergy. You will need high energy to work long hours and have the endurance to keep it all going when things go wrong.
- **T**enacity. Even if you miss your target, have the tenacity to dust yourself off and try again.

In conclusion, if you think you are ready to take the entrepreneurial jump, you will need a steady hand, practice, discipline, pivot options, marketing skills, mentors, teamwork, and vision. Remember tenacity is always required even if you are having problems achieving your business TARGET.

Wishing you much success on your entrepreneurial adventure.

Dr. Deborah Ferber

97

Derreck A. Ford

Derreck Ford is founder and CEO of JETEC Corporation. The company is headquartered in Costa Mesa, California and can be found at www.jetec.com

JETEC was started over 25 years ago to provide industrial manufacturing companies world-wide with the highest quality and most reliable product identification solutions available. Simply put, its mission is to provide its customers with a one-stop shop for state of the art, turnkey parts marking solutions equipment, services and accessories.

JETEC's suite of integrated industrial ink jet, laser and dot peen marking solutions have been designed to meet the unique and changing needs of aerospace and defense, automotive, electronics, medical, pharmaceutical and PCB manufacturers. The company motto is, IF YOU CAN MAKE IT WE CAN MARK IT.

Derreck's quest towards entrepreneurism started while growing up in the Soundview projects in the South Bronx, NY. His first exposure was being a paperboy where he had to deliver the morning paper and perform monthly collections.

While attending high school and college,Derreck held various positions in supermarkets. He learned the importance of customer service. Derreck earned his BSIE degree at the New Jersey Institute of Technology and later an MBA at Pepperdine University. Derreck feels fortunate to have worked for such prestigious companies as Armstrong World Industries, McDonald Douglas, Rockwell and Hughes Aircraft Company before he embarked on his entre-preneurial venture.

He reflects, "Giving back to the community has always been a very important part of my life. For over 15 years I mentored African American males who participated in the Passport to the Future Program offered by the Orange County Chapter of the 100 Black Men of America. In 2003 Dr. Ames asked if I would be a mentor at CSUF's entrepreneurial program and I have been participating off and on ever since."

Derreck is a motivational speaker and personal coach for high school and college students, as well as individuals who desire to become entrepreneurs. He is author of The Entrepreneur's Survival Handbook, A Deck of 52 Insightful Pointers from an Experienced Entrepreneur.

Derreck offers this advice to aspiring entrepreneurs, "**Prepare** yourself to have the skills to run your enterprise. This means master your strengths and plan on hiring your weaknesses. **Observe** and study other entrepreneurs. **Serve** your community; always Jump at the opportunity to *Pay it Forward*."

JETEC

Dear Founder:

Congratulations on taking that leap of faith on becoming an entrepreneur. You are embarking on a journey that will cause you to expand your knowledge of yourself beyond the self-imposed constraints of your current beliefs. I remember 25+ years ago leaving a very secure position with Hughes Aircraft Company to embark on my entrepreneurial journey. I was eager, over confident, motivated and crudely prepared. What allowed me to sustain my capital equipment, systems integration based, enterprise through three recessions was my ability to repeatedly recreate myself and my business while holding onto my moral, ethical and spiritual values. I encourage you to consistently remind yourself of what's important to you; know your core values.

No man or woman is an island, so I strongly recommend that you establish an advisory board consisting of legal, finance, business strategy, marketing, sales and human resource professionals that act as the lifeline of your enterprise. These are your Go-To people who are not afraid to tell you No and who know how to support you in meeting your business objectives.

People are your most valuable asset. Reward those who are loyal to the company, and quickly remove those who show they are cancerous to your organization. One bad apple can spoil the bunch. I treat my employees as family, and for the most part, I have experienced loyal employees over the years. Learn what motivates your employees and don't assume it is always money. Giving them time off or allowing them to have a flexible work schedule and not to miss their child's play or school event can be more valuable to them than monetary compensation.

You always require more financial capital than you think. What's comes faster than a speeding bullet and is more frequent than you can imagine? Fixed expenses for payroll, payroll taxes, rent, insurance and utilities. You may want to consider maintaining a reserve fund where you habitually put away a small percentage of your receivables to cover unexpected cash flow shortages. Cash flow is the lifeblood of any organization. Plan your cash inlays and outlays and you are essence controlling your stress levels.

Entrepreneurship is a journey for both you and your enterprise that requires constant cultivating. There are many avenues available to you to garner additional skills essential to staying abreast of the various aspects of your business. I enjoy being a mentor to CSUF's entrepreneurial program. My involvement allows me to stay current with today's technologies and I have access to the vast minds of the students. I encourage you to find a source that fits your personality and needs.

Once again, congratulations on having the courage to go after your dreams.

Most successful regards

Derreck A Ford
CEO/Founder

Professor and Business Developer

Howard Forman, Ph.D. is an Associate Professor of Marketing at California State University, Fullerton and an entrepreneur. He began teaching at California State University, Fullerton in August of 2007. As an associate professor in the Marketing department, he has taught classes in Marketing and Technology as well as courses on Marketing Principles, and Retail & Marketing Channels Strategies.

 Prior to joining the faculty at Cal State, Howard was an Assistant Professor of Marketing at Drexel University in Philadelphia and an Assistant Professor at The Pennsylvania State University, Worthington Scranton.

Howard earned his Bachelor's degree in Business Logistics from Pennsylvania State University, followed by a MBA in Logistics, Operations, and Materials Management from George Washington University. He went on to earn his Ph.D. in Marketing and International Business from Temple University in 1998.

Howard began his career as a pricing analyst at the CSX railroad, where he constructed and negotiated intermodal transportation rates with FORTUNE 100 companies. He went on to be a procurement agent at the Department of Defense. Later he was a contract administrator at Motorola. Before entering academia, Howard managed the contracts department for an environmental company, writing and negotiating contracts with major oil and chemical companies.

Howard leveraged his education and experience as an entrepreneur. His start-up experience ranges from co-founding an antique retail and wholesale business with his wife to a successful consulting business with

Good Hockey - Good Whiskey
Since age ten, Howard has been a passionate fan of Hockey and the Philadelphia Flyers in particular. His passion for fine whiskey began in a similar way with his first adult sip of a single malt scotch.

worldwide leaders in their fields such as General Motors, Ford, Meredith Baer, and Arkema. More recently his business development activities include Glueper, Charglet, and his latest ventures, CommunityFavor, Sukkah Hill Spirits and CALI Distillery.

Howard's passion for teaching is apparent to many. He states that he truly enjoys being an educator and believes that by being one he can make a difference in other people's lives. He feels a great sense of pride when he witnesses one of his students graduate or continue their academic careers by striving for an advanced degree. When asked to provide one piece of advice to students, he advises "peruse something you are passionate about."

CALIdistillery

Dear Founder,

I am very excited to share a few thoughts about being an entrepreneur. For the better part of the last twenty-five years I have always been wanting to start a new business. In that time, I was part of several start-up companies with varying degrees of success—as measured by dollars—from virtually nothing to hundreds of thousands of dollars and a potential for several hundred million. However, when I look back at each of these, I realize that HONESTLY, all of them were a success; it just depends on how you define success. I define success in terms of not only monetary success but also in terms of education. Without learning from my past experiences, I would not have been able to continue to persevere, and continually strive to succeed on as many dimensions as possible. Without question, you need to be able to and willing to work hard, any time of the day or night, but hard work is not enough because it is easy to get burned out. Here are a couple of quick thoughts that I hope you take with you as you travel down your entrepreneurial path.

You probably heard the old cliché, "honesty is the best policy". Well it is, but as an entrepreneur, the most important person you need to be honest with is yourself. This is the first lesson. Many young and first-time entrepreneurs get very excited about their ventures, as they should. Unfortunately, it is likely that one or more of your ventures will not work out. You have to be honest with yourself to recognize and know when a venture is not going to work, and get out. This is the second lesson. It is a tough decision to make, but one that is crucial for your success, no matter which venture you work on. I learned this lesson from lingering too long on a venture that ultimately failed because of, among other things, lack of funding, poor product development, and slower than expected diffusion.

The last thing I would like to share with you is to help you with your perspective and how you should frame the evaluation of your venture. By that, I mean how you evaluate success. Success should not be measured solely in terms of profits and losses, revenue, or market share. That is because these are not the only take-aways you should be getting from each of your ventures. Do not underestimate how much you learn from your experiences, especially from those ventures that do not work out quite as planned. These experiences and the education you glean from them are invaluable as you progress and grow as an entrepreneur. Many people like myself will give you tips about what you should be and could be doing to make your business a success. The value of experiential education should not EVER be underestimated. Learning what works and more importantly what does not, will help you as you grow in your ventures. By defining success to include my education and personal growth as an entrepreneur, I was able to capitalize on that and add value to the current team I am working with at Sukkah Hill Spirits/Cali Distillery. The result, it is paying off and I am adding value to the team that money cannot.

Best of luck in your ventures,

Howard Forman, Ph.D.
Business Development
Sukkah Hill/Cali Distillery

8950 W. Olympic Blvd, Suite 179, Beverly Hills, CA 90211 424.286.2474
CALIDistillery.com @Calidistillery info@calidistillery.com

101

Fratzke Media

James and Ryan Fratzke, also known as the Fratzke Brothers are the founders of Fratzke Media.

Fratzke Media is a Strategic Storytelling Agency that helps refine every touchpoint a company has with consumers, both internal and external. Fratzke Media helps their clients reduce workloads and curate beautiful brand experiences that drive financial growth. Its marketing expertise includes all aspects of the consumer's digital experience. Aspects include digital marketing, email marketing, social media marketing, local search marketing, website development, search engine optimization, online reputation management (reviews) and content marketing.

Although Fratzke Media is James and Ryan's latest venture, it's not their first. At 13 the identical twin brothers started mowing lawns, at 16, they were painting fences and landscaping, and at 18 they capitalized on Black Friday with a graphic design company at their local mall.

During their time at CSUF, the Fratzke Brothers worked fulltime at the Disneyland Resort as Special Event Marketing Coordinators during the day and full-time students at night. After making a connection in their Entrepreneurial Marketing class both brothers accepted roles at Brandify, a local orange county digital marketing technology company. Both twins served Fortune 500 brands like Walmart, Advance Auto Parts, and Disney Stores in their roles as Strategic Account Managers. Throughout their three-year tenure, both earned the right to say they were the highest grossing account managers in the company's twenty-year history, trading the honor in back to back years.

With that, the scene was set. The Fratzke Brothers identified an opportunity to provide outstanding service and to help brands better tell their stories across the multiple Channels of Digital media. Fratzke Media was born.

In 2014. James and Ryan delivered their graduation commencement speech for the Mihaylo College of business and Economics. In front of thousands of classmates and their families, they spoke of their parents and the College. "Our mother is the definition of a dreamer," said James... "She always taught us that no dream was too big, and if you are shooting for the moon, you're not shooting far enough." "Our father, on the other hand, taught us strong follow-through, hard work, ethics and how to look at things in a practical way," said Ryan. He added,"Our parents shaped our personality, and Mihaylo taught us the language of business. I am proud to say that James and I are the first in our immediate family to graduate from college."

Dear Founder,

So you're starting a new venture? Welcome to the club! There's no turning back now. Creating our business, Fratzke Media, has been one of the most rewarding journeys of our lifetime, but it's also had its challenges. Here are three of the most impactful lessons we've learned so far, we hope they help:

- You need to play by your own rules
- Go one-inch wide and one-mile deep
- Bridge the gap to success

Let's unpack these:

Play by Your Own Rules: Life has rules. You should not play by them! We're sure you've heard of David and Goliath. The giant challenged Israel's greatest warrior to a winner-take-all battle royal. Instead, a shepherd boy stepped forward. Why did David ultimately win? Because he played by his own rules, not Goliaths. Instead of engaging in hand to hand combat (a battle David would have lost) he shot Goliath right between the eyes with a slingshot. When we explained our vision to help Fortune 500 brands use storytelling to better connect with their customers, some people reacted like Goliath. They didn't believe we could do it. "Keep your jobs and punch the clock" was the rule they wanted us to follow. But we played by our own rules and our business has seen gigantic growth.

Go One-Inch Wide and One-Mile Deep: What does that mean? First, keep your business and audience simple and clear. Second, dive deep to provide the most value possible. Remember your new venture can't be everything to everyone. As Leonardo da Vinci said, "Simplicity is the ultimate sophistication." Our first concept for Fratzke Media felt like five different companies trying to be one. We realized the importance of striping out the parts we knew we couldn't be great at. Now we only focus on the things we know we can do better than anyone else and we work to perfect the processes around those things.

Bridge the Gap: Imagine you're standing on one side of the Grand Canyon and you decide to build a bridge to the other side. When you get halfway across, you realize you don't have all the materials, tools, and skills to finish. In case you missed it, the bridge is your business in this metaphor. As the founder of a startup, you can't do everything. Take inventory of your strengths and weaknesses and then ask for help. We're lucky because there's two of us and we have complimentary skill sets, but we also know when it's time to ask for help. Some of the most fruitful advancements in our business have come when we faced the cold hard facts and realized we couldn't build the bridge by ourselves.

We want to leave you with a quotation from Theodore Roosevelt:

"It is not the critic who counts; not the man who points out how the strong man stumbles, or where the doer of deeds could have done them better. The credit belongs to the man who is actually in the arena... who at the best knows in the end the triumph of high achievement, and who at the worst, if he fails, at least fails while daring greatly, so that his place shall never be with those cold and timid souls who neither know victory nor defeat."

Until We Meet Again,

James Fratzke & Ryan Fratzke
Founders of Fratzke Brothers Media

Making a Positive Impact

Charlie Gallagher is an Orange County native and a California State University Fullerton alumnus from the Mihaylo College of Business and Economics. He currently is a classroom mentor for CSUF Entrepreneurship

Charlie's parents operate a successful, family-owned, pools and spas business in the City of Orange. It has served commercial and residential clients for over 40 years. Charlie attributes his work ethic and entrepreneurial skills to his father and his compassion and patience to his mother.

His parents raised Charlie in the city of Orange. He attended El Modena High School, where he was captain and MVP of his water polo team. He grew up as a member of the Boys Scouts of America and earned the distinguished rank of Eagle in 2004. He went on to play water polo for two years at Fullerton Junior College. Charlie transferred to CSUF where he majored in business administration.

Upon graduating, he traveled to Germany and Croatia for several months. The experience abroad permanently enhanced his perception of life. After his return he became a financial services professional with New York Life Securities, Inc.

Charlie now works at the Costa Mesa office of Thrivent Financial, a Christian not-for-profit financial planning firm. Thrivent Financial is a financial services organization that helps Christians be wise with money and live generously. It offers a broad range of products and services – including life insurance, annuities and mutual funds. It serves 2.4 million member-owners nationwide. Charlie loves his career and where he works because

he gets to make a positive impact in people's lives every day. He specializes in raising money for faith-based organizations such as churches and youth organizations. He creates or enhances their endowments through planned giving.

In his free time, Charlie gives back to and serves the community in many ways. He is currently a Council National Eagle Scout Member and a Volunteer Chair of the Eagle Recognition Dinner. Charlie is a youth leader for the Anaheim YMCA and a Villa Park Rotarian. You can also find Charlie in the hills behind Irvine Regional Park. He enjoys mountain biking with his close friends or in boutique spin studios to maintain his cardiovascular conditioning between rides. Charlie likes to read, especially books that transcend generations. Two of his favorites are The Four Agreements by Don Miguel Ruiz and How to Win Friends and Influence People by Dale Carnegie. Charlie is also a member of the Center Club in Costa Mesa. It is a business social club which acts as a hub for his philanthropic work.

Charlie Gallagher
Orange County, California

Dear Founder,

Achievements matter, but connections we make along the way are invaluable. The right connections will open opportunities in ways you cannot imagine to help you conceptualize and create new ventures. As entrepreneurs, it is of the utmost importance that we continuously strengthen and nurture our relationships, both personal and professional.

The following methods have personally helped me build lasting connections, which I have turned into meaningful relationships. By sharing, I hope that they will also work for you in helping you expand as a professional and grow into a superior entrepreneur.

Sometimes less is more. Because we have a finite amount of time and energy, there is a limit to how many connections we can make and manage. In my experience, finding the right balance of quantity and quality of connections is the best approach. Knowing a select few very well is more fruitful than having many surface level relationships within large networks.

Think positive. Steer clear of those who are negative, talk bad about others or are otherwise toxic to your relationships. Do not be afraid to fail. Think of your "failures" as opportunities so that you do not repeat your mistakes and keep working until you figure things out to succeed in your endeavors. Always believe in yourself because it will be that much harder for others to believe in you if you do not.

Help others. I have been volunteering for a long time at local charity events, annually at the YMCA summer camp, and grew up participating-and now volunteering as an Eagle Scout-in the Boy Scouts of America (the "BSA"). The BSA taught me not only about entrepreneurial skills and ethical principles, it instilled in me a desire to help others and to make a positive impact in my community while making important connections with like-minded people along the way.

Just show up. Sometimes, luck is on your side and you just need to show face.
They say that luck is what happens when preparation meets opportunity, so stay prepared because the next opportunity might just pass you by unexpectedly. There are several examples where I have made life changing connections by deciding last-minute to go to an event when I could have more easily slept in or just hung out with friends instead.

Personal development. As a final word of advice, I recommend that you take the time to work on yourself. We all have room for improvement and there are many books to help you on this topic. To get started, I highly recommend that you read the book, How to Win Friends and Influence People by Dale Carnegie. You will thank me later.

Sincerely,

Charlie Gallagher

HX Works

Matthew Gallizzi is an alumnus of Mihaylo College of Business and Economics (2009). He studied entrepreneurship, but he started his entrepreneurial journey twelve years before. At age nine when he set out to wash cars in his neighborhood. $2 for a car wash, $4 for a truck. Matt spent his earnings on a BMX bike, a calculator watch, and many computer programming books. He did freelance computer programming work with global clients throughout his early teens.

In 2003, at age sixteen, Matt founded Notix Technical solutions (NotixTech). The company helped hundreds of startups and businesses with strategy and execution. NotixTech led projects for international clients. It coordinated multinational teams to deliver on six-figure web projects.

As the leader of NxTech, Matt was a frequent speaker and panelist at conferences and events. He served as webmaster for the Southern California Linux Expo for two years while running his company and attending college. Matt's thought leadership around technology reached tens of thousands of readers. NotixTech handled projects touching millions of lives. As Matt describes in his letter, in 2013 he realized it was time for something new. In 2014 he wound down his successful NxTech operations and founded HX Works.

Matt believes that we create the world we live in. The mission of HX Works is to equip extraordinary people with insights that serve their future. Insights bring more freedom and greater impact to strengthen a future vision. HX Works does this through meaningful conversation, unique experiences and its powerful technology. Clients include entrepreneurs, visionaries, creatives and other exceptional people who see the future.

In 2009 Matt teamed with an entrepreneurship classmate Daniela Bolzmann to present Mihaylo College's Commencement address. In his part of the address he said,
"My tough time was back in 1999 when a house fire took everything my family and I had. We were left with nothing but the clothes on our backs. Through this, I learned about what matters most in life. It's not stuff. It's not materialism. It's not money. It's relationships -- Family -- Friends -- Colleagues -- Neighbors -- Loved ones. Remember this, happiness is only real when it's shared. A leader named Anthony Robbins puts it this way: 'The quality of your life is the quality of your relationships.' Are you pursuing happiness in your life by sharing it with others? Power of mind is key. If you can dream it, you can achieve it. Remember, you are limited by nothing but yourself. This mindset helped me conquer 54 units in 2008 so I can graduate today and it WILL carry me through the rest of my life."

HXWORKS

Dear Founder,

These truths I am about to share have allowed me to become more powerful in who I am and what I do.

Let's begin with a moment. I was on my nightly walk. It was June 13th, 2013. 9:30pm. This dark night was windy. Aged green leaves danced around the floor dimly lit by streetlights. Large trees stood watching over as I walked and came to a realization. I realized I created a life and business I didn't want anymore. I was chasing what I thought I should be chasing. This carrot, it turned out, was not life-giving.

The first truth I learned was to know what I want out of life -- to know what I want out of how I invest my time. I learned the power of purpose and honoring my vision.

I knew I wanted to feel calm and present. You see, I used to talk fast. Think fast. Move fast. Build fast. Read fast. Act fast. I took 54 upper division units in one year at Cal State Fullerton in 2008 so I could finish fast. I took pride in how fast I was.

First responders don't enter a burning home fast and the navy seals don't enter enemy territory fast. They build habits over and over and over again. They train for the blink of an eye life or death moments by deliberate practice, deliberate movements, with an intention for desired outcomes. I learned how to slow down to speed up.

Lastly, I realized a truth that would change everything for me. It changed how I view my world. And it changed my relationships. With strangers, friends, family and myself.

A musician plays music with a combination of sounds. A chef creates a masterpiece with various ingredients. An author writes a book with arrangements of letters. An artist makes art with water colors. Each creates a larger piece of art from smaller pieces.

I discovered the words that describe the world I see create my world. Changing my words changed my world. I examined my sight and refined it with this provocative question: "What is my payoff for seeing this way?"

Knowing what I want, slowing down, and changing the way I see my world, continues to serve me in creating the world I believe in.

Godspeed on your adventure.

SCORE Volunteer

Like Warren Buffet and Meredith Whitney, **Robert Godlasky** began his business career at age nine on a newspaper route.

His professional career spanned forty plus years in retail with national chain stores including Alpha Beta, Albertsons, Sav-On Drugs, Longs . He worked in various roles beginning as store manager.

Over those 40 years, he held a variety of leadership positions. One of the most interesting roles was Senior VP of Marketing for the Intermountain Division of the holding company, American Stores.

The division operated 254 stores in 57 markets. From town to town, the major competitors tended to be local chains or independents; so the division's business model was extremely entrepreneurial.

Currently, Bob is a Small Business Counselor at the Service Corps of Retired Executives (SCORE). As part of that responsibility he is Director of Academic Mentoring.

Bob coaches students at California State University, Fullerton's Entrepreneurship Center in the Mihaylo College of Business and Economics. He also mentors residents of the CSUF Start-up Incubator.

In addition Bob counsels students at the Chapman University, Leatherby School Entrepreneurship. He also helps at the University of La Verne.

Since 2013, Bob has mentored marines at Camp Pendleton. The Marine Corps sponsors a Transition Assistance Program for veterans wanting to start their own business.

Bob has been recognized for his 'Lean Start Up Business' approach. Many of his students like his willingness to help them with career counseling.

Bob's mantra is:
"I Empower Entrepreneurs."

Bob at Lake Mary just below Mammoth Crest on the Mammoth Lakes Loop trail. (Bob says that at 9,000 ft elevation he was NOT smiling four hours later)

Bob Godlasky
Yorba Linda, California

Dear Founder,

What I Wish I Knew When I Was 22.

Shortly after retiring in the Spring of 2009, I found myself watching a business news program on TV. I was watching my 401k become a 201k. A guest speaker on the program was an H.R. exec from a Wall St. company. She pointed out that of all U.S. college graduates in 2008, only 54% landed a job! She went on to state that of the 54%, only 32% landed jobs in their field of study. I was stunned. By that evening I had decided I would volunteer some of my retirement time helping university business students get a stronger start in their business careers.

I'm not going to teach you or preach to you -- your faculty and parents can have that honor. Rather I wish to share a few concepts that could add value to your career.

1. Foster Collaboration:
In life and especially in business, relationships matter. Create allies.
All of my great friends, my best employees, my most loyal customers and my wife -- ALL started out as strangers.
Be happy every day. People gravitate towards happy people. They avoid unhappy.

2. Keep It Simple:
When you graduate you will find that life has a way of getting very complicated. I think that in California most people would tell you they have more money than time. As a marketing exec, my company performed annual surveys and focus groups to understand what consumers valued most. Year after year, convenience outranked price as a reason where people choose to shop.
There are only 7 colors in the rainbow. Look at what Rembrandt and Michael Angelo were able to create starting with only 7 basic colors. There are 8 notes on the musical scale. Look what Mozart and Beethoven created.

3. Do What's Right:
Without parents and teachers around some people create daily habits of cheating. We see it in people's driving habits. We often hear stories in the news. Make it your habit, your personal brand to do what's right. There's never a right time to do the wrong thing. There's never a wrong time to do the right thing.

Finally, Care About People:
You will enrich your life and strengthen relationships by showing you care (it feels good). Show your family you care. You better care about your employees and your boss. Show your clients that you care about them.
"No one can care about everyone, but everyone can care about someone." ~ President Ronald Reagan

Sincerely wishing you success and happiness in your future,

BOB GODLASKY

QuickBridge Funding, LLC

Ben Gold is a founding partner and President of QuickBridge, a privately-held financial services firm founded in 2011. The company provides smarter short-term working capital funding solutions for small to medium-sized businesses nationwide.

QuickBridge is the brainchild of innovators in the business lending field. They noticed that amazing companies, through no fault of their own, couldn't access working capital through the usual sources. Ben and his fellow founders set out to fix three key elements broken in the industry: mountains of paperwork, long delays and bait-and-switch offers that weren't in the best interest of the borrower. The goal was to make funding smarter and 'walk the walk' of offering superior service.

Out of that commitment to improvement came an award-winning lending platform. It allows the company to make uniquely designed working capital loans to small business borrowers. This lending innovation makes the application process easier, approvals faster, and has enabled the company to service customers much more efficiently. Instead of waiting weeks to obtain much needed financing, customers can receive funding in as little as one day.

The QuickBridge founders have shaped a culture that is even more important than process improvements. As Ben describes it, hallmarks of the culture are, "fierce transparency, unrelenting professionalism and unwavering dedication to providing the highest levels of service. The goal at QuickBridge is to be an extension of customers' businesses—becoming an integral part of why they grow and thrive."

Based on its growth, QuickBridge has ranked two consecutive years on the Inc. 500 Fastest Growing American

Companies list. In 2015, The Orange County Business Journal named QuickBridge the County's 2015 Fastest Growing Mid-Size Company.

Ben holds a B.A. in Marketing and M.B.A. from California State University, Fullerton. When he isn't at the office, or spending time with his wife and two young children, Ben gives back to CSUF. He serves as Treasurer for Mihaylo College of Business and Economics Executive Counsel and is a friend of CSUF Entrepreneurship. In addition, Ben is actively involved in the Southern California Chapter of the Young Presidents Organization.

410 Exchange, Suite 150
Irvine, CA 92602

888.233.9085
quickbridge.com

Dear Founder,

You are about to read a long-winded letter from a guy you don't know. So I'm not going to bury the lead. If you take just one piece of advice from me, let it be this: Integrity above all else. That's it. Living by the Golden Rule has paid me incalculable dividends in business and in life. Here's my nutshell of a story:

When I started my career in finance, I was a college kid with mounting student loans driving a beat up Nissan Altima. In the world of hard money, there was (and still is) this mentality of doing whatever it takes to make a deal, always in the name of personal gain. That never felt right to me. So from day one, I focused on making ethical decisions, treating everyone with respect, and building a network of mentors as I slowly worked my way up the ladder.

Less than a decade later, the relationships I made and the knowledge I cultivated came together in a perfectly-timed business opportunity: I was invited to be a founding partner of QuickBridge. I believe my commitment to integrity changed the course of my life (and eventually allowed me to buy a slightly more dependable car). It's the reason I enjoy any measure of success, even if "success" is only defined by my ability to look my kids in the eye when I get home at night. What I'm saying is, start there. Let integrity be your guiding principle as a leader.

Still with me? Cool. Let's talk about you. There's an often-cited Les Brown quote: "Shoot for the moon. Even if you miss, you'll land among the stars." It's a nice enough metaphor: this idea that, somehow, simply putting effort toward your goal will guarantee good things. But when it comes to founding a business, missing your mark could lead to debilitating challenges, if not outright failure. I do not recommend winging it.

Forget Brown's quote and remember this one instead (I wish I knew who said it): "Starting a business is like launching a rocket ship. If it's off by an inch at launch, it'll be off by miles once it gets into orbit." In other words, you need a rock-solid business plan and a path to scale. You need trusted advisors to review your plan and provide honest feedback. Then, once you get going, you need to regularly measure results against the plan and course correct as needed. Good data and adequate funding are imperative to this equation.

Now let's assume you are already an expert in the field of your new venture (you should be), you have a solid plan, and enough money to get off the ground and grow. Start small and be prepared to DIY in the early days. QuickBridge started with two guys, a phone, and a laptop. We succeeded because we knew plenty about how to sell and underwrite business loans. As our product became more desirable, we defined and prioritized new objectives and added people to fit our needs. As a leader, I recognize most of these awesome people won't stay with us forever. But I have committed to making a positive impact on their career so they, in turn, make a positive impact on the business. As an example, in the early days of our company, we hired a brilliant mind to help create the first generation of our lending platform. He eventually moved on, but his efforts gave us a leg up in our space and we are better for it, even years later.

In closing, whatever you set out to create, do so with a strong plan and the guidance of people wiser than you. Then, make your company a place people want to work and be grateful to those that choose to work with you. Finally, don't forget your roots and if you do end up finding success, please remember to send the elevator back down.

Best of luck,

Ben Gold
President, QuickBridge

Live is Better

Duane Gomer is Owner and Founder of Duane Gomer, Inc.("DGI"), a California Education Provider. The company was formed in 1963 in the San Fernando Valley as a Real Estate Syndication and Property Management firm. To build the company Duane taught at the UCLA Extension at the Anderson School of Business and wrote a weekly Real Estate column for the Daily News.

After 15 successful years, in 1978 the company went in a different direction. Enjoying students more than tenants, DGI became sponsors of California Department of Real Estate Courses. The company moved to Mission Viejo in 1985 and was also approved to present California Notary Licensing and Federal Approved Mortgage Loan Origination Courses. All classes are available online and as correspondence home study, but DGI is best known for their LIVE presentations. (LIVE IS BETTER).

Today, the corporation employs a staff of 10 W-2's and 22 1099's as speakers. This outstanding cadre of speakers presents LIVE classes from Santa Rosa to Chula Vista. In one month last year they presented over seventy classes.

Duane's entrepreneurial journey started in Racine, WI. Park High School and then to Indiana University to play tennis and basketball. After Indiana he secured a prestigious teaching assistantship with Dr. Ralph Barnes at UCLA. After completing his MBA, he became a Navy Supply Corp Officer and served in Germany at the Rhine River Patrol.

Coming back to California he passed tests for his Insurance, NASD, and Real Estate Licenses and went to work for two years at Forest E. Olson in Van Nuys as Director of Property Management and a Commercial Salesperson. He left Forest E. Olson to start his own company over 56 years ago.

Some honors Duane has gathered of which he is proud; Big Ten Medal at IU (most outstanding senior athlete), Valedictorian at Navy Supply Corp School, All Navy Tennis Team. Eight State Tennis Championships, Hall of Fame Youth Football Coach, Six Little League and Pony Championships, Beta Gamma Sigma, set Wisconsin Community College Basketball scoring record, college level basketball official and Realtor Emeritis.

Duane is a long time friend of CSUF Entrepreneurship and has helped out in the classroom many times. DJ, his co-owner wife, and Duane live in Coto de Caza, California. They enjoy their four children, Debra Struhs, David Gomer and wife Lisa, Danny Gomer, and Melissa Moore and of course, more importantly they dote on their five grandchildren; Lindsey, Ashley, Kaylee, Grant and Brooklyn.

DUANE GOMER SEMINARS

23312 Madero St., Suite J • Mission Viejo, CA 92691 • (949)457-8930 • (800) 439-4909
Fax (949) 455-9931 • E-mail: Duane@DuaneGomer.com • Web site: www.DuaneGomer.com

Dear Founder:

First, I would like to thank John Bradley Jackson and Michael Ames for asking me to contribute a letter for their *Creating New Ventures* book. It is both an honor and a privilege to be included.

I have been an entrepreneur since 1963, without partners or shareholders. I am still working. Pundits say, "You learn from your failures". I agree, and I have learned so much from mine. Reacting to success is easy, reacting to failure not so much. You must learn to be creative in your thinking, then react to crisis.

A mantra that I heard before I went into business was, "Find something about which you are passionate and have talent to accomplish, and then find a way to get paid well for doing it." In other words, find your niche. I would have liked to be a Big Ten Cornerback, but I was small, skinny and slow. Not so good. But I had quick hands, good coordination, quick first step, and perseverance. So tennis.

It is my opinion; sports and business have many of the same characteristics. For example, "Be on time and be prepared"; "Understand you will not win every game"; "Need a game plan and be able to make adjustments quickly when your game plan does not work"; "Perfect practice makes perfect"; "Recruit, recruit, recruit, in business and sports you need the best".

Find mentors: I have been lucky to always find someone to help me find my way. Their assistance and encouragement is so appreciated. This includes Rich Robinson for Continuing Education, Theresa Ballard for NMLS Education, and Stan Jones for Property Management.

Learn to delegate and give out authority. This is not a 9 to 5 job, be prepared to put in extra time. Learn to be an outstanding interviewer as personnel is most important (you want to find a Montana or a Brady in the later rounds). If they are outstanding you have to sell them to join your firm.

Most important: Balance your work life with your home life. An extremely successful work life and a very poor home life is really not good. Learn the words: Date Night, Baby Sitters, Fidelity, Vacations or even Staycations, and Fun. The life you save may be your own.

And remember when you lay awake at night wondering where you are going to find the payroll money, no one can ever fire you, tell you to move to another city, or to retire. You are the owner, your name is on the door. Good luck, and may the wind be always at your back and the California sun always be shining warm upon your face.

Best Regards

Duane Gomer

Duane Gomer

Tech Coast Works, L.L.C.

Jeff Greenberg is the founder and Managing Director of Tech Coast Works, L.L.C. He formed the company to help the University of California, Irvine commercialize some of the university's inventions.

Jeff's most significant achievement to date for Tech Coast Works is the launch of Hiperwall. He grew the startup from an academic research project into a global multi-million-dollar business. It now has customers in 58 countries around the world, without the need for any outside investment.

Jeff began his career as a software engineer, working for large enterprises like McDonnell Douglas, Xerox, Toshiba and Canon. Over time, he transitioned to a technical marketing role, then to product management, brand management, strategic planning and eventually into general management. In 2000 he shifted his focus to the world of hi-tech startups. Since then, he has worked exclusively for emerging companies as a consultant, employee, advisor or founder. During his 30 years as corporate executive, entrepreneur, and industry consultant, Jeff gained considerable experience at accelerating growth, entering new markets and implementing turnaround strategies.

He has had significant startup success. For example, he was part of the four-person team that launched the Westinghouse line of flat panel televisions. He was involved in the startup Dayflo that PC Magazine named software company of the year. At Zetera, he was responsible for all international sales and manufacturing agreements. He was part of the team that raised over $20 million in venture capital.

In Jeff's view, the foundation of his career advancement is a strong educational background. It includes a bachelor's in computer science from Rutgers University, a master's in computer science from U.C. Irvine and an Executive MBA from Pepperdine University.

Jeff holds multiple patents, with additional patents pending. He is a published author whose work has appeared in publications such as PC Magazine, U.S. News & World Report, PC Computing and Digital Signage Magazine.

Jeff gives back to the community as an adjunct college professor, teaching start-up skills to would-be entrepreneurs. At California State University, Fullerton, Jeff has been a mentor for the entrepreneurial marketing class and a guest speaker for the Start-up Incubator.

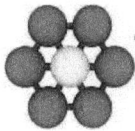

Tech Coast Works
Commercializing Innovative Technology

Dear Founder,

Archimedes said "Give me a lever long enough and a fulcrum on which to place it, and I shall move the world." While he didn't actually use the word, he was referring to leverage – the ability to gain maximum advantage from a resource to complete a seemingly impossible task.

This concept is extremely important to most startups, where there is usually an endless supply of impossible tasks and a constant shortage of resources. Success in this type of environment depends on maximizing the leverage you can get from the resources you have and the resources you can access.

Maximum leverage on your existing resources can be viewed as working smart instead of working hard. Each person on the team should work on activities for which they are particularly well suited. This requires the ability to delegate work to others, and allow them to execute with as much independence as possible, freeing you up to work on the more strategic or complex issues. To maintain high efficiency, you should consider setting aside some time each week to review progress on critical activities, re-evaluate the relative priority of the company's key initiatives, and change assignments when necessary. This concept is fairly ordinary management, although it is easy to forgo this type of management review in the heat of the battle.

In order to really increase performance, you should also consider how to leverage external resources. If a specific task is not a core competency of someone in the company, then you should consider the value of keeping it in house, verses assigning it outside. This can involve hiring an outside agency or consultant to complete the activity, but this can consume another precious resource: money. Another possibility is to use the resources of your suppliers, partners and distribution channels. They often have complimentary skill sets to yours, and may be willing to provide access to those resources if the result will benefit them as much as it benefits you. The resources are usually there, and you just need to identify them, make a compelling pitch to their management regarding the shared benefit, and be prepared to manage resources that are not under your direct control. The result can provide significantly improved leverage beyond the capabilities of your overextended startup.

Best of Luck,

Jeff Greenberg
Managing Director
Tech Coast Works

Guchereau Investments

Ken Guchereau founded Guchereau Investments in 2008. The company provides Startup Capital and Bridge Financing to small startup companies that demonstrate talented leadership, desire, and have a product that is scalable.

Ken has thirty plus years of experience as a Certified Public Accountant. He worked with an international CPA firm before becoming a founding and managing partner of Guchereau & Nettles, CPA's. The firm was a local Orange County firm. It provided consulting, tax and accounting services. It served clients that ranged in size from small to $1 billion in assets.

Ken is one of the five founding partners of Craig Realty Group ("CRG"). They started CRG in 1996 with no ownership of property, but had a vision and dream of what they would accomplish. Ken was its Chief Financial Officer.

CRG grew to own, operate and manage nearly 4.0 million square feet of retail outlet centers in the U.S. During its growth, CRG capital formation was solely from family and friends of the founders and did not use institutional investors. Today, CRG is a full-service real estate development and management company specializing in income-producing upscale factory outlet centers. CRG properties contain quality branded merchandise in an architecturally themed environment that offers shoppers ease of accessibility and convenient amenities. As CFO and cofounder, Ken was responsible for strategic planning, capital structure and formation, lender financing, investor relations, acquisitions, dispositions and corporate administration. He retired in 2008 and still consults with CRG.

Ken is an alumnus of California State University Fullerton (1974). He enjoys giving back to CSUF, the place where he started his career. For the past 15 years, Ken has given his time, talent and financial resources to the Mihaylo College of Business and Economics. He is an active member on two advisory boards, Center for Entrepreneurship and Accounting Department. He was the founding member of the Center for Entrepreneurship board. Ken has served as mentored student teams in the Entrepreneurship concentration's Entrepreneurial Accounting class. He has also sponsored the CSUF Fast Pitch Business Competition and other events.

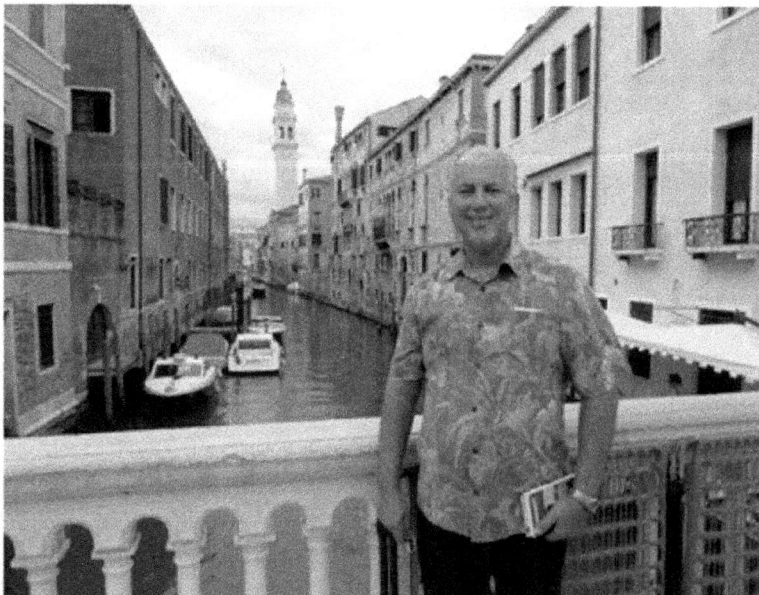

Ken in Venice, his favorite Italian vacation destination.

116

GUCHEREAU INVESTMENTS
LAGUNA NIGUEL, CA 92677

Dear Founder:

In my career as a small business consultant and founder of two companies, I have learned certain lessons about entrepreneurship. Becoming a successful entrepreneur is mostly about your psychology, passion and determination. I call these the "entrepreneur personality".

As a CPA, I watched many businesses fail because the entrepreneur did not realize how hard it is, how much you have to be all in, and how much effort it takes to be successful. You need to work hard to understand what it means to be an entrepreneur. You need to understand the total scope of work that's going to be required. This could mean such things as your overall investment in time and money, your plan of action, and your personal capabilities.

When I was looking for a business to start, I looked for a business that I truly loved and had a passion for. There will be disappointments and failures along the way. If you're not in love with what you are doing, you will give up before you succeed and will not learn from your mistakes. If you are passionate about your business, you will work hard and have the perseverance to think outside the box in finding solutions.

A motivating factor for me was the feeling of fearing failure. Or to say it another way, I always felt the hunger for success. These are motivators to help you do what is necessary to be successful. The Fear never leaves, but does not Lead me in my life.

I did not succeed by myself. I surrounded myself with individuals that mentored me in all aspects of business that I did not fully understand. Find the right people you can trust that will mentor you in the process of building of your business. This will reduce the number of mistakes you make and help avoid pitfalls that could derail your plans.

I started two businesses with partners so I could share the burden of the creating a new company. Consider starting your business with partners. Choose partners that balances out your strengths and weaknesses, someone you trust and respect, and ultimately, someone with whom you want to share both the positives and negatives of owning a business. Partners can lessen the burdens of a startup by sharing responsibilities. Partners will be a great source to share ideas and problem solving.

The biggest risk is not taking a risk. The only way to learn is by doing, so you can't afford to sit around waiting for someone else to help you execute your idea. Assume that if you do not start that business, someone else will. As Franklin D. Roosevelt said, "The Only Thing We Have to Fear Is Fear Itself". Don't be afraid of getting started.

Lastly, you need to stay balanced in your life while you are seeking success. It was, at first, very difficult for me to stay balanced in my life between work, my family, my social life and my hobbies. My work became primary and the others became secondary. When I recognized this, I worked hard at staying balance in all areas of my life. If you can balance your life, you will be able to better focus on processing new information, making decisions and creating adjustments in your plans accordingly.

I hope this letter gives you some insights into what I think is important in an entrepreneur personality, motivates you to set goals, learn from your mistakes and get started.

Sincerely,

Kenneth W Guchereau
Managing Partner

M Gutierrez Investments, Corp.

Monica Gutierrez Hernandez, is co-owner of Victorian Realty, M.G. She is co-founder and owner of several other S-Corporations and Limited Liability Corporations involved in real estate investments and business opportunities.

Monica began her entrepreneurial journey at a young age. She sold treats to her fellow classmates in middle school, and purchased and resold many items for profit on popular e-commerce sites.

Monica found a full-time job at a popular fast food restaurant in the midst of her high school years. Meanwhile, she fed her hunger for business development and investment by consulting at a real estate firm. Real Estate has always been the one business Monica believes will give her secure, high return investments.

Monica continued to venture out throughout the end of high school and all of college. She became a manufacture's representative to various Multi Level Marketing companies. Monica decided not to continue with such business models and terminate her partnerships. However, she took a lot of value and knowledge from those experiences and has applied her learning to new ventures.

Monica graduated from California State University, Fullerton, with a concentration in Entrepreneurship. During her course of study, Monica was involved in the development and improvement of many business plans. Her passion for business grew tremendously. Monica quit her full-time job at the fast food chain soon after collage and became a Realtor.

Real estate investments have always been Monica's main focus and where her forte lies. Both as a business student and realtor, Monica networked and partnered with many individuals. She has inspired many individuals, her age and older, to become entrepreneurs themselves by setting an example for them.

Monica's real estate career has allowed her to become an investor and aid others to do so as well. She motivates and assists her clients in acquiring and/or creating business opportunities. They range from purchasing a lot and developing on it, to purchasing a business for sale. Monica continues to seek such opportunities and share them with others.

At the age of 26, Monica is working on several business plans for ventures, which she hopes to soon launch as sole owner. Her long-term plan is to create a conglomerate consisting of diverse business models and business profiles. She hopes it will aid and inspire others to become entrepreneurs themselves.

Monica remains actively involved with the Mihaylo College of Business and Economics. She aids student entrepreneurship activities.

Dear Founder,

Like many entrepreneurs, I have felt the need, love and passion for business since a very young age. Becoming an entrepreneur has been as simple as baking a batch of cookies from my mother's kitchen and selling it for a profit. I have come to find that the opportunities are endless.

Needless to say, I have had a rough start in my journey as a young entrepreneur. I have come across times of doubt, fear, anxiety and even depression. All of which is normal. Starting a business is easy, growing and maintaining it is hard. The real struggle of becoming a successful entrepreneur lies in feeding and conserving the success of a venture in which one has committed to.

I would like to share some of the factors that have enabled me to overcome the struggles of becoming a young-successful entrepreneur. Many of which I hope will help you as well.

Detaching your personal self from your professional ventures...
 Only invest what you/your family does not depend on. Then consider it a (personal) loss.
For example, I have always had a so-called "steady job" to provide for my daily needs. My rule is to only invest/risk the extra cash made on my side ventures. I then consider it a loss I am willing to take, because I do not depend on or plan on seeing that investment until my venture has grown enough to repay me. This has allowed me to maintain a clear focus, relieving some of the stress that comes along with investing/risking money.
 Be objective. Make sure to treat every venture as a business, not as your "baby". This means to know when it is time to make the tough decision of letting go of an idea or even the business as a whole when it is no loner viable.
Plan on failure in order to succeed...
 Whether it is one strategic plan or an entire venture, have a plan INCASE it fails, and plan to learn from it. My entrepreneur mind is filled with a whole lot of new ventures and ideas. I do not let that comfort me into failing, but I do allow it to motivate me into seeking every learning opportunity any time something does not go as planned. Like any great product, even a currently successful business can become obsolete over night. So plan your next move!

Take partners and WHATEVER feasible opportunities come your way...
 Opportunities are knocking on your door! Perhaps you have and idea and your friend has capital to invest. Maybe your sister has a great product, but only you know how to turn that into a successful business. Being a true entrepreneur means being strategic and innovative, not just owning a business or an idea that sits idle and steady.
 I dislike red meats. The smell, the blood, the fat that smothers them, everything about red meat grosses me out. I came across a man who wanted me to sell his meat market. It had a great butcher, lots of space, a little bit of meat and a small clientele. I had previously sold 2 meat markets and immediately noticed the potential it had. I had zero experience dealing with meat nor did I have the desire to do so. However, there was a great butcher and a lot of opportunity. Long story short, I partnered with another individual who produces organic-exotic fruits and veggies. The butcher, agriculture engineer and I purchased the meat market and quadrupled its income in less than 3 months.

I hope you find my experiences of help. Remember that wealth does not always measure success.

Sincerely wishing you true happiness and prosperity in your future ventures,

Monica Hernandez

Bringing Innovation to Life

Michel Haddad is a 2011 entrepreneurship graduate of the Mihaylo College of Business and Economics. Currently, he is the Entrepreneur in Residence at the FastStart.Studio technology incubator in Irvine. He is also a Partner at CalTheory in Irvine. CalTheory's mission is to transform startups with imagination, experience and execution. It helps startups to boost their growth and have successful seed and series A funding rounds.

In addition, Michel advises several early stage startups. Names include MonsterVR, Naiad Physics and Industrial Optic.

Michel specializes in business development, go-to-market strategy, and execution for early stage ventures. Previously, in 2013, he founded and served as CEO for DirectEffect TV a crowd funding video platform for conflict resolution. In 2014, he became a co-founder and the Chief Marketing Officer for AquaCloud, Inc. The company makes cloud-based monitoring systems to provide real time data and analytics to water managers about their water quality. AquaCloud, Inc. Spent sixteen months at the Lemnos Labs hardware incubator in San Francisco and Michel raised $1.9 million in venture capital. He brought the product to market by securing government contracts with different counties across California, condensed the sales cycle with municipalities and refined the product features and road map through his "customer discovery process."

He is the co-founder of OCVR, a community of virtual reality developers and enthusiasts. OCVR positions itself as, "the lexus point for virtual reality technology and gaming." They have co-hosted events with Oculus, hackathons with UCI, and established themselves as thought leaders in an emerging industry. Michel has been on the "Road to VR" podcast and interviewed by Re-Code about his role in starting OCVR.

Michel has consulted for UNICEF to increase engagement with their public audience. He also consulted for Muirsis where he identified the medical market segments for their touchless faucets.

As Michel notes in his letter, that what he liked most about the CSUF entreprenurship program was the opportunity to connect with "determined people who want to do something big." His major take away from the curriculum? Michel's LinkedIn profile cites, "Hands-on experience in consulting and bringing innovation to life."

Dear Founder,

Starting a new venture is a roller coaster, a grind, and a hustle. Many of the lessons can be counter intuitive and some are straightforward. Here are the 3 points that I believe are the most crucial…

Above all else, it's the people you choose as co-founders that determine the success of your journey. You have no idea how much of a resource the entrepreneurship department is for finding determined people that want to do something big. The density of brilliant minds all in one place gets harder to find after your college years go by. Take advantage of it now. Now's the time to be cognizant of which colleagues you truly respect and enjoy working with. They are the prime candidates to start a company with. The emotional rollercoaster can be high one minute and drop to a low point the next so the bond between the founders will carry you through it. Choose these people with this in mind.

Intelligence is important… but determination is what counts. Once you hit a certain threshold of intelligence, it's determination that takes over. Startups and new ventures are riddled with difficulties and ambiguities. It's these times that will test how badly you want it. A founder might quit, venture capitalists won't want to fund you and the release of your first "hacked together" product can fail. All these are headaches but can be resolved if you keep gnawing at the problem. You'll be surprised at how many problems will topple by the amount of persistence you and your team have. The consistent grind of solving problems you have never faced before will sharpen you for future obstacles down the road.

Move fast and stay close to your customers—these go hand in hand. The first release of your product should be quick and minimal. See how your customers react to the first version and build off their reaction. This will help ensure you're building the right thing, creating a set of happy customers, and iterating quickly. Don't pay much attention to competition or raising money at first. Let me re-iterate how important it is to stay close to your first set of customers. You'll be happy you did when venture capitalists want to call your customers and interview them for their own due diligence.

Lastly, here is my favorite quote from Travis Kalanick: "Fear is the disease, hustle is the antidote."

Sincerely wishing you all the best,

Michel Haddad

Aspiring Tech Entrepreneur

Munir Haddad is an entrepreneurial minded millennial. He has over a decade of experience that extends across sales, marketing, business development, management, and operations within the tech industry. He's hired, mentored and led teams, managed projects, and has developed concepts from idea to reality. He however, considers working with TP-LINK - a world leader in consumer network products - to be his most interesting experience.

Munir was part of the founding team at TP-LINK USA (TP) that helped scale USA operations. Its employee count went from ten to over a hundred employees. Its revenues from single-digit millions into triple digit millions.

Throughout his time at the company, Munir wore multiple hats and pushed himself to sharpen his skill sets. The experience challenged him to remain aligned with the company's vision and principles. He had to learn how to engage with the inherently different cultures of a foreign company expanding into a new market.

Munir is a 2003 BS graduate of the New York Institute of Technology. To meet the challenges at TP, he practiced self education and validated learning to support the organization's internal and external growth goals. Simultaneously, he earned his MBA from California State University Fullerton (2015). He took the opportunity to apply what he learned from the MBA program to TP. Topics like change management, leadership, new venture management and operations helped him positively impact the company, his team, and career.

Munir's experience eventually led him to work on his own ventures. He experimented with different ideas, ranging from simple e-commerce sites to hardware inventions, to find his calling.

In 2013, Munir co-founded O2Free, a venture focused on the preservation of perishable liquids through an innovative container design. The venture went through two rounds of incubation, first at the CSUF Start-up Incubator then at the Cove in Irvine. Incubation involved patent applications, prototyping, and market surveys. The company ended in 2016 due to financial barriers and complications with product design.

Munir's new venture creation experience taught him the principles of starting a business. He learned how to develop ideas into products. He also learned how to adjust his mind-set and think like an entrepreneur.

Today, Munir continues to involve himself in ventures. True to the words in his letter, he first seeks ventures that are trying to find solutions for big, painful problems in large markets. Next, he decides if he can bring value and further develop himself.

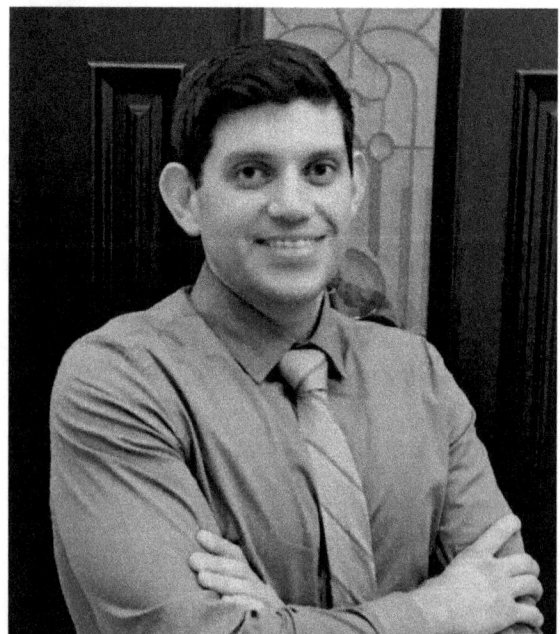

Munir Haddad
Baldwin Park, California

Dear Founder,

Rather than fit a solution to a problem, find a solution to a problem. A common saying among entrepreneurs is that ideas are worth nothing, and that value rests within the execution. While this is true, it is common to see ventures with the most impressive ideas and the best execution strategies struggle; one major reason behind the struggle, is because they begin to build without a deep understanding of the problem that their idea will potentially solve. Whether the idea is to improve an existing product or to create a new unique product, ask yourself: **What problem does this solve? Who experiences the problem? How painful is the problem?**

I co-founded an innovative container solution venture that helps prolong the shelf-life of wine after popping the cork. Our early research led us to see overwhelming opportunities for the invention. We collected ideas for specifications and features, and we built prototypes and surveyed the market. After interviewing with friends, family and potential customers, it was apparent that our friends and family were providing biased results, and that the potential customers, for several reasons, did not connect with the problem we were attempting to solve (Search: Cognitive Bias and Confirmation Bias).

Deep into the interviews, we realized that table wine was so affordable that the typical wine consumer was not significantly interested in increasing their shelf-life. On the other hand, wine aficionados - those who consume expensive wines - actually buy into the wine drinking experience, and so, they didn't care for our product as it doesn't enrich this experience. In reality, we built a product that solves a problem that never really existed.

Unwilling to give up, we searched for other potential applications for our product, but were unsuccessful finding a solid match. The venture failed because we attempted to fit a solution to a problem. I noticed the same flawed approach was adopted by other entrepreneurs, and this prompted me to write on this.

As a fellow entrepreneur, before you begin building, I advise that you adjust your mindset and take a step back to analyze and thoroughly understand the core pain points or real problems behind the ideas you are developing. As you progress, you'll receive requests or generate ideas for particular specifications or features to integrate into your product, which at first glance, will sound reasonable. In reality, these requests may merely be symptoms of a deeper underlying problem.

For example, your young nephew asks you to help tie his undone shoelaces. You do it, but then, the next day, he comes to you with the laces undone again. Obviously, you haven't solved your nephew's problem; all you did was react to his request to tie his shoelaces. The actual problem is that your nephew is tying his shoes incorrectly, so the actual solution would be to teach your nephew how to do it correctly. Think about this for a second. Although this example sounds silly, in the context of entrepreneurship, this happens often.

A simple and effective method to get to this underlying problem is to consecutively ask the source of the idea, "why?" The more you ask "why?", the closer you get to the root cause and understanding of the pain point. Clearer understanding of the root cause leads to better decisions made when deciding what specifications and features are most important to your customer. (Search: 5 Whys Approach)

While you may be on the right track with the solution you consider building, a major influencer of success will be from your venture's ability to identify the real needs of the customer. The process of developing a product consists of continuous learning and improvement. So, change your mindset, reach out to as many potential customers as possible, and study the topics of lean startup and product management. Do your best to understand the problem before you build the solution.

Wishing you success on your venture,

Munir Haddad

Chamber President and CEO

Theresa Harvey has served as President and CEO of the North Orange County Chamber since 2005. She is an alumna and longtime supporter of California State University, Fullerton.

Under Theresa's direction, the North Orange County Chamber has developed the organization's core programs. It has sharpened its focus on representing business interests to government. Increased advocacy aims at creating a strong local economy. Theresa has led the organization in updating the association's membership model, positioning the chamber to better help businesses.

Theresa partners with the City of Fullerton in its business recruitment efforts and currently serves as a member of its Economic Development Commission. She develops relationships with the international business community, highlighting opportunities made possible through trade agreements and global markets.

In evidence of extraordinary service and professional accomplishments, the YWCA of North Orange County named Theresa Business Woman of the Year. The 65th District also named her as Woman of the Year.

Recognized within her industry, Theresa currently serves on the board of the Association of Chamber of Commerce Executives (ACCE). She also serves on the board of the Southern California Association of Chamber of Commerce Executives.

At California State University Fullerton, Theresa has twice served as President of the Alumni Association. She currently serves on the University's Auxiliary Services Corporation Board.

In 2017, the CSUF College of Communications inducted Theresa into its Wall of Fame. Recognized as one of the University's 50 Women of Distinction, she has served on the University's board of governors and milestone anniversary committees.

Dear Entrepreneur:

In my position, I have many opportunities to interface with a variety of business owners and entrepreneurs. Most recently, I spoke with an owner whose comments rang true. She stated that for the first five years, the company's ownership felt like they were living in a fog. Struggling with the many aspect of business development while keeping focused on their goals. In this case, success has followed the hard work. The company has grown from three employees (all owners) to a staff of 500 and a major international presence.

This example, unfortunately, is not the outcome for many. What is it that separates successful entrepreneurs from those who struggle or fail? Below are some of my observations from years of being a business consultant, observer and supporter.

1) Be Passionate. Starting a business takes time. There is no get rich quick scheme and many successful business people faced failure before finding success. You need to love what you are doing. Thinking about your business day and night will be difficult to do if you are distracted along the way. Passion will aid in your efforts to be creative and maintain the energy it takes for success.

2) Be innovative. How can you be the best at what you do? Make sure you are offering fresh products, new services and unique ideas. By continually innovating, you will be able to anticipate the marketplace and adapt to new opportunities. Innovation wins.

3) Take risks. Mark Zuckerberg once said, *"The biggest risk is not taking any risk...In a world that's changing really quickly, the only strategy that is guaranteed to fail is not taking risk."* I add, make sure you carry a parachute. Great risk can also mean great failure. As an entrepreneur, you must be willing to take great risks...financially and personally. I know successful business people who didn't have a support system to assist them through difficult times. Whether that is a financial backer or a person willing to listen and lend their shoulder to cry on. Develop your support system.

4) Be a leader: Positioning yourself as a leader does not mean you have all the answers, but establishing yourself as one who is capable of being confident in the decisions you make can help establish your reputation. The relationships you establish as a leader help you build loyalty and trust among your employees, your customers and your investors. Your ability to establish yourself as leader gains your company credibility, loyalty and strength.

5) Seek guidance. Whether it's at your local Chamber of Commerce, your SCORE office, the SBDC or a trusted friend, talk with those who can assist you along the way. There is no shame in asking for advice. Look for mentors who can guide and assist you as you fulfill your dream.

Whatever you do, I wish you success with your entrepreneurial endeavors!

Sincerely,

Theresa Harvey
President & CEO
North Orange County Chamber

Woman Healthcare Entrepreneur

France Dixon Helfer is a California State University Fullerton alumna in biologic sciences and member of the Center for Entrepreneurship's Advisory Board. France has over thirty years in the Healthcare Industry, over twenty as a senior level executive. Currently she is CEO of TinyKicks.

The company is developing wearable flexible health-monitoring smart sensors that capture fetal movement and uses machine learning to predict and guide healthy pregnancy outcomes. Following birth, the wireless sensors will monitor an infant's health during the first year of life. The technology is UCI developed and EvoNexus Incubator houses the company. France leads the TinyKicks effort to take UCI engineering, know how and intellectual properties, "productize" them, and launch a sustainable stand-alone company.

She brings much to her current endeavors: C-level business leadership, Corporate and Business Development, Operations Management, Product Development, R&D, and International Sales and Marketing expertise for high growth Fortune 500 companies and start-up companies. She is a very experienced entrepreneur. France has been involved as a founder or founding team member of six companies. She has raised over $80 Million in funding from angels, corporations and venture capitalists. She is also an active angel investor.

Before TinyKicks, France was CEO of Halo Healthcare, a breast care predictive diagnostic device turnaround. She revived the technology, and launched overseas sales with a distribution organization, establishing a solid revenue stream. Her career includes executive level positions at: Medtronic, Xenotech Labs (founding employee, acquired by Medtronic), SORIN, Eclipse Surgical (where she guided strategy leading to a successful IPO), and MDDataDirect. As Founder of Pegasus Biologics, she raised $32M. In under three years, built the company into an emerging growth company with a solid product pipeline that Baxter Healthcare acquired.

France is a frequently invited executive panelist and speaker at medical industry events. She serves as a board director for several medical device companies and non-profit boards. France has been a frequent student mentor and judge for many entrepreneurial programs and related business plan and fast pitch competitions. She lectures and writes about female leadership and entre-preneurship in the medical industry.

What is France proud of? How her work builds value in healthcare. Plus the positive affects from her promoting and mentoring of female leaders as entrepreneurs and executives.

Dear Founder,

Accolades for deciding to take the leap to start a Company. Begin by verbalizing this to all those around you, it helps you to commit!

Choose to Lead or Choose to Follow. I have been leading companies and start-up's for a very long time, and I have always believed, and shared with all those I mentor, that you are an entrepreneur, or you're not, and that inside each of us, we know if we have the desire and skillset required. We are not all cut out to take the high risks associated with founding a company, and there is no shame in choosing a career path that provides you with more security than does a start-up. Understand also that working for a large company provides you the discipline to know how to manage your start-up in the future. For example, you'll learn fundamentals of budgeting, fund raising, HR, and management. You will observe and learn formal process and product development, marketing, sales, product lifecycles.

However much you know, things change when you start a company from the ground up. Understand clearly that your path will be challenging and more difficult than you anticipate.

Everything costs more and takes longer than you expect. So plan and budget accordingly for all contingencies-have your Plan B in mind. There are aspects of a start-up business that you solely control, and others that are outside your control, such as actions of the US Patent Office for your Intellectual Property, or US FDA if you require healthcare approvals. And be nimble, the beauty of a start-up founder is the ability to change directions if external forces require you do so; don't fight the changes, anticipate and accept as early in your Company's lifecycle as possible.

Surround yourself with people smarter than you. Understand that at some point you may need to step aside and let someone else lead your business with you. This does not take away from your leadership abilities or from your venture, however, as the founder, you have core strengths in an area that enabled you to found a business, but not in all functional areas required to grow and sustain a business. For example, if you are a highly technical engineer starting a device business, you may not understand customer acquisition, marketing, spreadsheets, manufacturing optimization-and the list goes. You may need to hire someone with a deeper and broader network with resources. Learn from that person and become his or her right hand person.

The Priceless Value of your Network. As early in your career as you can, including as a student, build your network! Start filling your contact folder with as many bright and diversely skilled people as you can. Collect business cards and keep notes on them. Stay in touch with all those you meet who may be of value at some point in your company's lifecycle. Be gender blind, and hire the right person for the job. Join the LinkedIn network and alumni associations from your schools, and reach out; never be afraid to ask for guidance or support.

And finally, learn every day from your founder's experience, and enjoy the ride.

Respectfully,

France Dixon Helfer
President and CEO

StrategyIP

Rose Hickman is the Founder and Managing Partner of StrategyIP. The firm specializes in all areas of Intellectual Property protection. Its services range from protecting brand names, through trademark clearance and registration, protecting inventions, patent opinions and prosecution.

StrategyIP clients are from all corners of the world. They range from individuals to multinational companies. The firm also handles inventions in a wide range of technologies, including electrical, mechanical and software.

Rose has a B.S. in Physics from the College of William and Mary. At NASA Langley and the Georgia Institute of Technology, she worked on satellite technology/remote sensing. Then she attended law school at the University of Southern California. Before forming StrategyIP, she was a Partner at Karish & Bjorgum PC, and an associate for Hogan & Hartson LLP and Christie, Parker & Hale, LLP.

Rose has helped her clients secure and enforce monopolies on their ideas and protect the goodwill of their brand names for fifteen years. Many sources recognize Rose as a top Intellectual Property attorney. Her honors include receiving a perfect 10/10 rating from AVVO. Los Angeles Magazine listed her as one of the "Top Women Lawyers in Southern California." Coast Magazine described Rose as a "Top Attorney in Intellectual Property." OC Register Metro recognized her as a "Top Attorney in Patent Applications," and a "Lawyer of Distinction in California" (an honor reserved for the top 10% of attorneys in the State). Super Lawyer Magazine named Rose a "Southern California "Rising Star" each year from 2004 to 2012

(an honor reserved for the top 2.5% of attorneys under 40).

In her patent work, Rose has handled a wide range of technologies, such as software, integrated circuits, fuel cells, flat panel displays, interplanetary rovers, medical devices, complex mechanical systems and computer implemented business methods. In her trademark work, Rose has helped clients from individual startups to international corporations secure and enforce their trademark rights from initial trademark selection to litigation. She has also advised and advocated for her clients on domain name issues, such as selection, transfer, and enforcement.

Rose has had the honor of serving on the Executive Committees for two sections of the Los Angeles County Bar Association: Entertainment/Intellectual Property and Barristers. She also served in the leadership of the International Trademark Association. Rose has been a frequent guest speaker for CSUF Entrepreneurship.

STRATEGY*IP*
Intellectual Property Law Firm

Orange County Office
2372 Morse Ave., Suite 326
Irvine, CA 92614
424.256.8010 Tel
424.251.8360 Fax
www.StrategyIP.com

Rose Hickman
Managing Partner
424.256.8011 Direct
RoseRigole@StrategyIP.com

Dear Founder:

Congratulations on starting your own business! As you know, this can be an incredibly creative and exciting time. It can also be filled with stresses, sacrifices, and pitfalls for novice and expert alike. You have tight budgets and big goals. You want to do it right, but no money to bring in the support you need. I hope this letter will provide you with some timely advice to help you prioritize your decisions regarding patents at this crucial time.

Your big idea is valuable. It might be what makes or breaks your company. It can help you get investment. It can open the door to a monopoly, which you may need to compete with the larger companies who can copy your idea and undercut your pricing. When you are prioritizing spending, start with protecting your big idea. If you don't, you may lose your biggest asset before you're even up and running.

With patents, time is very much of the essence. In the United States, you have one year to file a patent application after you publicly use, publicly disclose, or offer embodiments of your invention for sale (collectively, "barring activities"). If you file one year and one hour after any of these activities, your invention is dedicated to the public and cannot be protected. "Public disclosure" is any disclosure made without an obligation to keep it confidential. This can start the clock ticking, so make sure you have your non-disclosure agreements ready or some documented understanding that what is said will remain in confidence. In some other countries, you have no grace period. Without a patent, anyone is free to copy your idea and undercut you. Merely being first on the market, or first with an idea, gives you no protection.

Beware of provisional patent application scams. The US Patent Office allows filing a "provisional" patent application, which sits unexamined in the Office for one year. Within that year, you may file a regular ("non-provisional") patent application claiming the provisional's filing date, which might be needed due to a barring activity. There are very few formal requirements for provisional applications, and you could attach a cover letter to a napkin drawing, file it, and have a "patent pending." Because of this, some people offer bargain basement provisional application filings, which are little more than this. Many inventors and small businesses file these due to budget concerns, with the hope that they can file a non-provisional after they get more investment. The problem with this is that, in order to get the provisional's filing date, the claims in the regular application must be *fully supported* by the description in the provisional. This means that the provisional should be as packed with disclosure as a regular application would be. Many inventors and small businesses find this out the hard way: over a year after a barring activity, they attempt to file a regular application, hoping to claim the provisional filing date, only to realize that they are now barred from claiming anything not fully supported by their bargain basement provisional.

Have I scared you sufficiently? Good. Patent protection is and should be one of the central investments for your new company, if it is based on a big idea. Do it right the first time, and it will save you time and money. Find a good, strategic, efficiency-minded attorney who will make sure your IP fits and grows with your business model. Start off with this as your solid foundation, and then use it as a runway. Good luck!

Very truly yours,

Rose L (signature)

Rose Hickman

Affluent Target Marketing

Wally Hicks is the founder and owner of Affluent Target Marketing, Inc. (ATM). It is the parent company of Affluent Living Publications. He has been a supporter of CSUF Entrepreneurship for over twenty years.

Wally began ATM in 1980 on his dining room table here in Orange County. It was a direct mail magazine program for the affluent homeowner market. By April of 2008, the Company had expanded to thirty-six separate magazines in sixteen states reaching over 3.6 million affluent homes via direct mail. Since then, ATM has adjusted size and circulation to reflect today's current market conditions. The company has added review and social media components to the magazines. Wally is developing a new web-based networking and information sharing site.

Wally is an alumnus of California State University, Long Beach where he majored in Business Administration and Marketing. Before that he studied computer science at Compton Junior College.

During his college years, Wally started his career with IBM's office products division fixing and working on magnetic tape word processing machines. While he was at IBM, he moved into sales of office products and office equipment and became a lead closer of preventive care contracts. Xerox later recruited him to work on new product sales development (selling their new fax and word processing products).

After college graduation, Wally took a leave of absence from Xerox to start a silk screening business. He pivoted to selling support hose to the nursing industry. He pivoted again to selling burglar alarms to homes, and finally he started Affluent Target Marketing.

Wally is a founding board member of the Center for Entrepreneurship at Mihaylo College of Business and Economics. He has been on the board for over twenty years. He serves on the boards of three other charitable organizations.

Wally has been a mentor for CSUF Entrepreneurship since the mid-1990s. He coaches entrepreneurial students on student consulting projects and new venture creation and funding.

He served as a Newhope Church phone advisor for twelve years. Wally took incoming calls from those with hurting hearts and shut ins.

Wally has coached youth soccer (both boys and girls) for the Junior United Soccer Association since the 1993 season. He believes in the value of advancing and promoting the physical fitness of youth in the community. As both a coach and mentor, he uses organized soccer competition to teach teamwork and other important life lessons.

Wally Hicks III
Orange, California

Dear Founder,

I offer you seven business tips:

1) Don't just create one idea. Create many and pick the best from the group.
2) Pick a set time for idea brain storming and business planning.
3) Don't just get up in the morning and roll the dice. It is better to have a plan that you can adjust as circumstances dictate.
4) Evaluate your talents, strength and weakness. People have a difficult time figuring out what they want to do. So, I suggest writing down what you _don't_ want. You'll find that what's left are "feasible" options that fit you.
5) If you have $10,000 to play with, I would suggest spending $2,000 per option/idea and give yourself five chances to win .
6) I recommend integrating two or more ideas to make a new option. As an example, the cell phone started off as a combination of the walkie-talkie and a traditional phone. Another example was Redbox – a vending machine with DVDs that helped to put Blockbuster out of business. Both examples above are not creating something brand new and unproven which can be very risky. Rather, both examples represent "reinventing." They combine components that are already available and improve on them.
7) Know you fears. Write about them. Develop plans to minimize your fears. Additionally, you should know the _cost of not acting_ versus moving forward and taking that risk!

Finally, remember the words "customer driven" when starting your venture. Starting a new venture is like riding a racehorse. You have to give the horse some freedom to go where it wants, just like customers will point you in the direction they want your venture to go.

Saddle up and enjoy the ride,

Wally Hicks
Owner

Improv For Health

Nanciann Horvath is a CSUF entrepreneurship guest speaker and improvisation coach. She is the owner of Improv for Health. She founded the company in 2005.

Nanciann describes herself as a nurse, actress and comedian. She was born in Bethlehem, PA to a theatrical Hungarian/ Slovak family. She decided at age five to be a nurse, "when I saw those great, white, crisp uniforms!"

After graduating Sacred Heart Hospital School of Practical Nursing, she moved to Morristown, NJ, where she did both nursing and local theater. She also started taking classes in New York City for acting, commercials and improvisation ("improv").

Nanciann moved to New York City. There, she worked for an oncologist, studied at the HB Studios, and worked at Radio City Music Hall.

She moved to Los Angeles. It proved to be a good decision. Since Nanciann had already joined the American Federation of Radio and Television Artists (AFTRA), her Screen Actors Guild (SAG) card came a short one year later.

Nanciann has always seen the need to live in the moment. Nursing has shown her that we are all here to make a difference and each day is a gift.

She did improvisation with the LA Connection Comedy Theater and other LA groups. Soon, she started reading and doing research about the health benefits of improvisation and founded Improv for Health.

Her business has been building for years. She serves health groups, businesses, church groups, schools, senior centers and anyone interested in obtaining better total health.

Today, Nanciann is a working SAG actor, and a set baby nurse at NBC, and a mom to two sons. She has been married for over 25 years. Her family lives in Orange County.

Nanciann says, "I teach improv for health to regular folks. They can learn to think fast on their feet, laugh and enjoy the moment. Life has many ups and downs. With a little improvisation we can all learn to take the bumps along the road of life and see the fun in the moment."

Nanciann's mantra is,"Life is 10% what happens to a person, and 90% how they react to it."

IMPROV FOR HEALTH

WWW.IMPROVFORHEALTH.COM

Nanciann Horvath-Owner

714-394-4989

Lake Forest, Ca.

Dear Founder,

My business is teaching other business owners to think fast on their feet and adapt to the many changes that may come their way. Improvisation is the art of improvising or composing without any previous preparation.

When we have improvisation in our lives we don't carry negative feelings towards others and thus there is room for being open and positive towards others. I use the example many times of being on a bus and someone steps on our foot. If we say "ouch" and they say sorry it's over, however imagine we hold that in and weeks later we see that person and the hurt and anger flare up. They probably don't even remember us or the incident but it eats away at us. This happens in business or families all the time. By speaking the open truth and handling the problem immediately it doesn't grow and fester.

Here are some practical ways to incorporate this every day:

* Speak the truth using fewer words

* Repeat back what you just heard from the person so it's clear to all

* Use YES AND, when trying to convince others while being open to their points of view.

This takes some practice and might be a challenge at first because it really is developing a muscle like any other muscle we use. It does get easier with practice. Also with ease comes the fun of always being ready!

Improvisation brings a mind and body change for the positive which we can use every day in business and personal situations.

Professionally Yours,

Nanciann Horvath

Director, Professor and Entrepreneur

John Bradley Jackson ("JJ") is Director of the Center for Entrepreneurship at California State University, Fullerton. He is a professor of entrepreneurial marketing, new venture creation and new venture launch.

JJ brings startup experience along with practical marketing and sales knowledge to the classroom. He has worked in both Silicon Valley and Wall Street.

Recently JJ was awarded two grants from the National Science Foundation. The first was for the I-CORPS program which embraced "Lean Startup." The second was a $1,000,000 I-Test grant. This grant stimulated junior high students to learn more about Science, Technology, Engineering, and Math (STEM).

JJ's career began in high technology sales in the semiconductor industry at Signetics Inc., but he soon moved to high technology market research with Dataquest Incorporated. At Dataquest, he served as Vice President for nearly ten years and held a variety of roles in sales, marketing, and research. Later, he joined Bowne and Company, the world's largest financial printer, and served as Senior Vice President responsible for sales, marketing, and operations. JJ also was Sales Director at Forrester Research Inc., an Information Technology advisory firm.

As an entrepreneur, JJ founded The BirdDog Group, a marketing and sales consulting firm that specializes in helping small and medium sized businesses with marketing and sales strategy. In particular, he is an expert in digital marketing including social media, web development and search marketing.

JJ has published four books, First, Best, or Different: What Every Entrepreneur Needs to Know About Niche Marketing, Déjà New Marketing, Socially Close: Social Media Marketing for Small Business and Your Entrepreneurial Journey: Fifteen Guiding Principles (co-authored).

JJ is extremely active in the Southern California business and philanthropic community. He has served on many boards. They include, Titan Angels LLC, TriTech SBDC, Aidtree Incorporated, Small Business Development Center (SBDC), Global Vision Holdings, Inc., O2Free LLC, BrandMixer, Inc. Southern California Junior Achievement, Los Angeles Triathlon, Southern California Committee for the Olympic Games, Los Angeles Sports Council, Los Angeles Venture Association, Orange County Venture Network, and United Way.

JJ is a blogger, public speaker, angel investor, and horseman. He owns a small horse ranch in Norco, California where he lives with his wife and daughter.

CALIFORNIA STATE UNIVERSITY, FULLERTON

Mihaylo College of Business and Economics
Center for Entrepreneurship
P O Box 6848,
Fullerton, CA 92831

Dear Founder,

Often new business founders find themselves needing advice and counsel; worse, they are just plain lonely. This vacuum can be very prevalent at small businesses and, by definition, exists for the "solopreneurs" (the individual business person).

Frankly, few of us truly are multi-talented and this can quickly be brought into focus when you start a company or go off on your own in a small business. Running your own business requires you to be an accountant, marketing guru, an operations manager, and a human resources manager, to name a few of the skills required.

You really have no choice but to look outside and ask for help. You can pay for this counsel or you can get it free; either way most of us need it. I recommend that you set up your own personal board of directors. Look for people who know what you don't. This could include law, managing people, sales and marketing, finance, spirituality, real estate, technology, and others. They must be willing to help you. You probably have friends who support you already. What I suggest is that you take the next step and formalize the relationship.

First, you need to identify the people who have the knowledge, expertise, and contacts that you don't. They could be friends, relatives, neighbors, colleagues, or strangers. Just about all my friends started out as strangers, so don't let the fact that you don't know someone stop you. You are looking for people who also have the desire to coach, teach, or share.

Next, meet with them in a casual setting one on one. I like a business lunch best, but that is up to you. At this meeting, a key objective is to explain your admiration for their skills and how you don't have the same skills. This disclosure can be powerful for you and for them. Most people need to be needed and will bend over backwards to help you. Ninety-nine times out of one hundred, your prospective personal board of director will be complimented by the words and they will admire your self-disclosure. Most will agree to help you on the spot. It is just that easy.

From there, it is up to you, but I recommend that you make a point of meeting, phoning, or e-mailing your individual board members monthly. Keep them updated on your progress, successes, and failures. Be gracious and thankful. Look for ways to give back and help them. The goal is to set up a friendship or bond similar to that of a coach and player. The coach gives and the players gets. My personal experience as a coach is that I have been paid back in full many times over. You will find this same attitude with most people who are willing to join your board.

John Bradley Jackson
Director, Center for Entrepreneurship
Professor, Entrepreneurship
jjackson@fullerton.edu

135

Jafari Law Group

David Jafari is an attorney licensed in California and the District of Columbia. He started Jafari Law Group, Inc. in June 2005. His firm has been a CSUF Entrepreneurship student consulting client. David is a recent speaker at the CSUF Start-up Incubator.

David's practice as a lawyer has focused primarily on intellectual property, business law, and employment matters. He has also served as a mediator and helped clients settle cases outside of court, avoiding costly and unnecessary litigation. David holds a Certificate in Mediation from the Orange County Human Relations Council. He is a part of the Mandatory Fee Arbitration committee of the Orange County Bar Association, and is also associated with Quality Dispute Resolution Services and IVAMS Arbitration and Mediation Services. Mr. Jafari has represented clients in over seventy litigation cases.

Prior to establishing his own practice, Mr. Jafari lived and worked in Washington D.C. for four years as an associate trial attorney in the intellectual property, media, and technology groups at McDermott Will & Emery, an international law firm with a diversified business practice. Prior to this position, Mr. Jafari also gained experience as an associate patent attorney by drafting and prosecuting technological patent applications for Blakely Sokoloff Taylor & Zafman, a national law firm. Mr. Jafari and his firm have prepared and filed over 150 patent applications.

Mr. Jafari earned his JD degree from Western State University College of Law where he graduated cum laude, ranked third in his class of 122 students. He clerked for the Honorable Justice Sheila Prell Sonenshine at the California Court

of Appeal in Santa Ana, California. David was admitted to the State Bar of California on June 19, 2000 (member number 207,881) and was registered as a patent attorney on August 5, 2002 (registration number 51,839). He is also admitted to practice in the US District Court for the Southern District of California, the US District Court for the Central District of California, the District of Columbia, the District of Columbia Court of Appeals, the US District Court for the District of Columbia, the US Court of Appeals for the District of Columbia Circuit and the US Court of Appeals for the Federal Circuit.

Previous to attending law school, David received a BS in Electrical Engineering with an emphasis in Computer Science, and an MS in Communications Engineering with an emphasis in Coding Theory, both from George Washington University. He speaks fluent Farsi.

JAFARI LAW GROUP®

A Professional Law Corporation

18201 Von Karman Ave, Suite 1190
Irvine, CA 92612
Telephone: (949) 362-0100
Facsimile: (949) 362-0101

David V. Jafari
Attorney at Law
djafari@jafarilawgroup.com
www.jafarilawgroup.com

Dear Founder,

The single most important step you can take to assure success or avoid failure when starting a business venture is proper planning. Everything must be planned. At a minimum, you must evaluate and address three different categories of issues.

First, you must determine the amount of money needed. It is easy to overlook this question and hope for the best. It is also easy to overstate the revenue that the business will generate. But that will be disastrous. The last thing you need is to run out of cash once you are half-way to breaking even. Details, detail, details. Everything must be written down. Numbers must be as close to reality as possible. Assumptions should be made for the worst-case scenario.

Second, you must have a marketing plan. The market is so much easier to reach now digitally than it used to be. An interactive website where your customers can communicate with you directly, where they can pay their bills, where they can order products and services, and tell you how you did is a must. Even better is a website that is optimized for mobile devices. Your site must be easily found on Google. Social media is another aspect of the marketing that did not even exist a few years back. You must have a YouTube channel where you can post useful videos that your customers can use to solve their problems. You must have a Facebook page, an Instagram account, a Twitter feed, and the list goes on and on.

Third, you must address legal issues properly beginning with an intellectual property (IP) strategy. Begin with your trademark, your name. Your brand is your identity and you must be diligent in picking your identity in a way that is not confusingly similar to others lest you receive a nasty letter from a lawyer demanding that you cease and desist using your name. This could be devastating, especially at the early stages of your business where your attention has to be on growing your business, not the bank account of your lawyers. The next thing to worry about are patents. A patent portfolio will go a long way to increase the value of your enterprise, the chance of raising capital from VCs, and will keep competitors from stealing your ideas. If you are going to be selling goods, you must make sure that your products are not infringing on you competitors' patents. Think of lawsuits as hurricanes. One direct hit can knock you off the map or drown you in sewage water. You must also be aware of other legal matters, starting with which business entity to choose, to whether you have a proper employee handbook. From reviewing your lease agreement, to drafting contracts that clearly define your rights and obligations. If you are not going it alone, picking the right partners and having the proper legal documents in place, such as a shareholder agreement, is critical.

Bottom line: plan, plan, plan. That starts with educating yourself and your partners on issues that are dominating the business scenes of today, not those of the past. Having a solid business plan, understanding your financial and marketing strategies, procuring and protecting your IP, and securing your legal rights and understanding your legal obligations will go a long way to increasing the odds of success in a tumultuous and unpredictable road of the startups autobahn!

Wishing you all the best in your endeavors,

David Jafari
President – Jafari Law Group, Inc.

Next-Gen Inventor and Founder

Dalip Jaggi is the founder of Devise Interactive. The company is a next-gen brand and digital agency. It gives clients innovative solutions designed to capture audience attention, improve brand perception, and collect meaningful connections. Its campaigns increase clients' brand value and customer loyalty.

Recognized as a young entrepreneur, at age 28, Dalip is an active soul who is always looking to do more and get better. He is a member of the Young Entrepreneur Council. It is an invite-only community of the world's top, young entrepreneurs.

Challenging himself as an inventor, in 2014, he invented the world's first smart shower device, and co-founded EvaDrop (Smart Shower) to produce and sell it. EvaDrop saves water and provides an enhanced shower experience. It has an advanced sensor system which automatically adjusts water flow to each user's custom specifications. EvaDrop has blue tooth pairing. The user can track how much water they save daily and connect to other smart home products. EvaDrop even has its own on line community.

Dalip founded Fraxtion based on another of his inventions. It offers an interactive kiosk for brick-and-mortar shops. The Fraxtion kiosk features capabilities that enable it to interact and engage in-store customers. It aims its next-gen consumer experience at invoking increases of sales and brand awareness. It communicates promotions, products, and service. Shops can connect with its in store audience on a new level without hiring another sales agent.

Fraxtion empowers customers to take and share a branded photo directly to their social wall. They become brand socialites for the shop. Customers can use the promotional check in module to increase the shop's social presence, boost its profits, and encourage customers to become proud patrons. Fraxtion also collects customer contact information via its newsletter module.

Dalip enjoys building. In 2013 he co-founded Forge54, a nonprofit, that hosts a 54-hour hackathon weekend to provide a marketing make over for one nonprofit organization per year. This allows him to stay very active within his community. He hosts monthly networking events and is on the board of the Ad Federation chapter in Orange County (Ad 2 OC). Dalip has been well received as a guest speaker at the CSUF Start-up Incubator.

Dalip is a 2014 alumnus of CSUF's Mihaylo College of Business and Economics. He earned his BBA in Management and Operations. He enjoys spending time with his family and friends. He plays chess and the saxophone. Outdoors, he is a snowboarder.

Dalip Jaggi
Orange County, California

Dear Aspiring Founder,

My name is Dalip Jaggi, and I am the founder of Devise Interactive, a brand and digital agency in Orange County, CA. Given that I am a relatively young entrepreneur, many inquire about my path and how I made my dream of opening an agency a reality.

Growing up, I was the stereotypical nerd--always experimenting with different technology into the wee hours of the night. I found solace in learning about the digital world and making virtual friends that shared the same passion. After working online with Randy, the now Creative Director at Devise Interactive, for years, I knew that our dynamic was the start of something really amazing. Fast forward to today, only 3.5 years later, Devise Interactive stands ten team members strong.

Founding a company will always have a learning curve--just like anything else in life, you win sometimes, and you lose sometimes. It's absolutely critical, however, that you learn from every success, misstep, and always strive to better your craft. What does that mean exactly? Focus your time and energy on providing the best service possible to clients. Naturally, it is a must to consider company profit, but by no means allow that to be your driving force. Passion shows. And it always wins.

Even more important than building your client base, however, is nourishing your ecosystem-your team. I take pride in fostering a work environment that is conducive to personal and professional growth. I am every team member's biggest advocate. I believe in each person's abilities, but always look for ways for team members to gain new knowledge and skill sets. When you invest in your team, both the extrinsic and intrinsic rewards are truly incredible.

Lastly, building your network organically will take your company far. How can this be done? Get out of your comfort zone and be social! Your social presence and confidence will be a magnet to all of those around you.

I hope that this letter will provide you with the stepping stones needed to take that leap of faith! Always be patient and kind to yourself. Remember, "Rome wasn't built in a day." I assure you, great things are yet to come.

Cheers!

Dalip Jaggi
Founder of Devise Interactive

Clearly Innovative

Ken James is the founder of KBJ Enterprises LLC, d.b.a. Clearly Innovative Home and Office Products("CI"). The privately held company was formed to manufacture and distribute tempered glass chair mats as high-end replacements for plastic chair mats. Ken is a 1969 Business Management alumnus of California State University Fullerton.

Throughout his career Ken was in direct contact with customers, and had P&L responsibility. Ken recalls, "Both prepared me to own and operate my own business. Serving customers and understanding the "numbers" are critical core competencies for consumer ventures."

Ken's career path started in a family business, serving as General Manager at River View Golf Course in Santa Ana. He then moved to E-Z-Go/Texron, starting as a Sales Representative. He soon became a branch manager, and was promoted again to Western Regional Manager.

In 1983, he joined American Golf Corporation as a regional director. He became its Senior Vice President- Public Golf Operations in 1990. In 1999, Ken sold his interest in American Golf Corporation and retired.

After retirement, Ken became a Residential Real Estate Associate with First Team Real Estate -Newport Beach. He founded CI in 2007. As he describes in his letter CI had a long ramp-up. He received his patent in 2012, had to pivot from the supply industry to the furniture industry, and eventually had to manufacture off-shore to keep costs down. In 2015, CI began distributing through SP Richards Company. SP Richards Company is the second largest national distributor of business supplies and furniture.

In 2016, CI contracted to private label a chair mat product for Deflecto, LLC, the world's largest manufacturer and distributor of plastic chair mats. Today, CI's glass chair mats are featured in all major business supply and furniture catalogs under the Deflecto brand.

CI has been a profitable venture since 2012. CI's company philosophy is, "Our very existence depends on satisfying our customers with solutions to their problems, by offering products and service that exceed their expectations."

Ken's firm has been a Small Business Institute student consulting client. He is a friend of CSUF Entrepreneurship.

Ken is married to Debbie. Together they have five children, and nine grandchildren. They reside in San Clemente, California.

Ken at the Dead Sea ,Israel (2017)

Clearly *Innovative*
GLASS CHAIRMATS™

Dear Founder:

My venture started in 2007 after I had been retired for ten years. Looking back, this could have been a disaster if I had not come across CSUF Professor John Bradley Jackson's book, <u>First, Best, or Different,</u> <u>"What Every Entrepreneur Needs to Know About Niche Marketing"</u>. I am sure I would still be on the lauching pad scratching my head without this resource. Thanks John!

I have a patented product that I have manufactured overseas and distribute in the business supply and furniture market. It is the very definition of a "niche product". I use clear, beveled-edge, tempered glass to make chairmats as a replacement for cheap plastic and vinyl chairmats. The Mercedes of chairmats. The product name is Clearly Innovative Lifetime Chairmat. The annual market for all chairmats domestically is $125 million. You can go to www.chairmatsofglass.com to learn more.

Here are the lessons I want to share with you as my business evolved:
<u>What I did right:</u>

> I didn't need to make a profit for five years (I was able to self fund).
> I avoided having fixed overhead, employees, or inventory to keep costs low (only inventory commitment has changed in ten years).
> I sought advice from SCORE.
> I protected my idea by filing for a patent (even patent pending has value).
> I out-sourced everything I could from the beginning and personally handled much of the business.
> I chose an importer that I could trust almost like a partner.
> I brought in a "sweat equity partner" to handle day-to-day operations, so I could concentrate
> on business development.

<u>What I should have done better:</u>

> **Product Positioning and Messaging** – I thought my product was a supply item, really turned out to be a furniture product. It's difficult to to reposition a product after launching.
> **Distribution Logistics** – I didn't factor in the high cost of single piece shipping and how distributors solve this problem (a unique problem for us due to our oversize product).
> **Marketing Reps** – I hired reps that called on the supply industry (see above) instead of the business furniture industry.
> **Internet Marketing** – I thought the internet was a low cost marketing tool on a level playing field, it is not.
> **Manufacturing** – waited too long to manufacture off-shore to bring manufacturing costs down.
> **Pricing** – I set pricing for immediate profit instead of setting down-stream sales targets and pricing accordingly.
> **Marketing Channels** – I should have worked with distributors who operate in the right channels (small guys are at a serious disadvantage).
> **Personal Time Investment** – I should have dedicated myself to my venture with a make or break horizon.

In summary, I should have done more homework to vastly shorten my ramp-up, and should have realized a great product does not sell itself. I now understand Steve Job's frustration with VC's who could not visualize a Mac Computer in every home!

Today our product is private branded by the largest manufacture of plastic chairmats, and is listed in all the national distributor and dealer business supply and furniture catalogs that thousands of dealers depend on to choose the products they resell.

Good luck with your venture,

Ken James, Founder/President

Be A Good Human

Bo Jones is the founder and President of Staceye, Inc. "(SI"). SI is a consulting firm in Orange County, California. He is also Vice President of Investors' Property Services ("IPS"). IPS is a real estate service company head quartered in Southern California.

SI engages with individuals and small start-ups. It provides guidance and framework for ventures to launch and execute their business plan during the initial 24 months of operations. From concept to reality, SI provides insight and assistance in four areas: business plan formation, budget creation, investor structuring, financing, real estate/ location sourcing. SI offers ongoing business consulting.

IPS is a boutique commercial real estate firm headquartered in Southern California. Its operations span the nation. IPS specializes in managing real estate income properties. It provides property management and property repositioning. IPS implements growth oriented real estate investment strategies.

While attending CSUF, Bo earned his real estate sales license and specialized in multifamily real estate. He joined Real Estate Partners, Inc. There he learned how to structure deals, do market research, underwrite investments and make presentations. Simultaneously, in college Bo concentrated in Entrepreneurship. His course work included multiple student-led small business consulting projects. He learned the fine points of small business consulting.

Upon graduating from CSUF, Bo joined IPS and managed day to day operations of projects. He earned his present position in 2013.

As the Vice President of IPS, Bo is primarily responsible for key client relations, technology adaptation / roll-outs and multifamily operations. He leads a team of approximately 150 individuals employed across the country.

Before his present roles, Bo spent twelve years creating companies, servicing needs in multiple sectors. Included were fitness/ martial arts, apparel design, automotive engineering and marketing.

Since graduating from the CSUF Entrepreneurship program in 2007, Bo has given back. He acts as a mentor and consultant for the Center of Entrepreneurship. Bo is married with two children and lives in Orange County. He enjoys spending time with his family, advancing his jiujitsu, mountain biking and of course pursuing his ultimate passion - all things automotive.

A photo from Bo's engagement shoot, after which, "Life really began to escalate and elevate personally and professionally."

Bo Jones
Trabuco Canyon, California

Dear Founder,

Since I graduated from CSUF, I have been involved in many entrepreneurial and managerial roles. In each I find that my effectiveness hinges on three factors. First in importance for me is my belief that we must be good humans. Second is my passion for my craft. Third, is my perseverance.

Be a good human. I am responsible for a hundred and fifty or so employees across the country. In business, when I point out the importance of striving to be a good human, I call it the human factor. I stress that the human factor means putting people first. That sounds very easy, but we often find ourselves in situations where putting people first is hard. For example, our real estate operations are a people business. Much of what I do is dealing with people. With residents, we are talking about their homes, the places where they raise their kids and families. We are talking about life changing situations that can dictate their paths through life. We really need to put people first. We must have human compassion. Our employees who work for us serve our customers. The mind set that I work hard to instill is "treat the janitor like you treat the CEO." I mean that. If we can treat everybody the same, we can gain momentum as an organization and a company culture. Put people first. You can still take care of business, but you can do it with compassion. Approach things from a human perspective. You will find you have things in common. You gain better control. Don't prejudge people, try to overcome your preconceptions. Be more understanding. Being good humans goes a long way to resolving situations and revealing the value in people.

Have passion for your craft. To realize your dreams you must have passion. You must do what you love. One thing that has gotten me through some incredibly difficult times is my passion for my craft. I do the work when things are not looking great, and when things are looking amazing, tempting me to take an extra day off. You have to have something that moves you and I firmly believe that it can't just be money. Strive to know what drives you. Passion comes naturally if you do what you love.

I have discovered that you can't teach passion or buy passion. Passion comes from within you. Over years we have hired people who may not be the best leaders or workers. They succeed because they have that something about them. They are passionate about the work and the clients they serve. I hang onto those people for dear life. I can teach someone to be a good manager, a better book keeper, or consultant. I can't teach someone how to be passionate about their craft. I cherish that fire within people. I know they will not give up or cut corners.

Persevere. Most entrepreneurs I know say perseverance and its synonym persistence are essential. You can't overstate that. Starting in 2006-2007, we launched several startup companies. Some did well, some have not. Some have done well over a long period, others did well only for a short period. What is important is to make sure that you keep your eye on the prize. Persevere and do what you have to do. I have heard hundreds and hundreds of "nos" in the last twelve years. It's not easy. Doors close frequently. The idea is to find the ones that are opening. Seek expert advice, be flexible, change lanes when needed but stay on the road to your dream.

I chuckle a bit when I look back at my idea of success years ago. Now I laugh when I think about all the times I thought I would quit and I didn't. You will find a long road ahead that changes daily. Moving forward with your entrepreneurial journey will require human perspective, passion and perseverance.

I wish you the best,

Bo Jones

143

Stay on Target with Your Passion

Greg Jordan is a California-based sales and marketing professional.

Greg is adept at distilling complex initiatives into a manageable and measurable pathway to success. With a strong foundation in consulting sales, and hands-on experience in marketing, Greg is accomplished at closing high-value enterprise engagements.

Beginning in the 1990s, Greg began working as a salesperson in the IT market research and consulting world. In the early 2000s he was Business Development Manager for SUGO a music and multimedia agency specializing in sensory marketing campaigns. Next, he served was an account Executive Forrester Research, Inc. for selling Forrester's full suite of products: syndicated research, data, consulting, and executive programs to C-level executives at $500 million+ companies.

In 2006 Greg was recruited to direct big brand advertising campaigns for Yahoo. As Senior Account Executive he grew and strengthened interactive advertising partnerships in Yahoo!'s most strategic and valuable advertising tier, including Mazda, Land Rover, Jaguar, Suzuki, Kelley Blue Book.

After Yahoo, Greg founded Greg Jordan Design, a marketing consultancy for small to mid-sized companies, where he spent six years working with a broad range of brands and product companies. He helped clients with lead generation strategy, email marketing campaigns, search engine marketing, and landing page design. Deliverables included planning services, digital marketing assessments, consulting, and campaign management.

In 2016 Greg returned to Forrester Research, Inc., where he is currently a content marketing consulting specialist, working on a team to develop B2B campaigns for global tech titans.

Originally from Southern California, Greg has made the San Francisco Bay Area his home, where he resides with his family. Greg has been a guest speaker for CSUF Entrepreneurship and a consultant to the Center for Entrepreneurship.

Greg Jordan
Burlingame, California

Dear Founder:

As you enter the whirlwind of activity that comes with being an entrepreneur I'd like to offer up some helpful coaching that I've found to hold true over the years. None of these principles are new, and they are all things I've learned from people far more successful than myself.

You can be moderately successful on your own, but you can soar to do great things once you begin working with a team of trusted colleagues. When you launch your business it's likely you'll have to bootstrap your new venture and do many things on your own. But eventually you'll be in a position to grow. Do this with a select few intelligent people, and be sure you trust them with your livelihood. Some of the people you partner with will be part of your direct company, and others will be part of an extended, yet tight circle of partners, like a banker, a lawyer, and a CPA. Keep these essential people close and communicate frequently and honestly.

Remain focused on what you do best. At many points along the way you'll be lured to stray from your organization's core expertise and test new grounds. Your temptation may be piqued because you're enjoying success and you're eager to see what more you can do, or you may have become anxious to accelerate for other reasons. New technologies, new business partnership opportunities, and employee ideas will be important for you to carefully evaluate before spending too much time on something that distracts you from being the best at what you and your company truly do best. Stay on target with your passion.

Develop your company around a distinct competitive advantage, and something you can continue to improve. Be extremely competitive and more expert than your competition. Develop a voracious appetite for knowledge and read more than you ever have, even at CSUF! You'll become smarter than you thought possible by reading what others have already learned. Nurture mentor relationships with people wiser than you. Model your business after ones more successful than yours.

Once you're ready, come back to CSUF and share what you've learned with the next generation of entrepreneurs!

All the best,

Greg Jordan

dbk Associates, Inc.

Dave Kinnear is the founder and CEO of dbkAssociates, Inc., a change management consulting and executive coaching firm for leaders in small and mid-sized enterprises. He is a board certified business advisor, mentor and executive coach. His firm is affiliated with Vistage Worldwide. Dave convenes and facilitates peer advisory boards of business owners, company presidents, general managers and chief executives dedicated to becoming better leaders who make better decisions and achieve better results. He also provides one-to-one mentoring for these highly successful executives.

Dave has more than three decades of leadership experience at some of the world's largest semiconductor corporations including Toshiba America Electronic Components, Advanced Microdevices, Fairchild Semiconductor, and United Technologies. His career has spanned Electronic Design, Application Engineering, Procurement Management, Sales and Marketing Management, Business Systems Implementation, Analysis and Operations.

Dave holds a Bachelor of Science degree in Electronics Engineering and a Masters degree in Business Administration. He is a Board Certified Coach (BCC) with the Center for Credentialing & Education, and a Certified Veteran Development Coach. He is a life time member of the Institute of Electrical and Electronic Engineers (IEEE).

Dave sits in several private-for-profit boards. He also sits on not-for-profit boards, including the board of the California Conference for Equality and Justice (CCEJ).

Dave serves the community as a mentor and coach for college students. He is an executive-to-executive mentor to Executive MBA students at the UCI Paul Merage School of Business. In addition, Dave coaches students at California State University, Fullerton's Center for Entrepreneurship and holds open office hours at CSUF's Start-up Incubator.

Dave's mantra is, "Creating a better world one leader at a time."

dbkAssociates, Inc.
25422 Trabuco Road
Ste 105-316
Lake Forest, CA 92630
(949)436-0222
dave@dbkassociates.com

Dear Founder,

Congratulations on creating your own venture! You are in for an amazing time, one with highs and lows. Most importantly, if your experience is even close to my own, it will be a highly rewarding time as well. I hope you are open to my sharing a few observations on the world of entrepreneurship.

To be sure, if I had it all to do over again, I would take the same path I've taken to create a successful Executive Leadership Coaching practice. Yet, there are some things I would work on in a different order. I would, for example, take the time *up front* to deeply understand my own core values and how they created my company culture. Company culture trumps everything! Values underpin vision which in turn informs the mission of the organization. So, values are the foundation on which all else is constructed. It is much easier to build the right culture in the beginning than it is to undergo culture change later.

This may sound trivial or perhaps obvious. Yet, I can tell you from more than a decade of working with founders that they had thought little about their own core values until challenged to define them. They found that once they understood what drives them to make decisions the way they do (their values), it positively affected the way they chose potential partners, interviewed for hires, mentored and trained their employees, engaged advisors and how they decided which clients and/or markets to pursue. And when they hired employees who shared their values, they could confidently delegate major assignments--thus allowing autonomy. This is no small advantage. The founders "got their life back" by being able to confidently delegate tasks so they could concentrate on culture and strategy.

A second lesson I learned, a bit late in the game, was that I did not have to "grow it alone." Once I began assembling a network of peer advisors that I could lean on for advice, my business world became a lot less lonely, and my practice grew much faster. Even as you realize your days are full to the max, you may well find that something is missing—perhaps what is missing is sharing your experience with someone who truly understands what you are going through. So, build your own *diverse* group of colleagues who have gone through what you are experiencing. The common thread for this group is that they have your best interest at heart. The more diverse their backgrounds are, the more creative their ideas will be.

There, then, are a couple of ideas you might consider. First, your real task as a founder is to actively manage the organization's culture. In fact, the larger your successful organization grows, the more time you must spend on that task. It is imperative that you be self-aware and know your core values. Second, remember that no one of us is as smart as all of us. Surround yourself with trusted colleagues who have your best interests at heart. A shared journey is often more pleasant and productive than a solitary one.

Warmest regards and wishing you the best of luck,

David B. Ki

CEO, *dbkAssociates, Inc.*

COO and Mentor

Charles Kissel is associate executive director and COO of the CSU Fullerton Auxiliary Services Corporation (ASC). The ASC is a not-for-profit corporation with the sole purpose of supporting California State University Fullerton (CSUF). He teaches corporate finance part-time at CSUF.

Chuck is a CSUF alumnus. He holds aB.A. in Entrepreneurial Management, a minor in Chemistry and an M.B.A. in Finance -- all from CSUF.

Chuck has been at ASC for over twenty years. His oversight includes commercial operations, property development, information technology, payroll and human resources. He is responsible for approximately 1,600 employees.

He sits on the board of directors for a for–profit startup subsidiary (indiCo). He serves on the Executive Committee of a small not-for-profit organization (Auxiliary Organizations Association) in California.

Chuck has previously been President, CFO and Chair of the Finance & Finance, and Audit Committees of two other corporate boards of directors/trustees with combined revenues of $120 million. He He has special expertise in not-for-profit startup organizations.

Prior to joining ASC, Chuck worked for Sunkist, a small privately owned family business with two locations within Disneyland, CA.

Over the years, Chuck has mentored aspiring founders in CSUF Entrepreneurship's New Venture Launch course. He is also a supporter of the CSUF Start Up Incubator.

Chuck lives in Yorba Linda and works in Fullerton. On weekends, if not vacationing at a tropical location, he can be found in his garage turning wrenches on any one of the classic and antique cars in his collection.

Chuck acquired his latest vehicle, a 1930 Kissel 5-Person Sedan 8-95, while traveling to Denmark as part of a father-son bucket list trip. This car is one of three; the only one on the road as the other two are in a museum. It is the last known car off the assembly line to still exist. Together, Chuck and his father display the car at Concours shows throughout California.

Charles Kissel
Yorba Linda, California

Dear Founder,

Starting a new venture is an exciting yet challenging time. Many people will say that, "where there is a will there is a way," and "a great idea makes millions." Though there is some truth to those statements, most startups simply don't succeed despite the great idea and individual willpower behind them.

My undergraduate research project was to help a close friend launch his own business. He had worked for others as a marine/automotive mechanic for many years and felt it was time for him to work for himself. Unfortunately, the more research I did and further into my project I got, it became clear that he should not start his own company. So, why was I thinking this way?

Unfortunately, this friend did not have a good business plan. When asked to provide critical information, he was at a loss. He had limited capital at his disposal and no clear competitive advantage. He was always starting a new project without having finished the last one. The few times a project was completed, it was always at the last minute and usually late.

What does it take to be successful? Passion and a committed work ethic are critical. Individuals can learn skills or even hire the skills when needed. Excellent customer service and time management are needed in the service industry. Founders need to be able to communicate and connect an idea, product and business model to others. You need to be able to differentiate your idea and core competency from others in the market place. While mentoring, I have seen this first hand. A student has a great idea but is challenged conveying and/or selling the idea to group members. Ultimately, the group struggles.

Get excited about your venture, take time to plan your business and consider all the possible challenges you may encounter. When possible, create strategies to overcome those challenges in advance. Be passionate and take ownership of your idea. Have a great work ethic. Remember that founders are leaders and the best leaders lead by example. Be prepared, as well as one can, for the curve balls that life will throw your way. Most of all, remember life is short; have fun and enjoy what you do.

Wishing you success in your venture,

Charles Kissel

An Expert At Raising Capital

Guy Knuf is a partner at Hein & Associates. He leads the transaction advisory services group in Southern California.

Guy is a 1987 alumnus of California State University Fullerton. He earned a Bachelor of Arts Degree in Business Administration with a concentration in Accounting. Guy has been a Certified Public Accountant since 1987. He is a Certified Merger & Acquisition Advisor, and Certified Global Management Accountant. He holds an MBA with a concentration in Finance and Venture Management from USC.

Guy began his accounting career with eight years at a local and national accounting firm (Kenneth Leventhal & Co.). Today, He has over 25 years of experience advising entrepreneurs, private-equity and strategic investors, lenders, and other capital providers. He has expertise in merger and acquisition, divestiture, and ESOP transactions ranging from $10 million to $1 billion in enterprise value.

Guy has served both high-tech and entrepreneurial clients within the manufacturing, distribution, retail, service, contractor and real estate industries. Before joining Hein & Associates, he founded and managed successful advisory and business consulting practices at national, regional and local CPA firms.

Guy has extensive experience in growth and exit planning, merger and acquisitions, valuation, due diligence, budgeting and forecasting, and deal structuring. He is a member of the American Institute of Certified Public Accountants, the California Society of Certified Public Accountants, the

Turnaround Management Association, the Association of Insolvency and Restructuring Advisors, Alliance of M & A advisors, and the Beta Gamma Sigma national business honor society.

Guy is a past member of the Dean's Advisory Board at Mihaylo College of Business and Economics. For many years he served as an Adjunct Professor for California State University, Fullerton's Entrepreneurship concentration. He taught the Entrepreneurial Accounting class.

Dear Founder,

You are not alone, if you find that your new venture is under capitalized. Most new ventures have insufficient capital to achieve their strategic plan. It is true that "Cash is King" because it's the company's lifeblood. You may not run out of energy, but you can definitely run out of cash. Utilize your cash flow wisely, because everything stops if you run out.

With this fear of survival, many new ventures focus on doing whatever it takes to raise capital. They spend countless hours chasing angel groups, attending investment capital pitch nights, and deal their inadequate business plans to whomever will listen. Your idea may be great, but work smart when you start chasing capital.

Before you go to the capital markets, spend the time building products and services with competitive advantages and really perfecting your business model. If you can truly prove to me on paper that your business model successfully works; I guarantee you that you will raise investment capital. However, this is easier said than done. Do your homework and do your research, because investors will do theirs.

Most importantly, be prepared for the third question. Question #1, you will be asked, what is the gross profit margin of your products? You may proudly claim that your gross profit margin is 50%. Then you will be asked, Question #2, how many products do you have? Again you may boast that you have 25 products. You will then be asked, Question #3, what is the gross profit margin of each of your products? Hence, this deal breaker third question is where the rubber meets the road. Typically, you hear the lights buzz when you ask most entrepreneurs this question. However, if you respond that the majority of your products have 70-85% gross profit margins, but you have one main product that has a 10% gross profit margin. This is because you bundle this lower margin product with your higher margin products to build competitive advantages and barriers to entry. Congratulations you have an investor's attention because you have demonstrated that you not only know your company, but you also know how to build and sell competitive products within your targeted market within your industry.

Apply this third question philosophy to all aspects of your company including raising capital. You know you will be ready to go to the capital markets when you can accurately respond to he following three questions. First, how much capital do you need? Secondly, how will you use the funds that you receive from investors? Finally, what type of return will you provide to the investor?

Be prepared and good luck, I wish you the best of success in your new venture

Best regards,

Guy W. Knuf
Partner, Transaction Advisory Services
Hein & Associates, LLP

Marketer, Communicator and Mentor

Teresa Koch is the assistant vice president of member engagement and communications at Orange County's Credit Union (OCCU). She is a marketing and communications professional with over twenty-five years of experience in the financial services industry. Teresa has been with OCCU since 2003.

She continues to bring a wealth of knowledge to OCCU, a $1.5 billion credit union with 100,000 Members and ten branches in the Orange County area. Its portfolio includes auto, home and small business loans. Its mission is, "Simple banking, for people, not profit." Prior to Teresa's start at Orange County's Credit Union, she served as vice president and senior marketing officer of First Citizens National, a $700 million community bank with twelve branches headquartered in Mason City, Iowa.

Teresa is responsible for the creation and implementation of OCCU's strategic roadmap for member engagement and communications. Currently, she leads a team of five and is in charge of executing the annual marketing plan, including digital media buy, trigger email, social media, reputation management, content creation, branch collateral, public relations and reporting. Teresa is also the co-author and co-oversees OCCU's annual LIFE Game Plan, an internal, award-winning leadership program for all Associates.

Throughout her time at OCCU, Teresa's work on the LIFE Game Plan has helped rank OCCU as one of the top credit unions by The Orange County Register four years in a row. With the help of her diligent work ethic, Orange County's Credit Union was a recipient of the Peter Baron Stark Companies Workplace Excellence Award in 2013 and 2016.

Teresa is an honors graduate from the University of Northern Iowa. She majored in Accounting and minored in Communications. She also serves as a member of the American Institute of CPAs, Credit Union National Association and the Marketing Association of Credit Unions. Teresa believes in the value of having a Personal Leadership Brand Statement. Hers is, "A strategic leader with deep industry knowledge, empowering and inspiring others so together we can see the future, be creative, and foster powerful Member engagement."

OCCU has been a CSUF Small Business Institute student consulting client. Teresa guided the process. She has been an Entrepreneur in Residence (mentor) for CSUF Entrepreneurship.

Teresa lives in Dove Canyon. She enjoys spending time with her kids, reading, walking and whale watching.

Dear Founder,

I spent the first two years of my career as a CPA. However, my creative side won out and I transitioned from being the internal auditor of a community bank to being the bank's marketing director. Since then, I've spent the past 25 years as a marketer of banking services. To me, marketing is the next best thing to being an entrepreneur; to owning your own venture. You have the opportunity to make something out of nothing and use creativity and hard work to build something of value. I currently lead the award-winning Member Engagement & Communications team at Orange County's Credit Union, the largest community-chartered credit union headquartered in Orange County, California.

In addition to my role as marketing director, I have greatly enjoyed my numerous semesters as a mentor and Entrepreneur in Residence at Cal State Fullerton. It's with fondness and appreciation for my past students that I offer my personal insights to future founders.

1. Ideas are your natural resource.
Keep the creativity flowing – brainstorming is your friend. Research brainstorming techniques and then practice them. The best ideas come when you're relaxed and thinking about your objectives. But remember, you don't have to act on every idea. Pitch your ideas to your spouse, your friends, and other business associates. Watch their reactions. Gauge their interest. Go back to the drawing board when you need to.

2. Keep the word "pilot" in your vocabulary.
The need to get things perfect before you act can be a big roadblock. Take the pressure off by calling your project a "pilot." Everything doesn't need to be perfect or completely vetted before you launch. You can learn a lot in a small rollout and gain a competitive speed to market.

3. Take a stand – transparency is important in today's marketing.
Today's values-based consumers want to do business with brands that stand for something important. Whether it's righting global warming, the humane raising of animals for food consumption, or human rights issues – consumers want you to take a stand on issues that are relevant to your brand and genuine in their intention. Find out what your customers care about and show that you care about it too. Be ethical. Be relevant. Be proactive.

4. Be good to your staff.
Not only do consumers want to do business with companies that treat their employees well, your team will be the most productive when they feel valued. Take the time to hire the right people and hold them to high standards – then make them feel appreciated. They will go above and beyond.

Wishing you creativity and success in your exciting new endeavors!

Teresa Koch

Teresa Koch

Innovative Initiatives

Robert Kovacev Sr. has professional experience as a technologist, program manager, and international marketer for technology firms. He has served firms ranging from high tech start-ups, to turn-arounds, to Fortune 50 technology companies. Bob founded The Innovation Initiative Consulting Group in 2010. He is a principal consultant for the firm.

Bob has had multi-disciplined corporate experience in such industry-leading firms as Boeing, Northrop-Grumman, Rockwell International and Printrak International. His experience includes positions as a technologist (research physicist and systems engineering manager); Director of Program Management for major U.S. defense and Canadian Law Enforcement system development programs; and International Marketing and Business Development Director with experience in Mideast, European, Asian, Australian, and Canadian markets. Bob is a member of the Board of Directors for two Southern California firms.

He has a BA degree in Physics. He also has a MBA-Marketing from California State University at Los Angeles, and a DBA from the University of Phoenix with an emphasis in entrepreneurial organizational behavior. His dissertation is entitled, Encouraging Employee Entrepreneurial Spirit in a Process-Oriented Technology Enterprise. Bob iwas a featured speaker at the American Institute of Information Management (AIIM) Conference in New York and many other professional and business venues. He has published several articles on marketing, management, program management, computer peripheral technology, law enforcement technology and laser communication.

Bob has taught undergraduate and MBA business courses at California State University and Chapman University for over twenty-three years. He currently teaches finance, marketing, entrepreneurial marketing and entrepreneurial finance at the Mihaylo College of Business and Economics.

Bob has mentored many start-up and small businesses through CSUF Entrepreneurship and SCORE. He is a mentor at the CSUF Startup Incubator.

THE CENTER FOR ENTREPRENEURSHIP
Small Business Institute, SGMH-3280
Mihaylo College of Business and Economics
800 N. State College Blvd.   Fullerton, CA 92831

CALIFORNIA STATE UNIVERSITY
FULLERTON

Dear Founder,

What is the most valuable asset in any new venture?

The answers most people will give to this question are likely to be: intellectual property, the marketing strategy, or the customer and prospect lists. While these are certainly critical assets for any firm, new or established, these are not the most valuable assets.

The most valuable asset a start-up or even an established enterprise has is the entrepreneur's time. Since 2009 I have led student teams consulting with over fifty companies, done one-on-one SCORE mentoring and have been board member of several founding teams. One thing I have noticed is that most entrepreneurs are continually inundated with urgent tasks that demand their immediate attention . . . tasks that could be handled adequately by others. These include such tasks as management of the firm's social media networks, writing checks, resolving product technical issues, or finding facilities and negotiating rents and running the daily operations of the firm. This urgency generally relegates the important entrepreneurial job to spare time (if there is any).

The real job of the entrepreneur has very few elements. The four most important are:
(1) Maintaining close relationships with customers [particularly during the lean start-up phase of developing the minimum viable product (MVP) and analyzing customer feedback for subsequent iterations].
(2) Maintaining close relations with current investors and seeking follow-on investment.
(3) Controlling cash flow and making key decisions for major expenditures.
(4) Developing the vision and strategy for the future growth of the enterprise.

Why does the primary CEO/entrepreneur need a partner?

Leading a start-up or small business enterprise is a complicated job. Many of the most successful companies in the technology, financial, entertainment, and other fields were founded and led by teams of two or three primary leaders. These include Microsoft, Apple, Berkshire-Hathaway, Disney, and Home Depot. The common thread for most of these teams is that one member was the "outside" person, responsible for the company vision and tasks external to the firm, while the other team member was the "inside" person.

One solution to the dilution of the CEO/Entrepreneur's time and attention from the tasks that are his or her real job described above is to have a COO partner to handle all of the operational tasks and crises that come up on a daily basis. This COO partner is an integral part of the executive leadership team and participates in defining the vision and strategy for the company's future.

You have taken on the role and big challenge of being an entrepreneur, a role crucial to the future of America. I wish you the best of success in that venture and hope that this letter has given you something of value toward that success.

Dr. Robert J. Kovacev, Sr.

Tax Incentives In The Tax Code

Rob Kovacev is a tax partner in the Washington, D.C. office of the law firm Steptoe & Johnson, LLP. He provides advice to established and startup companies. He is an expert regarding innovation tax incentives such as the research tax credit, the domestic production activities deduction, and alternative energy tax credits. Rob graciously agreed to prepare a letter that shares his expertise for educational purposes. He helps us better understand tax incentives that may apply to new ventures.

Rob also defends taxpayers in IRS audits and in the courts. Prior to joining Steptoe in 2013, he was a senior litigation counsel in the United States Department of Justice, Tax Division, responsible for some of the largest and most complex civil tax cases in the nation.

Rob is a strong advocate for innovation tax incentives as a vehicle for fostering entrepreneurship and economic growth. He is an active speaker, author and commentator on tax issues. Top news and media outlets have frequently interviewed and cited Rob.

Steptoe is a multinational law firm with a reputation for vigorous advocacy in complex litigation and arbitration, successful representation of clients before governmental agencies, and creative and practical advice in guiding business transactions. The firm has more than 500 lawyers and other professionals in offices in Beijing, Brussels, Chicago, London, Los Angeles, New York, Phoenix, San Francisco, and Washington D.C. Steptoe is known for its ability to help clients solve high-stakes, multi-dimensional problems, particularly those with a governmental aspect. In particular, Steptoe's tax lawyers bring to clients

decades of consulting, transactional, and advocacy experience in all substantive areas of federal and state taxation, including corporate, partnership, state and local, compensation and benefits, tax exempt and international tax. Steptoe is a forceful and effective advocate for its clients before the IRS, the Treasury Department, state departments of revenue, the courts, in Congress and state legislatures.

Robert J. Kovacev
202 429 6462
rkovacev@steptoe.com

1330 Connecticut Avenue, NW
Washington, DC 20036-1795
202 429 3000 main
www.steptoe.com

Steptoe
STEPTOE & JOHNSON LLP

Dear Founder:

The last place any entrepreneur would expect to find help is in the tax code. In fact, there are tax incentives at the federal and state level designed specifically to support innovation, and even startups may benefit from those incentives.

For example, there is a federal tax credit for research expenses. Basically, if you incur expenses (usually wages and supply costs) as part of a process of experimentation to discover technological information to resolve uncertainty, when that information is intended to be useful in the development of a new or improved business component, you may be eligible to claim a percentage of those expenses as federal tax credit. The credit is not limited to high-tech companies – research expenses in any industry may qualify.

The research tax credit was originally designed as a credit solely against federal income taxes. While this was useful for established, profitable companies, it left many startups in the cold. While a company in a loss position can carry research tax credits forward for up to 20 years, most new ventures can't afford to wait that long. As a result, the research tax credit was largely ignored by entrepreneurs building new ventures. But a recent change in the law puts the research tax credit within reach of startups as well as mega-corporations.

For tax years starting after December 31, 2015, the research tax credit can now be used by startup businesses to offset federal employment taxes, even if the company doesn't owe federal income tax. A startup is defined as a taxpayer earning gross receipts for five years or less, with under $5 million in gross receipts on average over the past three years. If your company qualifies as a startup under these rules, and has qualified research expenses, it could claim up to $250,000 a year in credits against federal payroll taxes for W-2 employees.

There are other tax incentives for renewable energy, for domestic manufacturing, and several other types of entrepreneurial activities. Many states offer innovation tax incentives as well.

Of course, when it comes to taxes, nothing is simple. Maintaining books and records substantiating research expenses is essential, and there are technical rules that must be followed. If you think you may qualify for one of these incentives, consult a tax professional – and when you do, ask that they look for any innovation tax incentives that apply to your situation.

Wishing you the best of luck,

[signature]

Robert J. Kovacev, Esq.

*This letter is for educational purposes only and is not intended, and should not be relied upon, as legal or tax advice. Consult a tax professional for specific advice tailored to your situation.

OPUS Productivity Solutions

Robert (Bob) Kreisberg is founder and president of OPUS Productivity solutions. OPUS is a management consulting firm that helps its clients make better hiring decisions. The firm then assists in maximizing the productivity of the client's new and existing people.

OPUS offers specialized products and services that it gears toward these goals. Clients range in size. OPUS serves small entrepreneurial companies with less than ten people. It also serves corporations with over one billion dollars in revenues.

Bob started OPUS after spending 17 years in the high technology industry. A Drexel University grad, Bob started his career selling computer systems for ITEL Corporation in New York City. Bob was the top performing salesperson in the country two consecutive years. ITEL promoted him, at the ripe old age of 28, to run the New York City Branch office. At age 30 the company moved Bob to Chicago to run the Central Region.

He subsequently changed companies while in Chicago, and headed MAI Basic Four's largest office in the country. It had well over $20 Million in combined sales and services revenue, more than one thousand customers and close to 80 people. Bob's next move, at 33, was to come out to California to take on national sales responsibilities. Bob did this for six years before starting OPUS.

OPUS began in 1989, and to date the company has served more than 650 client companies. OPUS has served many companies for more than 10 years. It has also maintained ongoing client relationships with executives as they have made changes in their career. In fact some managers have worked with OPUS for more than 20 years, while working for four different companies.

The OPUS client base continues to evolve. Bob has found that, "Literally every type of organization wants to make the right hiring decision. Then they want to have their new hire be a productive member of their staff for an extended period."

Bob first experienced the services of CSUF Entrepreneurship many years ago. He sponsored a student consulting project at OPUS. The experience inspired Bob. He offered to volunteer his personal services to mentor students working on additional projects. As a result, Bob has been providing volunteer services to CSUF Entrepreneurship for more than a decade.

Bob resides with his family in Carlsbad, California. He is an active member of the Carlsbad Hi-Noon Rotary Club, and the Carlsbad Chamber of Commerce.

Dear Founder,

You're reading this, and, clearly, I don't know you from Adam (or Eve, for that matter). And I have no idea what your brilliant, or maybe not so brilliant, product or service is that you plan on building your business around. But the advice I have for you is universal, no matter what your product is, or who you are.

If you are going to have a successful venture, you're going to need to "sell" your prospects on what you've got. Maybe the idea of having to sell anyone on anything is right up your alley – maybe you've been selling "stuff" forever, from Girl Scout cookies to dog walking services to esoteric software solutions. So the idea of having to "sell" is great.

However, many people are actually quite uncomfortable with the idea that they need to sell someone on their ideas, and that might be you. Perhaps you don't like the potential rejection that comes along with sales. Or maybe you feel that if the product or service is truly worthy, it will "sell itself" – i.e. "build a better mousetrap and people will burn a path to your door". Good luck with that one ...

The truth is, you have to sell your product (service). You need to be able to clearly articulate the "problem" that exists today that requires a solution, and then how your product solves that problem. And you need to be able to qualify what circumstances need to exist to determine if your potential buyer has a problem to which you have a viable solution. Not everyone will qualify, and not everyone who has the problem will perceive the solution to be greater than continuing to live with the problem. In any selling environment, inertia (getting people to change what and how they do something today) is always your biggest competitor.

Maybe you don't see yourself as a salesperson? Well, maybe you're not the caricature of what you think is a salesperson – loud, obnoxious, overly friendly, aggressive. Here's the point – **everyone can sell something they genuinely believe in**. How you approach it has everything to do with your own behavioral nature. Your personality determines your selling style. You can sell anything you believe in by harnessing your own personality style. Maybe your strength is "taking charge" of a situation and having people follow you. Maybe your style is to build on your natural likeability, and have people get caught up in your own natural enthusiasm. Maybe people will buy from you because they feel you've taken the time to understand what they genuinely need. Or maybe people will buy from you because you've worked out a logical game plan, and the logical solution for people that have the need for what you've got is to end up buying it. You can be a successful salesperson simply by being yourself, and by "sticking to it."

Speaking of "sticking to it" – Yikes! There isn't anything more important to your success than your ability to stay the course. You must believe in your venture, and you cannot let other people's doubts or actions get in the way of your success. One of the most important lessons my very first manager taught me was this – "Nobody cares what your batting average is   all we care about are hits. If it takes you more at bats than anyone else, who cares?"

So get out there and sell something. Find a selling style that most naturally fits who you are, and go make it happen.

Good luck to you. If you believe it, **you can** do it.

Robert S. Kreisberg

President and Founder, OPUS Productivity Solutions

Consistent Founder

Ash Kumra is the co-founder and CEO of Youngry™. The company provides original content, events, and e-commerce for its united community of entrepreneurs to, "hustle, profit, expand and inspire."

Youngry™'s mission is to help every early stage entrepreneur (Young in experience, Hungry in ambition) be successful. It is positioned as the inclusive global entre- preneur media brand. It's equalization focus and mission are envisioned as a social impact inspiration. Youngry™ is a full-service digital agency. It is built to deliver explosive growth for clients whose brands target Millennials and Generation Z. Services include, launch strategy, live video, marketing automation, premium content, mobile ads, viral marketing, influencer marketing and Ecommerce.

Prior to Youngry™ Ash founded two other companies. During college, he founded DesiYou, Inc. It curated Indian entertainment and distributed it to content providers around the world. His business plan was winner of the 2010 Irvine Entrepreneurial Forum. The success of DesiYou was honored by Empact 100 as one of the top companies in the nation run by entrepreneurs under 30. Ash was also co-founder of DreamItAlive.com; an online community dedicated to guiding people to create, believe and live out their dreams using virtual dream boards.

Ash is an award winning entre- preneur, author, speaker and talk show host recognized twice by the White House as an entrepreneur making an impact. He spreads his message and invites collaboration via http://ashkumra.com and www.Youngry.com.

Ash is the author of book series "Confessions from an Entrepreneur." He makes himself available for speaking engagements for corporations, schools and cause related organizations on topics around entrepreneurship, social media and self branding. He has spoken to over 10,000 people on entrepreneurship, written over 100 articles. Ash has conducted over 1,000 interviews with business mavens, entrepreneurs and celebrities who have achieved their dreams and goals. He has been featured in 100's of articles including Forbes Magazine, Huffington Post, American Express Forum, Entrepreneur Magazine, Startup America/ Up Global, LA Times, OC Register, Tedx and The White House.

Ash is an active advisor – organizations include Tie, Woman Economic Forum, UC Irvine's Merage School Of Business, FWD.US, Clinton Foundation 20/30 Initiative & OC Tech HH. He helped launch the California team for the White House/ Steve Case "Startup America" initiative.

At CSUF, Ash has been a panelist for the Business Plan Competition and a guest speaker for CSUF's business plan class and the Start-up Incubator.

YOUNGRY

Dear Founder,

You are about to embark on the most exciting journey of your life. You'll get a whirlwind of experiences and an opportunity to make an impact. I was once in your shoes and am continuously learning how to improve. But this is for you: the first-time founder. This is for you as the person who is about to begin entrepreneurship. This is for the ambitious who want to change, make an impact, and initiate a movement.

To become successful, first get over yourself. I know, you're great which is why you can strive and be a successful founder. But, so is the rest of the world. Live to serve others, not yourself. You need to develop a selfless mentality and by doing so, you will experience the positive domino effect: a great impact on your state of mind, the people who will work with you, the customer growth, and the product outcome. Everything will fall into place, but if you go out there believing you are superior than everyone else, then your focus will shift to trying to prove yourself to everyone, ignoring the details behind entrepreneurship. This is a business decision, what I'm telling you, it's not an egotistical comment, but it's meant to truly help your business. The more selfless you can become the better your business will be.

Secondly, build a business for passion not for trend. I always say this to early stage founders, entrepreneurs and other people. If you create a business that is based on something you are truly passionate about regardless of the state of the economy or the audience numbers or your surroundings, you will find a solution. But if you're doing this based on a trend, you will easily fall behind due to environmental factors. Sometimes when those factors affect your business such as ad rates falling to low or a company with a bigger audience appears with a highly competitive and similar product, you'll feel defeated and shut down the business. But when you're passionate, you'll find a way. You'll pivot, find the solution, and come up with something better.

Thirdly, team work is everything. The team is essential to your business. You are the founder, co-founder, or you might be the reigning voice, but regardless without your team it won't happen. All the strategy, visionary thinking, and hard work you're doing will turn into dust. Be a smart founder. Pick people that are amazing, who excel in areas that you fail in and they allow you to focus on the one or two tasks to make the company a success.

Finally, have fun. This is a journey that is never going to end. You found this business, so you'll experience it all: discouragement, rejection, loss, and success. You will see things in your personal life that will get you through these moments, you'll learn lessons, meet amazing people, make an impact (big or small) but, above all, you'll experience opportunities that come out of your business. You'll reach a certain point down the road and you'll go out to write a letter like this to your younger self as a reminder to have fun, be humble, and stay focused.

Sincerely,

DocuSigned by:

A. Kumra   10/3/2017

C424F4794FA0412

Ash Kumra
Consistent founder, Youngry CEO co-founder

LaCount Law

Stephen LaCount founded LaCount Law in 2005. Before founding his own boutique firm, he was affiliated with Nixon Peabody LLP, a top-50 international law firm headquartered in the Northeast.

Stephen was previously a partner (and member of the firm's Executive Committee) at Arter & Hadden LLP from 1992-2003. He attended Boston University (B.A.), New York Law School (J.D.) and New York University School of Law (LL.M. Trade Regulation).

Stephen has served as in-house counsel with many prominent multi-nationals, including Studebaker-Worthington, Inc., Westinghouse Electric Corporation and Esterline Technologies. In 1987, Stephen relocated from Connecticut to Irvine, CA to join AST Research, Inc., a Fortune 500 personal computer company. He served as General Counsel for three years before entering private practice.

Stephen's practice emphasizes domestic and international business transactions. He has helped clients with acquisition and sale of technology assets, general counseling with emerging growth companies, intellectual property protection and exploitation, technology licensing and development, software transactions, information technology contracting, outsourcing, strategic partnering arrangements, internet, e-business, privacy, data protection, antitrust, and regulatory matters involving International technology transfer.

Stephen is a member of the American Arbitration Association's National Roster of Neutrals. He has arbitrated disputes involving intellectual property rights, technology, franchise-related agreements and transactions.

Stephen has served in leadership roles for associations related to technology companies. He co-founded the High-Tech Innovation Awards, an annual Orange County technology company showcase, In may of 2007, Tech America awarded him its prestigious Community Service Award. Stephen is a nationally recognized lecturer and author on technology contracting and international trade subjects. Who's Who Legal ranked him as one of California's top Information Technology lawyers for the past 16 years.

Stephen gives back to the community by teaching. He served as the Laspa Visiting Professor of Entrepreneurship Law and Practice at Harvey Mudd College (the engineering and science school of the Claremont college consortium). Stephen teaches law-related courses at Chapman University and at California State University Fullerton's Mihaylo College of Business and Economics.

LaCount Law
Tech Transactions • Intellectual Property • International Trade

October 1, 2017

Dear Founder:

I was accused of being arrogant when I was young (and even when I was old). But it is not a desirable quality in a founder or leader. Displaying outsized confidence, or an exaggerated sense of one's own abilities, can put a target on your back and discourage veteran service providers (e.g., lawyers and accountants) from working with you. Be mindful of the 'known unknowns'. Seek out and respect the advice of wise counselors.

My representation of startup companies and their founders goes back to the early 90s and peaked in 2008 when the Great Recession tanked many of my small client relationships. I have been in law practice for over forty years, as in-house counsel with multinational corporations, partner in a national law firm, and currently, as principal of a boutique law firm. For the past five years, as an adjunct professor, I have taught the required "Legal Environment of Business" course (MGMT 246) at CSUF's Mihaylo College of Business & Economics. From 2013-2016, I also served as visiting professor at Harvey Mudd College in Claremont where I taught a course that I created ("Law and the Technology Entrepreneur"). I have learned that each new generation of founder/entrepreneurs and investors brings different approaches and expectations to the client relationship. And frequent "pivots"!

Recruit and settle on a business lawyer who you can trust and who will be dedicated to serving your (and your company's) interests. Sometimes, this attorney may be a friend, colleague, or former classmate who went on to law school and is now associated with a reputable law firm. Sometimes, he or she may be a senior attorney recommended by a business executive or other professional that you respect and hold in high esteem. One key point to remember: business law is highly specialized; no lawyer can do it all. I have yet to meet a corporate securities lawyer, for example, who can draft and negotiate international partnering or technology development agreements. Whoever you engage as 'general counsel' must be willing to steer you to (more) competent counsel, as necessary.

A final word about legal fees. Assuming that you are not engaging a trial attorney to handle a personal injury case (typically performed on a contingency percentage), most business attorneys bill their time on an hourly rate basis (but many will quote fixed fees or 'hard estimates' on routine projects). Some folks gage the quality of a lawyer based on how elevated his or her hourly billing rate is ... wow, that $1,000/hour New York lawyer must be a miracle worker! This is misguided, of course. Assessing a lawyer's value should always focus on the quality of her or his judgment, experience, efficiency, and results.

Sincerely,

Stephen H. LaCount

A Seasoned Small Business Lender

Andy Lamb has been in banking for over thirty years. He is Senior Vice President at South County Bank.

Many of Andy's years in banking have been with community banks. They include, Pacific Mercantile Bank, Sunwest Bank and South County Bank. Bank to Bank he has been a commercial loan officer financing small to mid-size businesses. He has financed clients in a wide range of industries and at various stages of the business cycle from start-up companies to mature.

Andy has also worked as a sales team manager at an import and distribution company. The company, M-S Cash Drawer, sold point-of-sale equipment domestically and internationally. During his nine years at the business, it grew from $10 million in annual sales to over $20 million. He still provides advice to the owner when asked.

For over twelve years, Andy was a mentor for California State University, Fullerton's entrepreneurship program. He served in the entrepreneurial accounting class, coaching several student consulting teams that aided small businesses. Through this program he prepared future founders for their foray into the world of commerce.

As part of his community outreach, Andy is on the boards of two nonprofit organizations. NeighborWorks of Orange County, is an affordable housing service. The Chance Theater, is a community theater based in Anaheim.

Another of Andy's service commitments is as a loan committee member for the Small Business Financial Development Corporation of Orange County. It is an agency that gives financial institutions loan guarantees backed by the State of California. The loan guarantees provide a means for banks to lend money to small businesses that would not otherwise qualify for conventional bank financing.

Andy is married with two children. He has been a resident of Orange County for over thirty-five years.

Andy at Avebury Stone Circle, UK.

(Or, Andy preventing crushing loan debt from falling on a new venture)

South County
BANK

Dear Founder,

I come to this venture not as an entrepreneur starting up my own business, but as a seasoned banker. During my 30 years in banking, I have seen numerous small businesses in various stages of evolution. So my perspective is from being a counselor who has viewed the ups and downs experienced by the business owner, not with equity at risk, but with loaning depositors' money to a business as my risk. My job requires me to be, in the worst case, 99.9% accurate in financing a business and getting the loan repaid.

I will be the first to admit that I am too cautious and risk averse to take that deep breath and jump into the unknown of starting my own business. And that leads me to a key observation – get smart and learn all you can about the industry in which you intend to compete and the associated risks, internal and external. Knowledge is a powerful tool. Being prepared will go a long way to helping you meet the challenges. You will have a better chance of achieving a successful outcome.

The successful business-owners that I have worked with surround themselves with people who will provide them with sound, candid advice. You must be prepared to ask the questions, and no question is wrong. As a banker I am often asked by clients, some with years of experience operating their own companies, for input to help them make a decision that will be best for their business. The experience I have gained from banking businesses in a variety of industries has provided me with an awareness of many scenarios that present themselves to a business-owner. While industries vary, the context of the scenario may be similar. I believe that establishing a relationship with a community banker can be a valuable asset that helps your business succeed.

Another observation is that the time and energy you put into your business will be the best investment you make. Owning and operating your business is a commitment. You will have to negotiate with yourself the balance between the time and energy that is devoted to making your business succeed versus the other commitments to yourself, family and friends. Your business can consume your life 24 hours a day, 7 days a week. There are situations when the time and energy commitment is needed, but the rewards will become apparent.

Finally, the primary reasons I have seen for a business to fail are poor cash management and lack of capital. Be sure that you have enough cash, or access to cash, to see the business through opportunities and challenges. Too little cash can mean missing an opportunity to grow the business or not having the ability to overcome an unexpected expenditure. Retaining the earnings in your business is a good investment. After paying yourself for your living necessities, rather than withdraw the profits from the business, keep the excess cash in the company and build capital. The return on your business success will be far greater in your earlier years than you can get from outside investments. Plus, you have complete control over the investment in your business.

I wish you all the success in your adventures into the business world. It can be an enormously satisfying experience. You will have an impact on the local, regional and national economy no matter the size of the business.

Sincerely,

Andy Lamb
Senior Vice President

2 Venture, Suite 120 ✑ Irvine, CA 92618 ✑ phone: (949) 766-3000 ✑ fax: (949) 766-3098

Lawler Capital

Jesse Lawler is the Founder/President of Lawler Capital Inc. and Co-Founder/ Finance Director of Maverick Real Estate. Both companies are in Orange County, California. Jesse graduated from CSUF in 2010, with a concentration in Entrepreneurship.

Jesse was unsure of what industry he wanted to pursue, but he knew three things: he wanted to be his own boss, he was interested in Real Estate, and he had an inclination for numbers. While working two low paying jobs (construction and retail: 60-70 hours per week), Jesse began taking his Real Estate course work online and prepping for the BRE licensing exam.

Jesse searched for a job in the Real Estate industry. In September of 2010 - after countless job interviews- he landed a job. He became a personal assistant for the President of a private mortgage brokerage in Laguna Hills. This was a turning point in his entrepreneurial journey.

While this job only started with a $25K annual salary plus performance bonus, Jesse viewed it as the opportunity of a lifetime. He could learn the day to day operations from a veteran entrepreneur in the Real Estate industry. Over the next two years, he learned the "in's and out's" of the business, moving up through the company ranks to Director of Finance. He oversaw the entire loan production of the company -$100 Million+ in residential loan volume per year. He also assisted in marketing campaigns, annual reporting, client relations, and social media presence. In

three years, Jesse was originating his own deals and ready to move up again.

Jesse, obtained his BRE Loan Originator license and worked for two years at a national lender. He was no longer receiving a salary plus bonus or working with leads that his boss obtained. The new job required him to generate his own leads and work on a commission only basis. However, he was closing deals in his own name and working as an Entrepreneur.

In 2015, Jesse formed Lawler Capital, Inc., a full service direct lender. With this new endeavor, the daily business operations were similar to the national lender with one major difference – Jesse was operating as Lawler Capital, Inc. This required more time and costs, but the return was worth it. Jesse is currently on track to reach $50M in loan volume in 2017.

Recently, Jesse and a business partner launched Maverick Real Estate - a Real Estate Brokerage Firm. The new venture allows Jesse to handle both the financing aspects and the real estate buying side of clients' transactions. His goal is to launch one new office per year. Lawler Capital will match the growth of Maverick Real Estate by sharing office space, marketing expenses, and other resources.

LAWLER CAPITAL
"Direct Lending Simplified"

Dear Founder,

I'll get straight to the point, here's my mantra: "Provide something of value for free and people will pay you for more." It's a little vague, but that's good! The vagueness allows it to be applied to almost all business applications (especially start-ups) and definitely my industry – Real Estate/Lending.

Every day I give clients and potential clients things for free: credit reports, advice about financing options, appraisals, and possibly the most valuable item – my time. These items are valuable because it helps my clients achieve their goal(s) of buying a home, saving money on their current mortgage, or simply being able to make a decision on what to do next. It does not always result in an immediate sale, but it creates a bond between myself and the client; it puts me in a position to be their ongoing resource for information and direction. That is powerful!

Sometimes the information I share with these clients is not always what they want to hear (i.e. "you don't qualify"). But I give them the truth, followed immediately with a game plan on how to achieve their goals. This has paid dividends for me and my business. I have clients who I've worked with for over 2 years, helping them improve their poor credit, teaching them how to save for a down payment, and so on; all the while giving them free info and my time with no immediate monetary return. Throughout the process they almost always refer me to their friends, family, and co-workers. These referrals are the life blood of my business!

There is something magical about referrals. Ex: *Jim trusts me → Jim refers Tim → Tim trusts Jim → Tim automatically trusts me.* I have literally heard these words straight from a new referral client's mouth. It's trust by association. This makes the selling process light-years easier. I guess I should have started this letter by telling you all, I don't practice "hard selling." It's not me and it never will be. I focus on being honest, straight forward, and helpful to everyone I meet. People sense this when they meet you; it's something they can hear in your voice and read on your face.

Lastly, I use a multitude of various ongoing marketing campaigns, which are rarely sales letters to strangers. My marketing efforts are via Facebook posts of business/personal successes, monthly newsletters, thank you cards to past clients, follow up calls to check-in with clients, birthday cards, and so on. You will notice that these items have one unifying theme: generating continued awareness. It reminds clients and prospective clients that, "My name is Jesse and this is what I do for a living." Case in point: Sending a client a hand written birthday card shows them you remember and care, but it also reminds them who you are and what you do. I have literally received new deals and clients by simply sending out birthday cards.

In a nut shell, I've learned that people do business with someone they know, like, and trust. My goal in everything I do is to allow people to <u>know me,</u> be friendly and helpful so they <u>like me,</u> and be honest at all times so they can <u>trust me.</u> I hope this letter will be helpful in all your business and personal endeavors! Cheers to your success!

Sincerely,

Jesse Lawler
President | Lawler Capital Inc.

Nine Lives and Still Learning

Rrandy LeSage Like most entrepreneurial and ambitious people, began paid work for others at age ten. Across the next 60 years his responsibilities and duties grew with the experiences gained. Randy went from yard clean up to enterprise president and from neighborhood endeavors to global enterprise. His employers were micro-cap firms to the FORTUNE 500. He was also self employed.

Randy recalls that, "Too late in life, a Strengths Finders 2.0 (Gallop) taught me my greatest strength - Learning. I loved to learn. Regrettably, it was also my greatest weakness. I lost interest in endeavors once I had mastered a full understanding of the driving factors in their sector. I would then desire a new experience." Randy believes such motivation caused complications for him, "Enterprises don't wish to retain those over 30 years of age who want to learn. They want only those who will teach something."

For Randy, college was not an option at the close of high school. During military service he discovered night school. During his work career, he acquired schooling after a fifty-hour work week and after 7:00 P.M..

Randy graduated from California State University with a BBA in 1983, twenty years after high school. Says he, "This was the second most important achievement of my life. The first was marrying the girl in the picture!" (His wife Kitty)

Randy's learning interest drew him into nine different occupations across a dozen different markets. Typically, he was a good wingman for an owner or executive with huge goals laid before them. Too often the smaller firms were at the brink of failure and needed guidance back from the abyss. When no one else would have him, Randy would establish his own proprietorships based on skills learned from the past.

Randy is "retired" now. He owns and operates LeSage Carpentry Arts which offers small local job repairs and re-do's to discriminating and caring customers only. Randy still very much enjoys speaking with, and encouraging, folks with entrepreneurial interests. He says, "Such occasions seem to happen monthly and it still gets my motor running! It takes me back to my many evenings as Entrepreneur in Residence in John 'JJ' Jackson's evening classes at CSUF."

Randy and Kitty LeSage,
forty-five years of partnership

LeSage *Carpentry Arts*

Dear founder,

During my career I helped recover or grow nine enterprises. How did I do it? I have organized my thoughts on this question. They boil down to a list of eight insights that work for me. I share my list with you now.

EMBRACE CHANGE. Everything around you and your enterprise will be undergoing change. Remain flexible yourself. Keep your enterprise flexible. Make strategic change when appropriate.

BE TRUE TO YOUR SELF. Keep your strategy private. Keep the reasons for your successes secret. Being proud and boastful will invite competitors to create counter-strategic actions.

KEEP RELATIONSHIPS APPROPRIATE. Betrayal and pain comes from those we care for and trust...especially employees and subordinates. Use relationships outside your business for ego and emotional support.

EMPLOYEES. Teaching a tiger to sit is much easier than teaching a snail to run. Encourage retention of those who bump into you and your rules of business. Discourage relationships with those who acquiesce to nearly anything. The former will help your business thrive, while the later will encourage the status quo.

KNOW YOUR NUMBERS. Numeric results are the life blood and heartbeat of your endeavor. Know and understand your accounting (i.e., quick ratio, retained earning, cash, and so on).

KNOW YOUR 4 P's. The names of concepts change across the decades, but the essence remains the same. Know how well your business is aligned to it's "Pricing, Place in the Market, Product Features/Acceptability, and how Promotion is deployed successfully in your venture."

BECAUSE YOU CAN, DOESN'T MEAN YOU SHOULD. Manage your resources carefully and ask yourself "Should We?" Each use of resources blocks that resource's use elsewhere.

RECOGNIZE TRUTH. Low revenue, cash flows, or profit, means your belief in your skill and/or product are flawed. Start at the top again.

Good luck with your life's pursuits,

Randy LeSage

Bolcof Plastic Materials

Jay Lieberman, his wife and brother-in-law joined Bolcof Plastic Materials (BPM) in the mid 1970s. It was a small family business. The founder was Jay's father-in-law.

Like many small business founders, Jay's father-in-law preferred to hire family in key roles when his business started to grow. He knew them well and could trust them. Even if they had limited business experience, they were family. They had a psychological stake in the business and would stick by him through everything. While this logic is sometimes more dream than reality, it worked for Jay's father-in-law. Consider Jay's resume.

Jay worked assorted part time jobs while earning his BA from San Diego State University: including a brief stint as a salesman at Bond Stores. He joined the Air Force in 1966 and had ground duty. In 1969, Jay began teaching at Anaheim Union High School District. While working at the district he earned a MA, worked in curriculum development, taught history and English, and became a high school counselor specializing in ROP. Then came his father-in-law's offer.

Jay's first job for BCM was part-time sales. Sales of a product he knew nothing about. However, he made good entrepreneurial choices. He took advantage of his teaching/counseling skill set, and he used his own version of conceptual selling to move on from there. He sold full time for BCM for ten years. In 1986 Jay became VP of sales and marketing. He was eventually responsible for the development and execution of a world wide sales and promotion program. His wife, brother-in-law and he became principals in BCM in the late 1990s. They sold BCM in 2014.

Jay has been involved in his community since the 1970's. He served in Cub/Boy Scout leadership positions for nine years. He then joined the Anaheim Hills Lions Club and the Anaheim Hills Rotary Club (AHRC). Jay served as president of the chapter in 1987. The chapter named him AHRC Rotarian of the Year in 1989. In 1996, Jay helped establish the Villa Park Rotary Club and served as its' charter president. He was awarded Paul Harris Society membership in 2002, and White Hat Society membership in 2012. Since 2014, Jay has been the assistant governor of Rotary District 5320.

At California State University, Fullerton, Jay has been a mentor and coach for entrepreneurship courses since 2008.

Jay's mantra is, "Don't take yourself seriously." He illustrates how his bio could list his early jobs, but does not.
Street Corner Sales (paperboy)
Literature Distribution (paper route)
View Enabler (self employed window washer)
Gas Station Attendant (windshield-washing specialist)

Jay Lieberman
Villa Park, Ca.

Dear Founder,

Often, I would think that if it wasn't for our suppliers and customers, my business would have been fun! Stress was the rule! This statement, I suppose, requires an explanation.

My company, (Bolcof Plastic Materials aka BPM), was actually founded by my father-in-law (who died about 20 years ago) back in the early 60's. My wife and I, along with my brother-in-law, entered the business in the mid 70's. Over the last 30 years, we brought the company from a small local distribution operation to an international organization that had yearly revenues in the $80,000,000 range. We recently sold BPM to a large, international holding group.

So, how did this all happen? Perhaps the easiest and most factual answer is both "by accident" and hard work. I was a teacher with the Anaheim Union High School District and was earning about $6,500 a year (1975 salaries). I was offered an opportunity to "sell plastic", part time. I knew absolutely nothing, at that time, about the products, however the opportunity to increase our income could not be ignored. I jumped at the chance.

Now this is the important part. I called on plastic molders in Southern California. I told them that, "I am a teacher doing this part time, and am trying to learn the trade. Would they talk to me about what they did and what they need?" The response was most gratifying. Most of the contacts took the time to teach me about plastics they used, and in the process, became supporters of my effort.

This resulted in an integral part of my success. By allowing the "molder" to become a "person of importance" and provide him the avenue to build his feeling of status, he became personally invested and supported my effort with plastic orders. I learned that allowing your customer to develop, maintain, and increase his feelings of self worth could pay off handsomely.

As time went on, I eventually "retired from teaching", and sold plastics on a full time basis. I continued to employ the philosophy that I was not a "salesman", but rather, became both a teacher, friend and a counselor. I truly felt that my role was to develop a relationship that would be beneficial for both of us. Individuals that I dealt with developed a sense of trust, and as a result, continued to "invest" in both my company and me.

The next 30 years or so provided me with an amazing variety of opportunities and challenges. I eventually assumed the role of Vice President of the company, responsible for our marketing and sales decisions and strategies. We prospered and expanded our influence, increasing our product line and customer base. Along with this came the inherent problems that I referred to at the beginning of this letter.

Our customers were both small and large molding organizations that had one basic overall objective, namely, to show a profit. Raw material was a huge, if not the largest expense and therefore, any reduction in cost was to their advantage. Likewise our suppliers (e.g. Chevron Chemical, Total Petrochemica, Phillips Petrochemical, etc.) wanted to obtain the highest price possible for their raw plastic. Thus the conflict. Since we operated in a highly competitive environment, we were constantly dealing with customers that wanted unreasonable cost concessions and suppliers that also demanded unreasonable pricing. Thus, we were under constant pressure to provide significant value beyond just that of the raw material.

This brings me to the point of this letter. As a business person, you must expect competition. If the only thing you provide a client is a lower price for your service or product, you will eventually lose to competitors. You must be able to develop the relationship and provide added value. Simply put, the added value of a product or service will eventually generate long term success and profitability.

Best Regards,

Jay Lieberman

Beatshare, Inc.

Barry Lieberman is currently President of two companies: Beatshare, Inc. and Advantage Plus Marketing Group.

Beatshare, Inc., is a 2015 start-up. It brings branded multimedia content to messaging ecosystems. The company found a way to unleash the power and potential of music within the evolving menu of messaging tools. Everyone using Beatshare is empowered to match clips from over 100 million songs to photos or videos in a way that elevates messages to a personalized art form.

Barry founded Advantage Plus Marketing Group, Inc. in 1992. It executes lead generation marketing programs for key brands (HP, Oracle, Sun, IBM, Cognos, etc.) in the Technology space.

Before establishing Advantage Plus Marketing Group, Barry was in key marketing roles at Avnet Computer and was a major account manager with Hewlett-Packard. Overall, he has 35 years experience at enabling technology organizations to scale and open new markets, become the go to industry brand, and to improve sales and customer retention by executing best in class customer care.

Over the past 9 years Barry has been in interim executive roles as a change artist to enable organizations (Western Digital, Targus, Q-See, ATEN/IOGEAR, etc.) to implement modern marketing, demand generation and customer care operations.

Barry is on the Board of Chapman University's Leatherby Center for Entrepreneurship. He mentors and guest lectures at Chapman and UCI. Barry is an active member of the Orange County Angel investor community.

At California State University Fullerton, Barry has coached and mentored students in the entrepreneurship program for over twelve years. He was an Entrepreneur in Residence in 2006-2007.

Barry continues to coach CSUF student consulting teams that serve the business community. He also is a frequent guest lecturer on campus in the areas of Go To Market , Commercialization, Demand Generation, Customer Care, Start-up development, Funding and Leadership.

Advantage ⁺⁴ Plus

MARKETING GROUP

Advantage Plus Marketing Group is a business unit of Advantage Plus Marketing Group, Inc.

Beatshare
music is the message

Dear Founder,

You have chosen to start a new venture. The path you are choosing is one where you will work harder and travel through more ups and downs than you ever have. It's a 24 hour by 7 day a week adventure. How do you thrive with that pressure and stress? Find "Fun" in everything you do. How? I found a few ways...

I chose the philosophy of "You don't know what you don't know."

"You don't know what you don't know" means I have to be humble, that I don't know everything and don't need to. That every person I meet, from the person who cleans the office, to our employees, partners, service providers, and consumers, to people on the street, all know things I don't. That knowledge helps me and the venture I am involved with to flourish and grow. By asking those people questions, listening to them and using that knowledge I get needed energy for both me and the venture. By finding interest in each person I meet, every day becomes "Fun."

It's more "Fun" to Orchestrate and lead than to "Manage," don't be the "Boss."

For me, my best days are where I can "orchestrate and lead" the actions of the venture. "Orchestrating" is not "managing", managing is not fun. I don't need nor want to be the "boss" nor the smartest person in the room. What's fun and exciting is setting the direction with the right people and watching them come back with "magic." Things I would never have thought of or making what I did think of, many, many times better. Those times are "Fun".

"Never Say Never"

If you had asked me three years ago that I would be co-leading a new venture that is in the music/entertainment industry, selling an app, begging for money (raising venture funds) and that my partner would be 35 years younger than me, I may have said, "never." Yet here I am. If you had asked me when I was 18 that over my 35-year career, I would be in sales, business development and marketing, I would have said "never." I was the kid who couldn't sell one greeting card or knock on one door for Cub Scouts to get my merit patch. Yet ten years later I was managing a major account for one of the world's leading technology companies, HP. Then four years after that I became the CEO of the first technology focused B2B Lead Generation company in the nation. Your business and career will take turns you never thought of. Please be open and "let it and yourself" take those turns. It's what makes it "Fun."

Most people don't connect "Fun" with new venture creation, yet it should be. Find "Fun" in all you do and the roller coaster ride of the business and your career will be the adventure of your life. I have and I am very grateful for it.

Yours truly,

Barry Lieberman

Entrepreneur in Residence

Travis Lindsay is an Entrepreneur in Residence at the Center for Entrepreneurship and the Startup Incubator at California State University Fullerton ("CSUF"). He is one of the founders of the CSUF Startup Incubator ("SI") and currently manages SI's Placentia location.

Through his work at CI and with CSUF Entrepreneurship students, Travis has helped dozens of entrepreneurs develop their business concepts into actionable plans.

Travis is a founding investor and one of the managing partners for the Titan Angeles LLC, a seed-stage investment fund. While unaffiliated with CSUF, the founding investors in the fund are CSUF alumni and the fund seeks to invest in startups connected to CSUF.

Travis is a California State University Fullerton Alumnus. He earned a BA from Mihaylo College of Business and Economics in 2007 with a double major in Finance and Economics. In 2009 he received his MBA in Entrepreneurship from Mihaylo.

Travis has worked as a consultant for small businesses, a researcher for Cal State Fullerton, and as the owner of a popular cigar blog. In 2011, he went to work for the Center for Entrepreneurship and was one of the founders of the CSUF Startup Incubator in 2015.

CALIFORNIA STATE UNIVERSITY, FULLERTON

Mihaylo College of Business and Economics
Center for Entrepreneurship
P.O. Box 6848,
Fullerton, CA. 92831

Dear Founder,

I am an Entrepreneur in Residence for the Center for Entrepreneurship and the CSUF Startup Incubator. I have been fortunate enough to have had a hand in the management of both, and the launch of the latter.

Having reviewed hundreds of business plans and consulted with dozens of entrepreneurs who are actively working on a startup, I have learned a couple of things that I think will help you. They are, in this particular order, the importance of people, vision, and metrics.

The Importance of People. Every startup I have worked with that went on to achieve success had good people. They worked well together, shared the same goals for the company, and were above all else passionate about what they were working on. The startups that I have seen flounder and fail usually did not have a team and if they did have a team they were at best dysfunctional. Building a powerful team is not easy, it takes time and effort to make sure that everyone is on the same page and aligned with the vision but it's worth it. It all starts with choosing the right partners and progresses on to hiring the right people and cultivating what it is that makes them excellent members of the team.

Vision. Vision is something that can be hard to articulate and, especially with first time entrepreneurs, that can materialize as a muddled statement of a problem that the entrepreneur knows to their core to be true but can't get beyond that. For me, vision is all about communicating "why" you are doing what you are doing. Your business isn't just about the perfunctory manufacturing of products or discharging of services; if that was the case your employees would quickly lose interest or, at best, perform at a suboptimal level. Maybe your business isn't inherently exciting (there aren't many that are when viewed from an outsider's perspective), but it is incumbent on you, dear founder, to communicate why your employees, partners, and customers should care.

Metrics- It is critical to have a strong team with a unified vision. During good times that will be enough, maybe. However, I have seen many businesses, from the freshest startup to the most stalwart of corporations, lose focus and falter because they do not have enough (or any) metrics. Metrics are important for companies in their totality, but you also need metrics for divisions and for the people within those divisions. Metrics have a way of focusing the mind on what is critically important and, if done right, focusing work on those tasks that provide the most long term value to the company. If something does go wrong, with metrics you can see where the problem lies; if you can't pinpoint the problem then you need to rework your metrics.

In my view, good people, leaders with a shared vision, and focused metrics are the three most important ingredients for any successful business. They will not guarantee success. There are things outside your control that can undermine your efforts. However if you give enough attention to cultivating these three components then you are going to be at least a few steps ahead of your competition. You will also have a more fulfilling entrepreneurial journey.

Best wishes,

Travis Lindsay
Entrepreneur in Residence

175

Business for Non-Business Majors

Jeff Longshaw teaches "Starting Your Own Professional Practice/Small Business."(BUAD 410) The course provides a cross disciplinary perspective on entrepreneurism for non-business majors. BUAD 410 was originally envisioned by the CSUF Health Science and Communications Deans for graduating seniors and graduate students who wanted support starting their own business. Jeff and the Mihaylo Center for Entrepreneurship Director John Bradley Jackson designed the course. The emphasis is on developing student-selected business plans that are usually team efforts. BUAD 410 is of particular interest to international students who, like the CSUF students in the class, have a wide range of backgrounds including engineering, prelaw, communications, gerontology, psychology, art and others.

BUAD 410 provides the business side of successfully going out there on your own. It is directly applicable to aspiring individuals who bring their ideas and concepts to the class for friendly advising and useful recommendations.

Jeff earned an MSBA (Entrepreneurship) from USC and an MBA from the Florida Institute of Technology (Marketing). He is a retired Navy Officer and Senior International Marketing Manager for Hughes Aircraft Company.

As he describes in his letter, Jeff founded Group L in 1993. While he has managed and participated in large scale proposals for Aerospace firms, he has also produced business plans for start-up companies. Jeff is both an entrepreneur and communications expert. He has been a part-time lecturer for CSUF's Communications Department since 2005.

Jeff holds volunteer Office Hours at the CSUF Startup Incubator. During these office hours, people who are new to entreprenership are able to talk to him about how to communicate the value in their business idea and discover the hidden gems that their idea may solve.

Since its conception, Jeff has been a donor and volunteer for the Phil Simon Clinic Tanzania Project. The project was founded by Dr, Kimberly Shriner, an infectious disease specialist at Huntington Hospital in Pasadena. It was Initially started to combat AIDS. The project has expanded to become a general medical clinic . Every year a team of doctors from Huntington Hospital run a two week clinic in Country. In 2018 the team will consist of a full surgery team and a total of 64 doctors. The project participants have trained and funded two Tanzanian doctors and the establishment of a new modern facility on land donated by the Zulu Tribe. Jeff says, "It is a source of great pride that I can be part of this organization."

176

Jeff Longshaw
Pasadena, California

Dear Founder,

I have owned my own business for twenty-five years and have three important lessons to share with you. First know that I am a business management and communication consultant. I teach proposal writing and composition and orchestrate proposal production. My work helps companies improve their win rate. This may sound as if I am a glorified paper pusher or ghost writer. However, the proposals I have managed or participated in are large scale proposals for major government contracts. I have served companies like Westinghouse, Lockheed, Bath Ironworks and General Dynamics. For each engagement I am the conductor. I must orchestrate the client's subject matter experts with my outside proposal team to hammer out winning proposals. Each proposal must be completed in a compressed 24/7 time window. Clients allot no time for doing it wrong and going back to do it again. Nor is time allotted to try to start with under skilled people and bring them up to speed. Bidding is highly competitive and the U.S. government does not accept late proposals.

Lesson one: You need to provide "on the deck" leadership for your venture. You have to be there and do it. You are the conductor. If you don't lead your composite team of stakeholders properly, you will just start badly and get worse. Get into the fray, provide leadership on the ground, move fast, and adjust quickly to changing dynamics. Evaluate your personnel's assigned roles on the fly. Make quick decisions about pulling out under performers and putting other people into those roles.

Lesson two: Ethics and reputation are your best marketing tools. I didn't market my company. People came to me. Why? They came to me year after year because they knew my reputation. They knew how ethical I was. They knew they would get a good product and it would be honest. Unethical people get caught. They are never used again. You are only as good as your reputation. The longer you are in the business and the more reputable you become, the less marketing you have to do. Things become much easier all around. For clients, it is easier because they do not have to look over your shoulder. Your reputation permeates your team. People you bring in benefit from your reputation, even if they are pretty expensive. People like to employ those they have used previously and know they can count on. Also, clients will give you the benefit of doubt. They will let you know when things are not right so you can resolve the problem yourself, not just suddenly lose your contract. Ethics and reputation, you cannot live without them.

Lesson three: I believe in the boy scouts' motto, "always leave your campsite better than you found it." I always leave my client, their proposal operation, and particularly the training of their people better than I found them. I would usually start with formal training. Next, I would go into how we were going to do it. Then, as the trainer, I went out and did it with them. The training became very specific and not academic. "This is the way it works and it works very well." You show them why it works and you go at it with them and make it work. What happens is the client team that you leave behind is stronger at proposal preparation. Hopefully you will get it the next time you come. They will just have to do a little refresher training. You have moved them up the knowledge scale so that every time you come and work with them, the proposals get better. Each time you can do even more training. Training and education were always components of my business plan. Always leaving your campsite better than you found it gets you invited back more often. Another fall out is that clients who know they will receive good value do not argue about prices. They are happy and don't bat an eye at high fees. You can only do that if they believe in what you are doing. They pay you whatever you ask and you never have to fight with them over money.

Best wishes for your success,

JS Longshaw

Jeff Longshaw

Why2Fail

Virginia Lorimor is the founder of Why2Fail. It is a consulting firm with an innovative mission.

Virginia is a serial entrepreneur. She is a thought leader, investor, entrepreneur, and change agent specializing in the hi-tech, land development, building, and retail sectors. She is a seasoned mentor for CSUF entrepreneurship students and a former incubator owner.

Virginia is a magna cum laude alumnus of the University of Southern California with a BSA. She began in Big 4 public accounting obtaining her CPA.. She quickly leaned towards strategic finance and operational aspects including strategic partnerships, buy and sell side mergers, acquisitions, joint ventures, fund accounting, IPOs, REITs and fundraising for businesses at all stages.

In 2016, Ms. Lorimor sold a group of nine companies that she had grown over the course of 10 years, known as "The WIN Companies." The companies centered around Business Acceleration Centers designed to help start up businesses bootstrap their way to success. The WIN Companies were a synergistic group of companies designed to accelerate the growth of an ecosystem of businesses, from start-ups to middle market, using a variety of financial and operational strategies.

Today, Virginia is moving forward with her latest venture, Why2Fail. Why2Fail is a consultancy that provides a series of VBlogs, Biogs, and publications on the new "F" word, failure (Visit the twitter page at @WHY2FAIL). The posts discuss how insights from prior failures can become the wisdom we grow from or, more commonly, are tossed by the wayside and become waste.

Virginia believes that failure is an opportunity. She says, "Why2Fail's consultative services focus on what many culturally see as a negative, failure, and turn it into a positive. Why2Fail examines and resolves human, system, and process errors in businesses. It helps clients create strong efficiencies in operations and increase profitability."

Further, Why2Fail stresses designing a culture where employees are encouraged (with consent) to engineer failure and push processes and boundaries. By embracing this dynamic environment, businesses retain their competitive advantage and discover new, industry-disruptive techniques and technology.

Virginia explains the mission of her new company succinctly. She says, "Why2Fail will make FAIL the new positive 'F' word."

Why2Fail

Dear Founder,

Launching a new business can and should be an exciting time in your life. It also can be isolating, overwhelming, and even scary. When launching a new venture, you invest 100% of yourself into it. All your passion, enthusiasm, energy and time tend to be diverted to the burgeoning vision that you are creating. Unfortunately, many times, I have seen founders invest 100% of their financial resources leading to their complete personal financial devastation.

So how do you create your new venture, staying invested, without destroying your health, family, and friendships – and why should you care? I recently read that you must work harder than everyone else to be successful as an entrepreneur and while I agree, you must work hard, you must also work smart. Surround yourself with a strong, well rounded, team of people that meet the needs of your venture at each of its stages. As your venture grows, so will the needs of your team. Running ideas by friends and family is a fine way to start, but bringing "gray hair" and well-rounded experienced professionals on board is imperative to the long-term success of any venture. Part two of this same concept of working smart is to take care of yourself. Get plenty of sleep, eat right, spend time with friends and family and don't isolate yourself (as many of us work from home offices), set aside time to think purposefully, and do what you need to stay at the top of your game. That is what you need to be to get to the top and make smart strategic decisions! Making decisions when you're isolated, exhausted, and overwhelmed will produce chaotic and misguided results.

When it comes to financially investing in your new venture, it is important to be invested yourself first. This should not, however, be to the complete devastation of your family! I've witnessed entrepreneurs spend every dollar they have, max out their credit cards, lose their homes, and then still lose the venture that they worked their every waking hour to create – and to what end? If your venture is going to be a success, then other people will want to get involved and it is up to you and your team to get the word out and to have other people begin funding your company. What that source of funding looks like can be very different depending on your venture and it's needs. For many ventures, grants are available. Depending on what stage you venture is in, you may be eligible for loans or micro loans. Often, ventures begin with quick funding from friends and family and online fundraising campaigns. However, the overriding goal needs to be to get revenue! One needs to revisit a venture model that doesn't produce revenue and profitability in a relatively short period (relative to the complexity of the product's development cycle).

Know that you are not alone as you walk this path. Build a solid team. Take care of yourself physically, mentally, and emotionally. Be sure to invest yourself financially in the venture before others and then trust that others will invest if your venture is viable. Know that not all ventures will be successful, but if you fall apart so will it!

Best Wishes in Your Future Endeavors,

Virginia Lorimor
Founder
Why2Fail

On-line Lifestyle Infulencer

Victor Macias is the co-founder of Male Standard (2009), founder of VM Consulting (2013), and co-founder of Keto Kookie (2016). Victor graduated with a Bachelor's degree in Business Entrepreneurship from CSUF where he co-founded MaleStandard.com.

Male Standard is a men's lifestyle website that enables men to become the best version of themselves. It has 150,000 targeted monthly visitors. Through Male Standard, Victor has collaborated with dozens of household brands including Gillette, Old Spice, Patron, Hilton, Heineken, AXE and Chevrolet. Victor is recognized as a leading men's lifestyle influencer and regularly attends press events throughout the United States and Internationally as a brand ambassador.

Victor is president of VM Consulting, an Online Marketing Agency that helps entrepreneurs and small business owners grow their business online. The firm's expertise includes: content marketing, blogging, video marketing, market research, search engine optimization, monetization techniques and website conversion.

Keto Kookie is a functional food company helping others improve their health with delicious treats. Keto Kookie shot into the spotlight with the success of its Kickstarter campaign which tripled its funding goal and rocketed low-carb, high-fat cookies into the media spotlight. Today, Keto Kookie continues to grow, selling its delicious low-carb, no sugar added cookies across the United States. The company plans international expansion in 2017.

Victor can often be found visiting coffee shops and microbreweries where he lives out his passion for the mobile lifestyle.

Victor shares his passion for entrepreneurship as a proud mentor for the Youth Entrepreneurship Program (YEP), further supporting his community-orientated, family values. Victor and his wife and children live in Orange County, California.

Dear Founder,

I'm excited to share with you hree strategies that impact my life as an entrepreneur. I hope they will impact your life also. The life of an entrepreneur is often an emotional roller coaster and at times can feel uncertain. However, with these three strategies, I'm confident you'll be better able to distinguish a path that leads you to meaningful and exciting opportunities, and grow to your full potential.

Focus on **90-day sprints**. When I was younger I would jump around from new idea to new idea. The result, I would get nowhere fast. It was shiny toy syndrome. As entrepreneurs its normal to want to run 20 projects at once. It comes from our drive and ambition to excel. However, some of the greatest entrepreneurs in history have the power of focus. Focus is what will allow you to gain traction and achieve your goals effectively. That's why I love the power of 90-day sprints. Here's what I do: Make a list of EVERY single project you're currently working on. Choose the one project that will have the greatest impact toward your goals (hint: it's usually the one that scares you the most). Next, focus on that one project for the next 90 days. Give it all your energy. If you get another great idea during the 90 days, add it to a list of future projects. At the end of 90 days, select your next 90-day focus and repeat.

Fear is the answer. Many times as entrepreneurs we say things like, "I can't start this business yet, I don't have enough money or I'll launch after I master this new skill." The truth is as entrepreneurs we procrastinate out of fear of failure. T this is normal end something that every entrepreneur faces each day. Tim Ferriss says, "what you fear is what you should most be doing." The most successful entrepreneurs I've met face fear. We all feel fear. I face it every day, but I also try to welcome it. Because thatr which you fear is often what you should most be doing. Here's how to do this. Each morning. Make a list of what scares you the most.

What you fear is the answer. What you consider a barrier, is actually an opportunity. Are you a female, are you too young, too old? Do you not have enough money? Something I've learned from entrepreneurship is that opportunity is where you look for it. What some look at as a weakness, others will look at as a strength. Are you too young? Great, that means others will want to help you more. It means that you're an inspiration for others. Are you broke? Great, that means that you're forced to be creative. The founder of Alibaba said, "being broke was the best thing we had going for us." The key takeaway is...successful people in general look for opportunities where others see pain and disadvantage.

Leverage outsourcing early. While at CSUF I was a starving student with a desire to grow my business. With little money and a full time school schedule I knew I had to get creative. So I decided to outsource help to the Phillipines and hired my first Virtual Assistant (VA). I still remember being in class and knowing that I had someone on my team working full-time on my projects. Today, our team has grown but VA's remain at the core of how I manage my time. VAs will help you leverage the skills and knowledge of an ample team. Use the internet to build a team to help you grow. Doing this will not only help you grow, but you'll learn how to delegate and manage at a young age.

Being an entrepreneur is exciting, but it can also feel intimidating and overwhelming at times. The strategies above are designed to help you cope and use what you feel as a strength. Before worrying about too many tactics, learn how to manage yourself - your emotions and your brain. Everything becomes easier after that.

Victor Macias

For in depth discussion of these topics by the author, please go to https://bit.ly/creatingnewventures

Be a Better Version of Yourself

Raj Manek, is Vice President of Vesuki Inc., based in Southern California. He has over twenty-five years experience as an executive. Raj has a rich history of bringing unique solutions to clients. He serves a varied portfolio of clients around the world, especially within sub-Saharan Africa.

Growing up in Nairobi, Kenya, Raj inculcated and refined an entrepreneurial mind set. He required it to both navigate and succeed in his environment. It is fraught with unique challenges steeped in long-held traditions, language barriers and a culture unique to Africa. Raj is fluent in Swahili and other local dialects. He continues to travel to East Africa several times a year to manage his investments. He provides cutting edge solutions to the aviation and other sectors that he has vested interests in. These include export, retail and wholesale of consumer goods, real-estate (commercial, residential, mixed use), consumer products marketing and distribution, and franchising.

Raj earned a BS Degree in Management, with an emphasis in Entrepreneurship from California State University, Fullerton. He changed his major three times. Say's Raj, "I felt boxed in when having to declare a major with a singular discipline." He recalls the cross disciplinary entrepreneurship emphasis was like hand in glove. "I loved it. This holistic approach is what business schools should teach every student. Students are prepared to handle business *life* after school, not just a career."

Raj is the recipient of several awards for his academic achievements including two

Raj at a giraffe sanctuary in Nairobi, Kenya. He is neck-and-neck with a Rothschild giraffe, an endangered species.

from the Small Business Administration. He also earned an Executive MBA degree from the UCLA Anderson School of Management.

Raj is active in Toastmasters International. He does charity work in eastern Africa with organizations like Rotary International. He is a founding investor in Titan Angels.

At CSUF, Raj is a founding Advisory Board member for the Center for Entrepreneurship. He calls the Center nothing less than "a guiding angel to assist and nurture ideas into viable businesses that are the very future of America. Being a part of a group who wish for future business-school graduates to be more savvy and bold, armed with the knowledge and tools that will assure their success is very important to me. Entrepreneurship is a common thread that touches every Cal State Fullerton student."

Raj Manek
Brea, California

Dear Founder,

As you shape your new venture, I hope to give you guidance about how to succeed. I write from my perspective as an immigrant to this great country. I am a grateful member of a family of entrepreneurs. My branch of the family came from humble beginnings. During my lifetime we have journeyed forward from these circumstances to launch and build many enterprises. In my view, success is the realization or fulfillment of one's talents and potentialities. I strive for success every day. I know I must make success happen for myself. I also know I cannot do so without help. My guidance for you is, (1) don't forget your roots, (2) be bold, have courage and explore and (3) work with people that elevate your game.

Don't forget your roots. Wherever you come from, your journey necessarily describes who you are. Your roots weave your identity, your origins and your traditions together like a fine fabric. Appreciate your fabric for what it does. You stand on the shoulders of those in your past. Don't get caught up in trying to reinvent yourself. Appreciate that who you are today is actually very good. What you should do is develop a better version of your current self. If you stay grounded in who you are, and are humble, you can constantly improve. If you take a big urgent leap to reinvent yourself, you will often trip and fall, forget who you really are and become disheartened. Skipping glamorous big leaps in favor of a series of small steps is OK. Choose small steps that will surely get you to the point where you need be.

Be bold, have courage and explore. Explore new subjects, new ventures, new places and new ideas. It is easy to become stuck. We are conditioned to become experts in a niche and we start to feel at home. We feel comfortable, and we miss the opportunities that are just outside that comfort zone. School is necessarily a discomfort because you are learning. The key is that when you graduate, when you are out there, learning has to continue. It HAS to. It has to be an ongoing process. It has to become part and parcel of your daily routine. A regular exploration of what is out there intellectually and spiritually feeds the soul. It also connects the dots and reveals business opportunities that would otherwise go unnoticed.

Work with people that elevate your game. When you give birth to a venture, figuring out how to make it work is fun. If things go well, you will reach the point where what was exciting to set up becomes a profitable routine. At that point you need to evolve. You need to hire good people and coach them on how to handle the minutia that you have been so accustomed to doing yourself. You need to trust them to make the business work and give you the space to evolve into a visionary leader. Their good work will give you time to breathe and absorb what's happening in the distant horizon and around you. The key is that once you have mastered the things that you really do well, delegate it out. In your office keep really good company. They will feed you and you will feed them. If you hire smart, dedicated, people that are self initiated, willing learners, then they will take on the mundane and report to you. Elevate yourself to a position where you have time to think. Take the time to see the horizon in the distance. New beginnings will inevitably present themselves. Think critically about what is coming. Invest your time in order to take your ventures to the next level.

I wish you success,

[signature]

Raj Manek '94

Fifty Years in Sales and Marketing

Alan Mannason is a WWII Army veteran. He began his business career in 1946. He took a job as an office boy with Schenley Distillers in Los Angeles, CA. Within a few months, he began working as a liquor salesman with the R. E. Spriggs Company. Alan called on bars in Hollywood during evening hours. In 1948, he became a Territory Salesman for Simon Levi Company, the top liquor distributor in Southern California.

In 1959, Alan bought a liquor store in Canoga Park, CA. At that time, it was an equestrian area and customers arrived on horseback! In 1962, he went to work for Fontana-Hollywood Company selling Italian wines in Southern California. He found success in selling to Italian restaurants and delicatessens. Additionally, he had a line of French wines. The company sent him to Italy and France in 1963 to meet the suppliers of the wines he represented.

In 1965, Bohemian Distributing Company offered Alan the position of Branch Manager. He won a trip to the Carribean that year in recognition of his success. In 1967, he went to work for Paterno Imports as a Western Division VP. There he sold sparkling wines and also Veronese wines and vermouth. His territory now expanded to 11 western states. By 1967, his position included marketing. He found success traveling to Italy and began suggesting marketing strategies to suppliers while searching for new brands. In 1968, the Italian Trade Commission awarded Alan the Bacchus de Oro for the amount of Italian wine brought into California. In 1978, Heublein bought Paterno. Schieffelin Imports offered Alan a position as Central Division Manager in Chicago, IL. There he was the VP and General Manager for Pacific Wine (a division of Paterno Imports). In 1983, Gaetano Cordials offered Alan a position as Vice President and National Sales Manager. He enjoyed traveling throughout the USA as their representative.

Alan's motto is, "Common sense is not so common." Alan always made his business decisions using common sense and this is what he continues to advise students and people in business. At age 93, he still sends daily marketing and sales information to people in the industry.

After retirement, Alan served as a SCORE volunteer for fifteen years. He served fourteen years as a mentor for CSUF Entrepreneurship's classes becoming the longest serving mentor in John Jackson's Entrepreneurial Marketing class.

Alan has sponsored fifty college scholarships. Recipients include students at CSUF, UCSD and the Ventura School of Nursing.

Alan A. Mannason
Former Vice President Sales and Marketing for Paterno Imports
Irvine, California

Dear Founder,

You are starting a new business. Marketing and sales remain the same whether you sell wine, canned vegetables or luxury cars. I will use marketing a new line of wine as an example. Say you represent suppliers selling to wholesalers and chain stores. Your business represents many brands and items. This is called "brokerage."

First: the bottle should have eye appeal, so attractive, creative labeling is very important. There should be point-of-sale material (supplied by manufacturer) during presentation. Second: salespeople should have a brochure with photos depicting what foods the wine is best paired with. Third: attractive floor display materials (ie shelf talkers placed on each bottle). There should be advertising allowances offered to merchants that will suggest pricing at wholesale and retail levels.

The product must be priced so both wholesalers and retail merchants can make a good profit. Price point does not have to be the least expensive possible. Items must be priced so there is room for designated sale days. Coupons are also an incentive that the manufacturer underwrites.

Another step is to sell to restaurants. I suggest targeting medium to high end establishments. Some will be open to using menu clip-ons. Choose restaurants wisely (examples: promote red wines at Italian restaurants and white wines at French restaurants). When making a presentation to your sales force, be prepared to display all point of sale materials in addition to suggesting where your product is most suited.

Taste testing is paramount! The three most important areas are eye appeal, aroma and taste. Don't use competitive brands to prove your point. They could be preferred.

Allow your pricing (supplier to wholesaler) to account for bonuses for salespeople for placements and total case sales. Your product knowledge and presentation of appropriate materials that will assist individual salespeople are critical points in the success of sales.

Remember that marketing and sales remain the same whether you sell wine, or any other product through distribution channels. **You represent your product.** The manner in which you present and conduct yourself will always be critical factors in your success.

All the best,

Alan A. Mannason

Alan A. Mannason

MyMetalBusinessCard.com

Craig Martyn, CSUF class of 2010, is a serial entrepreneur. He founded his first business in 2000 at age 15. Since then he has founded three more.

Since age five, Craig has been passionate about railroading and the associated modeling hobby. While attending High School, Craig started his first business – BLMA (Best Looking Models Around). The company started producing small, detail parts for locomotives that Craig hand-bent from scrap wire. Subsequently, while attending CSUF, he took classes in Mechanical Drafting and Design. Soon, he introduced machine-formed wire and injection-molded plastic parts to the BLMA catalog.

By 2015, BLMA was a leading quality manufacture of HO, N and Z Scale model train products. The company produced everything from detail parts, scenery accessories and freight cars. Its product videos were seen by millions on YouTube. The business, now had hundreds of products, thousands of dealers, dozens of distributors and regular, 20-foot container loads of deliveries from factories in China. In late 2015, Craig sold BLMA to a leading competitor. Craig continues as a paid consultant to the purchasing company.

In 2011, Craig launched MyMetalBusinessCard.com (MMBC). Over the last six years, he made MMBC into the world-leading provider of metal business cards, metal membership cards, metal VIP passes, metal invitations and much more. Recently, Craig launched two additional websites: MyPlasticBusinessCard.com and MyWoodBusinessCard.com.

Craig has been active in the entrepreneurship community. He competed in the Global Student Entrepreneurs Award – a competition of 1,500+ student business owners. He made it to the Global Finals two years in a row. After competing, Craig was one of 12 student entrepreneurs selected to represent the USA at that year's Young Entrepreneurs Summit. (Part of the G20 Summit in Nice, France.)

Craig is a member of the Entrepreneurs Organization (EO) in the Orange County chapter where he has served on the board as Communications Chair. (EO is a global organization with 160+ chapters and 12,000+ members, with an average revenue of $4.7M each.)

At CSUF, Craig has been a frequent guest lecturer in two classes: Mass Communication in Modern Society (COMM 233) and Advanced Business Communication (BUAD 301). He is a mentor for CSUF Entrepreneurship and coaches up-and-coming student entrepreneurs. Craig helps them create businesses from the ground-up, including all of the necessary planning, structure, and so on. Over one semester, the students watch their business go from concept to launch-ready.

Currently, Craig and his wife reside in Fullerton, California with their labradoodle.

Metal BusinessCard.com

Dear founder,

Here are the most important things I've learned in my 16 years as an entrepreneur. Hope you enjoy.

1. THIRST FOR LEARNING: It's said that experience is the best teacher. I have NO doubt this is true. To that end, I continually seek information from people who have walked the walk – don't reinvent the wheel on your own! Yes, you need a healthy ego to start a business, but you must keep that in check to realize you don't know everything. Learn from leaders and innovators; soak up their experiences in any way possible, and at any time possible. You don't need to remember every bullet point, just the general ideas to help shape your ideology. Finally, find your PASSION here – it will push you through long nights and keep you excited when business struggles would bring any ordinary person down. Four things I have learned: CONNECT: Join organizations or clubs to connect with other business owners who will inspire and mentor you. READ: Don't like to read a book? Try listening to books on a service like Audible. DO IT: Sometimes YOU need to dive into things and just figure them out. BEG FOR IT: Many people in this world can't take constructive criticism; don't be one of them.

2. WATCH YOUR MONEY: Don't get caught without cash because you blew it on trivial things or became a victim of your own success. Four things I've learned: MARGIN: You will NEVER make up a bad margin with quantity. Make sure your margins are solid; the bigger gross profit, the more fluid everything will become. Don't sell yourself or product short and make no apology for charging what you must to make ends meet, and make money. LOANS: Make loan terms work for you. Interest rate too high? Negotiate! Or, find another lender that will work with your terms. EQUITY: I have owned both of my businesses outright. A partner could be great, but could be detrimental as well. Remember, equity is cheap now, but expensive later. ACCOUNTING: Make sure you have a good bookkeeper and CPA. These people should advise you when they see problems in your business.

3. DELEGATION & ACCOUNTABILITY: You can't do it all on your own, and there are people out there who can do each task better than you. Find them. Hire people who are naturally motivated and dedicated to their work. Four things I have learned: DELEGATE: Understand your strengths AND the fact you can't do it all. Trust others to complete tasks when assistance is beneficial. Set up the proper systems and you'll be pleasantly surprised. INSPECT WHAT YOU EXPECT: Your job is to delegate and then inspect the work. Analyze the work, the process, and look for ways to lead each individual toward better work. REACH OUT: Need quick work done on an Excel file, or new blogs written for your website? Look to websites like www.upwork.com to connect with experts in many fields. You don't necessarily HAVE to do it all in-house with the employees you have. Keep costs low and keep things simple. SYSTEMS & PROCESS: Lastly, but definitely not least, create systems and provide checklists to check different parts of a process. Love or hate McDonald's, that company has systems down so well, you can bet the taste of a cheeseburger in California will taste the same in China (believe me, I've done it). Think about that. Systems allow for scale.

Best regards,

Craig Martyn

Craig Martyn

For in depth discussion of these topics by the author, please go to https://bit.ly/creatingnewventures

187

Piano With Jonny

Jonny May is a co-founder of PianoWithJonny.com,(PWJ) a piano instructional website. The site, launched in 2013, offers piano tutorials, sheet music and a piano community for students. Jonny's YouTube performances have reached over 17 million views and 105,000 subscribers to date. With the PWJ membership, students pay monthly and get streaming access to PWJ's entire catalogue of content.

PWJ's cofounder is Jonny's brother-in-law Yannick Lambrecht who edits and produces videos, manages the PWJ website, and works to keep customers happy. Yannick sings professionally throughout California and has taught voice and piano classes. The two co-founders bring extensive musical knowledge to PWJ, with over 25 years of collective teaching experience.

PWJ 's piano tutorials flip traditional "piano lesson" ideas on their head. With a light-up keyboard and an overhead angle of Jonny's hands, students can learn their favorite songs even if they can't read sheet music. Students learn "guitar hero style" wherethe notes fall down onto the keys, and PWJ offers high-quality downloadable and streaming sheet music.

Jonny is a world class pianist. He was the youngest pianist hired by Disneyland at age 18. He entertained guests as the Ragtime Pianist on Main Street and various entertainment groups.

Jonny has played piano at Universal Studios, The Kennedy Center in Washington D.C., on Comedy Central, and with artists such as Grammy Winner Lari White, Tony Winner Lin Manuel Miranda, actor/comedian Tom Wilson, and the band Postmodern Jukebox.

As of May 2017, Jonny is a Summa Cum Laude honors graduate from California State University Fullerton. He earned his Bachelor's Degree in Business Administration with a Concentration in Entrepreneurship.

The PWJ team was awarded a scholarship to be residents in the CSUF Incubator (December 2016-May 2017). In March 2017, PWJ placed in the top five in the country for the Global Student Entrepreneur Awards. PWJ was also the 1st Place Winner in CSUF's Business Plan Competition in April 2017.

Jonny loves spending time with his family, volunteering at his church, and snowboarding. He is happily married to his lovely wife and biggest fan, Crystal May.

Dear Founder,

My name is Jonny May and I am an artist and entrepreneur. I say that with pride, but it took me many years to accept this dual identity. You see, I always felt like I had to choose between my two loves: creating music and being an entrepreneur. They felt incompatible — how could I create and share my music with millions across the world and also build a multi-million-dollar company? The decision felt paralyzing because I didn't want to give up one ambition for the other. Then, something struck me one day. I was playing piano professionally at Disneyland, and I realized that Walt Disney, one of the greatest entrepreneurs of the 20th century, was also an artist. But his art wasn't just a hobby — no, he actually built his empire on his artistic creations: Mickey Mouse, Minnie Mouse, and the gang of Disney characters. It was at this moment that I realized that I could build my own business on my love for music, and several years later, I now have a thriving online music education business and a huge artistic presence on YouTube. The more my business grows, the more my artistic reach grows, and vice versa. It is a beautiful symbiosis.

I share this with you because I want to dispel a myth that I believed for many years — that I must choose between an artistic career and an entrepreneurial one. Even after Disney built The Walt Disney Company into a multi-million-dollar enterprise, he was still involved artistically with the business, helping create characters, craft stories, and collaborate on the music in nearly every film. He created a perfect synergy of his loves: the more successful his artistic creations were, the more successful his business was, and vice versa. It was a beautiful symbiosis.

Every human being on the planet is an artist in some way — they receive joy in creating something, whether it is music, fashion, cooking, or architecture. But many entrepreneurs with an artistic bent are told to "do their art on the side". The truth is that you don't have to give up your artistic passions to be an entrepreneur, and you don't have to give up your entrepreneurial dreams to be a creative — you can have both. The trick is designing a system whereby your creativity fuels your business, and your business fuels creative freedom. Before I started my business, I thought I was pretty fortunate to make a living as a musician, but I had little time to create and little say in what I created. Now, my business gives me more time to create and more creative control. Sound too good to be true? Not at all.

Now, I'm not saying that if you love making bracelets, you should start a jewelry business — oftentimes, business owners who make their art their business end up with less creative time and freedom. What I am saying is that you can integrate these seemingly opposed loves in a novel way such that growth of one perpetuates growth of the other, and you end up with a business that gives you more artistic license — not less. If you are searching for your next business idea, consider not only doing what you love, but also designing your business such that it produces more artistic freedom. It is in this symbiosis that I have found ultimate fulfillment as an artist and entrepreneur, and I believe it is possible for anyone.

Artist or entrepreneur? I say both. Now go out and find your beautiful symbiosis.

Jonny May
Founder, Y &J Music
PianoWithJonny .com

Capital Partners Worldwide, Inc.

David McConnell is a founding partner of Capital Partners World Wide, Inc. (CPW). He serves as a CPW Managing Director. The firm is a U.S. based multi-sector business advisory firm. It consults with clients who seek capital for projects or ventures. They raise funds from private sources. Amounts range from $1 million to greater than $100 million USD.

CPW has confidential sources of funding for projects for growing businesses, concentrating on 1.) Medical and Pharmaceutical, 2.) Energy, 3.) Communications and Media and 4.) Information Technology and Emerging Technologies. CPW brings a worldwide network of established contacts and proven business performance to the evaluation and preparation of its client's candidate's Capital Campaign. Through our affiliated partnerships, CPW can prepare a client for IPO.

David worked at Rockwell International during NASA/Apollo manned lunar missions.

He has performed functions in Sales, Marketing, Development and Operations, and also private Medical Consulting in the medical technology sector for over 25 years. He has arranged sales and installation of hundreds medical technology products worldwide.

David was National Sales Manager for TomoTherapy, Inc., an Image Guided Radiation Therapy system for Oncology. He was a founder of Apollo Cancer Centers of America, Inc. It is physician owned. Its centers are freestanding. They specialize in high technology radiation oncology treatment.

David has access to developers of new technology in biosciences, electronics, computer software, and communications. He has knowledge of startup businesses and has consulted for companies such as G.E. HealthCare.

David has a MS in Physics from CSU Los Angeles. He is fluent in Chinese, Mandarin, English, French, and Russian. He has conversational command of Spanish.

At California State University Fullerton, David has mentored for CSUF Entrepreneurship. He also has served as an investment panelist.

Capital Partners Worldwide, Inc.
www.dlmcpw.com

Dear founder,

Many founders know they will need a successful capital raise to fund their new venture. However, they lack understanding of what the "money people" use to measure the venture's chances of success. I am one of the "money people." Below, I share with you four salient points that I first presented to Tech Coast Angels in 2013. These points hold true today. How do you measure up? What will you do to improve your chances?

- 1) **RESPONSIBILITY** FOR RAISING CAPITAL

One person shall be responsible for the Capital Raise and that is the CEO. This is usually a fulltime job. The Founder cannot usually remain CEO and get the job done.

- 2) **COST** TO RAISE CAPITAL

It should not be expected that raising capital will have only "success" fees that you pay after your new capital is deposited in your bank account. A Budget needs to be set for your Capital Raise.

- 3) IDENTIFY A STRONG OPERATIONAL **TEAM**

It must be clear who is hired and what important positions are yet to be filled. Do not name "phantom" team members who are working elsewhere now. The team's job is to work together on the execution phase of the Business Plan. As seen by funding sources, advisors and board members do not have as much importance as your operational team.

- 4) **VALUATION** MUST MAKE SENSE

Use commonly accepted multipliers of earnings or EBITDA or **justify with rational thoughts.**

Regards,

David L. McConnell, M.S.

Multiple Careers Spanning 50 Years

Don McCrea considers himself fortunate to have had at least twelve different careers over a five decade span. His latest venture is Your Business Legacy. Its mission is to ensure successful transitions and lasting legacies for family businesses.

Don received an AB in Mathematics from Humboldt State University, and a MS from the University of Michigan. After college he worked for the National Security Agency as a computer systems programmer and systems designer. At other major companies, Don initially did the same type of work. He then moved into systems development management, overseeing planning, design and implementation.

Don pivoted into product management at NCR Corporation. He soon realized that he knew professional staff and budget management, but needed business knowledge. To fill this gap, he entered the EMBA program at the Peter Drucker School at Claremont Graduate University.

During eight years at Digital Equipment Corporation, Don managed district and regional marketing units. He implemented three internal startups in his region and oversaw a countrywide sales support effort for one of these startups. He realized that teaching and consulting were his passion. He transferred from his EMBA program into the Drucker School's PhD program. He moved to a five-year teaching career with Pepperdine University's Graduate School of Business. Don then managed the Drucker School's graduate degree programs, rebuilt and grew UC Irvine's Executive Education Division. Next, he led UCLA Anderson School's custom executive education program and clients, and the Anderson School's corporate director's program, guiding this program from regional to national prominence over five-years.

All along, Don gave back to his industry, consulted with small businesses and guided nonprofit programs for founders. His pioneering efforts resulted in his election to the board of directors for UNICON, the premier executive education industry trade association. Don consulted with small and mid-size businesses on their sales and marketing strategies, plans, and programs. He served as vice chair of the Orange County Workforce Investment Board, guiding the WIB's strategies and research efforts. He joined the advisory boards for two of the SBA's Small Business Development Centers in Orange County. At CSUF, Don served for three years as mentor for student project teams in the Entrepreneurship Program.

Recently, Don moved to the San Francisco Bay Area to be with family and grandchildren. He contracted with UC Berkeley's College of Engineering for a short period of time to develop a portfolioof engineering executive education programs. Then he founded Your Business Legacy, his current company.

Your Business Legacy

Dear Founder,

There are four significant principles that have emerged over the span of my life and career. These are:

1. Follow your passion.
2. Follow your heart—take guidance from your higher wisdom, not just your mind.
3. Create significant value wherever you find yourself.
4. Help others succeed, be they employees, students you mentor, colleagues, or any others you encounter.

Follow Your Passion

When you are passionate about what you are creating or participating in, it will never seem like work. You will wake up every morning and be able "to play!" Your passion also comes from a much deeper place than what you think about. It opens you to all of your creative aspects, including those you may not be aware of.

I've had the good fortune to follow multiple passions throughout my career, and this has resulted in a profound sense of fulfillment many times over.

Follow Your Heart

When you create and act from your heart, you are drawing upon a higher wisdom that encompasses a far greater perspective than you are able to perceive with only your mind. Your vision, mission, purpose, and actions take into consideration all those affected by your company, its products and services, and its inputs and resources.

I had the very good fortune to have been taught directly by Peter Drucker while he was still teaching. One of the many things that has remained with me from Peter is his observation that "The purpose of a company is to create customers. Profits are the measure of how well you do so." Peter meant "customer" in the very broadest sense of that word.

Create Significant Value

Wherever you find yourself, have an attitude of "How can I create value in this situation?" This is especially important for your customers, but it also important for your employees, your suppliers, the environment, and your "purpose-driven business ecosystem." If you can't create true value for your customers, reconsider what you are offering them.

One of my greatest builders of customer loyalty has been when I referred a potential customer to a competitor who could solve their current problem when I didn't have a specific solution that fulfilled their need at that time. It almost always resulted in them returning when they had another need that I could fulfill.

Help Others Succeed

As a business leader, you are charged with creating success—not only a successful company, but success for your employees, your investors, your suppliers, and all your stakeholders broadly defined. It may be in the volunteer work that you do, and certainly as a parent.

You do not need to take credit for the success of your company or your efforts. Be willing to give that credit to all those who supported you—in the broadest sense—in that success.

I wish you the most outstanding success in your business, in your career(s), and in your life!

Warmly,

Don McCrea

SCORE Volunteer

John "Jack" McSunas is a seasoned SCORE volunteer. It was CSUF Entrepreneurship's good fortune that Jack joined SCORE as CSUF launched the Entrepreneurship concentration. He has participated in many programs for CSUF Entrepreneurship.

During his business career, Jack bought or sold 13 companies or business units. He started four businesses from scratch. Jack attended Northwestern University on a U.S. Navy scholarship. He spent three years on active duty as a Navy Officer before starting his business life with the S.C. Johnson company. There in ten years he held Sales, Marketing and General Management positions including V.P. & Director General of their Mexican Subsidiary.

Jack managed Latin America and Corporate Marketing for a writing instrument company. Later, he was Vice President of International Sales for Dunham and Smith Agencies. The company sold to U.S. Military commissaries, clubs and exchanges in twenty-nine countries during the Vietnam War.

Following that, Jack began his thirty-year entrepreneurial life as a management consultant, taking line assignments in companies during periods of critical change. Consulting assignments included liquidation of the Indian Motorcycle Company for Bankers Trust, establishing a moped company to distribute throughout the US with the Indian name.

One career highlight for Jack was the management of a company without funds for a bank group. The group had loans outstanding to a company producing animal feed ingredients. It processed agricultural waste in the U.S., Brazil & Argentina and sold ingredients in Europe and Japan. Within five years under Jack's management he made all parties whole.

At the same time, Jack bought civilian sales and distribution companies in Hawaii, Alaska, Puerto Rico, Guam and Thailand. He expanded those businesses to include representing the sales of American manufacturers in the free trade zone of Mexico.

Since he joined SCORE fifteen years ago, Jack has mentored close to 2,000 clients. He has managed Membership and Counseling for SCORE Chapter 114. Jack was involved in the Business Plan Competition at U C Irvine. He developed "Business Plan Express" to help participating teams write their Business Plans. Jack has worked on a program to assist the Marines at Camp Pendleton in their transition to entrepreneurial lives. He also brought SCORE members together to form CEO Forums and has facilitated forum groups over the past nine years. Jack states, "My greatest reward is seeing my clients succeed."

Dear Founder:

What is the secret to success in founding your own business? Everyone would like to know that answer, if there is one. Personally, I have come to the conclusion that success comes from the sum total of all the little things that go into who you are and how you look at the world around you. You start out as a privileged group with a college degree. I know how hard that may have been, maintaining scholarships and working part time jobs, but now you are there. Where do you go?

Listen and learn. Pay attention to that which is presented to you by the world about you. Watch and observe the things that work and those that do not. Try never to make the same mistake twice.

Respect the people around you, your family, friends, co-workers, customers and those to whom you report. Respect what they have to say and learn from what you hear.

Work harder than those around you. Be a little bit earlier than others, stay a little bit later.

Try to make life fun. Whether at work or play try to enjoy what you are doing. You will not be very good at something you don't like to do. The hardest thing that you will encounter is to manage your impatience. For successful founders, nothing will ever happen fast enough to satisfy you. Accept that fact and learn to live with it and keep your impatience under control.

There are no secrets, just hard work and perseverance.

Sincerely,

Jack McSunas

Jack McSunas

Stretch Out of Your Comfort Zone

Charlesetta Medina is the Small Business Specialist and an Entrepreneur in Residence for CSUF Entrepreneurship's Small Business Institute. She Implements the Institute's strategic marketing plans. Charlesetta recruits small business owners and matches them with business classes that offer affordable student consulting. Charlesetta assesses each owner's situation and, based on their needs matches them with business classes that offer appropriate, affordable student consulting. Class topics include, operations, accounting, finance, marketing, leadership and strategy.

With Charlesetta's expert assistance, CSUF Entrepreneurship's student consulting program consistently recruits 100+ businesses each year. It greatly benefits both the businesses and the students. Since 2010, Charlesetta has served over 1,000 small business clients.

Charlesetta is a 2010 Alumna of Mihaylo College of Business and Economics. Her concentration was Entrepreneurship. She understands the student consulting experience from the students' point of view.

She dedicates many hours to mentor and support student consulting teams from initial client meeting to final client presentation. Charlesetta's mission is, "to be a resource to help advance and develop the local small business community while positively influencing and mentoring CSUF business students."

Since 2003, Charlesetta has had her own direct sales business representing one of the top five global skin care brands. She enjoys offering her services to a growing customer base and is always excited to find new ideas and strategies to generate increased business.

In 2017, Connected Women of Influence awarded Charlesetta the Women of Influence award. It recognizes an active member who exemplifies the characteristics, behavior and attributes of a woman of influence. Charlesetta continues to find ways to stretch out of her comfort zone. In 2018 she will serve at the Host for the Orange County Women of Influence Awards.

When asked, Charlesetta will tell you, "I was an average student with a strong desire for being a positive example to my three AMAZING, now adult children. Through my professional development in the direct sales space and CSUF's Entrepreneurship's student consulting, New Venture Creation, and New Venture Launch projects, I identified my key strengths. Those strengths led me into being a resource for and connector of businesses and people. Building a strong professional network is about your ability to build an impactful relationship. Whether on the giving or receiving side, how you show up in that relationship will determine the relationship's longevity and impact. I believe that, armed with a CSUF Mihaylo College of Business degree and a clear understanding of self, our graduates are truly Ready to Work and Ready to Lead."

CALIFORNIA STATE UNIVERSITY, FULLERTON

Mihaylo College of Business and Economics
Small Business Institute/ Center for Entrepreneurship
P.O. Box 6848, Fullerton, CA. 92831-6848 / T 657-278-8243 / F 657-278-7858

Dear Founder,

It appears that you have that entrepreneurial spirit in you! That thing that gives you the ability to turn an obstacle into an opportunity, that fearlessness that has you willing to leap before you see the completed path. Welcome!

Growing up in Oakland, CA I wasn't surrounded by folks that called themselves Entrepreneurs, or so I thought! It turns out I was surrounded by individuals who were passionate about their craft be it making clothing, creating expressions of art, doing hair, you name it! Today, we call it a side hustle. Unexpectedly, my side hustle became a passion.

Over the past 14 years of building my own business and earning my business degree, I learned that I would face obstacles that would make my knees knock and teeth chatter out of fear or frustration. Eventually, I would realize that I had a decision to make on how I would respond in the face of these challenges...real or perceived. You too will face many obstacles on your journey.

A lesson that has served me well came from a mentor who shared with me that there is no growth in your comfort zone. I had to learn how to embrace being uncomfortable. This was a lesson that I had to reteach myself from my much earlier athletic days of competing in track and field. What I found was that in being willing to be uncomfortable, I developed the confidence in myself to find solutions, support, and strategies to keep moving forward. Frankly, that's how I began working in the Center for Entrepreneurship. I said "YES" to an opportunity that became my New Venture project.

My Second lesson was about being ALL IN. What I mean by that, is that there is no plan B. So when I was faced with the obstacle of being academically disqualified (statistics was my kryptonite), I could have just given up. However, failure was not an option. Entrepreneurs learn how to find a way or make a way and I did! I'll save that story for another day. Be ALL IN on your journey and surround yourself with others who have the same mentality. Remember, iron sharpens iron.

The last lesson I want to share from my entrepreneurial journey is to find ways to be of service to others. Whether you are one of the hundreds of CSUF Business Students, Small Business Institute clients, or amazing professionals in my network, my goal continues to be to find ways I can be of service. As you find ways to be of service to others you will be surprised at the professional growth you will experience in the process.

Be encouraged to discover your own lessons as you continue on your entrepreneurial journey. I'll leave you with one of my favorite quotations. "It always seems impossible until it's done." – Nelson Mandela

Passion & Belief,

Charlesetta Y. Medina

One Realty Group

Sue Mehta is the CEO and Broker for One Realty Group and Veritas Escrow in Brea, California.

At the age of 17, fresh out of high school, Sue got her start in the real estate industry. She became a loan processor for a local mortgage company. After learning the ins and outs of residential mortgages Sue went to work for a large nationwide lender as an Account Executive. Four years later, after training in all areas of residential mortgage lending, Sue decided to leave mortgages and enter residential real estate.

Shortly after the infamous Real Estate Market Crash of 2007/2008 Sue did not leave real rstate as many of her colleagues had. She joined forces with four other partners and started Real Estate Xperts Inc., a local real estate firm based out of Fullerton, CA. The company was focused on helping homeowners avoid foreclosure and Sue started specializing in short sales. When the market began to recover, Real Estate Xperts started to grow and move out of short sales and into mainstream residential real estate.

Sue sold out her shares in the company in 2014 and started One Realty Group. Sue's experience drove the business model for One Realty. With over 17 years in the industry, Sue had the privilege of being exposed to key aspects within the real estate umbrella. It was that knowledge that fueled her in her pursuit of creating a firm built on high ethical standards and good practices.

One Realty Group Started in 2014 and in 2017 grew with the addition of Veritas Escrow. In Sue's view, client management and customer service have declined over the years in real estate. Too many brokers and agents are commission driven and unfortunately, consumers suffer. She did not model One Realty Group to be a large firm. Sue designed it to be a small boutique firm focusing primarily on client care and service.

Sue believes that both knowledge and integrity are essential when providing a service to the community. Understanding the fundamental aspects of a real estate transaction are essential for running a real estate firm. Only then can it provide the highest quality of service to its clientele. Integrity is essential. Self-serving choices are not acceptable when it comes to interpretation of the many aspects of Real Estate ethics and law.

Sue graduated in 2003 from CSUF, as a member of the founding class of the concentration in Entrepreneurship. She serves as a Mentor for CSUF entrepreneurship. She is a Southern California native who runs her business and lives in Orange County. In 2014 Sue started a foundation that puts on local athletic events to help in raising funds for animal cancer research.

ONE
REALTY
GROUP

Dear Founders,

When I started in the work force I was under the impression that corporate life was the life for me. A steady paycheck, benefits, and a five-day workweek sounded blissful. However, working for someone else was not what I had imagined. I had too many ideas and opinions on how to improve workflow and I quickly realized that my opinions mattered very little to upper management, let alone the owners. The timing could not have been more perfect as I had just entered into the Entrepreneurship program at Cal State Fullerton. And thus my journey began.

I wish I knew then, what I know now. The idea of self-employment sounded very appealing, even glamorous to some. Ideas are amazing. Putting them on paper is exciting. Opening up shop is exhilarating. But working the 12-14 hour days, seven days a week only to break even or to just stay afloat; those were lessons that school had not prepared me for. I gave up a few times but I didn't know that each time I gave up I was actually so much closer to my goal had I just stuck it out. I learned slowly that it takes a combination of consistency, risk and internal happiness to truly make it work.

Consistency- They do not stress this enough in the world. I opened up shop, once again, but this time with partners and a plan. Then I saw what I had wanted to see for so long; success. Success does not equate making millions. For me, at that time, it was simply just making a profit. Operating in positives versus being in the red. All this came with consistency in marketing practices, in operational practices and in leadership. Consistency is what made me finally successful in business.

Risk- Seven years I stayed in that partnership. I took a huge risk leaving the comfort of the success we had built and taking the tools I now had in my toolbox to make my own path. I started my next venture and with the lessons that I had learned and made a leap of faith. That was the best decision I ever made. It was when I took that jump, that I found my true happiness in work.

Happiness- Intrinsic happiness in what you do and who you are, will translate into success in your path. As cliché as that may sound, it rang true for me. If you truly enjoy your work, your entire idea of success will change. It will become a passion for you and that passion and determination will be driven by that internal happiness.

While many entrepreneurs may feel they could do these things without a formal education; my time at Cal State Fullerton in the Entrepreneurship program gave me tools that led to my success. If I had it to do all over again, I would choose this path time and again.

I don't claim to have the keys to success, but can only share my journey with you. I hope you find your own happiness and success in your entrepreneurial path.

Warm Regards,

Sujata Mehta

Restaurateur and Entrepreneur

Lynn Melton and her husband purchased Joaquin's Mexican Restaurant in December of 1980. It was on Main Street in Yorba Linda, CA. The first six months were physically grueling but by the end of the first year the restaurant was making a small profit. Within three years of the purchase, sales exceeded the previous owner's sales by more than three times.

Following the birth of two daughters and due to the sale of the building that they leased, they applied for, and received an SBA loan. They moved the business 2.25 miles to its current location in Eastlake Village, Yorba Linda. By 1987 and following a divorce at age 27, Lynn was a single mom running the business on her own. In 1989, the Yorba Linda Chamber of Commerce gave Lynn its Business Woman of the Year award.

After remarrying and raising four children, Lynn returned to California State University Fullerton to complete her BA in business. She was a founding member and served as president of the Young Entrepreneur Society (YES). Lynn was a member of the inaugural graduation class of the entrepreneurship concentration in 2003. She took a short educational pause before returning as a mentor for that same program.

Continuing her post graduate education at CSU Long Beach, Lynn earned a teaching credential. She taught high school mathematics for the next few years while her husband handled daily operations at the restaurant.

As a local business Woman, Lynn has been and still is active in many charitable organizations and community clubs. She has served in many leadership roles including president for the Yorba Linda Rotary Club (2003/04), the Yorba Linda Chamber of Commerce (2013/14) and the Alta Vista Women's Golf Association (2012-2014).

Today Lynn enjoys a round of golf or a trip to foreign lands when it fits into her schedule. She is a mom to four adult children all of whom are college graduates and gainfully employed. She is also a proud grandma to their seven adorable offspring.

Over the past thirty-seven years, Lynn has employed, trained and mentored hundreds of teenagers. She has sponsored scores of youth groups and sports teams, and donated thousands of meals "for a good cause." Lynn works with her husband and a strong team that includes many longtime employees. They continue to serve delicious Mexican food and refreshing margaritas to residents of the local community at Joaquin's Mexican Restaurant.

Dear Founder,

I am writing this letter to share my personal insight into one route of preparation and execution of running your own business. I do not claim that the pathway that I followed is the best road to success but it is one set of guidelines that I found to be quite effective. In addition to the following recommendation of "to-dos," I've also included a few "don't-dos." If I could change major decisions in my past they would be to finish college before getting married and before launching a business and to not open a second location while raising three middle-school-aged children.

Be Frugal But Not Cheap. My recommendation would be to have a nice nest egg to cover twelve months of personal expenses plus six months of fixed costs of your business operations before launching. If you can keep your personal expenses low (AKA live with parents), your chance of success should increase. Think of the long run and be cautious when spending each penny. Remember that cutting your purchasing costs goes straight into your profits. Likewise giving away free stuff can put you out of business very quickly. Create a written list of the pros and the cons before making a major financial decision. Make the decision; reflect on that decision and do not dwell on mistakes but do not repeat them either. Be honest and ethical in your dealings but do not assume that others will be. Negotiate when appropriate and remember that the lowest price is not always the best price.

Be Kind But Strong. Use the Golden Rule: "Do unto others as you would like them to do unto you." It is applicable while handling both employees and customers alike. Never ask an employee to do anything that you are unwilling to do yourself. Having the personal experience of performing every task is likely to help you garner a certain level of respect from your employees. In addition, gaining true insight into the level of difficulty and time required to perform the specific task should help with scheduling and provide confidence in setting appropriate wages for the various job positions. If you do not have time to learn every aspect of your business, you may need to have extra money to pay for over-staffing or the unexpected replacement of a key employee. You are the financial, emotional and intellectual safety net for your company. Be strong.

Be Respectful Always. Even with the high level of energy, stamina, self-determination, and passion of the entrepreneur, it is highly likely that additional people will be needed to attain success. A major input to the success of my restaurant is the incredible family support that I have had. My parents loaned me the money, all of my siblings, my children and many cousins, nieces and nephews contributed their time and talents. Today my husband is my supportive co-owner. The point is to encourage you to appreciate your family and let them help. Be sure to pay them for their services. Let your employees contribute their ideas. You very well could learn from them. Listen to your customers too. They sometimes make great recommendations. These recommendations may come in the form of a complaint. Do not take it as personal. Use the opportunity to put yourself in their shoes and try to understand their point of view. Think of your employees as both your representatives and potential customers. Their opinions should be valued and included in your decision making process. That sense of importance and being part of a team is a very powerful contributor toward job satisfaction. People skills may be your greatest asset. Handle both employees and customers with care. Treat them well.

Set your policy, then periodically evaluate your policy with an open mind. Be flexible to make changes as you see fit. As the boss, you set the company tone and culture. Remember to be frugal, kind and respectful.

Wishing you the best of luck in your entrepreneurial endeavors.
Sincerely,

Lynn T. Melton

Lynn T. Melton

Her Own Boss

Angeli Menta is a is a 2012 graduate of Cal State University Fullerton's College of Business and Economics with a business administration degree in entrepreneurship and a minor in philosophy. Since graduation her career exemplifies success in the "new economy." Angeli is a busy freelance business consultant. She consults with organizations such as Anna's Linens, DishClips, Nogalis, Inc., Delicious Table and more.

Angeli mostly provides consulting services remotely. They fall into six categories: business plan write-up, presentations and trade shows, content marketing, social media and branding, Email and marketing campaigns, and website development and design.

Currently Angeli provides administrative, marketing and social media assistance to Nogalis, Inc., including maintaining the company's website on a daily basis. Located in Newport Beach, California Nogalis, Inc, is a global IT service provider specializing in Infor, Lawson, and ERP solutions. Nogalis, Inc's clients range from Fortune 1,000 companies to emerging industry leaders. Being a smaller sized firm, Nogalis provides a unique one on one experience that larger firms cannot give to each client. Recently, Nogalis, Inc. Became a proud partner of *Infor Partner Alliance* and *Microsoft Dynamics Partner Program*.

Angeli co-founded Fuss and OC Forward, two burgeoning start-ups based in Orange County. Her work with these businesses involve every aspect from operational and website development strategies to online presence and brand identity through social media.

Angeli is a long-term volunteer as a Catechist/religious education teacher for her church. She began volunteering when she entered high school.

CSUF Entrepreneurship recognized Angeli's exceptional skills and invited her back soon after graduation to serve as a volunteer mentor. She continued to do so until relocating to Washington State in 2016. Angeli mentored a student-led consulting team to national first place in the 2013 Small Business Institute Project of the Year Competition. In 2014, she mentored an online-based start-up business, which went on to earn a US Bank Start-Up Scholarship from an investment panel at Cal State Fullerton.

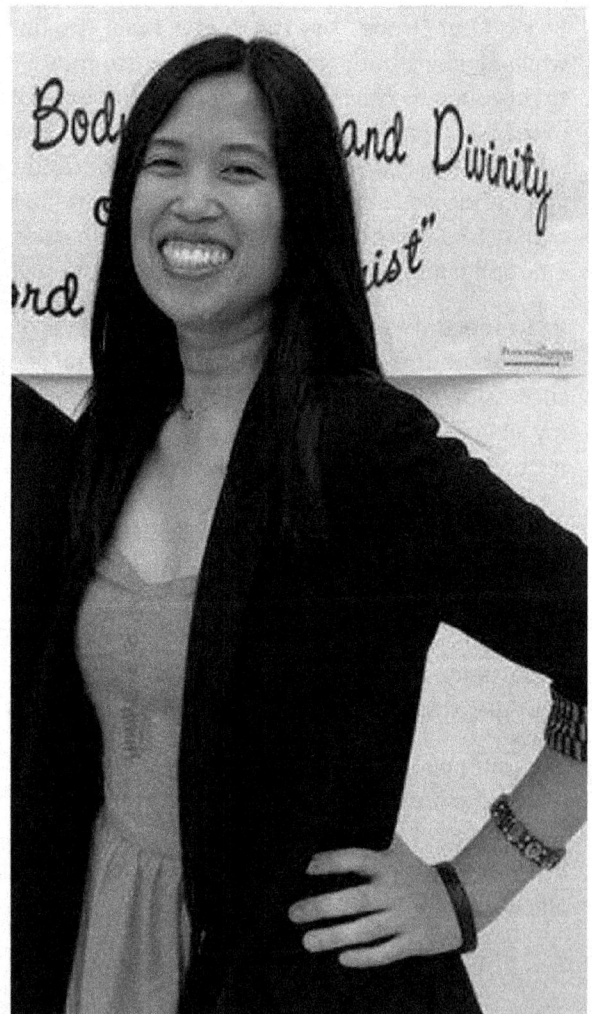

AM

ANGELI MENTA

Dear Founder,

If you're reading this letter, it means you've got more guts than your buddy in your Mgmt 339 class because one day you believe that you will be your own boss. I was once in your seat, hopeful and willing to do whatever it took to succeed. Professors, friends and mentors helped me along the way and without them, I wouldn't be able to say today that *I am my own boss*. So here's some advice, entrepreneur to entrepreneur, I'd like to share to help get you started.

1. **"Chase the vision, not the money, the money will end up following you"** Zappos CEO Tony Hsieh said. I was in marching band in high school. All I wanted was to win every competition. Having fun and enjoying myself came second. It wasn't until my senior year that I realized how much time I wasted working for that trophy instead of expressing my passion. Once I changed that, everything flowed easily. That year turned out to be the best year because the vision to entertain and express the music was my goal, and the rewards followed. So when you think of your business plan, think of all the people you'll positively impact, not just the numbers on your P&L statement.

2. **Value relationships** - When I was younger my mother told me to chose my friends wisely because who I surrounded myself with, I'd eventually become like them. I didn't really understand that because my friends and I were complete opposites – introverts vs extroverts, athletes vs book worms, etc. It wasn't until college when I realized how *right* my mother was. I even heard in the back of my mind her voice saying "I told you so!" It's not the person that you become, it's the mentality and mindset of those around you who influence your own attitude. LinkedIn co-founder Reid Hoffman said, "the fastest way to change yourself is to hang out with people who are already the way you want to be." That's why relationships are so valuable. The mentors who took me under their wing, classmates who supported my ventures, and professors who recognized my talents - I don't know what I would've done without these relationships when I was 21.

3. **Stay grounded** - When you're on this new journey, you can get side tracked. Sometimes you make "exceptions" hoping that it will benefit in the long run. But at the end of the day you're going to be the only one living with these decisions. Remember why you started this venture in the first place. Stay true to your roots. Don't forget to take a little R&R once in a while. Just do you and the rest will work itself out.

In business, like in life, we will face many obstacles. Sometimes we have to look at it the analytical way and often times the moral way. My last piece of advice is this: There is a difference between doing things right and doing the right thing. Whatever choice you make, just make sure it's the right choice for you. Best of luck!

Sincerely,

Angeli Menta

Angeli Menta

How to Generate Great Ideas

Scott Merritt is President of Meritocracy Consulting ("MC"). MC helps companies develop technology roadmaps and technology based marketing campaigns, plus offers database design/support and custom software development. Recently, MC has provided social media consulting, event marketing campaigns, facebook apps, custom kiosks, video capture touch screens, custom databases for real-time direct response marketing analysis and even merger and acquisitions analysis.

A repeat entrepreneur, Scott spent years developing custom social networking products in the early 2000s for a wide range of communities including college campuses, non-profits, businesses and membership organizations (such as the YMCA).
He has a broad range of experience starting companies and running organizations. Between 2003 and 2012, he personally founded three companies He sold one, merged one with a competitor, and the third failed.

For almost a decade, Scott ran After School Sports Connection, one of USC's neighborhood Outreach Programs. It was a 50 person non-profit that specialized in youth sports outreach. As Director, he interviewed, hired and trained over 500 employees, and helped the program triple its outreach.

Overall, Scott is most motivated within innovative organizations that are taking on either large issues, strong competitors or billion dollar opportunities. Can he find pleasure in optimizing relatively static operations? Scott says, "Sure, and I have done so as a consultant, but I know myself: my work ethic and drive, each function best when there is a mission or some sense of urgency. I enjoy smaller teams pursuing time-sensitive

opportunities, and too often that attitude is not present within mature companies."

Since 2012, Scott, has focused on writing (including fiction, non-fiction, and corporate strategy). Today, he is a CSUF Start-up Incubator Resident generating his next great idea.

Scott Merritt
Fullerton, California

Dear Founder,

In 2003, I started my first business, a social network similar to Facebook. The company grew at a very rapid rate reaching a fairly dense customer base at fifty universities. Shortly after we launched, a random site from Harvard was announced called TheFacebook.com. Though we were growing over 100% per month, as we grew, Facebook grew faster. In 2009, we sold our company to a slightly larger competitor in what marked a moderately successful exit and an end to my first entrepreneurial adventure.

Based on my experience, I believe the product discovery process is highly formulaic and thus there exists a usable framework that should aid you in the recognition and design of great future business ideas. Below are the steps I took as a senior in college to identify social networking as a compelling market.

1) I made a list of communication services only available to the very wealthy
2) I made a list of features and functionality that were not yet being used by individuals, despite existing widely in corporations (i.e. I asked myself what B2B services might provide value if packaged for the B2C market?)
3) I made a list of customer data not yet being shared, and ranked that data in order of how much utility it would provide if it WERE shared (i.e. What information would make it easier to communicate and socialize more effectively?)

Once I had those three lists, I generated specific ideas that hit on many of the identified concepts, settling on the creation of a new consumer facing service that could be delivered inexpensively. We packaged everything in a fun, easy to use interface, and a major innovation was the introduction of profiles that were relevant to the groups people belonged to (their school, class, sports team, sorority, etc...). Once we had a solid product idea, we focused on how to grow it. For example, we permitted large groups and organizations to setup accounts for ALL of their users at once.

I believe the techniques I used provide a timeless framework for idea generation. One key lesson is the importance of being customer focused. A second key lesson is to align your short-term goals with very ambitious long-term industry inevitabilities.

In summary, a good idea requires strong execution, but contrary to what is often said by prominent investors (that ideas don't matter, only the quality of the team, etc....), I disagree. I believe that a great idea can make it easier to bring people together, raise capital and achieve escape velocity in terms of customer adoption. I hope you, as one of the next round of ambitious and creative entrepreneurs, will find my tips helpful as you look to jump start your first (or next) venture.

Best regards,

Scott Merritt

For in depth discussion of these topics by the author, please go to https://bit.ly/creatingnewventures

A Banker Who Fosters New Ventures

Peter Meyers is the senior commercial lending officer in South Orange County for Farmers & Merchants Bank of Long Beach. His bank provides complete commercial banking services for entrepreneurs, middle market companies and experienced real estate investors. Peter started in banking in 1982 as a teller with Security Pacific National Bank and became an Operations Officer. Soon, the bank transferred him into its Industrial Engineering Group to measure and recommend operational efficiencies in the branch system.

In 1987, Peter joined First Interstate Bank of California as a project manager and implemented three automation projects over a two-year period. He then rolled back into the branch system. Peter eventually became one of only three branch managers in the First Interstate system to manage multiple offices in a hub and spoke format.

Next, Peter joined the largest office of Home Savings of America. The branch had over $850 Million in deposits and a staff of 43. He implemented that Bank's first large accounts-receivable-based line of credit for a packaging company.

In 1998, Peter joined City National Bank as the manager of their Irvine Office responsible for small business lending and cash management relationships. In 2000, the bank named him Line Officer of the Year and declared his office the Branch of the Year. In 2005 he joined Security Bank of California and finally joined Farmers & Merchants in 2013. His branch, was the number one branch for loan growth in 2016.

Peter uses his banking expertise to support his community. He volunteers as the Chief Credit Officer for the Small Business Development Corporation (SBDC) of Orange County. This nonprofit administers the State of California Loan Guarantee Program for small businesses. It gives community banks up to an 80% guarantee on loans and credit lines. Funds go to start-ups and businesses seeking to expand that do not normally qualify for a traditional bank credit facility.

In addition, Peter volunteers for the Entrepreneur Program at the Mihaylo College of Business and Economics. He serves in three ways: as a guest lecturer in the Venture Launch classes, as a panelist for Venture Launch presentations, and as a judge in the College's annual Business Plan Competition.

Peter lives, works and worships in the City of Lake Forest, where he and his wife Jennifer have lived for more than 18 years. They have four children. Their youngest son will start at CSUF in the Fall of 2017. Peter and Jennifer enjoy cooking, horses, gardening and wine.

Farmers & Merchants Bank

California's Strongest, since 1907.

Dear Founder,

In 1982, I graduated from Loyola Marymount University with majors in Business Administration (Accounting Emphasis) and Liberal Studies (Philosophy Emphasis), and a minor in Fine Arts (Photographic Arts). These three areas of study could not have been more different. I landed my first job as a teller in banking and never left. I strongly feel the reason for this is that I never have stopped my thirst for knowledge and applied all facets of my collegiate studies to banking in creative ways. As a budding entrepreneur, I encourage you to apply **everything** that you have learned in your Titan years towards your goal and challenge yourself daily to learn something new about your industry.

Banking is a commodity product. Checking accounts, savings accounts, credit cards, online banking, loans do not differ; however the way they are presented and delivered can differ widely. In 2005 I was approached with a wonderful opportunity to join a team of experienced bankers in forming a new bank in the Inland Empire. We wanted to make a difference. We opened our doors with just one branch and 12 employees. Within 18 months we grew to $150 Million in Assets with positive retained earnings. By the time I left the bank in 2013, we had amassed $650 Million in Assets and had opened a total of six locations, despite the 3 turbulent years of the Great Recession which stunted the growth of most banks.

What was the reason for our success? I attribute much of it to one word: **TRUST**. There were a number of key managers when we opened our doors. Each of us had critical areas of expertise. Our Bank President was responsible for running our Board of Director Meetings (regulatory requirements) and managing our Deposit Operations Team. Our Chief Banking Officer coordinated our product offerings to create a mix that was attractive to our primarily business clientele. Our Chief Commercial Lending Officer and Chief Credit Officer developed loan structures that gave clients financial flexibility to excel in their line of business. Finally our Flagship Office Branch Manager had the responsibility to get out in the community, spread the word about our bank and bring in the business. Each of us worked individually and as a team to meet client needs in personal and professional manner. The trust that each of us had in each other's capabilities created a leadership team that excelled even in trying times.

Jim Kouzes and Barry Posner developed a leadership model in 1987 called the Five Practices of Exemplary Leadership®. The model shows how these five key practices develop behaviors up and down your business that encourage and invigorate each team member to do their personal best. The five practices are *Model the Way, Inspire a Shared Vision, Challenge the Process, Enable Others to Act*, and *Encourage the Heart*. Our banking team took each of these practices and shared and implemented them with the rest of our individual teams to make our bank successful. My personal favorite of the five is *Enable Others to Act*; this concept immediately infers my key word mentioned above - **TRUST**. The entrepreneur cannot do it all on his or her own; know your weaknesses and bring together a team of trusted advisors and subordinates who can fill the gaps; provide these key people empowerment. This is one of the major reasons that CSUF Entrepreneurship Program's signature course, New Venture Launch, consistently requires students to create teams to develop their fledgling businesses.

Titan Entrepreneurs, it is my hope that as you bring your fledgling business to fruition you remember to never stop learning, never stop trusting and always empower your team to do their personal best.

Peter J. Meyers

Crexendo, Inc.

Steven G. Mihaylo (Class of 1969) is a serial entrepreneur and philanthropist. He has been the CEO of Crexendo, Inc. since 2008.

Crexendo Inc.is a full-service cloud solutions provider. It delivers critical voice and data technology infrastructure services to the start-up, SMB and enterprise markets.

Steve's path to business success began modestly. Following graduation from high school, the budding entrepreneur spent three years in the U.S. Army's 101st Airborne Division. He was a Radio and Radar technician. Steve took on tailoring jobs for additional cash. He attended Cal State Fullerton on the GI Bill and supported himself by working the 11 p.m. to 7 a.m. shift at Douglas Aircraft in Long Beach. Steve spent the last two years of college working full time and cramming every spare minute with schoolwork to complete his accounting/finance degree. Steve then turned down an offered accounting job with a major firm to follow his dream of building his own business.

Steve recalls, "I knew that in a large organization, it could take a long time to get established. With my degree and the experience I had working in the technical field and in sales, I felt that I had all the ingredients to be an entrepreneur."

Steve moved out of Orange County to Phoenix. There he founded Inter-Tel in 1969 as a division of Panoramic Audio — a company he had worked for while attending college. By 1972, the company had sales revenue of $1 million. He served as CEO until February 2006, the year annual revenues topped more than $458 million. Steve sold the company in 2007.

Since then, Steve has been actively engaged with several businesses. He sits on multiple boards of directors.

Steve has been active in and supported many educational charitable endeavors during his career. He generously supported CSUF's College of Business and Economics which is named after him. Steve joined the graduation processional with the Entrepreneurship class of 2005. He then went to the stage to receive his Honorary PhD, Doctor of Humane Letters from CSUF.

"Over the years, I have been grateful for the education that I received at California State University, Fullerton and for the opportunities that were afforded me," Steve said. "It is an honor to support the mission of the College of Business and Economics and to help support the growth of an institution where all students have the opportunity to succeed."

Crexendo, Inc.
1615 S. 52nd Street
Tempe, AZ 85281

Dear founder,

At heart, I am a salesman and an entrepreneur. My flair for sales led to positive financial results working for others, which in turn led to my entrepreneurial decision to raise my sights and start my own business. Over time, I was able to grow that business from just me to nearly tthree thousand people working at the company. I matured into an effective CEO of a publically traded company. I attribute that successful growth to the lessons I learned at California State University Fullerton. My studies in finance and accounting prepared me to run and grow a business.

For me, two key factors sparked my entrepreneurial spirit: Adversity and Limits. I believe that how I addressed adversity and limits changed my life.

My parents divorced when I was nine years old and that had a profound impact on me. I made the decision to not play the victim and take on the added responsibility that comes with being the underage patriarch of the family. It wasn't easy but I decided that I would take on a job as a newspaper delivery boy and salesperson.

Looking back on it now I am convinced that facing this kind of adversity has helped me immeasurably in my life as a man and an entrepreneur. Facing difficulties is a fact of life and instead of bemoaning that fact I made the decision to do something proactive about it. I could have despaired during my journey through multiple foster homes. I could have taken refuge in all manner of vices but I didn't. If you want to be successful in this life you must take adversity head on. Continue to better yourself. Nothing will be given to you.

Given my circumstances at age nine, I was confronted by limits, real and imagined. Today, I'm known as "No Limits" to my friends for the simple reason that my goal is to always be the best. Being a paperboy, especially when you are nine years old, isn't a glamorous job. There definitely weren't any high expectations that followed me into the job. But even though there was absolutely no prestige to the job I took it on with the determination to be the best.

At first, this meant being able to deliver more papers on my bicycle than adults were delivering in cars. My tenacity in this task easily extended to the other side of the newspaper business for me: sales. After getting the direction from my boss that we were to sell newspapers in addition to doing our paper routes I asked him "What is the record for subscriptions sold in a day," to which he replied "Fifty."

That is all I needed to hear. On my way home that day I planned out my Saturday for selling newspapers. If I started at 6:00am and finished at midnight that would mean I would need to sell about three subscriptions per hour in order to beat the record. And that's what I did. I targeted apartments because I would be able to sell subscriptions more efficiently and proceeded to sell for about eighteen hours. This activity taught me the power of setting goals and the bigger the goal the better.

When I next reported for work my boss had us all report on how many sales we had made. Every other employee was at or around 10 subscriptions sold and the boss seemed happy. I told him that I sold 53 subscriptions and he was flabbergasted, "I was joking when I said the old record was 50, the old record was 15." That was a real eye opener for me. It proved to me that I needed to keep on setting bigger goals for myself. If I hadn't done that then I don't think I would have ever started my own business. You are only limited to how much your brain thinks you can accomplish. If you expect great things you will achieve great things. If you only take one thing from this, then let it be this quote from Sir Winston Churchill who ended every broadcast he made to his people during WWII with, "Never, never, never give up."

Respectfully,

Steven G. Mihaylo, CEO

For in depth discussion of these topics by the author, please go to https://bit.ly/creatingnewventures

TriTech

Mark Mitchell is director of the TriTech Small Business Development Center (TriTech SBDC). TriTech offers no cost, individualized and confidential one-on-one consulting. Senior level consultants deliver consulting services to high technology businesses with economic growth potential. TriTech serves both existing firms and start-ups.

Mark took over the reins at TriTech in 2006 when TriTech relocated from Orange County to the Inland Empire. When he applied for the job, he realized that no other viable candidates were applying. He soon found out why.

Mark's first three years at TriTech were challenging. Funding was insufficient for fast growth. Economic impact in the early years was only $2 to $3 Million. To receive the federal funds promised by the U.S. Small Business Administration, Mark had to raise dollar for dollar matching funds from sponsors.

The service model for TriTech has been wildly successful for its clients. However, despite its effectiveness, the year-to-year grant contract has not grown in proportion to the increase in economic impact. TriTech is increasingly dependent upon sponsor donations for growth.

Facing these realities Mark operates Tri-Tech as a continuous startup. He bootstraps growth with limited human and financial resources. Somehow his team manages to serve all of Orange, Riverside, and San Bernardino Counties.

Fast forward to 2017. Currently Mark and his team of senior consultants have achieved $485 million in economic impact (equity, loans and increase in sales); plus the organization has created/ retained over 3700 jobs. TriTech has become a significant catalyst for building the regional economic ecosystem for high-growth techbusinesses. TriTech is the fifth highest producing SBDC in the nation. It is the highest performing SBDC in the nation based on return on investment (ROI). Mark credits TriTech's success to its team, "The TriTech team is second to none. It is made up of former CEO's and serial entrepreneurs. Everyone is obsessed about making a difference. The result is TriTech helps business owners and entrepreneurs turn their enterprises into hyper-growth firms. The beauty of TriTech is that owners receive world-class consulting at no cost."

Mark is an alumnus of CSUF's Mihaylo College of Business. He earned his BA in Management and Marketing. He has an extensive background in entrepreneurship, marketing and sales. Mark's mantra is "Allow yourself and organization to be pulled by a great vision".

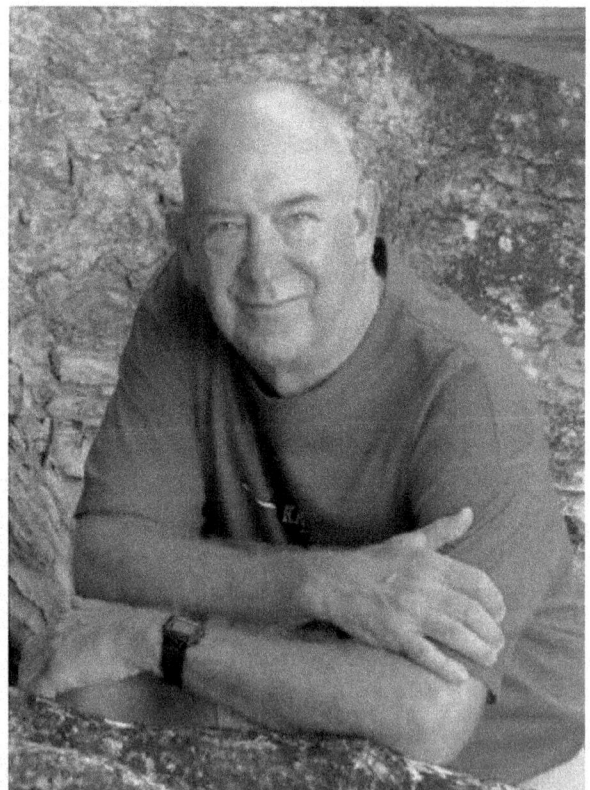

Mark feeling the Aloha spirit in Kawai, Hawaii

Dear Founder:

There are several foundations that have driven the success of the TriTech Small Business Development Center (SBDC) since I took the reins in 2006.

The first step was to create a team of senior consultants that shared the same core values as myself. In nature, a tree decays from the top. In an organization, the decline of the organization occurs at the top as well; so if you want to grow a dynamic organization you need to be a strong leader with solid core values. Your values will send a message internally to your team and externally to your customers, which tells everyone what you believe in and stand for. An amazing thing happened over the years at TriTech, that is, quality consultants came to us and wanted to be part of the team, plus we attracted high caliber clients that wanted to engage our services. People connected with TriTech because the brand became a trust mark rather than just a trade mark.

Another component that has contributed to the success of TriTech and resulted in the organization being one of the top five highest producing SBDC's in the nation, was the creation of a value monopoly. One of my favorite quotations comes from the famous architect Buskminister Fuller when he said, "You never change things by fighting existing reality. To change something, build a new model that makes the existing model obsolete". This is exactly what we did at TriTech. We built a business model and continued to morph the model over the years to provide unique and unparalleled consulting assistance. The key element that worked for TriTech is simple in theory but hard to execute. We continue to change how we think about different business problems. I found that how I thought became the lens through which I solved organization and client problems. As I continued to alter my perspective new solutions began to emerge.

I cannot end this letter without mentioning the most important ingredient that contributed to the success of TriTech. It is my passion for entrepreneurship. Knowing that I am making a difference makes my heart sing. I believe that of all the things that I have done in my career, being director for TriTech has been my single most fulfilling endeavor. I invite you to look for the touch stones in your business and determine what gives you the greatest pleasure and makes your heart sing.

Sincere regards,

Mark Mitchell
Director
TriTech SBDC

PS: May your heart be pulled by a vision that takes you beyond the impossible into the possible!

Orange County's Credit Union

Shruti Miyashiro is President and Chief Executive Officer of Orange County's Credit Union (OCCU). OCCU is a $1.5 billion credit union with 100,000 Members and ten branches in the Orange County area. Its portfolio includes auto, home and small business loans. Its mission is "Simple banking, for people,not profit."

Shruti's appointment as OCCU's CEO in 2007 marked a return to OCCU for Shruti who, from 1999 to 2002, held executive positions at the Credit Union and served as President and CEO of the subsidiary organization, Orange County Group, Inc.

Prior to returning to Orange County's Credit Union, Shruti was the President and CEO of Pasadena Federal Credit Union and Service Plus Credit Union.

Shruti holds a master's degree in Business Administration from the University of Redlands and a bachelor's degree in Philosophy from the University of California, Riverside. She is also a proud graduate of Western Credit Union National Association (CUNA) Management School. She received the school's prestigious James D. Likens Alumni Recognition award in 2017.

Shruti currently serves as a Board Chair for Jack Henry & Associates, Incorporated. She is on the Foundation Board for the Children's Hospital of Orange County. Shruti is a Board Member for the Filene Research Institute, and was appointed to the State of California Credit Union Advisory Committee for the California Department of Oversight.

In the past, she has been on numerous committees at the state and national level for the California Credit Union League, the and Credit Union National Association, the Board of Trustees for

Western CUNA Management School, CO-OP Audit Committee and Board as well as community board positions, including Pacific Oaks College.

Miyashiro resides in Newport Beach with her husband and young son and enjoys spending time with her loved ones, traveling, volunteering, and reading.

212

Dear Founder,

"When you hit a closed door and it doesn't budge, just rear back and kick it in – but hold it open so others can follow you."

These words from Muriel Siebert, the first female member of the New York Stock Exchange, hang on the wall in my office as a reminder that success begins with giving our best to one another. Many conclude that success is all about, "climbing up the corporate ladder," but it is imperative to remember to lend a helping hand, for nothing is ever achieved alone.

I was lucky enough to find my purpose early on in my career and that has led me to where I am today, the CEO and President of Orange County's Credit Union. It was not my intention to build a career in the credit union industry, but over time I have fallen in love with the industry's values. I believe when you're surrounded by good people and are doing something you love, you can become truly accomplished.

Over the years I have formed a few simple principles about leadership and success.

1. Be genuine; that's the easiest way to lead. Quiet confidence and humility are virtues; arrogance is not. Be honest because people really can handle the truth.
2. Synergy is powerful; cultivate it. My team is extraordinary. Their commitment, integrity, and drive to serve our Members and our community are at the heart of who we are. Together, we have passion for what we do and touch people's lives in the most meaningful ways.
3. Pay attention and you can learn something new every day. I believe leaders should observe everything, and copy nothing. It's important for leaders to synthesize information and form our own business model and strategic plans.

As you embark on your own ventures, know your own definition of success. Know that success is not defined by titles or money; it's about living your values. When I arrived, Orange County's Credit Union was already a great credit union and my goal when I leave is to ensure that it has remained so.

I leave you with this: go out and find a sense of purpose. True accomplishment and fulfillment will follow when you let your passion and values be your guide.

Wishing you the best with your future endeavors,

Shruti Miyashiro

BMooreCreative

Bruce Moore is a technology management executive consultant. He founded BmooreCreative in 2012. He has extensive business development experience. Bruce has taken systems, products and businesses from concept to launch and beyond. In recent years he has been an advisor, consultant, engineer, mentor and entrepreneur. Bruce's multifaceted volunteer services have been invaluable to CSUF Entrepreneurship.

Bruce has over 25 years experience consulting and working for Fortune 500 firms and entrepreneurial businesses. His past roles include Senior Manager for KPMG, and President of two L-3 companies.

Bruce has experience in multiple aspects of technology management. The list includes development of leading edge solutions for communications, sensor, power, energy information and situation display. He has managed breakthrough products for innovative growth with revenues up to $750M. He has also conducted POC and pivot point decision analyses for tactical and strategic monetization.

Bruce works with pre and post launch B2B, B2C companies on "go to market" acceleration in today's fast changing business technology environment. He is an expert at doing design reviews, proof of concept testing and evaluation, concept to launch, life cycle support, supply chain management and go to market process design. Bruce has conducted financial and document reviews for many firms. Review clients range from early-stage start-ups and turnarounds to large US and overseas manufacturers, distributors, retailers and service corporations.

At CSUF, Bruce has served for three years as a mentor for entrepreneurship classes. He is a mentor for residents in the CSUF Start-up Incubator. Also, Bruce serves as judge and panelist for business plan and funding events.

BMooreCreative

Dear Founder,

The traditional 9-5 employment model is changing. The "gig economy" is not new but its expansion is being made possible and popular through Internet and technology enhancements with advancements that continue to allow the freedom to be self employed, working on your passions, any time and place you chose. Working remotely on laptops and desktops as freelancers writing, editing, coding, consulting and researching among other creative services are providing gig money income for many.

Make your own schedules (flexibility), chose projects of interest, work remotely, and experiment in different trades are a few of the thriving gig economy benefits. Opportunities to work as an individual contributor or as part of a team are growing, allowing work - life balance and freedom. Intuit forecasts predict that by 2020 over 40% of workers will be independent contractors. Everyone has something (skills, abilities and unused capacity) that someone else needs and tasks they would prefer someone else perform. Freelancing in the new gig economy will continue to grow.

Attract, inform, engage, nurture and develop new value added client relationships in the growing gig economy. As a consultant, contractor, subcontractor, subject matter expert, thought leader or freelancer it is time to chart a new and changing career course. Consider your strengths and interests and develop your value proposition. Be prepared to pivot as your market grows and changes, always contributing to bottom line improvements or client cost avoidance. Continuously develop your problem solving, written and verbal communication skills to excel at winning proposals, reporting, estimating, budgeting, contract preparation, and negotiating.

An often asked question is: "What is a fair and reasonable hourly rate (gig money) to ask for services rendered?" Consider the following factors and then do the math. There are only about 2000 work hours in the year. Remember, you are usually only billable for 60% of those hours. There is a difference between working in the business and on the business. Every business has opportunity, overhead, taxes and marketing expenses. Your rate will always be compared to internal and competitive rates. Do the math. Start with 100.00/hour and compare. Try not to discount but be flexible in establishing your rates. Always collect travel and entertainment costs as agreed to, in advance, with your client and understand the IRS 1099 process. Invoice often and don't forget to collect.

Welcome to the new "Gig Economy,"

Bruce

Bruce Moore

SCORE Volunteer

William B. Morland (Bill) has been a volunteer business mentor with Orange County SCORE (Chapter 114) since 2002. Orange County SCORE is one of the largest and most productive chapters in the national SCORE organization with over 100 volunteer business mentors.

The SCORE Association is a nationwide nonprofit organization dedicated to the formation, growth and success of small business. It is a Resource Partner with the U.S Small Business Administration (SBA). SCORE provides free, confidential business counseling and workshops as a public service to all types of businesses, in all stages of development. Established in 1969, the SCORE Association has over 5,000 members nationwide, all volunteers with extensive business experience.

Bill served as Chapter Chairman for two years and under his direction the Orange County chapter was number one nationally out of 389 chapters in total services delivered to the local small business community. Bill served as District Director covering Orange, Riverside, and San Bernardino counties for three years. Bill recently took the volunteer position of Western Regional Vice President covering the states of Arizona, Nevada, Utah, California and Hawaii.

In addition to his volunteer leadership roles for SCORE, Bill has personally counseled 450+ local small businesses in a variety of business situations since 2002. Sales and marketing across a broad spectrum of products and services are Bill's core competencies.

Entrepreneurship is Bill's passion. He started and operated five small businesses over a period of twenty years. As President of one of the first contract employee services, he helped pioneer the concept of off-site personnel departments which are now known as Professional Employer Organizations.

Prior to his entrepreneur activities Bill was Vice-President of Sales and National Sales Manager for ITT Consumer Specialty Products. He successfully launched the concept of consumer telephones across the country through major retail channels such as K-Mart, Costco, Macy's and Target Stores.

Bill is an Alumnus of CSU, San Diego. He lives in Laguna Woods, California.

Commenting on Orange County SCORE's relationship with CSUF Entrepreneurship, Bill says, "Thanks for giving our SCORE members the chance to mentor and mingle with your students over the past 15 years." In turn, CSUF Entrepreneurship is grateful for the invaluable, volunteer support that Orange County SCORE members have provided to our students.

William B. Morland
Laguna Niguel, California

Dear founder,

American entrepreneurism is alive and well. If you are reading this you are either thinking of starting a business or are in the beginning stages of one. Well I started five businesses and had beginning business concepts for even more. Two of the five were non-profits. That wasn't because I had organized them as such; rather it was because I had to learn what I am writing to you about in this letter. The other three worked and provided enough success for me to be able to move onto volunteering for the SCORE Association and help aspiring and existing small business owners to make their way to success.

So here are the most important tips that I can give you about the process of business startup.

1. You can't do it all yourself! No one person has all the skill and knowledge that you will need to move from startup, through the growth stages, and on to success. So know what you are good at, and more importantly, what you are not good at. Then hire, contract for, beg for help from other people who have the skills and knowledge that you are missing. SCORE mentors are perfect for helping you through the startup and early growth phases of your business

2. Your most important asset at the beginning is time! Everything else is replaceable but if you waste one minute, hour or day you will never get it back. So from day one everything that you do should be focused on generating revenue. Don't sit around paying bills, talking to your best friend, texting, emptying the trash, etc. Do those things after working hours. Spend your work hours either communicating with someone who can give you revenue or preparing to talk to someone who can give you revenue. And by the way, the most important financial for you to watch daily is cash flow. Many small companies succeed themselves out of business because they book business on payment terms and then don't have the cash to create what they have already sold.

3. Drive to breakeven! You should have a financial plan so that you know how many widgets you need to sell at what margins, or how many hours of service you need to bill, to pay your costs of keeping the door open. Until you are there you are on the verge of failure. And no matter how well you plan when you start, what you assumed will change. So make your financial plan on spread sheet and update your assumptions every day.

I do have to say that while I went through what I have outlined above, I have enjoyed much more personal satisfaction during my 15 plus years as a SCORE mentor and volunteer. My relative success in business takes a back seat to my feelings about the successes of SCORE clients that I have mentored over the years. Without exception, SCORE volunteers, as a group, are the finest people I have ever known. These are people who devote countless hours to help others with no expectation or thought about any kind of personal remuneration. So when you think you have time please consider contacting SCORE and bringing the experience that you have acquired from starting your business to someone like you who is at a crossroads and only needs a few hours of your empathetic advice to help them move to the next level. You will know how because you will have done it yourself.

Good luck to you!

William B. Morland

Operations Manager and Mentor

Ryan Mueller has a background in Multi-Unit Retail and Operations Management. He has held roles of progressively increasing responsibility during his career for almost two decades.

Ryan's work experience started much like many entrepreneurs – with a small service business – in fact a few. In his early teens, he mowed lawns and taught private hockey lessons. Later, and while working a full-time job, attending school, and playing sports, he started a seasonal business installing Christmas lights. Ryan was completing small business consulting projects with colleagues during his early college years.

Over the past 18 years, he has worked for small to medium sized businesses, both public and private, including two Fortune 500 companies. Ryan has held a variety of leadership positions where he has experience leading operational and cross-functional teams.

His focus has been to support and drive top-line sales, while protecting the bottom line. He is expert at implementing efficiencies in operations to increase his business unit's profitability. Ryan has also had success in outside sales and business development roles which were very entrepreneurial in nature.

Ryan holds a B.A. in business administration and an M.B.A. from California State University Fullerton. He volunteers as a student mentor for the Center for Entrepreneurship. It is designated as one of the University's Centers of Excellence. In this volunteer role Ryan helps student-groups by serving as an advisor. He guides them through New Venture Creation Projects (from concept to launch), Student-led Consulting projects, and development of business plans and Business Strategy. He also served as a judge during the 2016 Titan Fast Pitch Competition.

Currently Ryan works as an Operations Executive for Ironwood Brokers and Insurance Marketing, a Wholesaler in Laguna Niguel, CA. He manages all operations of the company, including its Information Technology. He also oversees IT projects and support for Ironwood's sister and parent companies.

IRONWOOD
BROKERS & INSURANCE MARKETING

Dear Founder,

Congratulations on deciding to pursue your entrepreneurial instincts and start your own venture! Working for yourself and creating something that has the ability to outlive and outlast you is a thrilling adventure, and a lot of hard work. You will undoubtedly work harder for your new venture than you have ever worked in your life – but you will most likely find more satisfaction in it than anything else you have ever done. My advice is simple: be honest, have a plan, and remember that you can have it all, just not right now!

It is important to be honest with your customers, with your business partners, and others you will do business with, but be honest with yourself first and foremost. Are you providing a product or a service that is needed, or that is truly better than your competition? Is this a new idea? If so, why has nobody else thought of it – or if they have, why weren't they successful? If there is a market for your product or service, how large is it? Be honest about your potential – it is easy to get excited about your idea and decide that people "need" what you are offering – but be honest up front about what your target market really is, how large it is, and if you can enter that space and compete, winning market share with all the limited resources of a typical new venture.

Before you start, have a plan because being able to execute it will largely determine your success. Plan for change, and plan on re-working your plan often. Be fluid and be able to adapt and switch gears when needed. Don't get paralyzed by perfection because things aren't going to happen exactly as you had planned – make your plan work for you, use it as a guide, but be able to seize opportunity when it presents itself. If you wait for perfection before you act, you may be waiting for a very long time. One of my favorite quotes is from General George Patton: "A good plan, violently executed today is better than a perfect plan next week." It's all about execution – even violent execution! Have a sense of urgency about getting it done! A great idea without a plan is simply a great idea. The ability to execute your plan can turn your idea into a viable business.

Finally, remember this... you can (probably) have it all, but not right now! A new venture is going to have limited resources – limited time, limited personnel and, almost certainly, limited capital. Focus first on the most important things that are within your control – are you providing an excellent customer experience, so you can build a loyal following? Are you delivering on your value proposition? Don't risk your dream to put up a façade – too many people are too eager and dive into debt to finance their "wants." As you grow and generate revenue, budget for the "wants" but don't sacrifice the "needs" to get them. Remember – the corner office, big board room, and maybe a private jet will come with time... for now focus on operating within your means, and take small steps to build a foundation for your company that will ensure your success down the road - focus on your plan and never lose sight of your goals.

Wishing you success in your endeavor!

Ryan Mueller

Swaggle

Eric Niu is the founder of Swaggle. His start up company is a peer-to-peer fashion resale and closet sharing platform.

Eric is a Titan Alumni. He graduated in 2012 with a double major in International Business and Economics. Eric was the first recipient of the "Titan Leave Your Footprint Award" after serving as the President and CEO for the Associated Students Incorporated, CSUF, where he managed a $7 million dollar non-profit organization.

After college, Eric moved to Washington DC and worked in President Obama's Administration at the U.S. Office of Personnel Management. He founded Alakai (means leadership in Hawaiian), an elite innovator's community of practice to cultivate an innovative, collaborative and open ecosystem in the Federal government. Eric also led a Knowledge Sharing Workgroup of President Obama's Second Term Management Agenda Initiative focused on a knowledge and talent sharing economy for more than two million federal employees.

After public service, Eric joined Deloitte Consulting LLP as Senior Consultant where he partnered with government executives and business leaders to align people strategies with business strategies. He provided strategic change, project management and technology adoption expertise, using data analytics that helped clients manage change.

As described in his letter, Eric founded Swaggle from a problem that he couldn't find a solution to when he first entered the workforce. As a young professional who recently graduated from college, he couldn't afford the designer look that he wanted. Consignment shopping is fun, but most men don't know where to start. At the same time, the majority of brick-and-mortar consignment shops don't have an online presence because the cost of establishing and maintaining an online store is costly and time consuming. Swaggle is a mobile marketplace connecting high-end men's fashion resellers with interested buyers for a curated and personalized shopping experience.

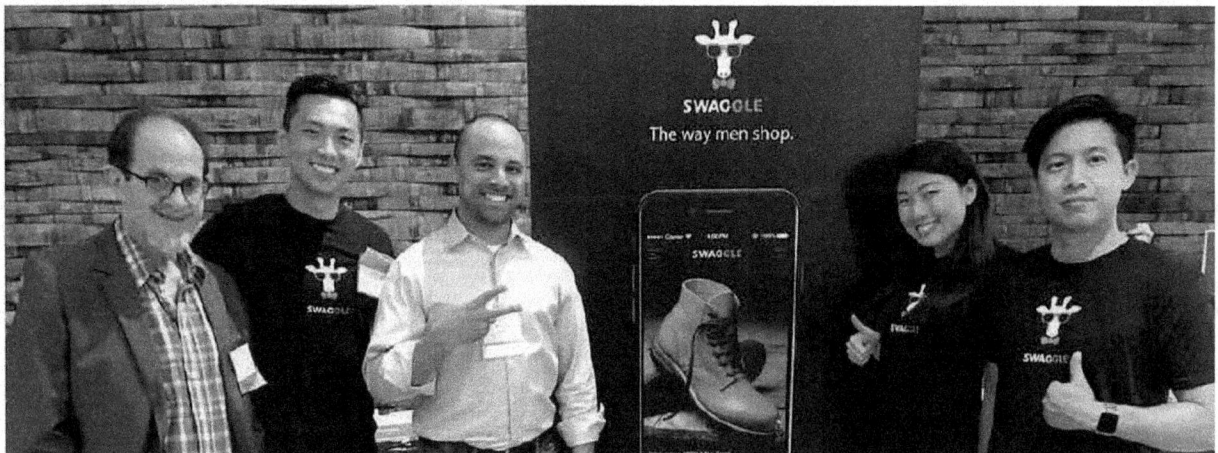

The Swaggle Team (L-R) Izzy Ezrailson (advisor), Eric Niu (CEO), Martin Sherene (CTO), Cindy Lo (Marketing and UX Specialist), Mokyi Chow (Chief Design Officer)

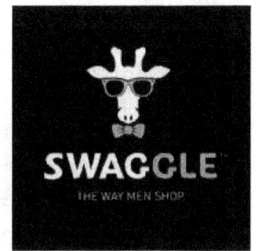

Dear Founder,

Have you ever asked yourself the question, 'What should I do?" Are you still feeling bad even when others are praising how good a job you are doing? As a founder, you are making countless decisions each day and many of them are based on minimal information. The most difficult thing is to **manage your own emotions** and make the best judgement that you can at the time. That takes experience, courage, intelligence and sometimes simply luck.

People often ask me what they can do to be a better founder or CEO. The honest answer is that I don't know, I am still learning. What I know is that everyone's journey is different and no one can teach you how to turn your idea into reality better than you. Using that same logic, you must be versatile as a founder and **constantly reinvent yourself**. It takes a certain skill to recruit others to join you when you just have an idea, it takes another type of skill to create something tangible and raise money. You can't be the same founder who leads a small startup and a CEO who manages a multi-million or even a billion dollar company. It's either you reinvent yourself along the way or your board will replace you with a more seasoned CEO. Here are three lessons learned along the way:

Start with a Question: Swaggle was founded because I was "too poor for Prada". I moved to Washington DC after college and worked in the Obama Administration. I was this young professional who wanted a designer look that I couldn't afford. Therefore, I started to swap, buy and sell clothes with my friends. As sharing economy platforms like Uber and Airbnb became a new normal, I realized the potential of a peer-to-peer fashion resale and closet-sharing platform. What can we do with the excess clothes in our closets? How might we create a better way to shop for quality menswear at discounted prices? Those are the questions that I asked myself. After some initial research on the market size and validation from friends and even strangers; I decided to do something with the idea.

Recruit a Team that's Smarter than You. Once I knew that I wanted to pursue the idea, my next challenge was to recruit a team. I needed technical coders that could create a tangible solution to solve the problem. I also knew the importance of building a team with a diverse set of skills and personalities. I started to pitch my ideas to the smartest people I knew and asked those people to recommend the smartest people they knew. That led me to meet my other cofounders, which ultimately turned Swaggle from our imagination to a functional product. As a founder, you never stop selling; starting from pitching the idea to a potential partner.

Invent Opportunities Relentlessly. As a two-sided marketplace, one of our biggest challenges is to ensure that we have the supply in place to drive the demand, and vice versa. In Swaggle's case, it was getting consignment shops onboard. I remember that we tried to get a particular consignment shop on board for weeks with no success. I was told by a team member that the owner of the shop was very private and did not want to be contacted. My team was also concerned that Swaggle was too early in the development stages to approach a consignment shop. Regardless, I picked up the phone and pitched Swaggle to the owner. The truth was that we were too early, and as a result the owner rejected our offer to join as a partner. The platform was not fully developed and we had nothing to show and prove that we would be an invaluable partner to her business. A week after our call, the owner of the shop reached out and introduced me to her husband who ultimately became our advisor. His advise helped shape the direction of the company and six months later the consignment shop became our first partner. I couldn't imagine where we would be today if I hadn't picked up the phone and called the shop out of the blue in the middle of a meeting.

As a founder, you can't expect everything to happen according to the plan. When things go south, you cannot afford to lose any opportunity that may turn your business around. When people ask me how is my day going. My response is often "every day is a grind." Don't get overly zealous when things are going well, because that's when bad things will happen. Don't lose hope when things are bad, pick yourself up and try to make the best judgement possible.

Go Titans!

Eric Niu

The Safariland Group

Scott O'Brien is president of The Safariland Group (TSG). The company is a leading global provider of a broad range of safety and survivability products.

In 1964, following his father's request for a custom holster, Neale Perkins launched a holster business from his garage in Sierra Madre, California. He called it Safariland. Scott joined Safariland in 1973 while a business administration major at California State University Fullerton.

When he graduated in 1977, Scott assumed many roles within the company in marketing, operations and manufacturing. He led the company through rapid growth. In 1993, the owners appointed Scott president and chief operating officer. He became a partner. They sold the business in 1999.

Scott remained a key leader both within the industry and in the company through diversifications and acquisitions by larger organizations. In 2005, the new owners asked him to again serve as president of TSG. He did so in 2006.

Today, TSG is a privately held firm. Its headquarters are in both Ontario, California, and Jacksonville, Florida. It has 2,200 associates and facilities throughout the US, Mexico, Canada, UK and Lithuania.

TSG is a manufacturer of premier products designed for public safety, military and outdoor markets. Its products range from body armor and flotation equipment to body-worn cameras, riot gear and gun holsters. Among the most recognized brands in TSG's product offering are Safariland®, Med-Eng®, ABA®, Second Chance®, VIEVU®, Mustang Survival®, Bianchi®, Break Free®, PROTECH® Tactical, Defense Technology®, Hatch®, Monadnock®, Identicator® and NIK®.

Scott is a member of the Young Presidents' Organization. He is Chairman Emeritus of the Toyota Motor Sales Supplier Alliance.

For years, Scott has been a dedicated supporter of the Mihaylo College of Business and Economics. He continues to play an active role as a member of the Dean's Advisory Board. CSUF named The Scott O'Brien '77 Family Innovation Center in Mihaylo Hall in honor of the gift he and his wife Deanna gave the College.

TSG also sponsors Mihaylo MBA student consulting teams. The college's Small Business Institute administers the MBA capstone experience. It is an intensive, semester long opportunity for MBA students to consult with companies and provide extensive research and analysis for real business questions. Each company pays a fee for these services. "It's been worth every penny," says Scott, "... they've done a fantastic job."

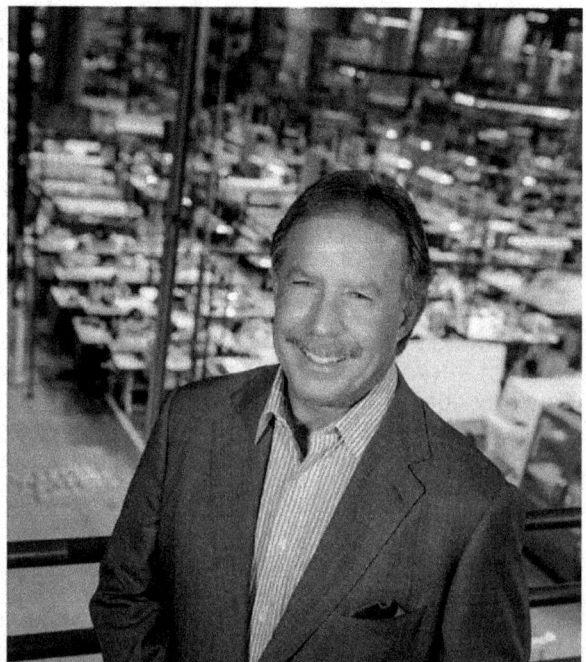

222

THE SAFARILAND GROUP

Dear Founder:

All my life, I've relied on my competitive spirit to drive success. As the athlete, student, or business leader, I love to win – I hate to lose.

I learned at a very young age that it takes certain behaviors to be competitive. Whether competing in a sport, taking on a new business venture, or striving for personal goals, the three behaviors that keep me focused and disciplined – inside and outside the boardroom are mental toughness, curiosity and perseverance. You have to compete every day.

As a business student at CSUF, I had the opportunity to work for Safariland. At that time, Safariland was a holster brand that was well recognized in the law enforcement community. As a young CSUF graduate, I was educationally prepared and eager to take Safariland to new heights. My curiosity led me to question, explore and develop products to better protect the good guys - our law enforcement community.

At the time that I started with the company in 1977, we did more than one million dollars in sales. Today, The Safariland Group operates worldwide with more than $450 million in sales. It is privately held with 2,200 associates in the United States, Canada, Mexico, Lithuania and the United Kingdom.

As a global leader of safety and survivability products, we protect lives. That is what we do. We are well focused on the significance of our work. Our products have saved over 1,985 lives, and that's why we work so hard to do it well. With each new SAVE, I am so humbly reminded why I come to work every day.

Each life that is saved is a win for the law enforcement officer and their loved ones. It is a win for our team and defines why we remain focused on our Mission "Together, We Save Lives." In my view as President of The Safariland Group, the foundation of our enterprise is built on relationships with our associates and suppliers, whereby we trust each other and hold each other accountable. We are passionate about our products and we are committed to be the best. Whether on the production line, in the boardroom or among our suppliers, each and every role is integral to our success.

Throughout my 40 years in the industry, we've had a lot of wins, but we've had our share of challenges. It takes mental toughness and perseverance to endure the challenging times and stay the course. As I mentioned, I love to win – I hate to lose, but regardless of the outcome, I always remind myself, tough times don't last; tough people do!

Best regards,

Scott O'Brien
President
The Safariland Group

Expert Networker

David Obstfeld is an Associate Professor of Management at California State University's Mihaylo College of Business and Economics. He is a member of the Entrepreneurship Concentration's Faculty. He teaches courses in entrepreneurship and strategy.

David developed a path breaking CSUF entrepreneurship course in lean start-up strategies. He networked with Center for Entrepreneurship board member and incubator owner Michael Sawitz to make the course a reality. David and Michael allowed student consulting teams formed in the course to serve FastStart.studio residents. Students applied what they learned in the class to benefit the resident companies. Michael personally took on a volunteer adjunct professor role. He teamed with David, presenting much of the course content and mentoring student consulting teams.

David's research examines how social network and knowledge processes interact to produce different forms of innovation in organizations, entrepreneurship, and collective action.

Multiple grants have funded his research. They include the National Science Foundation (NSF) and the Academy of Finland. American Sociological Association presented David with the W. Richard Scott Award for Distinguished Scholarship for an outstanding contribution to the organizational discipline. David's book-length study, Getting New Things Done: Networks, Brokerage, and the Assembly of Innovative Action (Stanford University Press 2017), focuses on how brokers and entrepreneurs coordinate action for innovation and value creation in complex organizational contexts. Leading management and social science journals have published his research. They include Administrative Science Quarterly, Organization Science, Strategic Management Journal, Research in the Sociology of Organizations, and Industrial and Corporate Change. He is widely cited across a diverse range of disciplines.

Before joining Mihaylo, David was a visiting faculty member at the Stern School of Business, New York University and at the Merage School of Business, University of California, Irvine. He received his A.B. from the University of Chicago and his Ph.D. from the Ross School of Business, University of Michigan. Before embarking on his academic career, he served as Director of Training and Development at The Federal National Mortgage Association (Fannie Mae) for ten years.

Mihaylo College of Business and Economics

Department of Management

800 North State College Blvd., Fullerton, CA 92831 / T 657-278-2251 / F 657-278-2592

Dear Founder

Given the mastery of any reader who is holding this volume (i.e., you!), what would I take this brief moment of your attention to emphasize? The importance of networks to new venture success is probably obvious but let me walk through some basic reminders:

1. ***Resources and ideas are accessed through relationships***. The basic building blocks of your network are "one-on-one" or "dyadic" relationships. Building a diverse set of dyadic relationships provides you with social oxygen by which you access ideas, resources and opportunities. Those conversations stimulate linear and non-linear thinking and learning.

2. ***Build relationships frequently***. You presumably know many of the ways to build ties – informal coffee, formal mixers sponsored by the Center for Entrepreneurship, but everyone needs to be reminded to stay in action, like we need to be reminded to work out. Initiate contact, ask questions, and listen.

3. ***Emphasize key relationships***. Those dyadic ties once created need selective cultivation – in some cases merely to keep relationships alive, and in other cases, developing them into ties of greater trust that support collaboration. The ties that are most important require more systematic attention though phone calls and follow ups … and patience. Don't be afraid to initiate more than once.

4. ***Assemble ties into clusters of three and greater***. With the ties you create dyadically described above, comes the crucial additional power of assembling ties in threes or greater, the root of collaboration and scaling.

5. ***Clustering involves unique skills***. One key skill is making an introduction between two parties who have never met, or who you will bring together to form a new collaboration. It also may involve knowing who to introduce and who to wait on, like the investor for whom you aren't quite ready.

6. ***Startups involve clustering.*** New ventures can be understood as the introduction of two or more founders, the ability to facilitate that activity over time, and the assembly of additional ties and participants over time. Individual building blocks are assembled into buildings.

7. ***Introductions of others is also a source of power and reciprocity.*** You may also create value for others in your network but step away afterward.

8. ***Locate the idea that motivates the networks you assemble.*** Assembly involves skillful talk – specifically analogies, metaphors and stories about how to grow. Skillful talk unites and motivates people.

Remember two fundamental network strategies, build dyadic ties and assemble those ties in clusters. Never stop practicing.

Good luck on assembling your success!

David Obstfeld

Axoro Management

Marc Pakbaz is a serial entrepreneur and a business consultant. He founded Axoro Management (Axoro) in 1994 and serves as its Managing Partner and Chairman of the Board.

Marc views Axoro as an business advising group with a new approach. Not only does it advise its clients on their day-to-day business or their strategy, but it also executes the plan and delivers the result.

Marc has owned and sold two companies, after facilitating their turnarounds from unsuccessful and unprofitable companies. He then became a specialist at "fixing failing businesses." He develops and executes plans to prepare companies to be "sellable."

Marc is a seasoned executive with over 30 years of experience in strategy, leadership, management, marketing, financial services and consulting. His resume includes expertise in areas such as starting businesses, mergers and acquisitions (M&A), business development, marketing and financial reporting systems. He served as Managing Director of Thomson Financial - Reuter in Paris, France.

With an abundance of international experience and speaking three languages, Marc has a strong understanding of many markets. The list includes markets in North America, Europe, Asia and the Middle East.

At Irvine based Axoro Management, Marc's team has worked with more than 300 companies. Clients range from small scale startups to mid and large size corporations. Axoro offers strategic and marketing consulting services across

many industries including: manufacturing, distribution, software development, transportation, real estate and professional services.

In addition to his executive career, Marc has taught at several universities, both in English and French. He holds an MBA and DBA from the University of Paris XII. Marc served for five years as an Associate Professor at the University.

Over the past thirty years, Marc has established himself as a thought leader in executive management, business development, marketing and financial expertise for business owners. He is a frequent guest speaker and lecturer.

AXoro
Management

Dear Founder,

It's a pleasure meeting you virtually. You may think, "All those founders are busy or they don't want to share their experience with me." Or you may guess that we are over qualified for your small venture. Wrong! We, founders, love to share our experience. We love to see others succeed and love to be a part of a successful venture.

You also may think, "Now is not a good time. I need to work first and gain more experience before strating my own venture. I don't have the time, money, knowledge, or experience to start it now. I plan to do it next year." Here is the problem: Next year, you will postpone it to the "next year" and another "next year" and so on and on.

Stop overthinking, jump in the water and start swimming. As long as you don't jump in the water and you don't swallow a few sips of water, you will never learn how to swim.

We have ALL been there. We have all paid for our mistakes and we learned from our mistakes. Don't even believe for a second that you will never make any mistakes. You WILL. So what? This is how you will learn.

Today's technology allows you to have access to endless information and experience and to read about many successful and unsuccessful experiences. The more you read, the more you realize what you don't know! However, If you have a good idea, if your idea is validated by a few experienced people and if you are passionate about it, just jump on it. Everything else will follow, including money.

Do you need to have a unique idea that not a single person has ever thought about? No! You don't need to be first. You just need to do it better or slightly, I said slightly, different than anybody else. Just DO IT.

My dear founder, If you jump in, a few years later you will say, "That was easy. Why doesn't everybody do that?"

Best of luck,

Marc Pakbaz
Managing Partner
Axoro Management
Marc.pakbaz@axoro.com

Husband and Wife Founders

Niaz Panhwar and Ayisha Fareed are husband and wife cofounders of Appoon, LLC (Appoon). Appoon is in residence at the CSUF Startup Incubator--Irvine Campus.

Niaz Panhwar is the CEO of Appoon. Niaz started his career as a Marine Engineer He has earned his master's in international business from a leading business school in London. He has held executive positions at many Shipping & Logistics companies and IT Companies in the United Kingdom and the United Arab Emirates.

Ayisha Fareed is the CTO of Appoon. She has a passion for technology and at a very young age she started work at Carrefour (a multinational retail giant today). She pursued a Computer Science degree while working full time. For nearly two decades, Ayisha's expertise helped provide excellent IT services to Carrefour. IT advances allowed the company to successfully expand from three stores to about 300+ stores in 16 different countries. As a senior executive, she managed big teams of three thousand users. She profoundly felt the very real pains experienced in the quest for team productivity. Pains that prevail in many organizations today.

Niaz and Ayisha have been entrepreneurs for the past five years. They founded and successfully exited from Dat Struct their award winning IT outsourcing company. It had won an award at the Gulf Cooperation Council's eleventh Financial Markets and New Economic Trends Conference. Niaz and Ayisha sold Dat Struct to a large regional player.

Niaz and Ayisha then formed Appoon in London. Its main product is TeamKnit, an all-in-one tool for communication,

collaboration and employee engagement. It helps enhance team productivity within all sizes and types of organizations. Says Ayisha, "It will help revolutionize the way work is performed in the workplace by teams like yours and mine."

When Niaz and Ayisha looked to move their North American headquarters from Toronto to Southern California, they chose the CSUF Startup Incubator in Irvine. Niaz explains the choice, "CSUF's incubator will give us a huge opportunity to work with the finest talent in the country. The excellent mentors and access to talented student consulting teams will help us grow much faster."

Appoon

Dear Founders

As we reflect on our own startup experience and what we have witnessed in other new ventures, we see some common elements for success: diversity, courage, and acceptance.

First, diversity is powerful. While cultural, racial, and ethnic diversity has great merit, so does diversity in mindset. Teams are enhanced by bringing together people with different experiences and life skills. As a husband and wife entrepreneur team, we each bring different approaches to problem solving. Ayisha is tech-savvy and deeply analytical, while Niaz is a sales and marketing executive who thrives on networking and meeting new people. Yet, as different as we each are, we are great partners. Our differences make for better, more balanced decisions.

Second, it takes great courage and self-belief to begin and sustain an entrepreneurial journey. Our advice to all new entrepreneurs is to just do it. Have the courage to try and the belief in yourself to pitch your ideas to others. Know that negative feedback and criticism will come, but you must suppress the tendency to resist or fight. Instead, welcome the feedback.
Consider each negative comment as a gift; these comments are tips about how to improve your business concept. Be brave and listen. You will be happy you did.

Third, you must accept where you are. Don't dwell on what happened a year ago, but instead stay in the moment. An entrepreneur's life is like the surf. It rolls in and pounds the shore and then quickly retreats back to the sea. This is normal. Know that this ebb and flow is predictable. Don't look too far ahead, or you might get hit by a big wave. Instead, focus on your daily tasks, be mindful, and celebrate your achievements day by day. This acceptance will allow you to be successful every day.

Diversity, courage, and acceptance are key ingredients for a successful entrepreneurial journey.

All the best,

Ayisha Fareed, CTO   Niaz Panhwar, CEO

US Office: 5754 Irvine Center Drive, Irvine, California, 92618 USA

Canada Office: 1801 Suite, One Yonge Street, Toronto M5E 1W7

✉ hello@appoon.com   🌐   ☎ US & Canada Office : +1 888 440 4833

Marketer and Volunteer

Clifton "Cliff" Passow received his BBA in Marketing from California State University Fullerton's Mihaylo College in 2008. He has undertaken many entrepreneurial ventures, worked for large corporations, and founded a content marketing agency.

Cliff's first entrepreneurial venture was selling his artwork at local comic book shops in middle school. He moved on to selling apparel in high school. Growing and selling corals and algae was his college venture.

Cliff has held many marketing positions in corporations within several industries. They include commercial real estate, aerospace, energy, retail, and sustainability. He was project manager for Sonfarrel, Inc.'s in house government contracts, and moved to marketing in 2007. He was a marketing assistant at Diversified Automation, handling all aspects of direct and SEO marketing. He served as marketing coordinator for Anna's Linens where he launched and managed Anna's loyalty/CRM program for over 300 retail locations. Anna's Linens promoted him to CRM Manager. He then became National Marketing Manager for Healthy Buildings where he manages marketing efforts for sustainability projects across the U.S.A.

After eleven years working for corporate America (plus some consulting on the side), he decided to launch his own business in 2013 – BrandGrew Strategies. He created a business that would let him do what he loves. He creates marketing content and strategies for amazing, genuine businesses. Cliff views himself as a motivated and calculated professional. In his words, "My ultimate goal is to continue growing, while having a positive impact on my community. I enjoy working with genuine, honest people who love what they do."

A big supporter of environmental awareness, Cliff also enjoys sharing knowledge and experience with future business leaders, fellow marketers, and entrepreneurs. In 2011-2017 he served as a mentor for California State University Fullerton students in Entrepreneurial Marketing courses. Cliff also serves as a Big Buddy for Comfort Zone Camp, a camp for children who have lost a parent, sibling, or primary caregiver. He says, "The weekend camps are life-changing, not only for grieving children but for their big buddies as well."

Cliff's other passions include producing and editing video, video games, and the great outdoors. Hiking and kayaking are his favorite outdoor activities. Cliff has enjoyed using Adobe products for the last 17 years, and absolutely loves Photoshop, Premier, After Effects, and InDesign. More than anything, he loves spending time with his son.

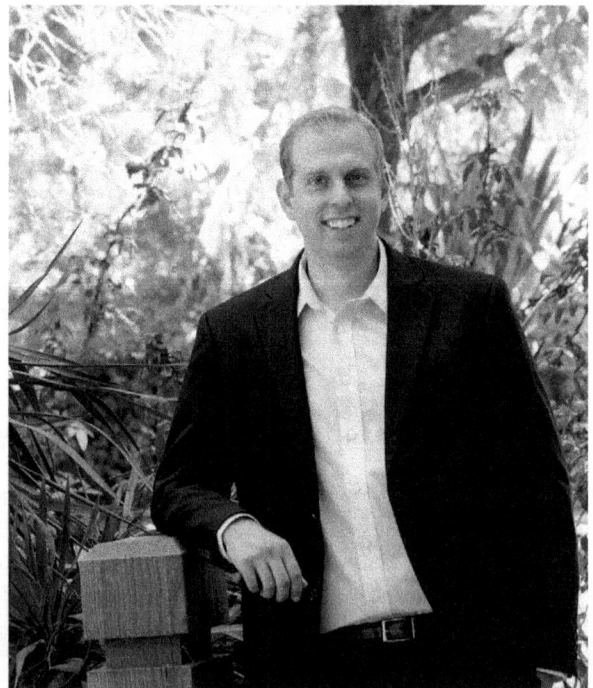

Clifton Passow

Trabuco Canyon, CA

Dear Founder,

What have I learned as an entrepreneur? Running a business is hard. *Founding* a business is grueling. In order to have the best chance of success, ensure that you really know yourself, and the business you plan to start.

From the moment you decide to start a business, your responsibilities will substantially increase. If you plan to hire employees, your duties will likely grow. During the course of my career, I have undertaken many entrepreneurial ventures and worked for large corporations, but I have only founded one company thus far. What did I learn about being a founder? In short, I don't want to be one...at least not alone.

When I founded BrandGrew Strategies, it was because I loved creating marketing content and strategies for amazing, genuine businesses. What I found through the formation of an S-Corp, which served as a marketing agency, is that it can be very inefficient to generate a worthwhile profit when starting a new venture. For most startups, it takes 2-5 years to turn a profit, if at all. I was able to do it by year two. With that said, the profit I was making was less than my previous corporate salary, and I was working far more than forty hours a week.

As a business founder, it is up to *you* to build the business' infrastructure from the ground up. Developing this infrastructure makes it difficult to focus on what you love when you're having to be a "jack of all trades" and doing accounting, IT, legal, HR, etc. If you love doing a little of everything, then founding a business could be right for you. For me, building the business' infrastructure was not fun, and took away from creating marketing content and strategies (which is what I consider fun).

You might be thinking "I will have partners/employees/vendors to take care of the stuff I am not good at." Finding the right people resources is key and no easy task. I learned the hard way that if you trust the wrong people to work on your business, it can really waste a lot of your time and money. Vetting good people takes time and trust, don't rush it.

Do not get discouraged, being a solo venture founder wasn't right for me, but it could be great for you. If you have a deep awareness of yourself and the business you want to start, and have really, *really*, **REALLY** thought through what you are about to do, then you might be onto something amazing.

I definitely don't regret starting my business, it taught me a lot of valuable lessons about myself and my passions. I am passionate about business ownership, creating marketing content and strategies, and running a profitable business. Starting a business from scratch...not my thing.

Best of luck in finding your thing.

Sincerely,

Clifton Passow
Entrepreneur, Volunteer, and Marketer

Emigrant, Banker and CEO

Ash Patel serves as President and CEO of Commercial Bank of California ("CBC"). CBC is one of the nation's highest capitalized banks and recognized as a BauerFinancial, Inc. "Five-Star Bank" for its financial strength and stability. It is a full service, FDIC-insured, community bank headquartered in Irvine, California.

CBC is owned, built and run by entrepreneurs for entrepreneurs. Local business leaders William Lyon, Paul Folino, and Alex Meruelo serve on the Board of Directors. CBC specializes in delivering customized, highly personalized banking services to small and mid-sized businesses in California.

Ash has over twenty years of experience in the banking industry. He immigrated from the Republic of Zambia in Southern Africa. Ash started as a teller at Bank of America. He had entrepreneurial drive and evolved into a seasoned CEO.

In 2001 Ash became the founding President and COO of Premier Commercial Bank. During his tenure the bank grew from $7 million in assets to over $480 million. It successfully maintained profitability in all quarters of operation since its inception.

In 2013 Ash became President and CEO of CBC. In 2015 he became Chairman of the Board of National Bank of California. He successfully entered into a definitive agreement in mid 2016 to merge National Bank of California with CBC. The combined bank had branches in both Los Angeles and Orange counties. Its initial, combined assets were $750 million. The goal is reaching $1 Billion in five years.

As CEO, Ash focuses on inspiring his team and clients to achieve their dreams. He leads by example, investing in building relationships and cutting-edge technology to enhance the client experience.

Ash and the team at CBC are endeavoring to build a bank that does not exist today. Their focus is on offering customers a high touch experience combined with high technology solutions. He has been at the forefront of the critical industry conversations surrounding FinTech and how traditional banking organizations need to evolve to embrace new technology.

In line with Ash's personal mission to empower people to achieve their dreams, he founded of the Siksha Foundation. It is a nonprofit organization that provides education through building schools for under privileged children in rural India and Africa. Right now, it focuses on Gujurat, India's westernmost state and Ndola, Zambia. To date the Foundation has built three schools in India and supported many local charities in Ndola.

Ash Patel
President & CEO
Commercial Bank of California

Dear Founder:

Some things in life happen by accident. And some things happen on purpose. But I believe the key to success is knowing when to seize an opportunity, no matter the circumstance.

My career began as an accident. I came to visit my brother in the United States from my home in Zambia, Africa. Before I knew it, my brother hid my passport and sent my resume out to a few banks. I'm not sure why he picked the banking industry, but a woman from Bank of America – who was also from Zambia – wanted to meet me. They had an opening for a teller position and I took it.

I called my dad back home to tell him and his response was "But remember, we are Indian and we are entrepreneurs. You can work for Bank of America, but I want you to find out how BofA actually makes money." With that, I was curious and determined to find out how banks make money.

My curiosity took me on an adventure. I asked every banking industry executive I met how banks make money. Most only understood the transactional side of the business. It wasn't until I received a job offer from the president of the Bank of Orange County that I got my chance to learn. I accepted a pay cut in return for a seat at the executive table and a 7-year crash course on how a bank really makes money. After years of fearless curiosity, the doors unlocked to a world of understanding that was pivotal to my success.

I set off to open my own bank and continued seizing the opportunities in front of me. I became the President and CEO of Commercial Bank of California in 2013 and invested in the CBC team by teaching them to lead with an entrepreneurial mindset by creating the initiative "Purposeful Journey to a Billion" (PJ2B). This approach not only inspired each person to take ownership in the bank's success, but it transformed the business. We grew from less than $200 million in assets in 2013 to more than $825 million at the end of the third quarter 2017. I believe regardless of the size of the company or how institutional it may be, you should always think like an entrepreneur. That insatiable sprit transformed my world and laid the foundation for my effectiveness as a leader today.

It is incredible to look back at my journey and think about my start in shoes very similar to yours. I attribute my effectiveness as an executive to my tenacious curiosity and steadfast hold to my entrepreneurial spirit. I never lost sight of *why* I was doing what I was doing. And today, I believe that this approach can be applied to any type of business. I bid you the best of luck and don't forget to believe in yourself, continue to investigate and never lose that spirit.

Sincerely,

Ash Patel

Global Women Foundation

Michelle Patterson is the founder of Global Women Foundation ("GWF"). It is a 501(c)(3) non-profit public charity created to bring women together to create global change by empowering them to transform their communities. GWF' mission is to support women to effectuate positive change. It serves as a world-wide conduit for connecting community, mentoring, education, and financial support.

Recently, Michelle took took over the reins of the California Women's Conference. She continues its thirty year tradition as the nation's preeminent conference for women.

Michelle Is a successful event promoter. She is a lauded business accelerator (she was the youngest Regional VP and National Sales Trainer for Robert Half, the world's largest specialized recruiting firm). She works with companies as a Strategic Advisor to help them get their messages out to the world.

Michelle is a sought-after media commentator (The Huffington Post, CNBC, Fox Business News, Bloomberg and hundreds of TV and radio stations seek her insights). She is an energetic and engaging public speaker and hosts a weekly radio show on Women Network Talk Radio.

Michelle is the headlining author for a women's anthology, Women Change the World, featuring notable celebrity contributors, and is in five other books. She was invited to be a keynote speaker to the United Nations on the topic of women and the difference they are making in our world. Michelle has received many honors. Recently the Los Angeles Business Journal awarded her its Corporate Advocate award at their 23rd

annual Women's Summit. She received the Women's Elevation Award presented by Pepperdine University at their Global Perspectives Conference. In 2014, Ms. Patterson was knighted Dame Michelle Patterson for her humanitarian work by the Knights of the Orthodox Order of St. John Russian Grand Priory, a thousand year old organization known for their work founding of hospitals. In 2016, Ms. Patterson was awarded a "Lifetime Achievement Award" by President Barack Obama and the Corporation for National and Community Service for her lifelong commitment to building a stronger nation through volunteer service.

Michelle is a board member for Loyola Marymount University's Bellarmine College of Liberal Arts. She is a past CSUF Entrepreneurship student consulting client.

Michelle is passionate about her family. She lives in Orange County, California with her husband of twenty years, Eric, a successful corporate CFO in his own right, and their two beautiful children, Jaclyn and Chase.

Global Women Foundation
27702 Crown Valley Parkway Suite D4
Ladera Ranch, CA 92694

Michelle J. Patterson, CEO

Dear Founder,

During my many years in the corporate world, and as the CEO of my own businesses, I have witnessed firsthand how executives who hold true to their values become successful in both their personal and professional lives. I myself hold many values close to my heart (and wear them on my sleeve), but the most important one that has helped me achieve my goals over and over is **PERSISTENCE**.

Persistence is one of the biggest keys to success. It means that you keep moving forward even when you feel like quitting. Many people give up on their dreams at the first sign of opposition or misfortune. Nothing in life worth achieving ever comes easily. Sometimes you need to fight for your dream. Sometimes you need to let your sheer will and persistence carry you through despite all the negativity and opposition you might face.

Since its founding three decades ago by then Governor George Deukmejian, the California Women's Conference had been bringing together women from all over the world to learn and to grow from each other. The event was organized by the first lady of California, the governor's wife. But in 2012, Governor Jerry Brown's wife decided to discontinue the event. Mrs. Brown's decision inspired me. As an experienced producer of large-scale events, I decided to take over the conference, determined to keep it alive. My team and I locked down a venue, developed a plan and started to execute. We had a burning desire and a definite plan of action.

Over the next few months, I signed up thousands of attendees, over 250 exhibitors, more than 150 speakers. Things were off to a great start. But as the event grew closer, things were not going according to plan. I had two major setbacks that jeopardized my dream and the event. First, the team outsourced to handle sponsorships grossly inflated their projections; they were nowhere near what they should have been. Second, the funding that was expected to come for the business failed to materialize. When a payment came due for the production, I realized we were $1.8 million in the hole. The conference was in danger of being cancelled and I had just 17 days to save it.

I had a definite goal – to put on this event and to provide resources to thousands of women who needed it. Against all odds I kept at it. No matter how many people told me to shut down the event, I pulled in all my resources and stuck to the plan. Persistence allows you to keep taking action even when you don't feel motivated to do so, and therefore you keep accumulating results. That's exactly what happened to me.

Together with my team of advisors, we went from nearly being shut down and considering bankruptcy to reducing the debt to $150,000. With persistence and a positive attitude we were able to make the 2012 California Women's Conference extremely successful and continue to produce the event, making it the largest 2 day Women's Conference in the United States. I often reflect on what would have happened had I given up out of fear and let my ego get the best of me, but by not accepting defeat, loss was nothing more than a temporary road block.

Whatever your goals and dreams are – make sure PERSISTENCE is one of the tools in your toolbox!

Michelle J. Patterson, CEO

Executive, Entrepreneur, Mentor

John Pietro started his career shining shoes in a barbershop. He liked being his own boss.

John's professional career of over 40 years was spent first as a Marketing Executive for restaurant chains like Wendy's, Denny's, and Bojangles Chicken. He then switched to the Advertising Agency business, working for a mid-sized agency. Next John joined Omnicom, the world's largest agency conglomerate. At Omnicom he worked on clients like Burger King, Denny's and Union 76.

At 51 years of age, John quit the corporate world and opened a small business, an advertising agency in Orange County California called AMP. He built the business over the next 12 years by working with clients like Cinnabon, Coca Cola, El Pollo Loco, Baja Fresh and Aramark. He sold the business 12 years later and retired.

After he retired, John became a SCORE Mentor in Orange County. Currently he mentors and gives seminars on Marketing Without Money. He has seen over 750 small businesses in the last seven years including many through CSUF Entrepreneurship. John has spoken to thousands of would be entrepreneurs in the last seven years. He has over 40 documented success stories with SCORE.

John has been married to his beautiful wife Anne for 47 years, has one son Michael and a granddaughter Elle. He is an avid sports fan and golfer.

John's best advice to entrepreneurs is simple: "Be Great at One Thing."

John Pietro
Mission Viejo, California

Dear Founder:

I had the pleasure of leaving Corporate life at 51 years of age and starting my own business. I thought I understood business from a 30,000 foot view, but was lost from a 500 foot view. There was no administrative assistant to handle my calls, appointments or correspondence. In fact, I was my own Administrative Assistant. We had no janitorial service, so on Saturday I cleaned the office. We had no payroll clerks, so I handled payroll to insure everyone got paid but me.

This sounds scary, but I enjoyed it immensely! I was my own boss. The first lesson I learned was humility. The second was to learn to manage risk. I made the wheels spin or they didn't spin. Any entrepreneur who thinks others will make the wheels spin is nuts! You are the catalyst. You are the best person to make sales. Others will follow your lead. It is your business! The internet will not make sales for you, but it might generate good leads. You have to turn these leads into sales.

The best way to make this happen is to have a plan. I like quarterly plans, they should include where we are today, where we want to be in three months and how are we going to get there. Once you make the plan, then own it. You are the rainmaker. This is a high risk, high reward business so develop a healthy appetite for action. Be great at one thing! Make sure that one thing is valuable to your customer.

Don't worry about future products or channels, worry about what you do best. Get to know your customers and let them know you. Relationships drive business more than you think, so start developing relationships with companies you want to do business with now. Seek mentoring from people who have more experience, listen more than you talk and put good ideas to work immediately. Learning is a continuous process, the more you learn the more you realize how much you don't know. Finally, make a commitment to yourself that you will do whatever it takes to succeed and don't give up.

Keep Your Eyes On The Prize!

Sincerely,

John Pietro

Entrepreneur and Intrapreneur

William J Purpura is both an Entrepreneur and Intrapreneur. As an Entrepreneur, at age 23, Bill was loaned out as Chief Engineer for a $1.5 M startup funded by his employer Southern California Edison. He played a key role in acquiring its initial funding. In 1983, Bill co-founded Dargon Development which currently manages a multi-million dollar boutique investment fund and offers Financial /Engineering consulting to outside firms. In 2015, he co-founded and self-funded Dynamic Archery Systems with a team of CSUF alumni engineers.

As a Intrapreneur, Bill worked at Boeing for 33 years.. He combined his entrepreneur skills with Boeing's resources to influence its future technology and new business thrusts. During his tenure at Boeing, Bill was recognized as the "key win factor" on many major Department of Defense proposal wins. He earned the designation Boeing Subject Matter Expert in multiple areas including advanced technology development, next generation net-enabled systems, cyber architectures, and new business pursuit. Bill's work was awarded 19 U.S. Patents (three more are under review) plus two Boeing trade secrets. He has been recognized by both Boeing and the aerospace Industry for his intrapreneurial achievements., Bill received the 2010 Boeing Supplier Management SAGE Award and the 2004 Boeing IDS Innovative Engineer Award. He was Profiled in the Project Management Institute's professional journal, "Imagination" in August, 2012.

At California State University Fullerton, Bill supports CSUF entrepreneur development. For five years, he was Boeing's liaison to CSUF's School of Engineering & Computer Science (ECS)

and the Mihaylo College of Business and Rconomics (MCBE). He continues to volunteer in this role since retiring in 2015. Bill's volunteer focus is on mentoring and sometimes sponsoring both senior ECS design teams and MCBE Entrepreneurship's student business case teams, student team entrants in the annual business plan competition, and student start-ups.

Bill also serves as a Director on the CSUF Alumni Board of Directors and is an enthusiastic CSUF assistant archery coach.

Dear Founder,

Over my 41 + year career as an Entrepreneur, Intrapreneur, and fund manager I learned more startups fail due to the lack of the right people in key functional positions than undercapitalization. Staff backed by relevant experience and proven capabilities is crucial to credibly filling the core functional positions:

General Manager: Often the concept originator, the one with the vision and understanding of the goals. The GM possesses the critical leadership and communication skills needed to recruit critical team members and convince investors to buy into the firm. It can be difficult for the concept originator to recognize that there is more to building a business than having a great concept or they are not qualified to perform every key function. Their daily role is to build and lead the team. They have ultimate responsibility for all cost, schedule, and performance goals.

Service/Product Producer: They are responsible for the content generation. This is the design, development, fabrication, generation, delivery, and support of the service or product that generates sales and income. They also ID/manage all personnel and assets needed at startup.

Marketing Lead: This person is responsible for developing and managing the firms initial marketing plan for the kickoff product or service. The marketing lead keeps the team focused on developing a product that meets the identified market desired requirements. It is easy to get distracted and build that product that you want, instead of the product that can make sales for the business. The marketing lead has full responsibility for advertising, social media, and sales campaigns until future growth can justify adding skilled staffing to assume these roles.

Financial Lead: This person wears multiple hats at startup, and will later grow to lead a team with specific financial responsibilities. Initial responsibilities include development of proforma budgets, financial analysis for income/expense projections, supporting the GM in locating and acquiring initial funding, as well as accounts payable/receivable during initial operations.

Infrastructure Support: All ancillary support such as legal (contract and Intellectual property), accounting (CPA, tax, payroll), IT, office admin support (often initially subcontracted services).

To be successful, all these positions must mesh their abilities, back each other up, and focus on getting the the job done regardless of traditional responsibility boundaries. The issue often missed by entrepreneurs is that smart investors FIRST evaluate the experience and capabilities of those to execute the business plan plan BEFORE they look at the service or product to be sold! Some of the most critical red flags found include:

- Clear evidence of Entrepreneurs's critical lack of understanding of what it takes to run a business
- Entrepreneur's inability to attract personnel with critical capabilities to be equity partners.
- Entrepreneur's belief they can effectively do all these functions while fulfilling their own role.

Successful Entrepreneurs understand it is the quality and capabilities of the proposed team that investors are betting on. A well-rounded team with past success, applicable experience, and ability to cross-support during a demanding startup is usually funded. However, an inexperienced team lacking critical core capabilities will almost always fail, even if it is fully funded (but it rarely will be). If you were considering investing your OWN hard-earned money would you evaluate a startup any differently?

William J. Purpura

239

Ultra-Research, Incorporated

John Rau is the President/CEO of Ultra-Research, Inc. (UR). The 33-year-old company provides consulting services in market research for inventors and start-up companies. The home base for the company is in Anaheim, CA.

John has over thirty years of experience in market research, planning, analysis and overall market assessment. His focus is on products, technologies and early stage ideas that could lead to patents. He and UR perform competitive assessments, business intelligence gathering, marketing planning, business pursuit planning and business plan preparation. John and his firm are expert at the identification and assessment of potential merger and acquisition candidates. Also, they do business proposal preparation in response to customer Requests for Proposals. He and UR also provide overall business planning about organizational structure and operational planning.

John has program management and business development assignments in the aerospace industry (Hughes Aircraft Company, Rockwell and the Boeing Company). He has extensive experience in the energy and environmental-related technology areas.

John is a member of the Board of Directors of Orange County Inventors Forum. He is actively involved in working with inventors who seek to bring their ideas into the marketplace.

John volunteers extensively. He is an expert volunteer mentor for both California State University Fullerton's Entrepreneurship programs and the University of California at Irvine's Applied Innovation Institute. He is a certified counselor and mentor for the US Small Business Administration's SCORE organization.

John's choice of the prefix "ultra" for his company name reflects his approach to business and community service. He writes, "The prefix ultra means 'beyond the range or limits of or beyond what is common or ordinary.' The business objective of UR is to provide research services of the quality and scope that are beyond the range or limits of what is common or ordinary."

Dear Founder:

Before launching your new business and venturing out into the world of "entrepreneurship", it is essential that you research your business industry, market and competitors. That's what market research is all about, namely, the process of gaining information about your market. The results of market research become the basis of your plan to move forward with your business. Without having performed adequate market research to give you information and some direction as to where you should be going with your new business in the marketplace, you'll be like Alice when she "came to a fork in the road. "Which road do I take?" she asked. "Where do you want to go?" responded the Cheshire Cat. "I don't know, " Alice answered. "Then ." said the Cat, "it doesn't matter."

To get started, you need to get yourself answers to some basic questions such as the following:

- Is my market clearly identifiable and who is my target customer?
- What is the size of the market and how fast is it growing?
- What are the characteristics that describe my target market in terms of financial trends, on-going technological changes, potential sensitivity to economic fluctuations and any potential governmental and environmental regulations that affect this type of industry?
- Who are the potential competitors in this marketplace and what products or services do they offer?
- What types of people buy these products or services and what do potential or existing customers like about my competitors' products/services?
- What are current buyers paying for comparable products/services and what factors are most important when buying these products/services?
- What makes my product/service unique relative to others in the marketplace -- in other words what are my discriminators, if any?
- What is required to succeed in this market and can the market support another player?
- How do my competitors reach the market and by what methods am I able to reach it?

The above is an illustrative, not necessarily complete, sample list of questions that's intended to give you a starting point relative to your market research efforts. You need to get answers to these types of questions in order to give you the basis and direction as to how you want to proceed with your new business. Don't be an "Alice" who had no idea where she was going.

John Rau

ULTRA-RESEARCH
INCORPORATED

Suite 1
6432 Via Estrada
Anaheim, CA 92807
(714) 281-0150 • Fax (714) 281-2549

P.O. Box 307
Atwood, CA 92811

For more insights by the author on what it takes to start a new business, please go to https://business.fullerton.edu> ...

Associated Group

Laurie Resnick is a California State University Fullerton alumna in Political Science. Laurie has served as an Entrepreneur in Residence for CSUF Entrepreneurship. She was a founding member of the Center for Entrepreneurship's advisory board. She serves on the Executive Council for the Mihaylo College of Business and Economics.

Laurie is a founding partner of the Associated Group (AG). AG is a full service commercial display firm that operates from a 55,000 square foot 1940's warehouse in Commerce, California. They create and deliver cutting edge decor designs for clients throughout the United States. A tailored approach ensures that each project is unique. AG's talented staff is adept at executing the most intricate customized displays for both intimate and expansive spaces. The company was founded in 1986 by Laurie and her partner Greg Salmeri. In 2001, Associated Group acquired the Rolling Greens brand and currently has three Rolling Greens locations in Los Angeles.

Under Laurie's leadership, Associated Group has built its reputation as a customer-centered and design-driven organization. She provides leadership for brand management, culture, marketing, design and finance. Over the years, Laurie has developed considerable financial expertise. She has used it in the analysis and eventual acquisition of several compatible service companies and Rolling Greens Nursery.

Laurie strongly influenced the formation of Associated Group's Display Division. Her creative guidance and drive to exceed customer expectations have led the division to industry accolades and many design awards. Clients include The Del Coronado Hotel, Ritz Carlton Hotels,

Venetian/Palazzo, Westfield Century City, and many cities, shopping centers, and commercial office properties.

Each year, Laurie joins the professor for a day program at Mihaylo. She has served as a classroom mentor and new venture panelist for CSUF Entrepreneurship. Laurie was honored in 2006 by the College for her business accomplishments and achievements.

Laurie has provided business expertise to The Midnight Mission in downtown Los Angeles. She has served on several trade and business advisory boards. She is a member of the Orange County chapter of Women Presidents Organization. AG is one of Orange County's largest women owned businesses. Smart Business Magazine recognized Laurie for her contribution to the Orange County business community. She lives in Newport Beach, California.

Dear Founder,

I count three types of founders. Type One includes the MBA folks. They crunch the numbers on market opportunities, analyze the data, select opportunities with high projected ROI and found companies to make money by meeting demand. Type Two individuals, maybe business school grads, use their skills to get a job. They go to work for a company. After a few years, they decide they can do it smarter, faster or better than their present positions allow. They launch their own companies based on industry experience. Finally, Type Three founders (which include my partner and me) just land on something that resonates with their passions and values. They take their passion and make it happen. The financial success rate of Type Three founders is probably the lowest. Nevertheless, I contend that our success came from following our core values and not knowing how to do it any other way.

My partner and I aspired to deliver the premier home and garden experience. We wanted to be the best at delivering inspired design in creative and unexpected ways. We were passionate about sharing our gifts with others. We grew our business, not with intention, not with a strategy, but by embracing the biggest challenges in the marketplace. We just said yes, yes, yes. We never said no to big design challenges. Then, we figured out how to do it. My partner and I had no professional training to do what we did. I majored in political science, he majored in fine arts, and we ended up doing landscape design. Today, everything we do revolves around design. Neither of us had ever taken a design class. Yet, we have made a living for 31 years by designing amazing things - landscapes, holiday displays, and interiors. We cater to the design trade, select corporations, and the discriminating public. We continue to delight our customers by under promising and over delivering with amazing design results. This is exceedingly difficult to do. However, our customers know that we are the premier operators in our field. They know that we really care that we put out a good product and we don't cut corners.

If you are a Type Three founder like my partner and me, I advise you to:
1. Select something you can be best at. Make sure your vision resonates with your passions and values. Your vision will be the guiding light for you, your employees and your stakeholders through tough times and distractions. Stay focused on your vision. If your instincts tell you that you are straying off course, adjust quickly. Strive to be the best in your category. It is not interesting to be a commodity. Be passionate about sharing your gifts with others.
2. Find beauty in things most people overlook. Embrace the imaginative.
3. Be authentic. Tell people what you can do, what you can't do, and why.
4. Care about putting out the best results.
5. Be courageous. Take the lead and stand up for doing things right.
6. Never give up. Be persistent, resilient and tenacious in pursuit of your vision.
7. Aspire to live up to your potential as an individual and as a company.

I wish you every success,

Laurie Resnick, President
Associated Group, Rolling Greens

Entrepreneur, CEO and Investor

JJ Richa is a seasoned entrepreneur. The logos on his letter represent only two of a twenty-five-year string of successful ventures: Trenchant Ventures, LLC and BusinessVision Advisory.

JJ is the Founder and Managing Partner of Trenchant Ventures, LLC. Based in Irvine, the company is a private equity firm. It acquires, restructures, and adds value to distressed and underperforming companies for the benefit of shareholders and stakeholders. The business steps are secure funding sources, find the right opportunities, inject qualified executives, and make a strategic exit. In short, the company invests both human and financial capital to transform underperforming businesses into successful enterprises.

BusinessVision Advisory is JJ's newest startup. Its offerings reflect JJ's accumulated accomplishments as a CEO. The company provides management consulting, online marketing services and custom development services for web and mobile. It helps businesses with planning, running, restructuring and execution. It's marketing service division helps businesses reach their target market using the latest in online tools, social media, SEO, and paid advertising. Further, the company provides web and mobile custom development services to fit today's robust business needs in a fast paced environment.

JJ's work as founder, CEO, and CTO of a SaaS/WaaS technology company is perhaps the best example of Richa's results-oriented approach to building businesses. He brought to market a new software product for the hospitality industry. His business plan and channel distribution strategy accelerated market penetration and brought the company to profitability. Leading national and local publications featured his accomplishment, including Hospitality Technology, Franchise Times and The Orange County Business Journal.

Besides his own startups, JJ has also served in senior executive roles for others. He led the restructuring and turnaround of several small to medium sized businesses in the retail and service industries.

JJ is a member of Tech Coast Angels, the nation's largest angel group. He serves on the Executive Committee of the Orange County Network. He has lead the pre-screening, screening and due diligence of prospect portfolio companies for several years.

Like many contributors to this book, JJ is a California State University graduate. He holds a Bachelor of Science degree and a Master of Science degree from CSU Long Beach, with concentrations in electronics and software. JJ is an adjunct faculty member at Concordia University, Irvine. He has been a panelist and speaker for CSUF Entrepreneurship.

Dear Founder:

We've heard it so many times and in so many flavors: The idea that entrepreneurs are born and not made. Regardless of the way it is articulated, it is my belief that entrepreneurs have many attributes that make them who they are. These include their tolerance and willingness to take risks, ability to be self-taught, leadership skills, motivation, inspiration, passion, creativity, confidence, and commitment.

After taking the leap and risking almost everything in order to reach your objectives, as an entrepreneur, you depend solely on your instinctive nature of self-motivation and inspiration. Motivation starts with the almost impossible task of motivating yourself and continues with the ability of motivating others. Starting, running, and growing a business is a daunting task, especially in the early stages. Businesses go through cyclical phases that create obstacles preventing entrepreneurs from attaining their ultimate goals. Without motivation, the ups and downs would most certainly put an end to those dreams.

I remember so many times during my entrepreneurial endeavors when I felt like giving up. If it weren't for the ability to motivate myself and others working alongside me, things would have been different. I can tell you with certainty that my original plan, when I started each one of my companies, was not what the ultimate business ended up being. Don't be misled, sometimes as an entrepreneur, you must stop. There is a fine line between perseverance and knowing when to cut the cord.

Motivation coupled with inspiration is the essence behind leadership. Leaders are masters at motivating and inspiring their peers and groups they lead. Entrepreneurs are masters at motivating and inspiring themselves. Entrepreneurship skills combined with leadership skills may be the formula for success.

Successful entrepreneurs love what they do. Inspiration gives entrepreneurs the fire to keep going. Inspiration is what makes entrepreneurs get up every morning, work 18-hour days, and go to bed anxious about starting the next day. Inspiration is entirely self-generated and comes from within.

As an entrepreneur, angel investor, mentor, and coach, I encounter many entrepreneurs with fire and excitement raging within them. It can only come from the fact that they are inspired. They love what they do and believe success is inevitable. Make no mistake about it, not all entrepreneurs are successful. It takes more than inspiration and motivation to be successful. It takes knowledge, intelligence, coachability, ability to execute, ability to be agile, pragmatism, objectiveness, preparedness, and timing.

For the most part, entrepreneurs come into this world pre-programmed with a special gift. The ability to inspire and motivate themselves and others may not be a part of that special gift. Motivation depends on coercion while inspiration is generated from a conscious decision that stems from within. That said, there are ways to assist you to motivate and inspire one's self and others: 1) Follow your dreams; 2) Choose your own destiny; 3) Create a plan; 4) Work out a schedule; 5) Set goals and objectives; 6) Love what you do; 7) Know yourself; 8) Understand the purpose behind your actions; 9) Answer the question to your why; 10) Find a mentor, an idol and a confidant; 11) Have a positive attitude; 12) Surround yourself with other individuals that are inspired and self-motivated; 13) Acquire the proper knowledge and experience; 14) Invest in yourself and keep learning; 15) Believe in yourself and your abilities; 16) Track your progress and make sure you are making headway; 17) Share your ideas with likeminded and successful individuals; 18) Take regular and consistent steps toward achieving those dreams; 19) Be humble, coachable and persistent and 20) Stop thinking about it and just do it.

Wishing you success,

JJ Richa

Celi International

Araceli (Celi) Rivas has a passion for entrepreneurship. Her maternal grand-mother ran an in-home neighborhood candy shop. Her paternal grandfather ran a seed shop cart around town. Her parents and various other family members were also entrepreneurs. By school age, Celi was starting small businesses.

In high school she joined her school's Business Academy, taking courses in business. Celi became the VP of Marketing for a school project and really enjoyed it. During a school trip to California State University, Fullerton, she learned about the Entrepreneurship program offered by Mihaylo College and the student-led Entrepreneur's Society. The trip inspired her. She was thrilled to receive her CSUF acceptance letter.

During her years at CSUF, Celi took advantage of every opportunity she could. She lived on campus, joined the board of the Entrepreneur's Society (Its President in her last year), studied international business for a year at SKEMA Business School on the French Riviera, received scholarship awards and earned a double concentration in Entrepreneurship and Marketing.

After graduating in 2010, Celi began a career in marketing - first building marketing plans for small businesses. She then worked for Experian Consumer Services, a Google Top 10 advertiser worldwide. Her passion and business training helped Celi to quickly succeed in her career. Experian promoted her often. She soon became a Search Marketing Manager, then a Bilingual Marketing Manager. Experian awarded her its Top 1% Employees Award. During this period, Celi also became a mentor at CSUF Entrepreneurship, coaching student consulting teams.

Although working for a top company was great, Celi's ambition took her back to Europe. There she spent time off traditional work to fulfill personal goals. In 2016 she made the move to San Francisco - the land of entrepreneurship, to focus more on her passion for startups.

Celi is currently still in marketing. She is "Manager-Paid Search and Social Team" at GroupM, the world's largest media investment group responsible for about one in three ads globally. She manages campaigns for several major brands.

Simultaneously, Celi is working on many entrepreneurial projects including Celi International, a marketing and talent management company. She hopes her efforts will evolve into real estate invest-ments and multiple business ventures.

Celi sets aside time to spend with family and friends between Southern California and Silicon Valley. She enjoys travel, fitness, learning, philanthropy, helping others achieve their goals and living life to the fullest.

Araceli Rivas
San Francisco, Newport Beach, CA
Email: contact@celiinternational.com
www.celiinternational.com

Dear Future Founder,

I admire your decision to be here this very moment as part of the Entrepreneurship experience. I admire your passion for wanting to create something, whether small or large, even if you don't already know what that creation will be. I admire your dedication for being here ready to learn and ready to do!

I'd love to share with you a couple things I've learned along the way in the workplace and in creating a venture.

1. Determine your motivation and remember it through the good and the bad. Even when times get tough, things will always get better. I promise.

2. Along your journey you may experience close trusted individuals, even a best friend, could put your ideas down. It does not mean it is not the next billion-dollar company. Don't let their negative opinions stop your creativity and from attempting to launch your idea. Find and continue to surround yourself with people, even if just one, who will not shut your ideas down, but who will help you find a way to make it happen. The worst thing you can do is not get started and lose your motivation simply because someone you admire does not have a similar vision. As the saying goes, it is better to fail and learn than to never try. You will become a better and smarter individual for your next idea.

3. If you take the path of working for a company first, like I did, may be to help fund the business or gain experience, in interviews do explain how the entrepreneurship courses have helped you. Example, consulting for actual businesses, finding problems and building solutions, or learning all departments of an organization which makes you understand business as a whole. This will make you more valuable to employers because you will actually have hands on experience.

4. When you are ready, buy a domain and get started on your business. It does not have to be perfect, you can edit and update along the way. This is to keep you on track on getting started.

5. Break your ideas into smaller chunks so that they are more digestible and don't seem so difficult to accomplish. For example, write down one major thing you want to accomplish each month for your venture. Block out time on your calendar to specifically work on things. Find places where you can focus, example coffee shops with wifi. Sooner rather than later you'll have something going.

6. Always have a passion for learning. Identify your weaknesses and work towards improving them. If you want to maintain a successful business or career you will always have to stay on top of trends and adjust your strategies to be relevant in this fast changing world. You can find relevant events in your area through the university, meetup.com or Eventbrite. Always keep an open mind and keep learning.

Do!

Araceli (Celi) Rivas

CSUF, 2010

Birch Capital

Ali Roushanzamir founded Birch Capital LLC, in 2008. It is a private equity firm concentrating on distressed real estate assets in the inland Empire of San Bernardino County and Riverside County markets. Ali has rehabbed and developed over 100 properties since 2008. He grew revenues by over 30% in 2017.

Ali views his financial successes as foundation blocks for building his legacy. He is passionate about deploying energy policies which are climate change friendly.

Ali grew up in the middle east, where both of his parents were agricultural engineers on government farm land. There, he developed his passion for the environment and natural resources. As an assistant farmer, Ali was involved in the analysis, testing and growth of organic tomatoes and strawberries, on traditional soil-based habitats.

In 2001, Ali earned a BA degree in Business Administration, concentration finance from CSUF. He built a solid finance resume by starting his career at the US Securities and Exchange Commission, as an Investment Advisor, Regulation. Next, he had success as a licensed investment advisor with large wire houses, including, Wells Fargo Securities. Ali then moved into insurance institutional asset management at American International Group (AIG), overseeing the investments of the Orange County Sanitation District in 2007.

Soon, Ali started his own registered investment advisory firm in Orange County, California. He is a firm believer in obtaining licensing and developing exceptional expertise in the many related aspects of financial advisement. Ali is a licensed California Bureau of Real Estate

broker. He holds numerous California Department of Insurance licenses. Ali passed many securities licenses and is a California Department of Corporations licensed investment advisor. In 2011 he earned his MBA from the University of Redlands. Ali is currently parlaying this experience to develop a socially responsible renewable energy fund concentrating on large scale micro grid systems.

In 2016, his private equity firm invested in 164 acre parcel of renewable energy land in San Bernardino County. The project is currently in the process of being developed for a commercial scale photovoltaic solar farm, generating enough electricity to power thousands of homes. Currently, Mr. Roushanzamir has connected with California State University, Fullerton's business incubator program to help position this $80 million plus solar farm for success.

Ali has a very special relationship with California State University Fullerton. He met his wife Traci at the CSUF's Pollak Library. They have two children, Grant and Riley. All are Titan Baseball fans.

BIRCH
CAPITAL

Dear Founder,

I am a founder of several organizations that leverage my own experiences and accreditations. I hope this letter provides significant insight for new entrepreneurs starting up.

I can attribute my own personal success, and accomplishments to three key characteristics: (1) My ability to draw upon my spiritual guidance, (2) My academic and professional education, (3) my personal intuition. These three characteristics enabled me to find success as an entrepreneur.

First, I would define spiritual guidance as God-given strengths in business. I can relate to this by going back to my early 20's when I discovered what my significant strength was. Working as an intern for, Dean Witter, now called Morgan Stanley Dean Witter, I went on a lunch break, found a Wall Street Journal in the break room and read it from front to back all the way through. My unquenchable thirst for financial knowledge is how I knew where my passion was. It is extremely important to find your God-given skills or traits so you can embrace and leverage them to build your business.

Second, the value of education and achieving mastery in your fields of endeavor are tantamount to your success as an entrepreneur. I found my success in education by studying business, at California State University, Fullerton. Education and professional accreditations are invaluable when it comes to building your business.

Third, the most significant characteristic needed to run a successful business is intuition or emotional intelligence, which can be defined as the ability to obtain information without having the proof or evidence at your disposal. Intuition and emotional intelligence, in my opinion, go beyond the realm of consciousness and tap into your unconscious mind. I find that by tapping into intuition I am able to enhance my day to day emotional strengths and refine my business acumen.

Finally, to be successful in business you have to have an unquenchable desire to overcome obstacles and find your success. In my perspective, finding your spiritual guidance (God-given talents) is important. Obtaining appropriate education and professional accreditations are significant. I cannot see anyone being successful in the business world without having intuition and emotional intelligence to help them overcome the daily obstacles.

Sincerely hoping for your success in mastering all of the challenges and gifts a business has to offer!
Best regards,

Ali Roushanzamir, MBA
CEO/Founder

Gigging and Grubbing

Shari Rudolph is an accomplished retail, digital commerce and media executive. She has a strong track record of building audience, revenue and brands.

Shari is co-founder and Executive Producer of Gigging & Grubbing, an omni-channel media enterprise. It developed a television show about musicians and their favorite places to eat while on tour. Gigging & Grubbing is syndicated nationally and has featured artists such as The Plain White Ts, Andy Griggs and BJ Thomas.

Shari is Chief Marketing Officer for nonprofit Good360, a leader in purposeful giving and product philanthropy. At Good360, Shari is focused on reinventing the philanthropic model to create a modern nonprofit committed to doing good through mutualism.

Shari was co-founder and Chief Marketing Officer of Bonfaire, a luxury e-commerce destination. At Bonfaire, she drove customer acquisition, marketing, branding, partnerships, and social media strategies. Bonfaire was acquired by its largest competitor, Moda Operandi.

Shari co-founded FreeRealTime.com, a first-generation web venture focused on the provision of information and tools for the individual investor. It was the first web site to offer real-time stock quotes for free and helped pioneer the online media space for financial information services.

Shari has also held executive positions with established companies looking for new opportunities to grow. As Vice President and Chief Marketing Officer for Gabriel Brothers Inc. ("Gabe's"), an off-price retailer with over 100 stores, Shari pioneered the lead marketing role. She led marketing for multiple new store openings, developed a comprehensive digital media strategy and introduced the company to new ways of driving store traffic. As Chief Marketing Officer for Kaboodle, Shari drove top-line growth in both revenue and audience share to help create the world's largest social shopping site. She came to Kaboodle from Hearst's Digital Media division. There she oversaw sales marketing efforts for the web sites of magazines such as Cosmopolitan, Marie Claire, Esquire, Good Housekeeping and Redbook. Shari's additional professional experience includes executive and leader-ship roles at both start-ups and large media and retail e-commerce companies.

Shari earned her MBA from The UCLA Anderson Graduate School of Management. She enjoys teaching as an adjunct professor in marketing, advertising and entrepreneurial studies. At CSUF, she has been a volunteer review panelist for student business plans and a frequent guest speaker. She and her husband Kenny (also an entrepreneur) have frequented the Start-up Incubator.

Dear Founder:

There are killers in our midst. They are cunning, wily and insidious, striking when we don't even realize it. Often, they come disguised as long-held thoughts and beliefs lurking in our own minds. Sometimes, they take the unassuming and unexpected physical figure of a friend, family member or colleague. Regardless of form, their aim is the same – to stifle and even kill our innate creative genius.

As an entrepreneur, creative thinking and problem-solving skills are critical. You know you are creative – you came up with a great idea you decided to pursue as a business! But creativity doesn't just apply to the generation of the original idea or concept. You will need to apply your creativity at every step of the way to bring that concept to fruition as a successful business.

The problem is that creativity killers are everywhere. And you need to fight back.

Perhaps most important, you need to watch out for fear of failure. When a scientist conducts an experiment and it does not produce the end result she hypothesized, is that a failure? No, it's an opportunity to glean new information and to learn. And that data may even lead to a valuable new discovery along a different path. The concept of "failure" has been given a bad rap when it's a natural (and productive) part of any creative process. Recognize the fear and be willing to engage with it. Devise small experiments to test your ongoing hypotheses. A landing page asking potential customers to take a specific action will teach you a lot very quickly and you don't need to build the entire platform.

Remember that creativity thrives on constraints. Don't get caught up in the "I don't have enough time, money, resources…" pity party. Limitations force us to think differently about how we can solve problems. Many of us do our best work the closer we get to a deadline. If we don't have a huge marketing budget, we get creative about guerilla tactics. Remember the scene from the movie *Apollo 13* where ground control solved a complex problem using only the items the crew had available on the shuttle?

Don't be a perfectionist. Many of us wear the perfectionism label as a badge of honor, but the truth is that perfectionism is a major creativity and productivity killer. Creativity requires curiosity, comfort with uncertainty, a drive to experiment and most importantly, a willingness to fail. The problem is that perfectionists are afraid to fail, even on a small scale. Instead of perfection, let excellence be the goal. Focus on learning and progress and don't pressure yourself (or others) to be perfect. Recognize, accept and develop a level of comfort with the fact that the creative process is messy and rarely, if ever, follows a straight line.

I wish you the best of luck in your endeavors, whether you start your own new venture, launch a new initiative in an existing company, or set about to reinvent something that has long been overlooked.

Go forth and create!

Shari Rudolph

Career Banker

Nancy Russell is Senior Vice president and SBA Business Development Officer at Seacoast Commerce Bank. She originates SBA commercial and industrial real estate loans in multiple industries across sixteen western states. Her duties include handling deal structure, pricing and loan eligibility/underwriting analysis. She monitors loan requests through each stage of funding.

Nancy began her banking career while in College. She was a part time teller at US Live Savings and Loan Association in La Habra. Nancy earned her BA in business administration from California State University Fullerton in 1980. She graduated with honors. After college graduation Nancy joined Mercury Savings and Loan Association. She started as a management trainee in the Savings Division. Within one year Mercury promoted Nancy to Vice President, Regional and Branch Manager in the Savings Division. In 1985 Mercury promoted her again to manage ten branches in Los Angeles and Orange Counties. In 1986, Mercury named Nancy Vice President, Business Development Officer at Mercury's Business Lending Division.

Nancy found her career passion in developing SBA small business Lending. She continued her career focus in successive, vice presidential SBA business development positions. She has advanced SBA lending at The Money Store, Comerica Bank, Umpqua Bank, Wells Fargo Bank and finally Seacoast Commerce Bank. Nancy remains deeply committed to serving the small business community. In 1997 Nancy won the U.S. Small Business Administration (SADO) Financial Services Advocate of the year Award. In 2008 SADO named her Financial Services Champion of the Year.

In 2003, the SBA awarded the Lead Small Business Development Center contract to CSUF. Since then, Nancy has been a member of the advisory board for the Orange County /Inland Empire Lead Small Business Development Center. She has served as the Chairperson for the board since 2008. She served as the lead judge for the Region IX U.S. Small Business Administration Business Week Awards since 2001 through 2015.

Nancy is a frequent guest lecturer for CSUF Entrepreneurship. She has been a judge for business plan and new venture launch presentations since 2004.

During college, Nancy became a Delta Zeta. She began serving as a national trustee for the Delta Zeta Foundation in 2008 and was elected Secretary/Treasurer in 2010.

Nancy lives in Yorba Linda, California a few miles from CSUF. She is a long time runner and loves to travel. Her daughter Brandi shares the same passions. She is also a runner, traveler and a banker who lends to businesses.

Brandi and Nancy during the holidays.

Dear Founder,

I am a career banker. The positions I have enjoyed most were my first job as a part- time teller during college and my positions as a SBA business loan development officer. All allowed me the opportunity to get to know my customers, advise them, follow their progress and learn from their experiences. I have observed many founders in action. Three success factors stand out.

First, having a working knowledge of their own business from a financial perspective is really important for founders. They don't need to know all of the line items in their financials. However, the founder must be able to answer financial questions about their business and describe the anticipated results for the bottom line. Whether the business is a start-up, plans to expand or needs to buy new assets the founder needs to explain why they need the money and describe how it will be spent. When a founder tells me, "I don't have a clue ask my accountant", I assign them fillable spread sheets and key financial questions as "homework". I counsel them that when they understand the broad scope of their numbers, it makes a huge difference in my ability to obtain a loan approval for the business. Confidence and strong communication skills while articulating their financial position to an underwriter will make a positive impression.

The second factor is the founder's ability to build trust through open communication with key stakeholders. For example, during the great recession, many of my client founders faced difficult times. Revenues and profits were falling and they faced hard decisions regarding employee layoffs. Those who kept open communications with the bank, accountant and/or attorney and treated us as trusted counselors had a better chance of survival. The goal of all parties was to help the founder and business weather the storm.

Third, is the founder's skill at surrounding her/himself with good people who are not yes persons. The founder's inner circle needs to include people who are skilled at operations, marketing, finance and leadership. Also, the founder needs an outer circle of advisors; experts who follow the company's progress, know what they are talking about and give sound advice when called upon. If the founder builds trust through open communication (the second factor) they will receive solid advice from their outer circle. This will occur not only from their banker, but from other experts who have been following the business and understand its strengths, weaknesses, opportunities and threats. Advice from the outer circle will often cost money. However it will help keep the inner circle from getting stuck in a rut and provide extra problem solving tools to the founder's tool chest. Often, the outer circle provides good solutions that the inner circle does not see.

Best wishes for your ventures,

Nancy Russell

Nancy Russell
Senior Vice President, SBA Business Development Officer

253

Triathlete, Founder and Head Coach

Ron Saetermoe is founder and president of Automotive Associates ("A2") founded in 1990 and Triathica founded in 2009. A2 provides marketing, consulting and training services to truck dealers. (www.AutomotiveAssociates.com). Triathica provides training resources for triathletes (www.Triathica.com).

A2 works exclusively with commercial truck dealerships to generate quality leads for its clients' sales staff. The company makes a niche market sales proposition. "We know how hard it is to keep your sales staff's calendar full - we can help... [We] craft solutions that optimize your success in the competitive commercial truck environment."

To serve its clients in a turnkey fashion, A2's services encompass multiple specialties. Five specialties are:
1-BDC services -highly trained call center staff specializing in commercial truck sales appointment setting.
2-PPC Management -expertly managed search engine pay-per-click campaigns.
3-SEO Management-enhancing of rankings in the organic search results.
4-Collateral-eye catching materials featuring business products and services.
5-Graphic Design- aesthetically pleasing design work.

Triathica Academy is an online triathlon training platform created for triathletes, by triathletes. Triathica Academy specializes in triathlon coaching, nutritional guidance, strength training, and networking with fellow triathletes. It designs its services to take subscribers' triathlon performances and enjoyment levels to new heights. The company mission statement reads, "Our mission at Triathica Academy is to get you ready to compete. Whether you choose to compete, or not, is entirely up to you, but we'll get you ready. At

Triathica Academy, you train like a triathlete." Triathica gives access to USAT certified triathlon coaches trained to teach athletes everything they need to improve their swimming, cycling, and running.

Ron Saetermoe is Triathica's Head Coach. He has been competing in the sport of triathlon since 1983. Ron is a top age-grouper and his passion for the sport is off the charts. He is a USAT certified triathlon coach. Ron works with a range of athletes -- endurance sports beginners to recreational competitors to elite athletes and long time veterans of the sport. All his clients are looking for that extra edge that comes with the highest quality of specialized coaching.

Ron is a longtime friend of CSUF Entrepreneurship. He has been a student consulting case sponsor multiple times, and has hired our graduates.

Dear Founder,

After a particularly exasperating day, I've decided one of the important lessons I've learned is you can't make people do what you want.

One of my employees came to me today with a situation she was dealing with, with one of her employees. This particular employee is a high-performer – when he wants to be. She has had problems with him ever since she became his manager, but not enough to warrant firing him.

We discussed the alternatives: write him up or have yet another discussion about his lack of performance. Writing him up could mean him getting defensive and perhaps repaying her with more of the same. Not writing him up meant she was certain to get more of the same.

I asked whether she was ready to have him quit or to fire him. She really couldn't decide because her performance is closely associated with his.

The fact is, none of us can really control others the way we sometimes would like. As a result, we have to make a choice – let them be them, or take matters into our own hands.

This situation gets to all of us. If only if everyone would do what we want them to.

When I was younger, and much more intense, I might lose it when I wasn't getting my way. Now that I'm older, with much less energy, I'm more apt to let it go. That doesn't mean I care less, it's just that I'm not going to let anyone else's behavior get to me the way it once did.

Sure, I've had to discipline employees, and fire them, but only after I gave them every chance to meet my expectations. It isn't easy, but I've learned to accept people for what they are.

Life is more peaceful now.

Ron Saetermoe

Food Safety Systems

Stacy Sagowitz is CEO of Food Safety Systems (FSS). She founded the company in 2001. FSS provides and implements a standardized food safety program across all K-12 child nutrition sites.

Many young children have dreams of their future and then as they grow, choose a different course for themselves. Stacy always knew that she wanted to be in the field of Domestic Studies, formerly known as Home Economics! Lacking the artistic skills to go into fashion, and not being very savvy in the kitchen, she chose a career in dietetics, food and nutrition. Her area of specialty has been feeding children in school grades K-12. She earned her BS in Dietetics from SUNY Oneonta. Stacy went on to earn her MBA from San Francisco State University with concentrations in operations and supervision.

FSS was originally founded under the name School Nutrition Services to provide consultative and marketing services to the food service Industry and to capitalize on the vast sales opportunities in the school food service segment. In 2015, the company pivoted and was relaunched as FSS. The new mission is to be the food safety and Sanitation resource to food service in southern California.

Currently, FSS provides Food Safety and Sanitation audits, assessments and training to over 50 school districts in southern California. It helps protect the food safety of almost 1 million school children.

Over the course of almost 40 years, Stacy has held many leadership positions. She has served as School Food Service Director for the Hayward USD and the Ravenswood City School District.

Her sales experience began with Lang Mfg. where she was instrumental in developing their sales of commercial cooking equipment with K-12 school districts across the country.

Prior to founding FSS, she was the manager of School Sales and Marketing for FoodSalesWest, a prominent food service brokerage firm. In that capacity, she consistently increased the sales of the school market segment for ten straight years.

Stacy is no stranger to the professional organizations in the school food service industry. She has served them well. In 2013, she received her most prestigious award from the School Nutrition Association (57,000 members). It named her Individual Industry Member of the Year. She is very proud of this honor.

On the weekends, look to find Stacy paddling her kayak on Orange County's coastal waterways.

Food Safety SYSTEMS

Dear Founder,

I'm sure you've heard the saying before, "If I only knew then, what I know now ..." In retrospect, I DID know then, what I know now. However, I didn't have the understanding that the three principles I incorporate into my business every day, are the three principles I have lived by my entire life, instilled in me by wonderful parents and mentors. They are the core values of my personal life and my professional life. In my business, I hire employees that share these core values; they can learn the specifics of the position later. Staying true to these values has served me well.

Believe in Yourself

I have worked hard to build a career and a profession. Throughout my entire career, I have worked in some segment of feeding children in public schools across the country. The contacts I have made and the experiences gleaned over the last 40 years have all contributed to my development of expertise in this niche field. Yet, it wasn't until I started to understand that others saw me as an expert and leader in this field, that I started to believe it myself. Once I turned that switch in my head, and started to let my belief in my abilities to control my actions take over, I've never looked back. Anything less leads to hesitation, second guessing and unclear decision making. Believing in myself does not mean I'm infallible or invincible; but it does mean that I believe whatever I choose to take on, successful or not, will lead me to a new action or decision, learning from the results of everything leading up to it. I know I cannot forget that my success is directly impacted by my belief in myself.

Meet Expectations and Commitments

I had taken for granted that everyone 'does what they say they're going to do.' NOT! I have been disappointed many times in my life, personally and professionally, by those who did not live up to that expectation. Meeting the commitments and expectations to which others have held me accountable, has allowed me to build a relationship of mutual trust, respect and consideration with those I do business. It is a foundation of my company. I am not afraid to admit I cannot do something, will not do something or need more resources to do something. By my doing so, everyone is clear on the expectation, and trusts it will be met.

Live with Integrity and Accountability

Last time I looked, we're all human, and we make mistakes. OWN UP, the truth will set you free! Walk the talk, and admit when you have not. Hold yourself to the highest accountability and standards. It will maintain the level of trust, respect and consideration you have with others. Most importantly, I can look myself in the mirror each morning, after sleeping peacefully each night!

Find your passion, live your values, and seize every opportunity. Wishing you much success.

Sincerely,

Stacy Sagowitz, RDN, SNS
CEO and Founder

Restaurant, Home Care and Clinician

Sadaf Salout is a 2007 CSUF Entrepreneurship Alumna. She earned her MBA at Mihaylo in 2010. In 2011 she founded Sadaf Restaurant in Encino, CA. She became a franchisee of Home Instead Senior Care (HISC) in Sherman Oaks in 2014. To better operate HISC, Sadaf earned a MA in Clinical Psychology in 2013 and completed her three-year marriage and family therapist internship in 2015. In 2016 she received her PsyD in Clinical Psychology. In short, Sadaf owned and operated two successful ventures before her 30th birthday and has just started a clinical psychology practice.

Ever since she was little Sadaf wanted to own her own business. At the age of eight she would gather things from around her house, place it on a pushcart and sell it to her neighbors. At times some of her peers felt she was bossy, and others regarded her as a leader in the group. Overall she was an entrepreneur in the making.

Her father had paved the road for her by owning and operating Darya restaurant, a successful well-known Persian restaurant for over 30 years. His restaurant was one of the first Persian restaurants in Orange County, CA. Sadaf always had a part in her father's business. She bussed tables, served guests, and managed day to day operations. She gained her experience working at her family restaurant while gaining her business knowledge from CSUF. She designed her own restaurant around Persian food but gave the ambiance and menu a modern twist. She picked a location in Encino that met her market specifications and would not compete with her family's restaurants.

While launching her restaurant, Sadaf decided to go back to school to get her Master's Degree in Psychology. She wanted to work in an industry where she could help people. A friend of hers, who was looking to retire, offered to sell his business. Sadaf thought she would be a good fit for the business, so she bought his HISC franchise. She hired and trained caregivers to give seniors care in the comfort of their own homes. Sadaf really enjoyed the business model as it combined what she had studied in business school with what she had learned in her psychology classes.

Sadaf continues to own and operate both HISC and Sadaf Restaurant. She is currently seeing patients in nursing homes across the San Fernando Valley. She continues to look for new ventures and brainstorm about her next ideas.

In her free time Sadaf enjoys exercising, cooking and eating at different restaurants. She has an identical twin sister, Darya, who she enjoys spending time with, along with her niece and nephew.

Dear Founder,

A failed business attempt doesn't mean you are a failure. If I had known this I would have taken the steps to starting my ventures earlier. A failed business attempt means you need to look at your business plan/idea, make changes where necessary and try again.

The three factors most important to my effectiveness as a founder were:
<u>Do Not Give Up</u>- Don't let others opinions and doubts make you doubt your new ventures and give up on them before you've even started.
<u>Have Passion</u>- if you don't have passion there will be days where you are just exhausted working at your business idea and you will give up trying. When you have passion for your idea (not passion for only money) you will start your business venture and see it to its completion. You will not give up because it is your passion.
<u>Surround Yourself With Successful And Motivating People</u>- Seek people who inspire you, push you to go forward and encourage you to do your best.

When I wanted to start my restaurant in Encino, CA, I bounced the idea off many people. My family told me it was too far (from Orange County), we didn't know the area (the Valley), and my family couldn't come out to help me because it was so far. I realized they didn't want me to move out to LA to start this new venture. Nonetheless, I did my research and saw there was a need for a contemporary designed restaurant serving high quality Persian food in Encino. I had to drive from OC to the Valley almost every day until the business was up and running. Only then did I decide to move to Encino. Once the restaurant was open, the customers began to learn about us and give us a try. From then on they were hooked! If I had listened to my family I would have never made the move to fill in the need for a Persian restaurant in Encino.

Ever since I can remember I was in my father's restaurant, whether it was flying paper airplanes into customers' foods (yikes) as an 8 year old with my twin sister Darya, or it was bussing and serving tables from the age of 16 to 23 years old. I loved being in the restaurant industry -- dining in restaurants, owning restaurants, cooking dinner at home. I love food and bringing those around me to love it as much as I do. I want my guests to enjoy our high quality food in our beautifully designed restaurant with our over the top Persian hospitality. I want them to have the "Sadaf experience." I enjoy watching them leave the restaurant stuffed and happy, with the promise to come back again. Even after the hectic and crazy days where everything goes opposite of what was planned, I still love waking up the next morning and going back to work.

The third factor that helped me start and operate my business successfully is that I surround myself with successful and motivating people. They inspire me, and push me to go forward and give it my best. Without the support system I have around me, I would not be where I am today. I spent time getting to know these people and what made them successful. I can relate to each and every one of them in some way. Some have failed once or twice, and had the courage to get up and give it another try. Others have successfully overcome tough times when they wanted to throw their hands up in the air and give up for good. The people I surround myself with all help me understand that I'm not alone in this business world.

These three points have been the main factors to my effectiveness as a founder.

Yours truly.

Sadaf Salout, Owner

FastStart.studio

Michael Sawitz is a serial entrepreneur and founder of FastStart.studio, a mixed use business incubator in Irvine, California. He has held founder or C-level positions for over forty years in the apparel industry, equipment distribution and retail arenas. Most recently, his Amailcenter Franchise Corporation, was the franchisor for AIM Mail Centers. He sold the brand in 2011.

National outlets have published Michael's writings. He has spoken nationally as a keynote speaker. Print and talk show media have also interviewed Michael on numerous occasions.

In the community, His extensive SBS volunteer resume includes President, National Alliance of Ship Centers and member, board of directors Tech Coast Venture Network. Michael is a member of Professional Mentors Advisors and Coaches. He is a Charter Member of TiE, the world's largest entrepreneurial education organization.

Michael is a frequent speaker at minority business development centers sponsored by the SBA and at Franchise Business Network events.

Michael cofounded CoderCoJoOC.com an organization that teaches computer skills to 300 plus elementary school children throughout Southern California. He is currently serving as a commissioner with the California State Bar Association's Franchise and Distribution Law Committee.

At California State University Fullerton, Michael is a member, board of directors for California State University Fullerton's Center for Entrepreneurship. He has advised several entrepreneurial graduates. Michael provides scholarships at FastStart.studio for top teams from CSUF's business plan competition. He offers select graduating residents of CSUF's start-up incubator the opportunity to transition to FastStart.studio.

Michael was also instrumental in the development of a path breaking CSUF entrepreneurship course in lean start-up strategies. The course allowed student consulting teams to serve FastStart.studio residents, applying what they learned to benefit the resident companies. Michael personally took on a volunteer adjunct professor role. He teamed with a CSUF Entrepreneurship professor, presenting much of the course content and mentoring student consulting teams.

Currently, Michael hosts an entrepreneurial podcast called FastStart.talk (FastStartTalk.podbean.com). His latest endeavor is as Chief Strategy Officer for The Laser DARRT a revolutionary medical device.

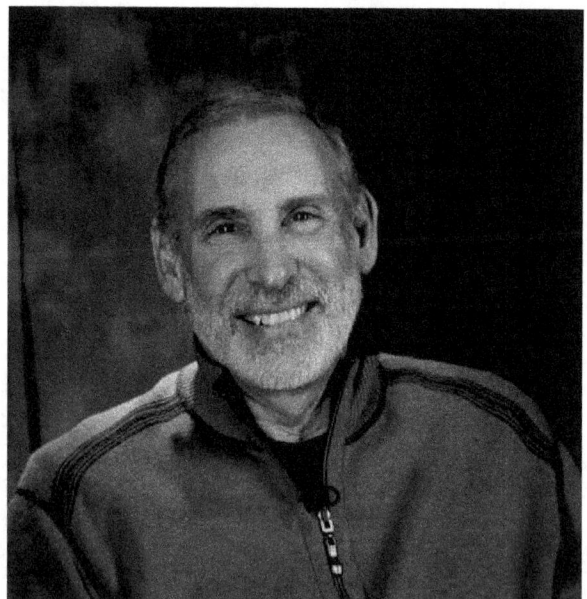

FastStart.studio

Dear Founder,

Welcome to an exclusive club composed of men and women who not only have a dream but more importantly have the drive, intellect and vision to bring that dream to the global marketplace.

Bottom line, everyone has a dream, but only few have the ability to execute. By execute I am including building and managing a team or teams of individuals who are committed to that shared vision. You cannot expect to be successful as a solopreneur. No one, no matter how talented can build a massively successful enterprise by themselves. Finding and leading teams of talented people is even more important than creating the Killer App. At the end of the day, it's about people.

Finding individuals that have the supreme skills the job requires and also who share in your vision is a daunting task.

To be successful in building highly effective teams for your startup begins with your own self-awareness. A tested and effective strategy is to bring on board the most talented people available. Spend time with them so they can know who you really are. Being really transparent is mandatory. You must become a skilled communicator and speak plainly about the problem you are trying to fix with your startup and how the world will benefit from that successful launch.

If that is indeed a shared vison with your new hire then the next step is to surround them with likeminded team members. Supply them with the needed resources. Arm them with a clear picture of the expected outcome. And then get out of their way.

Yes, get out of their way and let them create solutions that are in line with your vision of the company. That is leadership. You can only lead when you have given over control to those that are doing the work. Build teams of leaders, not followers.

Being a strong leader does not mean that you are doing the work or micromanaging. Being a strong leader is about making sure every team member has the resources and support to do their job.

Bring the light, bring the structure, bring the resources and a clear picture of the goal. Hire the right people and support them to the nth degree and you will have a chance at building something amazing.

I wish you great success.

Michael Sawitz

Chief Enthusiasm Officer

15550 Rockfield Blvd, Suite D, Irvine CA 92618 ·· 949-837-4151 ·· FastStartStudio.com

Private Client Advisor

Steven Shields is a 2008 alumnus of California State University Fullerton's Mihaylo College of Business and Economics. Steven concentrated in Marketing. He has been a guest speaker for the entrepreneurial marketing class and is a friend of CSUF Entrepreneurship.

While attending college, Steven worked with Cox Target Media selling advertising (2006-2008). He created and customized ad campaigns for small to medium sized businesses. Steven consistently ranked in the top 15 percent of Sales Representatives.

At graduation Steven was hired on by Ameriprise Financial as a financial adviser. He managed and maintained a portfolio of brokerage accounts, annuities, alternative investments, and insurance. He provided comprehensive financial planning for businesses and high net worth individuals. Steven also learned how to establish relationships with influential partners through networking. He participated in or hosted events with other colleagues and influential partners that addressed current events or specific topics affecting clients and prospects.

In 2010, Steven moved to J.P. Morgan Chase Bank N. A. Steven is now a

Certified Financial Planner™. He has grown his book of business dramatically during his seven years at JPMorganChase. In 2012, Steven became a J.P. Margan Private Client Advisor. He is now a Vice President Investments.

Steven lives in Orange County with his wife and son.

Dear Founder,

My road into the business world started at CSUF and it was an uphill battle. This built character and allowed me to gain confidence to become a business professional against all odds. I burned much midnight oil to learn the importance of being authentic, dedicated, and able to accept change. My story is about how I learned how to build something from nothing while pursuing my passion for helping others.

The course work during my senior year gave me confidence to make business decisions that have made a lasting impact on my life. For example, I was able to implement the statistics, marketing, management, entrepreneurial, finance, and economic learnings into a project. This project was in my entrepreneurial class. I interviewed a national trade association about their member enrollment problems, awareness issues, and organizational challenges. My group and I were able to formulate a plan that was detailed and concise about making their organization become more prevalent. To this day, our logo is still being used.

My experience with CSUF was something that was not given to me. It started with me talking to classmates before and after class about their thoughts and goals, discussing strategy with my professors and many long nights. I was once told "It takes a lot of mice to eat an elephant." This means that you will start out small in business and as time goes on, you will become great enough to challenge an elephant. In business, it is important to be authentic and to challenge yourself. Make something great of your vision and pursue your goals. For instance, I asked a professor what he thought about me becoming a financial adviser. He said, "Steven, you know that profession is very risky and not many advisers will make it. However if you are going to pursue your vision, this is the time!" I utilized that advice and took a risk in order to pursue my goal of helping others. Meanwhile, I was balancing work, attending class, studying for my series exams, and preparing for fun off-road racing.

After graduation, I was against a steep incline on my journey. I was hired as a financial adviser and had a bag of business tools with no blue prints. I knew I had to be "First, Best, or Different" so I took every opportunity to differentiate myself from other advisers. I studied the industry, worked long hours, and talked with every senior representative. Furthermore, I was weathering the great recession. I networked with professionals and asked prospects and clients questions that would allow me to understand their goals and objectives. For example, where do you see yourself in five to ten years? What are your concerns? Paint me a picture of what your retirement looks like. As a financial adviser, you need to learn about your clients and create tailored solutions. You have to have "IQ" (intelligence), but more importantly you need "EQ" emotional intelligence. Having empathy for someone will help you close business especially if they have had an unpleasant experience with an adviser in the past, have suffered investment loses, have made decisions on their own for the last 30 years, or are going through a tough time. All of these scenarios will change someone's beliefs and decision making.

Work hard, be comfortable with change, and become a student of your profession. My story is based on focusing on what I can control. I am thankful I attended CSUF. It helped me to follow my dreams. I have benefited in my career by asking my clients tailored questions and creating a life of balance. Every day is a good one and I make the best out of each day while pursuing my dreams.

Best wishes,

Steven Shields

Say Simon Homes

Charles Simon is the founder of Say Simon Homes. He is a member of the CSUF Entrepreneurship Class of 2009.

Charles values the knowledge he acquired from CSUF's entrepreneurship program. He views it to be a firm foundation for business start-ups. As he notes in his letter, he used it to start up his own real estate brokerage firm and and run it successfully for the past six years.

However, Say Simon Homes was not Charles' first start-up. He recounts his entrepreneurial journey as follows.

Before getting into real estate I pursued my class project, a designated driver service named SHMAXI. When I write about failing and learning from my mistakes I recall my experience with SHMAXI. Without a doubt I learned much from attempting to start that company. From knowing (or not knowing) my financial numbers and cash flow, to working with someone who was not vested in my start up, to getting into a business that did not suit my lifestyle. However, given my training, I was able to recognize the main causes of SHMAXI not working. It only took a short while for me to understand that the company was not going to work out for me and that I needed to look into other options.

I wanted to quickly find something else to jump into. I did have a job to pay the bills but that was not cutting it for me, I needed to be my own man. A close friend of mine, who was a mortgage originator, talked me into getting my real estate/ mortgage brokers license so that he could work under my license. I took the classes, passed the test and earned my brokers license, but at that point my friend took a job at a big name mortgage brokerage. It was an opportunity that he could not pass up. I had to move forward by myself.

It was the end of the recession and home prices were dropping fast so I decided to follow the real estate side of my new license and sell homes to take advantage of the next real estate cycle. I started Say Simon Homes and used my previous knowledge of setting up an entity, website, and a social media campaign. I was off to the races. I was not an immediate success, in fact, my company is still a work in progress but I enjoy the hustle and I am able to work with my baby. I literally take her with me to show homes and I would not have it any other way.

My future plans include trying to start up the mortgage brokerage side of my license with the same friend who left me earlier. He now has thorough experience and knowledge of how a large brokerage functions. This is great but it would be ideal if he had graduated from the CSUF entrepreneurship program because there is so much to be learned about starting and running your own company that is taught through lecture, text and the venture creation/launch classes.

Charles' positive experience with CSUF's entrepreneurship program is why he volunteers as a mentor in the new venture launch course. He explains, "I get to learn something new every semester and I get to network with future founders."

Dear founders,

My name is Charles Simon, CSUF Class of 2009, and the founder of Say Simon Homes with some advice for the program and your future as an entrepreneur.

1. **Don't worry about failing**. For some of us failing is an important part of learning. Learn from mistakes, learn what works and what doesn't work, learn to succeed.

2. **Networking**. Start off with all the amazing peers in the department. These can be guys who you can bounce ideas off of when coming up with a new venture. Maybe they end up being your clients as you might want to be their clients as well. Keep that networking going and meet as many people as you can because in entrepreneurship sales is the name of the game and the more connections you have the more likely you will be able to be introduced to your buyer.

3. **Believe in yourself**. You will receive a lot of criticism, not all constructive. Listen to what your critics have to say and be able to discern what is constructive and what is not.

4. **Keep it simple**. To get your point across start simple and go from there as needed.

With the knowledge acquired from CSU F's entrepreneurship program I have been able to start up my own real estate brokerage firm and have run it successfully for the past 6 years. Future plans include expanding into mortgage brokering along with growing through hiring more agents.

Charles Simon, CEO
Say Simon Homes

265

Mr. Charge Higher Prices

Scott Sorrell founded Sales Adrenaline("SA") in 2002. He serves as its Chief Sales Officer. Scott is a professional speaker and sales trainer. His collection of speaking engagements, books, seminars and SA sales training programs achieve documented sales increases. Clients served include Cisco Systems, MetLife, Canon, Chase, BMW, Rawlings, Time Warner, 3M, Vistage (TEC), and many more.

Scott has acquired the nickname, "Mr. Charge Higher Prices." He has identified more than eighty different techniques, methods and strategies for getting customers to pay more than they thought they would, but still be happy they did. He trains sales teams in the U. S. and internationally how to get to the top of their customer's price range. Also, how to stay there. Scott has written two books: Professional Selling Power: Keys to Maximizing Your Personal Profits - Guaranteed and The Power of Persuasion: How to Master the Art of Influence.

Scott gives back to his community by serving as a guest speaker and part time lecturer at local universities. His credits include, USC Marshall School, Chapman University Argyros School, UC Riverside, and Concordia University. Scott feels privileged to be a regular speaker for Orangewood Children's Foundation delivering seminars and workshops to staff, mentors and foster youth.

Since 2015 Scott has taught marketing classes at California State University Fullerton. He currently teaches Marketing for Entrepreneurs for CSUF's Entrepreneurship Concentration. Four examples of what Scott teaches in class include:
How to charge higher prices,

The power of persuasion, How to sell on value, not price and Professional negotiation strategies. Scott says, "My seminars are dynamic and humorous, but my training is also highly effective. I work with my corporate clients to hold their program participants accountable for implementing my tactics and producing results. They have no choice! -- and they make more money." Scott's approach is a good fit for CSUF's Marketing for Entrepreneurs class. There, coached by the classroom mentors, students immediately apply Scott's teachings to serve their consulting clients and move the students' own businesses forward. Scott reflects, "I find it very rewarding to bring daily, real-world best practices into the classroom. I help guide up-and-coming young professionals in the highly profitable art of entrepreneurial marketing. The class throws them to the wolves as consulting teams for actual companies. They deliver in stellar fashion. Teams develop a solid collection of customized marketing solutions for each business."

Dear Founder,

Want to be homeless? Sleep on the floor of your office? Scrounge food every night from happy hour buffets? Sneak into your local college gym to take showers when you're not even a student?

I didn't either. But that literally was my life during my first five years as an entrepreneur.

You might think it was because of my dedication to my startup, investing every penny of profit back into accelerating my venture's growth. But you'd be wrong. It was because for years I charged less than half what my competitors were charging, and was uncomfortable asking for even that little! Because I grew up in a middle class family with a thrifty lifestyle, when I got in business I assumed everyone else made their buying decisions on low price, too. I charged accordingly, and was always broke. It was painful and embarrassing.

My first piece of advice: _**Don't Sell with Your Own Wallet**_**!** Customers will pay good money for your value – often far more than you'd ever pay! But you must communicate your value by quantifying it in terms of the customer's ROI. That's when you'll really start to maximize their perception of your value, and be less afraid to ask for a nice, high price. Because boy was I afraid … deathly afraid! But, eventually, I forced myself to ask anyway. To be honest, when I started asking higher and higher prices, I was genuinely shocked when people said _Yes_. Still am sometimes, matter of fact. But the trick is to ignore the fact that you're terrified, take a deep breath, and just name the number you want – with as much nonchalance as if you're ordering a cup of coffee. And when they say _Yes_, act as if it's the answer you expected all along. I assure you, overcoming your fear of asking a high price definitely beats the discomfort of sleeping on a hard floor!

My second piece of advice: _**Niche Down and Price Up**_**!** First, make your niche as narrow as possible. There are two ways to do this: either narrow your market into a niche, or narrow your brand into a niche. I failed at both; I tried to be all things to all customers, and ended up spreading my brand so thin it wasn't recognized by any particularly exclusive group, nor was it recognized for any particularly exclusive thing. This taught me the hard lesson that if you stand for everything, you stand for nothing. And if you stand for nothing, you'll never command top dollar for anything. So niche down and price up! People in a tightly segmented group will pay a high price for a product or service tailored to their needs exclusively. And even customers in a wide, diverse market will pay a high price for a product or service that itself is narrowly defined and positioned as solving one particularly narrow problem for them. When I became Mr. Charge Higher Prices, I did the latter – because every CEO, from midsize to large, wants their reps to learn "How to Charge Higher Prices & Get Your Customers to Thank You For It." Just wish I'd learned this earlier. Niche it down!

My third piece of advice: _**Become the Authority**_**!** Don't settle for simply being a product or service provider. There doubtless are tens of thousands of those in your industry. Don't even settle for being an "expert" in your field. There are at least hundreds of experts. Instead, strive beyond expert status to Authority status so you can command premium prices for everything you do or sell. Achieve recognition as THE Authority in your niche by giving speeches on your narrowly defined topic, publishing articles, columns, books, etc. Becoming the ultimate Authority in a highly focused specialty will brand you as a very big fish in a very small pond (even if you don't adopt a catchy nickname, haha!). And when you become the recognized Authority, everyone will want to do business with you … in spite of whatever high price you decide to charge!

If you'll do all three things I've advised, you'll be well on your way to maxing out your target customer's WTP (willingness to pay) and, as a result, enjoying a lifestyle substantially above "floor level"! ☺

Warm Regards,

Scott Sorrell

Scott Sorrell "Mr. Charge Higher Prices"
CEO, Sales Adrenaline

An Aerospace Launch

Bernard Spear is the owner manager of BASA / b.a.spear &associates in Anaheim. The firm provides marketing and sales consulting to electronics and small systems Instrumentation manufacturers who target Aerospace. It provides advice concerning both domestic and international markets.

As described in his Dear Founder letter. Bernard started his career in Aerospace. He has spent his entire career pursuing his dreams in that arena. In total, he has more than forty years experience in sales, marketing and application engineering. His specialties are test & measurement electronics sold to aerospace companies around the world.

He joined Preston Scientific Inc. In 1964. He worked in marketing and sales while studying for a BA degree in operations and marketing at Tulane University. Eventually, Bernard became Vice President of Marketing. As VP he directed world wide sales representatives. In 1982, he formed Halear, Inc. To buy Preston Scientific. As part of the deal, Halear, Inc. retained the exclusive right to the Preston Scientific brand name

Bernard served as President and CEO of Halear, Inc. for twenty years. After the sale of the company in 2002, he spent eight years as Sales Director, International & West USA for Kinetic Systems. In 2007, he became a business consultant for DynamicSignals, LLC. After it acquired Kinetic Systems. In 2012, he formed BASA / b.a.spear &associates. His firm maintains close ties with Dynamic Signals.

Bernard first connected with CSUF Entrepreneurship while he was still President/CEO of Halear, Inc. His company was a student consulting client.

Since then, he has been a long term, steadfast volunteer. Bernard has been an Entrepreneur in Residence and has mentored student teams in multiple entrepreneurship classes for nearly twenty years. He has mentored residents of the Start-up Incubator since its inception.

Bernard's hobbies include back packing, hiking, people watching and humor. His favorite quotation is, "In humor we find truth and often wisdom."

Dear Founder,

My story is not about a new venture, it's about my lifelong dream. When I was growing up I was fascinated by planes. The way they sliced through the air was amazing and as I matured I began to realize how air travel was opening up the world. From a young age I knew that I wanted to work in the aerospace industry and that is exactly what I did. During my career, I worked for five different aerospace companies. It's a journey that I am proud of and I think you can learn something from as well.

Becoming an entrepreneur wasn't necessarily part of the plan but in 1982, with the help of a loan from Bank of America, I purchased the company that I had worked at for more than a decade: Preston Scientific. Preston Scientific developed sophisticated instrumentation for test and measurement applications for the private sector as well as governmental agencies like NASA.

During the twenty years that I owned Preston Scientific I had two clear mandates in mind: 1. Be customer focused and 2. Be employee focused. I readily admit that there were some people who questioned this decision by saying things like "How can you be customer and employee focused? Those two things just don't mix." But what I knew then, and more companies have thankfully come around to this point of view, was that if you treat your employees well they will help make your business more successful than you could imagine.

From the receipt of every order we worked with the customers to make sure that we made products to their specification and delivered the finished products on time. And then we supported those customers with 24/7 customer service to make sure that the products met their exacting specifications. After all, if our products didn't work as specified then people could get injured or worse.

In order to accomplish this difficult task we cross trained all of our employees so that they would have a better understanding of what the person sitting next to them or in the office down the hall was doing. In essence, we created a culture where every one of our employees treated each other like they were a customer or a supplier. This all resulted in a culture where employees, our suppliers, and our customers had equal importance to everyone.

Our culture permeated through to the design, quality, and on-time delivery of our products. Not only were all the stakeholders at Preston Scientific of equal importance, every step along the value chain assumed equal importance as well. As is the case with an airplane, every input at Preston Scientific had to work superlatively or the whole operation would inevitably fail.

To make all this happen we created a company where people really enjoyed their working environment. Preston Scientific was one of the first small companies to introduce a four day work week, we paid salaried-professional employees (engineers and managers) 1.5 times their salaried rate for any overtime hours requested. And, of course, we had sick leave compensation, paid vacations, and profit sharing.

The bottom line was that the difference between employee and customer was forever blurred. Both were treated as equals. We made Preston Scientific's work environment superior to most other companies and our employees were treated as part of the family.

The basic concept is that if you create an interesting, fun, profitable and healthy working environment you will have better results. And this is my best advice for founders: Pick something that you really enjoy doing because it will be your life and you will be a successful, very happy person working 70 hours per week.

Respectfully,

Bernard Spear

PTS Staffing Solutions

Ronald Stein is founder of PTS Staffing Solutions ("PTS"). PTS is a family business that provides Engineering, IT and Professional Staffing. Ron launched PTS in mid-career. First, he worked in the Engineering, Procurement, and Construction (EPC) industry for 20 years as a Project Manager. He acquired an in-depth knowledge of the petrochemical industry.

In 1995, Ron founded PTS to address the emerging need for a focused staffing provider. One that, unlike non-specialized staffing agencies, could partner with companies to provide them unique tailored, staffing solutions and address both their short and long term staffing needs. Today, PTS is one of the largest employment agencies in Orange County, and the primary supplier to to the petrochemical industry in California. Ron notes,

"PTS strives to provide not only quality engineering and professional staffing services to our clients, but to also think like a business partner and bring an array of best practices to our clients. PTS has experienced years of proven success from understanding petrochemical industry trends.

Employees that work through PTS, immediately gain access to PTS's comprehensive employee benefits package, known to be the best in the industry. Strong benefits combined with no waiting period makes PTS the choice amongst leading professionals in the specialized industries we service."

PTS is a family business. The company is a nationally certified Women Owned Business. Ron's wife June serves as President. Ron and June successfully delegated responsibility and authority for finance and operations to their sons --

Russell, VP of Finance, and David, VP of Operations.

Today, Ron focuses on nurturing client relationships and authoring Op Ed articles that enhance PTS's credibility. He actively shares his views about the energy industry and the economy. Ron was the Program Manager on the Oil Infrastructure Section of the ASCE California Infrastructure Report Card Update for 2016.

At CSUF, Ron is an Advisory Board member for three Centers of Excellence at the Mihaylo College of Business and Economics: Family Business, Leadership and Entrepreneurship. The Stein family is a supporter of the new Steven G. Mihaylo Hall. One of the 50-seat Lecture Halls bears the family name.

Dear Founder:

RE: Ingredients to enhance your chances to be an effective and successful Founder

For your reference, here are the fundamental ingredients that have contributed to the successes of PTS Staffing Solutions.

In the early years

- Before starting PTS in 1995, I acquired more than 20 years of experiences with a major international engineering and construction company that focused on major energy infrastructure.
- My Project Management experiences enhanced my abilities to communicate, coordinate, and prioritize activities to bring projects to a successful conclusion.
- PTS was created with knowledge of the industry leaders and the "pain" they had for cost effective staffing augmentation services to supplement their core staff.

Experience

- In any business, relationships are the key to success. To be able to communicate, verbally and in writing, training is recommended. Toastmasters training in my early years as an Electrical Engineer, lead to Project Management opportunities.
- Sales and Marketing Training after decades of Project Management experiences, enhanced my abilities to nurture relationships.
- The Toastmasters, and Sales and Marketing training were the fundamental building blocks for PTS.

Advice / Wisdom

- Give back to your industry, either through volunteering for a leadership position in an industry related organization, or by authoring oped articles that support the industry.
- Become a recognized "spokesman" for your industry.

Things to succeed in Family Business

- Start with a PASSION for your business to succeed.
- Pick an industry or service that you have a thorough understanding and familiarity with the players, leaders, practices, terminology, and applicable laws or regulations that apply to that sector.
- Hire the best, then delegate and develop their strengths.
- Treat new hires as an opportunity for a return on investment, rather than just an expense.

Ronald Stein

Ronald Stein, Founder

Mountaineer, Founder and CEO

Phillip Stinis is the co-founder and CEO of 52 Hike Challenge ("52HC"). It is the on-line community for a global movement that empowers individuals to take a personal journey. Members discover the physical, mental, and spiritual benefits gained through hiking.

Phillip earned his Master's of Business Administration (MBA) degree from California State University, Fullerton (CSUF). He later taught classes in Entrepreneurship at CSUF as an Adjunct Professor. He was the pilot resident of the CSUF Startup Incubator, which coaches aspiring entrepreneurs on how to successfully start their own venture and scale it. He is currently Entrepreneur inResidence at its Irvine location.

Phillip graduated college as an Electrical Engineer where he served as President for both the National Engineering Honor Society and the International Electrical Engineering Honor Society. He spent the first decade of his professional career working in Aerospace. He did early design work for NASA and Hughes Space & Communications on government satellites. Later he developed corporate strategy for Northrop Grumman.

In his strive for excellence in his work, Phillip neglected his health and found himself quite overweight in 2001. He decided to rebuild himself mentally and physically. He decided to get in shape by training to reach the summit of Mt. Whitney, the highest mountain in the contiguous United States. Lead by his ambition, he broke this goal up into manageable steps. He lost 40 pounds over eight months and reached the summit of that mountain.The story appeared in Men's Health Magazine as a motivational article. He continued to train hard and lost another 40 pounds, making his total weight loss 80 pounds over a two-year period. Continuously pushing himself, Phillip earned a position working for Nike as a Brand Ambassador and running pace leader. Phillip completed a couple of marathons and climbed progressively higher and harder mountains around the world. He joined an international expedition and reached the summit of the highest mountain in the Western Hemisphere. Aconcagua, in Argentina, is 22,841 feet high.

Phillip believes getting outdoors regularly can help build one's confidence within themselves and an appreciation for simple things. It alleviates stress and teaches people how to handle adversity. His passion for hiking lead him to introduce others to nature's therapy. He felt he could help make a better society by getting people outdoors more. Karla Amador, then new to hiking, agreed. They co-founded 52HC in 2014. 52HC works with several outdoor brands. It licenses their challenge to counties and municipalities, and firms as wellness programs.

Dear Founder,

As the founder of 52 Hike Challenge and one of the founding members of the California State University, Fullerton (CSUF) Startup Incubator, I have seen dozens of aspiring entrepreneurs over the years and can tell you the successful ones had three main characteristics in common. I believe these characteristics are: following your passion, being self-disciplined, and being relentless in finding out how you're going to make money. I'll explain why these three characteristics are important in the beginning of your venture so that you can have the best chance at being successful when you start your entrepreneurial journey.

Starting a venture is going to be very time consuming and it's going to try your patience, you're going to be pitching your venture to a lot of people and at the heart of it, you're going to breathe this business day in and day out. Having a passion for what you are trying to achieve is going to carry you through the long days. You need to be passionate to the point where you would do this job even if you didn't get paid for it, because it needs to be something you feel is making a difference in this world. You need to be so convincing with you mission and vision, that you influence teammates to join you, and customers are excited to buy from you. You need to have so much passion that you feel it would be a disservice to society if your venture didn't exist.

Being self-disciplined to get up and go to sleep working on your business is critical, especially because you have other things that will compete with your time. You will invariably have friends and family, maybe even pressure from your full-time work that will gnaw at your time, and they will push your venture to the back burner if you let it, but you must fight to make working on your venture a priority. This is about respecting the business and not treating it as a side hobby, but something that you carve out time for every day and work on diligently with goals and milestones. Those founders who came into the CSUF Startup Incubator on a regular basis saw a dramatic difference in their business. The culture they created by being present was invaluable – others started to come in on a regular basis and there were synergistic effects of founders sharing lessons learned, as well as helping each other grow their respective businesses. Showing up and being present is half the battle, starting up a business is not an overnight success, it doesn't work unless you work at it.

Most first-time founders have a belief that what they are doing is going to make them money, but they don't always understand how. Creating value by solving your customer's pain is paramount for the business to exist and thrive. In addition, the majority of the money you create should not be for relaxation time at the beach, it is for building an army and furthering your mission to make sure everybody who needs your business knows you exist. Having a customer base for one product is great, but you will need to keep reinventing yourself throughout time too. Think about Kodak, once the leader in photographic film products, who didn't change with the technology trends towards digital photography and lost significant market share. Around year two or three, you should be introducing a few more products, based on what your customers want (you always need to listen to your customers) to reinvent or pivot your business. Do keep in mind you will need to measure each of these products to determine the most effective use of your time and Return on Investment (ROI).

As a founder, you should always be learning and there are several other factors that can contribute to success, but I believe these three will help you get a great start. Enjoy the journey and be prepared for a wild ride!

Best of luck,

Phillip Stinis

www.52HikeChallenge.com   22921 Triton Way, Suite 231, Laguna Hills, CA 92653

Family Fun and Fitness

Chuck Su is a 2011 CSUF entrepreneurship graduate. He founded Family Fun and Fitness in 2015.

Creating a successful business is hard work. Chuck's start up experience is typical. While working a second job at night, Chuck works diligently on his own business during the day. He and his loved ones make the sacrifice with grace.

As an entrepreneurship student at CSUF, Chuck exhibited many hallmarks of an entrepreneur: creativity, tenacity, and a big heart. It was the last of these attributes that led him to his idea for a business at a time when he was least expecting it: during a reverse triathlon. Chuck recalls, "The light bulb idea struck me at the end of my niece's race. The reverse triathlon did not have a team race; however, they allowed me to participate with my 4-year-old niece in her race bracket. In the end, I realized the fun was running the course as a family. We had a great time and made everlasting memories."

Chuck wanted to help other families replicate the happiness and fun that he experienced with his niece. He began to lay out the main points of a business plan that revolved around a new idea of family time and fitness. Chuck then met with his mentors at Cal State Fullerton's Center for Entrepreneurship. He received good advice. The Center's staff helped him to solidify his business plan and provided Chuck with access to valuable resources and connections.

One of these connections was retired engineer and CSUF Entrepreneurship mentor Bill Purpura. Chuck says he sought out Purpura because, "He was the man who I thought would give me the best advice. He doesn't sugar coat things and has your best interest at heart. When I met with him, I was nervous but prepared." After Purpura's positive review, Chuck believed that his business plan was worthy of launch.

With a solid plan and a seemingly endless amount of passion Chuck began to build his own business. Its mission is to bring together family time and exercise. These two activities form the main pillars of Family Fun Fitness.

FAMILY FUN FITNESS

Dear Founder,

What does it *REALLY* take to be an entrepreneur? The truth about creating your new venture follows. Over the past 10 years, I experienced most of what can happen from having your own company. What I lost and gained along the way is the tale I will now tell.

IT TAKES TIME

It takes at least three years to see if a business is going to succeed. The founder has to spend a considerable amount of time researching the market and gathering resources such as people, capital, vendors, etc. Then, the company has to land its first customers. For example, it took me 18 months to truly understand my client base and offerings. Be prepared to fully invest yourself in the business for the long haul.

IT TAKES COURAGE

Like an actor on a stage or a minor-league baseball player, I have no choice but to pursue my dream. Achieving dreams requires courage. For me, it still takes courage to do three things:

1. Scrape, crawl and beg for money from family and friends to get my business ideas going.

2. Make cold calls when I am not in the mood.

3. Decline social invitations from friends. There is much work to be done. Friends understand sacrifice.

IT TAKES A SUPPORT SYSTEM

In the entrepreneurial space, it is a good idea to have a strong support system consisting of your significant other, family, friends and mentors. There are several positive benefits to building a support system such as reduced stress and a healthier lifestyle.

In addition, having more than one mentor can be a great resource to help you think through current challenges, manage a career strategy, or just vent frustrations. For instance, one of my mentors advised me on a market opportunity which will replace the stale and boring Jog-A-Thon at elementary schools. I listened and Fun-A-Thon was born. Shortly after, a school in Santa Ana liked the concept and wanted us to start right away. Mentors are very supportive and don't charge a dime, if you're nice.

It's all academic unless you take the leap and do it. It can take a long time. It can be hard and you can fail. However, you are not alone on this journey. Plenty of people will be there to help. Ask your friends, family, mentors, team, vendors and customers to pitch in. You'll be surprised how they will come to your aid. Through perseverance, you will find your way and achieve your own definition of success.

Regards,

Chuck Su

Chuck Su

Swartz Investments, Inc.

Sylvan Swartz, now semi-retired, is a serial entrepreneur. His entrepreneurial journey began in 1966 after he graduated from USC with a Doctorate in Pharmacy. .

Initially, Sylvan managed Pharmacies in Pasadena, Glendale and Beverly Hills. All for the same owner.

He then opened a drugstore in Santa Ana in partnership with a physician to service multiple convalescent hospitals. Sylvan soon found out the importance of working capital. Third party payers often took six months or more to pay for the large volume of prescriptions billed to them. His largest client and slowest payer was the State of California.

Seeking improved cash flow and closer connection with patients, Sylvan opened a deep discount pharmacy in Anaheim. He planned to be a membership-only retail store with a large vitamin section, augmented by a mail order operation. He intended the membership fees to offset low prices. Volume was good but insufficient to offset the low prices. Price Club opened and showed how it was done.

Sylvan obtained a real estate sales license in 1978 and soon followed with a broker's license. He started selling commercial property and found that sound business principles were the same for real estate as they were for his prior commercial ventures.

Sylvan opened Swartz Real Estate in 1982 to syndicate commercial properties in sun belt states. With several partners, he owned and operated Best Western Motels, Ramada Inn Motels, apartment buildings and an office building. Sylvan found that having so many partners, even limited partners, was not enjoyable.

In 1986, Sylvan started Swartz Commercial Real Estate and Swartz Property

Management to broker and manage commercial Southern California properties. He started purchasing properties personally. He based his companies in the Irvine Spectrum in his own 10,000 Sq. Ft. office building. In 1992, he started dealing exclusively with banks, selling commercial foreclosures and leasing space.

In 2010, Sylvan decided to close the office and semi-retire. He now works from home, and only does some property management, leasing and sales for existing clients. Sylvan believes that the guiding principals of his real estate ventures have always been the same. "Provide knowledge, integrity and the best communication in the industry to clients."

For many years, Sylvan has been a volunteer for CSUF entrepreneurship. He has been a Small Business Institute student consulting team sponsor, an Entrepreneur in Residence, and a steadfast classroom mentor. He says, "helping at California State University Fullerton has been an outstanding way to give back to the community and to future business people. Giving is always more rewarding than taking."

SWARTZ
COMMERCIAL REAL ESTATE
PROPERTY MANAGEMENT

960 North Tustin Avenue, Suite 350
Orange, California 92867
Phone: (714) 835-2400
Fax: (714) 602 9225

Dear Founder:

I believe that founding a new business is in some ways a throwback to the frontiersmen of the 18th and 19th centuries. If you want to eat you need to hunt but in this case not for food but for business.

One person along the path advised me to get myself into deep debt with a fancy new car and maybe a big home. In that way I would have to really work hard to figure things out and build a business. I do not recommend this incentive method, although I guess it works for some.

I also believe that making money cannot be the primary motivating factor to be an entrepreneur. Of course we all want to be financially successful but there are a myriad of easier ways to do that by simply working for others and not having to worry about meeting payroll or paying the rent.

One needs to believe deep inside that they can rely on their own instincts for their success and possibly failure (I never gave the failure part much thought). The Entrepreneur must be nimble and able to steer the business in a new direction if necessary. In my commercial real estate brokerage firm, when interest rates soared to 19% and 20% in 1979/80, I put together only deals where sellers carried back financing. When the real estate market collapsed in the 1990s, I started representing banks selling their commercial foreclosures. Be creative and use your skill set to meet your market's needs.

One last thought. If possible find a spouse or significant other that is supportive of all your efforts or at least as crazy as you are.

Sincerely

Sylvan Swartz

Professor, Coach and Advisor

Atul Teckchandani is an Associate Professor of Entrepreneurship at California State University Fullerton's Mihaylo College of Business and Economics.

Before joining CSUF Entrepreneurship, Atul was awarded his doctorate from the Haas School of Business at the University of California, Berkeley. He received a master's degree in Business Administration from the McCombs School of Business at the University of Texas, Austin. Atul also earned a master's degree in Electrical Engineering from Santa Clara University.

After graduating with his undergraduate degree in Electrical Engineering, from the University of California, Berkeley, Atul worked as a hardware engineer in Silicon Valley. Before attending graduate school, he worked for three three technology firms: Advanced Micro Devices, Altera Corporation, and a venture-backed startup (CoWave Networks).

Atul's approach to teaching entrepreneurship and coaching CSUF entrepreneurs incorporates his experiences growing up in a family of entrepreneurs. He has a deep understanding of the academic literature on entrepreneurship. Atul took many entrepreneurship classes in his MBA program and reads extensively about how founders practice entrepreneurship.

Atul leverages his diverse career in several ways. He writes academic articles about entrepreneurship and entrepreneurship pedagogy.

In the classroom, he teaches students to become successful entrepreneurs and he supervises student consulting projects.

Outside the classroom, he is an informal advisor to many CSUF Entrepreneurship Alumni. Most are early-stage entrepreneurs or have small businesses. While these conversations range widely, a popular topic is work-life balance.

Atul is married with two children. He enjoys spending time with his family. Both children are active in sports and he devotes time to regularly attend their games. Other family pastimes include going to museums, the theater, amusement parks, and trying new restaurants.

Mihaylo College of Business and Economics
Department of Management
P O Box 6848, Fullerton, CA 92834-6848 / T 657-278-2592 / F 657-278-7101

Dear Founder,

As you embark on your entrepreneurial journey, consider the following two pieces of advice:

1. Solve a problem.
Successful businesses solve a problem. Dropbox solved the problem of not being able to access your electronic files from anywhere. Google solved the problem of not being able to find things on the Internet. And even the local restaurant or coffee shop solves a problem by offering a unique product that can't be found elsewhere (e.g., pasta sauce made with a family recipe or a latte made with a Turkish twist), offering food at a much higher level of quality (e.g., WhichWich versus Subway), or offering complete customization of your meal (e.g., Blaze or Chipotle versus a traditional pizza or burrito joint). No matter what the industry, solve a problem.

2. Don't be afraid to pivot.
Most of us are not going to get it right the first time. Rather than getting overly attached to your first idea, pay attention to what actual and prospective customers are saying and adjust your business model accordingly. Starbucks started out as a store that sold supplies (coffee makers and espresso beans) to allow coffee connoisseurs to make gourmet coffee at home. But after seeing tremendous interest in a coffee cart that was placed in one of their stores, the company began focusing on selling coffee drinks and bringing the Italian café experience to the United States.

Not wanting to make changes to the business model is the cause of many early-stage failures. It is not easy for someone to admit that they are wrong. But remember that, at the start, almost everything in your business model is an assumption. My father hates the word "assume" because if you break it down, it essentially means that you are making an "ass" out of "u" and "me." As a founder, your goal is to gather data to support or refute all assumptions (and avoid being an ass).

A great way to validate assumptions is to leverage customer feedback. All learning depends on feedback. The learning loop consists of four stages: observe, assess, design and implement. Understand your customers by observing how they interact with your product/service. (If your venture is in the early stages and does not have a product/service, you can interview prospective customers to understand their needs.) Only after you understand your customers can you truly assess what problem your product/service should solve. Then you design a solution. And, lastly, you implement the solution by offering it to the world.

But this is a learning loop. After your solution is out in the world, you are back at the top of the learning loop – the observation stage. Every iteration of the learning loop will result in a new product, service or process. The result will be a company culture that values continuous learning and continuous improvement – which are keys to a successful business.

I wish you much success in your entrepreneurial journey.

Sincerely,

Atul Teckchandani

Alvaka Networks

Oli Thordarson is founder and CEO of Alvaka Networks. The company is headquartered in Irvine, California.

Alvaka is a leading provider of network management, security and integration services. Its core purpose is to constantly improve the way networks are managed and secured. Alvaka provides IT services for small to mid-size enterprises that rely heavily upon good system performance with high levels of uptime and strong security.

Alvaka fills a niche for services that are not economically provided by its client's' IT staffs. Key services are network and application performance monitoring, security assessments and remediation, IT system design, upgrade and installation (often referred to as technology refresh), service desk, and trouble-shooting of persistent unsolved problems.

Clients often cite peace-of-mind as a key value they receive from Alvaka Networks. They like knowing that there is "someone else" watching the network who they can lean on when needed. It is important for them to not rely solely on the knowledge and staffing they employ. Second opinions and the extension of additional expertise regarding IT matters provides them comfort. Alvaka Networks is what is often referred to as their trusted advisor.

In essence, Alvaka Networks helps executives overcome the fears and frustrations they feel from being held hostage by the mysteries surrounding their Information Technology so they can get back to controlling costs, making money and rest-assured that their business is running smoothly.

Oli has 30 years' experience running his own companies in the Information Technology industry and is proud of the success of his entirely self-funded companies. He has a history of involvement.

Oli was the founding chairman of the Intel backed Global MSP Network in 2001. He has served on the board of CompTIA, the Global IT trade association, as well as on national industry association boards and editorial advisory councils for computer industry publications. He has also served as chair of the Technology Leadership Political Action committee.

Locally, Oli has served on the advisory board of the Discovery Science Center. At CSUF, he sponsored student consulting for the Small Business Institute, and served as an Entrepreneur in Residence for the Center for Entrepreneurship.

Oli is married with 3 children. He lives and works in southern California and is an avid outdoorsman, races motorcycles off-road and races his Corvette in the Sport Car Club of America, NASA and Trans Am.

Alvaka Networks

Dear founder:

Building the right team is hard work but it will separate you from all your competition. Your team is your most important asset. They are the underpinning for every decision, action and result coming from your new company. Build the best team you can afford. Don't go cheap, hire the best you can get. If you build the right team and provide them with strong leadership you will always find a way to succeed.

How to shape your invaluable team? Three axioms work for me: *Hire slow, fire fast; Even one person can change your culture; Give your people, purpose, mastery and autonomy.*

1. Almost everyone hires too quickly. When we find ourselves understaffed and behind schedule the temptation is strong to find an expedient solution. Avoid that temptation. A wrong hire is really hard to fix later. You must design a hiring process that works for your business. Learn how to interview people skillfully. Understand how to measure candidates and assess how they will fit culturally. Talk to successful business owners. Read tips online and talk with consultants.

Most of us fire too slowly. We start to recognize a problem and don't deal with it swiftly with clear language and explicit expectations. We tolerate less than acceptable performance until it negatively impacts our organization. Then we might counsel the person or reprimand them, but in vague terms. They usually don't improve . We see the problem again, but put off confrontation. Waiting a long time to do the inevitable is very damaging to your company, your customers and company morale. Firing people takes discipline, skill and time. It is an event most of us want to avoid but is often inescapable. Make sure you have good legal counsel assisting you. There are many pitfalls in the hiring and firing process (and regretfully, you will find some of them the hard expensive way).

2. Be aware that every hire you make is going to change the culture of your company. Learn how to assess a person not just for their skills, but for how well they will contribute to the culture you need. Peter Drucker said, "culture eats strategy for breakfast." I agree. It is up to us as leaders to make sure we hire people that accrue to a stronger healthier company culture.

3. I strongly concur with Daniel Pink who writes in his book <u>Drive</u> that there are three primary things that motivate people at their work: purpose, mastery, and autonomy. First, people seek a sense of purpose when they come to work. Give them a purpose. Second, people strive for mastery. They need to be challenged by their work and feel like they are growing. Give them challenging work. Encourage them to get to their next level both individually, and as a team. Overcoming challenges will keep them feeling good about themselves. That happiness will keep them on-board and producing at high levels. Third, people need autonomy. Your company needs well-defined processes and procedures, but within the job role people need to feel they have some control and discretion over how they do their work. It is very demeaning and demoralizing to be micro-managed all day at work. Listen to their feedback and follow their suggestions. This provides them respect and you gain goodwill.

Most successful regards,

Oli Thordarson
CEO/Founder
Alvaka Networks

For in depth discussion of these topics by the author, please go to https://bit.ly/creatingnewventures

Administrator and Angel Investor

John Tillquist has been an active angel investor since 2003. He is a past regional President and a current member of the Board of Governors of the Tech Coast Angels. He has been CEO and founding president for two software start-up businesses in California and Canada. In 2016, John was the Director of California State University Fullerton's Office of Research and Development.

John holds masters and doctorate degrees in information & computer science from the University of California-Irvine. Before that, his background in Industry spanned over ten years as a corporate director and senior software engineer at AT&T, GTE and Ameritech.

John has over two dozen publications. He has spoken nationally and internationally about entrepreneurship, technology, organizational strategy and economic development.

For eleven years John ran six southern California centers for workforce training, entrepreneurship and business development, including oversight of the TriTech Small Business Development Center. TriTech focuses on high-growth, early-stage businesses and helps southern California entrepreneurs raise nearly $100 million in new capital and revenue growth annually. He has served as entrepreneur-in-residence or occasional faculty at local institutions. They include the Naval Surface Warfare Center-Corona Division, Chapman University and California State University San Bernardino's Entrepreneurship graduate program.

John's board service includes the CSU-SB Technology Transfer Office, the Council on Economic Development Advisors, the Workforce Advisory Board and the Alliance for the Commercialization of Technologies. He has been a mentor and judge for business plan competitions at the USC Viterbi School of Engineering, CSUSB Entrepreneurship, the Keck Graduate Institute of Claremont and the Peter F. Drucker Graduate School.

John is proud of his activities with The Tech Coast Angles. It is one of the largest and most active angel investment organizations in the U.S., with over 300 members in five regional networks. Members have diverse industry backgrounds, many are entrepreneurs with start-up experience and collectively they have invested in over 300 companies a total nearing $200 million. Tech Coast Angel portfolio companies have gone on to attract over $1.6 billion in additional investment capital.

John Tillquist
Riverside, California

Dear Founder,

Three philosophies define baseball umpires. "I call them as they are", "I call them as I see them", and for the fist-pumping umpire Bill Klem, "They ain't nothing till I call them." The game is about playing in a fast-paced arena where split-second decisions are made. Even a blown call is still a call but credibility forgives mistakes. Bill Klem embodied credibility behind the plate, making him one of the most respected umpires in league history.

Credibility instills belief and creates excitement. Fervent belief energizes followers and in so motivates action, instills trust, brings insight, and creates a willingness to invest time, resources, and access for the entrepreneur. Confidence in the entrepreneur overcomes doubt and mitigates the sense of risk. It encourages exploration of opportunities especially when aligned with others' interests and goals. It opens doors to resources such as capital, information, and access. Credibility is the single-most important tool to mobilize action.

How can you build credibility? In over a decade of equity investing and hundreds of pitches, I have found three practices that make a credible entrepreneur. First, decimate your assumptions. Don't assume that you will win over a specific percentage of the market; know how your market approach will operate, how you will create awareness, and how you will deliver. Obliterate nebulous assumptions about who will and will not buy your product and how you will overcome customer inertia. Know in painstaking detail what resources, abilities, and knowledge you have and those you do not, and for those you do not, know how and when you will get them.

Second, have a strategy and pursue it relentlessly. Henry Mintzberg of McGill University described strategy as "a pattern in a stream of decisions." You will need to adapt based on limited knowledge, changing resource availability, and shifting playing fields. Decisions must be based on a strategy which weaves a pattern through daily operations and through wholesale pivots in direction. A worthy business plan articulates your strategy, putting front-stage the goals and purpose of the venture versus a detailed set of tactics and actions that are outdated before the plan is even completed.

Third, build an evangelical following. Leverage high profile connections to industry and thought-leaders to attract attention and stir interest. Get everyone involved to use their resources and to achieve their interests by aligning with your juggernaut. Collaborate with customers to beachhead innovative products. Feed your network through media, high profile events, and constant interaction. To paraphrase umpire Bill Klem, make sure the guy in the cheap seats can hear your message as well as those in the box seats.

Credibility creates confidence, exudes trust, and energizes evangelical followers. The successful entrepreneur is the fist-pumping umpire that commands belief, keeps the game on-track, and thrills the audience.

All the best,

John Tillquist

Real Estate and Investments

Aaron Tofani is a 2006 alumnus of California State University Fullerton. He is the founder of ATE Real Estate and co-founder and CEO of Rance's Chicago Pizza.

While earning his Bachelor's degree in finance from CSUF with a 3.9 GPA, Aaron worked full time for his family's construction and engineering companies. He advanced to Vice President of GeoKinetics which offers geo-technical and environmental services.

After graduation Aaron became interested in real estate development. In 2008, he became Director of Acquisitions for Convergence Capital, LLC. It is a real estate private equity group investing in sale-lease backs of auto dealerships. He went on to earn a Master of Real Estate Development degree from USC in 2011.

Aaron founded ATE Real Estate in 2011. It is a real estate development consulting company. The company's focus is retail property development. Clients include Paragon Commercial Group and Spectrum Real Estate Group. ATE Real Estate has provided underwriting, due diligence, entitlement, leasing, project management and construction management services for over 1,000,000 square feet of retail property development in California with a valuation in excess of $400,000,000.

Aaron then parlayed his expertise and relationships in commercial real estate to enter the restaurant business. He and his childhood friend Rance Ruiz opened Rance's Chicago Pizza with an eye to expand throughout Southern California. Rance's Chicago Pizza has won many awards since the first location opened in Costa Mesa, CA in 2012 including the "Golden Foodie Award" for best pizza in

Golden Foodie Award for Best Pizza
Aaron Tofani (left), Rance Ruiz (right)

Orange County. Aaron's responsibilities include sourcing locations, store design, permitting, construction management, contracts, financing, and marketing.

Today, Aaron lives within a short walk of the second Rance's Chicago Pizza restaurant which opened in December 2016. Most of Aaron's time now is spent managing the development and opening of the 3rd Rance's. It is set to open in USC's new University Village in 2017.

As an undergraduate at CSUF Aaron was active in the Young Entrepreneur Society. Since graduation, he has sponsored multiple student consulting projects for CSUF Entrepreneurship students.

Aside from running the restaurant business and continuing retail property consulting, Aaron's hobbies include outdoor activities. His favorites are snowboarding, surfing, scuba diving, golfing and traveling with friends and family.

Rance's Chicago Pizza

Costa Mesa, CA (Costa Mesa Square)
Long Beach, CA (Belmont Shore)
Los Angeles, CA (USC University Village)
www.rancespizza.com

Dear Founder,

Doing what you love for yourself is fun and rewarding. However, this typically comes after years of hard work and sacrifice along the way. Make sure you are set up for success before you invest the time to launch a new venture. Two important factors that have made my restaurant business successful is having competitive advantages and complementary skill sets.

Competitive advantages come in many forms. In Rance's case, it's a combination of first to market, highest quality, uniqueness, and personal relationships. My best friend since the 3rd grade, Rance, is a highly-skilled pizza chef and more passionate about pizza than anyone I know is passionate about anything. He is a competitive advantage with genuine passion and skill that money can't buy. Plus Rance's is a unique name than shows up in the top of search engine results no matter where you are in the world.

Rance's other key competitive advantage is my commercial real estate expertise and personal relationships in the real estate community. The 2nd and 3rd Rance's Pizza locations are highly desirable A+ locations which were sourced off-market. Location is critical in the restaurant business, so controlling the best location in our respective markets is a huge advantage.

Selecting partnerships with complimentary competitive advantages will help set your venture up for success. Combining my real estate, marketing and finance expertise with Rance's cooking, operations, and personnel management skills give us the key ingredients in the recipe for a successful restaurant business.

Wishing you the best in creating your new venture,

Aaron Tofani, CEO / Co-Founder, Rance's Chicago Pizza

Have Faith in Yourself

Ray Valencia is a financial advisor with Integrity Wealth Management (IWM) located in Newport Beach California. IWM provides comprehensive financial planning services. They include investment management, risk analysis, distribution strategies, wealth transfer, and retirement planning. Ray helps successful professionals, business owners, and high net worth individuals. Says Ray,

"That's my "professional" blurb that I mostly took from my Linkedin page. I'm told that I reflect a growing demographic on campus so I'll level with you on how I got to where I am. Keep in mind I'm by no means done growing, or super rich, but my life is good and the start at CSUF definitely contributed.

I mentioned demographics. Both my parents were born in Mexico and I'm a first generation American. I and many of my first gen cousins have obtained college degrees. Some have PhD's.

Many decisions got me though the obstacles that came my way. The first was thanks to poor plumbing or lack of it. When I was five my father thought it a good idea to live in his home town in Mexico. A town that was many years behind the times. Mom having been raised in the U.S. was not too thrilled about having to walk to the river with a bucket to get water for anything. So two years later I'm back in the USA. Yeah!

From there I would say I had a pretty normal public school upbringing. Both parents worked so I had to pretty much take care of myself. We started off with not very much but my father ended up making a pretty good living as an automotive designer. I was a terrible student in high school. I only mastered ditching classes with my girlfriend. But I got it done and went to Fullerton CC.

I started out in psychology because it's fascinating but then I figured it wasn't going to get me where I wanted economically. So business entered the picture. I didn't know what kind of business, but I figured they all have the same bones. Details I'd figure out later. I worked a forty hour week during the day and went to classes at night. That helped keep the student loans in check. And the experience of working in a small business while taking business courses at night was a huge boost for me. I can't overstate that fact.

Six years later I graduated from CSUF with a degree in Business Administration and a concentration in Entrepreneurship. Two years later Dr. Michael Ames introduced me to a financial advisor at Edward Jones and my career in financial services started. Unfortunately, it started in 2008-2009 and if you recall the stock market plummeted. I was doing better than most in my cohort but not well enough to cover my expenses. So I wanted to find someone who was successful to see what they were doing differently and eventually I did. I worked with him for three years and then went out on my own. I've now been self employed for almost three years and things are better and better each day. Do I work more than I would as an employee? Oh yes, much more. But these are my clients and I'm building towards my future everyday.

The moral of this story? Have faith in yourself and never give up. Someone is going to tell you to get a job. I'm glad I didn't listen."

Ray Valencia is registered with and securities are offered through Kovack Securities, Inc. Member FINRA/SIPC. 6451 N. Federal Hwy. Suite 1201, Fort Lauderdale, FL 33308 (954) 782 4771. Investment Advisor Representative offers Investment Advisory Services through Kovack Advisors, Inc. Integrity Wealth Management is not affiliated with Kovack Securities, Inc. or Kovack Advisors, Inc.

INTEGRITY
wealth management

Dear Founder,

As I look back on what has helped me over the years the following comes to mind. Some of which seems like common sense to me today, but possibly not in my early youth. I hope some of these come in handy.

Read books on sales, even if you have the greatest product/service you will always be selling. No sales equals no business/company at the end of the day. At the very least you'll be selling yourself for the rest of your life. Want to get married and perhaps raise children? This training will be a great investment. (Time saver tip; purchase audio books!)

Have an important presentation to make? Do it from beginning to end no matter how much you stumble at least 16 times. If it's a power point introduce the next slide before you click on it and you'll look like a pro.

If you ever feel hesitant to pick up the phone and make a challenging call or asking something of someone else; remember these words: "If you do not ask, the answer will always be no". This will also help in your personal life.

Follow up!, follow up!, follow up! This will make or break you. If you don't, someone else will be following up with your prospect/client and they'll win the business. Life and business is a perpetual competition.

Dress and act the part. Every industry is different but in my field (financial services) most are not going to trust you with their money if you don't look trustworthy, sharp, and successful. Also, good luck getting more business if a client should see you acting like a fool at a bar or worse a nightclub. You are always on stage when in public.

Find someone to model; someone who is really good in an area you want to improve and copy them. No need to reinvent the wheel. Use this in all aspects of your life.

Be mindful of what you expose yourself to both internally and externally. Internal self-talk can build your self-esteem and also destroy it. Externally think of yourself as a piece of flypaper. Wherever you put yourself something is going to stick to you, both good and bad so be purposeful in where and with whom you spend your time.

Exercise. You won't have time but even 15 minutes to get your heart rate up will help you in all areas of your life. You'll feel and look better which will help you succeed. Plus it helps with stress.

Be trustworthy, open, and honest in all your dealings. Especially with costs and fees (money!), never run or hide from these, just be really up front. It goes a long way in building trust and generating future business.

Shut up and listen first. You are likely dealing with intelligent people. Let them tell you what they want and need. Then come back with a few options that address their concerns. If you listened carefully they will notice and be much more inclined to do business with you.

Admit your shortcomings. You can fake how you feel that day, you can fake self-confidence, but you cannot fake knowledge. If you don't know, you don't know, but you will get the answer.

Have a firm handshake and make eye contact with both men and women. You will be judged! My culture taught me to not look elders or "superiors" in the eye so if you're in the same boat get over it if you want to be successful.

Last, but not least make it fun! I bought the office a dartboard for the break room, soft tip of course.

All the best, and good luck.

Ray Valencia

Investment Advisor Representative

Valle Consulting

Francisco Valle founded Valle Consulting ("VC") in 2002. The company provides consulting services in strategy, developing sustainable competitive advantage and Hispanic marketing.

Francisco holds a Ph.D. in Management and an Executive Certificate in Strategy from Claremont Graduate University's The Peter F. Drucker & Masatoshi Ito Graduate School of Management. He also earned an M.B.A. from California State University, Fullerton, and a B.S. in Chemistry, Pharmacy, and Biology from the prestigious Universidad Nacional Autónoma de México.

After earning his MBA at California State University Fullerton in 1985, Francisco began his career in the oil industry. He held operations management positions at Mobile Oil, BP and ARCO. Francisco then joined Taco Bell as a market manager. Later he was a Regional Vice President of Operations at ARAMARK.

In 2000, Francisco became Chairman and CEO of SCDRG, Inc.a privately held consulting, advertising and marketing agency. Its list of clients included Adelphia, AT&T, Charter, Cox, Disney Channel, Fox Sports, HBO, Showtime and Time Warner. In 2001, he conducted the first Hispanic Marketing Master Course for CTAM executives (Cable and Telecommunications Association for Marketing). Cable Vision, Cable World and MultiChannelNews frequently quoted Francisco.

As President of Valle Consulting, Francisco provides project support, strategic planning, development of a sustainable competitive advantage, and design of marketing and advertising campaigns. The techniques applied by the firm include the identification and evaluation of innovative, synergistic opportunities for value creation and increased market share. Valle Consulting leverages complementary assets in a culturally relevant way. The firm enhances the results of strategic and marketing initiatives by applying big data, multicultural knowledge, and open innovation. Institutions advised include Tri-City Medical Center, major cable companies and programmers, Merrill Lynch, U.S. Tennis Association and Wal-Mart.

Francisco co-authored How To Win The Hispanic Gold Rush™, a book selected by Forbes Magazine's Book Club. He has earned multiple awards. They include the Merrill Lynch Global Leadership in Diversity Award, the 2014 Community Healthcare Champion by the San Diego Business Journal, the 2013 Health Professional of the Year Latino Champion Award by U-T San Diego, and the 2013 Inspirational Leader of the Year Finalist by the San Diego Magazine. He received four Palm Awards for advertising campaigns developed for clients.

Strategy and Marketing
Hispanic Market Penetration
www.ValleConsulting.com

Francisco J. Valle, Ph.D.
President
15270 Falcon Crest Court
San Diego, CA 92127
V (949) 500-8852
franciscovalle@cox.net

Dear Founder,

Congratulations to you for your plans to found a new company. I want to share with you three items that I believe are important for you to succeed.

First, realize that you need to run "the business with the head while sprinkling it with a little bit of heart" but not the other way around. During the start-up phase, entrepreneurs and business founders tend to invite friends, families, or prior business associates to join them. This is fine as long as there are very clear goals and objectives set up for them with clear QUANTITATIVE benchmarks determining whether they are "getting the job done or not". If an individual cannot "carry his/her own weight" and/or cannot achieve the quantitative benchmarks set up for him/her after having an opportunity to do it, then, the entrepreneur and founder must make a quick move and replace the individual with one who has the knowledge, expertise, and skills to achieve the expected results of the position.

Second, learn to determine the products or services that are needed now and in the future. When I co-authored the book *How To Win The Hispanic Gold Rush*™ (2003), I thought that what leaders of organizations needed to know about the Hispanic market to be successful within that market were the critical cultural, demographic, marketing, and motivational factors. What I learned later on was that what these leaders needed most was a framework with a clear description of what to do from A to Z to succeed in their pursuit of this ethnic market. Indeed, as Peter Drucker wrote in his book *The Ecological Vision* (1993), "The important thing is to identify the 'future that has already happened.'" Drucker meant by this that an organization has to be capable of leveraging the changes that have already occurred in the marketplace. How can you do this? Follow these steps: 1) Analyze and understand demographics and the major trends affecting them (e.g. currently the growth of the Hispanic and Asian ethnic groups in the United States; 2) Read and internalize futurist concepts found in TED speeches, the content of information published by organizations and sites such as Singularity University – a Silicon Valley think tank; and 3) Gather key industry insights from information you collect from speaking with authors and experts in your field. These three items have provided me with a foundation that has allowed me to develop unique business models that represent a sustainable competitive advantage for my organization.

Finally, acknowledge that no matter how smart one is, as an African Proverb says: "If you want to go fast, go alone. If you want to go far, go together." Therefore, to stay at the top, one needs to be surrounded by smart people who play valuable roles within the team.

I wish you all the best with your businesses as well as a future full of remarkable achievements and growth.

Sincerely,

Dr. Francisco J. Valle

Jackson Square Partners

Jeffrey Van Harte and his team of partners formed Jackson Square Partners (JSP) in 2014. JSP manages large-cap growth, smid-cap growth, all-cap growth, and global growth portfolios. The firm is a spin-out from Delaware Investments. It is majority-owned by its key personnel, many of whom have worked together for over 12 years.

Jeff leads the firm as Chairman and Chief Investment Officer. The investment philosophy that supports JSP growth equity strategies is not new. It has not changed since early members of the investment team started managing portfolios over 20 years ago. It guided the team first at Transamerica Investment Management and subsequently during a tenure at Delaware Investments from 2005-2014.

The team focuses on finding companies in industries with limited competition that are generating more cash than they're spending. Jeff says, "What we define as our measure of growth is cash economics, We turn past companies' earnings statements and go right to the cash-flow statement."

Jeff has been managing portfolios and separate accounts for 30 years. Before becoming a portfolio manager, He was a securities analyst and trader for Transamerica Investment Services, which he joined upon graduation from California State University at Fullerton in 1980. He majored in Finance.

Jeff gives time and money to many CSUF programs. He says the reason he began donating to the university is simple, "I just wanted to give back to something that gave a lot to me. Attending CSUF really was a life-changing experience. I am very much a believer that state schools are an amazing value to a lot of families who are good, working-class families. I think that the job they do doesn't get the credit that it should."

Jeff contributed to the Campaign for the College of Business and Economics and several other programs on campus. He also funded the initial startup for the college's Student Managed Investment Fund. Recently, Jeff made a major donation to help expand the College's student investment program and establish Titan Capital Management, an investment management center on campus.

Since 2011, Jeff has served on the Board of Governors for the CSUF Philanthropic Foundation, and has been the chair of the Board's Finance and Investment Committee.

Dear Founder,

We created our new venture, Jackson Square Partners (JSP), LLC in May of 2014. This came after long and arduous negotiations with our parent company. In short, JSP was created to preserve our culture and ability to grow given the pressures we faced being part of a larger organization where sometimes profit motives and cultures clashed. As part of the deal we committed to create a fully integrated investment management company within two years. Our client book of over $25 billion in assets needed a fully integrated investment management company to service it. We met our commitment in eighteen months. How did we do this?

Investment people, like entrepreneurs, are notorious for not being the best managers of people and not particularly interested in the day to day management of operations. We had to get interested quickly. The new functions that we had to create involved legal, compliance, finance, human resources, client service, client reporting, a new trading platform, and many other administrative functions that heretofore we never had to worry about as we were just an investment team within a larger investment company.

My message to would be founders and entrepreneurs is, GET INTERESTED!! You simply can't ignore what would be deemed to be "mundane" or "not germane" to how you want to spend your time if you are going to be a successful entrepreneur. To keep your team of entrepreneurs and creative people in genius mode, I can't stress enough how important it is find the right operational people to allow your team to stay in genius mode while the operational people actually run the company.

Your job as founder is twofold. (1) find one or more people that can focus on operations while you and your founding team of entrepreneurs and creative people stay focused. (2) protect and augment your founding team with new talent so there is a upcoming generation to take your company to the next level. As founder, you will always need to have an awareness of operational issues, even after you find the right people that actually do the day to day work of running the company. Further, you need to foster an environment where the operational personnel are respected by the entrepreneurial or creative people in the company. Creative people need to understand the value of great operational personnel in that they allow the creative people to focus on what they do best. Mutual respect helps ensure a healthy and happy company culture. When all your people feel valued, motivation is stronger and your people will invest more of themselves in your company.

Jeffrey S. Van Harte
Chair and Chief Investment Officer
Jackson Square Partners

For in depth discussion of these topics by the author, please go to https://bit.ly/creatingnewventures

Nusabi

Gonzalo Vasquez founded Nusabi in 2011 while he was a student at California State University Fullerton. Nusabi is a brand name for a philosophy. Its purpose is to inspire, motivate and empower individuals to find their way through life by sharing the Nusabi philosophy. Nusabi is based on one principle: Trust your intuition.

Through Nusabi Life Coaching (NLC), a subsidiary of Nusabi, Gonzalo targets the parents and educators of elementary school aged children and college students. The goal is to help young people to reach their potential and to become powerful.

At the grade school level, NLC currently teaches parents and educators how to improve young peoples' self esteem. NLC enters partnerships with school districts to teach parents how to find self-worth and value within themselves. With this knowledge, they can recognize the value in others, especially their children. The goal is to increase parent involvement in their child's social development.

NLC also focuses on helping college students to become self-aware. Gonzalo notes that "This segment of our population will have a direct influence on the direction of our society in the immediate future. NLC helps them to understand themselves and adopt an effective system for decision making."

Gonzalo has professional experience in public speaking. He has been an Admissions Advisor for private educational institutions. Gonzalo's "home team" includes his wife Nancy (a school teacher) and their three beautiful children: Dylan, Diane and Roxy.

Gonzalo's life motto is,

"Fate is something imposed. Destiny is something that you Chose."

292

Gonzalo Vasquez
Life Coach
www.nusabilifecoaching.com

Dear Founder,

Be patient. Your venture will revolutionize the industry, make you wealthy beyond your imagination and change the world for the better. .. in time. Meanwhile, there is a lot of work to be done and you must make the time to do it. You might even have to work outside your venture to make ends meet. That's okay. Your venture might take different shapes, forcing you to adjust and go back to the drawing board. That's okay. Whatever the journey throws at you, remember that success is a destination that is reached through many paths. You are going to be okay.

Be afraid. Work with a sense of urgency that if you do not create, nurture and develop your idea, somebody else will. Make *time* your ally and *procrastination* your enemy. Cherish your ally, but fear your enemy. It allows you to stay focused and busy. Treat each interaction with clients/ customers with ultimate professionalism and importance.

Planning is crucial, execution is critical. All the market research means nothing unless you apply it. You can get stuck overthinking and second guessing everything. One of the most important components, especially in the beginning, is to create momentum. File for your DBA, get your resellers permit, business license and whatever else you must do to get started. When preparation meets opportunity; they conceive success. The more you act on the small decisions, the more it will prepare you to take on the medium and large ones. Learning by doing is a catalyst in becoming an expert in your field. The goal is to become so efficient, that you transform conscious momentum building to autopilot.

I wish you the best in both your personal and professional endeavors. Trust your intuition.

Sincerely,

Gonzalo Vasquez

Veta Ties

Johnathon Veta is the founder of Veta Ties. He began his entrepreneurship endeavors on his high school prom bus. He realized that he and his fellow male classmates all wore baggy, poorly tailored suits with what seemed like five-inch-wide neckties. The idea struck him of transforming the appeal of formal wear for young men. After leaving the prom early, he worked 24 hours straight to design his first set of men's neckties and fashion accessories.

Using his knowledge from digital photography and background in psychology, John strived to set a new standard in men's neckwear applying innovation, concept and quality. With unforgettable designs, Veta Ties captures the essence of both traditional style and contemporary fashions.

John created the original line 'Power Ties,' which applies theories of color psychology to everyday life; behind each necktie is information about the subliminal messages conveyed by its colors. Learn what each color says about you on www.vetaties.com.

While continuing to build Veta Ties, John graduated from California State University, Fullerton (CSUF) in 2016 with honors and a concentration in entrepreneurship. He served as the President of the Entrepreneurship Society.

John entered the Boeing Case Study competition while at CSUF. Boeing awarded him a scholarship. After graduation he began work in the Boeing Company's highly competitive business career foundation program. He is now pursuing his other passion, aerospace.

John's current functions at The Boeing Company involve accelerating and perfecting business operations for both the U.S. Government and commercial customers. In his first two years, he has led initiatives in estimating, financial operations, supplier management, contracts, program management, sales and marketing.

When he is not working in aerospace, John continues to pursue multiple entrepreneurial ventures within the fashion, extreme sports, and franchise industries. As an undergraduate, John was a sponsored "research and development athlete" for MotoWorks Exhaust during national motocross competitions. He also has obtained aircraft pilot (private license) while in college. Today in his free time, John enjoys racing motocross, sport shooting, flying airplanes, painting, and traveling.

John describes his favorite action photo, "This photo is from the early days of starting my business. I wanted a self portrait that encompassed all my interests. Suit and tie on, but not without a cowboy hat and a motocross helmet while riding down a dirt hill on a big wheel."

Dear Founder,

You probably decided you wanted to be an entrepreneur so you wouldn't have to work 9 to 5, right? Well, you are correct, but instead, I hope you're ready to be working 7 to midnight. It takes grit to play here. Plain and simple.

But what is grit? Grit is one of those weird and almost immeasurable things in our lives that no one really knows the definition of unless you've felt it. I think in most cases it's the things that can't be measured in us that start to make an entrepreneur dangerous and disruptive, in a good way, of course.

To give grit some type of definition, I try to look at it as "Guts, Resilience, Instinct, and Tenacity." I didn't really know what GRIT was until I woke up one morning at age 16, realizing I had a supplier overseas back out of a deal with my first business. All the money I paid for tooling and product was gone. Try going to class that day with that on your mind, while your classmates are complaining about the B+ they just got on their English paper.

I was so motivated to make something of my idea that I went home that night and did the only thing I could think of at that time: pretend I had money and stayed up until 4 a.m. starting over with a new supplier.

Part of what makes GRIT immeasurable is that it is so unique to each of us. You may already know what GRIT is to you. If you do, great! If you don't feel like you've flexed it enough, don't worry. It will come. It will come in the form of flaky business partners, no money, lots of money, no ideas and lack of time. Building your business will test you in so many ways. Think of it as street smarts in a way. I always tell people that I learned more in the first two months of owning my own business than I did in my entire college career.

But what do you do when this GRIT runs low? What do you do when your creativity and motivation feels like it hits a wall?

I often fall into periods of "writers block" where I simply have nothing new coming to the table. No ideas. No drive. My motivation slowly slips away and I find myself sitting there on my couch re-watching episodes of 'Game of Thrones' waiting for this motivational burst to hit me like a hammer. As much as you probably love the idea of binge-watching your favorite show, I'll save you some time. It's not coming. Action does not come from motivation.

I challenge you to shift your mindset. Trust that motivation follows action. Read that again. Motivation FOLLOWS action. Take baby steps if you feel stuck. Those actions will create motivation. You'll find a new angle or a new idea when you just dig in for a second. I promise. If you sit there day after day finding excuses as to why you're "not feeling it," you'll never move forward. Take the action...and it will inspire you.

Here's my last piece of advice to you, as someone who often has a lot of ideas in my head at once. Be patient. You can't get everything done today or even this year. Don't fall into the trap of feeling like you have all this stuff to do and so many ideas you want to tackle. Grab one and go! Play with it. If it fails, drop it and hit up the next one. Worst case scenario, you spend a couple years of your life finding out what doesn't work for you and what you don't like to do. That's still a win.

There are no excuses out there in this world. If you want it, you can get it. Giving 100% isn't going to be enough. Flex your GRIT and get after it!

In the words of Eric Thomas, "When you want to succeed as bad as you want to breath, then you will be successful."

John Veta

Fairchild of California

Fritz von Coelln and his brother Frank bought 50% of Fairchild of California from Charlie Fairchild in 1985. The company, located in Whittier, California manufactured upholstered furniture, including sofas, love seats, chairs, ottomans and sundry other upholstered products. The process was wood and fabric, foam, and parts combined into the final product and shipped in company trucks to the ultimate furniture store.

When Fritz and Frank bought out Mr. Fairchild, Walt Haigh was owner of the other 50% of the business. After the purchase, Fritz managed the production process, Frank became a silent business partner, and Walt was responsible for sales and administration. Production at the time was approximately $3,000,000 in sales with 70 employees.

Business was slow in1985 and Fritz downsized the production staff commensurate with production and concentrated on improving quality. Over the years, the manufacturing process was improved and its administration computerized.

Under Fritz's leadership, the company greatly increased its production capability. For example, in 1998 the company received a Costco order for 6,000 leather sofas and love seats, to be delivered in a two-week period in December. A factory in Argentina provided the leather, some of it precut and sewn. The Tijuana factory cut and sewed leather parts. The Whittier factory, along with a contracted East Los Angeles Factory assembled the Furniture. To meet the delivery date, orders were warehoused at a national trucking company to ship to Costco stores across the continental US, Hawaii, Alaska and Japan.

At the time of Fritz's retirement in 2001, production was at an all time high of nearly 50,000 units a year and sales of $18,000,000. Employees increased to 130 locally and 30 in Tijuana, Mexico.

Customers included Ikea, Costco and numerous smaller sales companies.
In addition, containers of upholstered products were shipped around the world including Japan, China, Australia, Poland and Saudi Arabia.

Since 2001, Fritz, has volunteered for the Osher Lifelong Learning Institute at California State University Fullerton. He administered and participated in OLLI-CSUF programs and mentored many CSUF business students. He also has been a member of the Orange County Grand Jury, and served as a business management mentor for the Service Corps of Retired Executives.

Fritz also developed interests in writing and publishing and has shared his capabilities with OLLI members. He is a contributor and editor of five poetry anthologies published by CLE Press (OLLI-CSUF), Published children's books, "Rollie Pollie Rap" and "Charlie's Challenge" plus other books available on Amazon.com.

Fritz's life's purpose as a retiree, "To expand my knowledge and experience with topics that were 'overlooked' in my working years and 'give back' to my community."

Fritz and his wife Cindy in Antarctica

Fritz von Coelln
Fullerton, California

To Tomorrow's Entrepreneur

I didn't know that I wanted to be an entrepreneur nor did I take college classes that would direct me in that path. It was "a step at a time" that placed me into business.

Mentors paved the way although I did not know it at the time.
- My father taught me work ethics: arrive 15 minutes early, stay 15 minutes afterwards and work hard during your shift.
- My father-in-law taught me moral ethics: do what is right, be truthful, be honest in everything you do.
- My civil engineering professor at CAL taught me process: what do you want, how do you get there, have you accomplished the task?
- My boss (my first full-time job) taught me to work outside-the-box: take on any task, learn what you need to know to achieve it, take risks to make it happen.

That first job, lasting nearly ten years, paved the way for my future in business. My boss nurtured and then set me free to flourish. It was a small company and I did everything from designing and implementing, managing people and resources to cleaning the toilets. (Yes, I cleaned toilets and maintained facilities). Subsequent jobs expanded these skills. I worked at only four companies in 43 years but within each I was promoted or moved to focus on a new responsibility.

Over and over again I stepped into a vacuum where management was weak and ineffective. I became the "fire-fighter" to improve the department or company. Once managed I recognized that it was time to move on to another aspect of the company or to another company.

My last job was with Fairchild Furniture Company. I was responsible for everything but sales. In my last year before retiring we manufactured nearly 50,000 upholstered sofas, love seats and chairs. As an owner, It was a 6 days a week, 12 hours a day enterprise—whenever I languished so did the company. If I failed at anything it was the maquiladora in Mexico that supplied our factory in Whittier, California—it lasted four years and was not cost effective so I closed it before I retired. If I failed to be the most efficient manager it was my concern for my employees—I believed that they were my most important resource. At my retirement party I was told that they called me "poppy" (father) behind my back. The company went bankrupt after I left because, in my mind, they were concerned only with the bottom line.

Entrepreneurial vs. an entrepreneur. I guess I am in the former category since I never started a business on my own. I bought into the furniture factory so I experienced ownership: the challenges, the headaches, the rewards. I was passionate about my work. I loved it!

297

Micro Biz Coach®

Nicole Washington, M.S. is the owner of Micro Biz Coach®. The company works with micro and small business owners.

Nicole identifies strategies that ensure a successful business start-up or boost a veteran business owner's bottom line. She successfully works with business executives to leverage their business acumen and networks in order to fulfill their life's passion.

Micro Biz Coach® focuses on educating the micro and small business owner to leverage various aspects of internet technology in their business operations in order to maximize efficiency and to effectively compete with larger companies. Its clients have been featured on CNBC, Fox Business News, TheStreet.com and a host of Clear Channel radio stations.

Nicole has nearly 20 years of systems integration experience, including systems implementation, design and programming from her previous career with Ernst & Young, Whittman Hart, and MarchFirst management consulting firms. As a management consultant, she worked with several Fortune 500 clients including Sprint, Williams Corporation and Nationwide Insurance. She is the author of an ebook titled, <u>Best Kept Secrets of Internet Business</u>.

Nicole is also the founder and CEO of Nicole's Naturals® Inc. (Est. 2014). Nicole's Naturals is a gluten free food manufacturing company specializing in the development of gluten free grain products with the texture and taste of traditional gluten products.

Nicole is a member of the Ohio TechAngel Fund, the 2nd largest Angel Investor Network in the United States, where she served as the due diligence team technology lead for several years. She was also a member of the Ohio Women's Business Advisory Roundtable

Nicole currently serves as Chair of the Academic Committee and Trustee of the Board of Education for Samueli Academy, a Science Technology Engineering & Mathematics (STEM) high school that services a large population of underserved youth. She is also an Entrepreneur in Residence at California State University Fullerton.

Dear Founder:

Welcome to the world of entrepreneurship and the network of those who impact society in a significant way. It's bound to be an adventure!

Let me start by helping you understand **why the journey you are embarking upon will matter**. If you have been of working age during any part of the past decade, you have no doubt heard about the job crisis in the United States and ultimately around the globe. Have you ever stopped to think about where jobs come from and what a job means to most people? Jobs are created by the establishment of companies, organizations or governments that have a need for services and/or products. When you create a company, you create a job – an entity that not only allows people to use their skills and talents to provide for themselves and their families, but in many cases also gives people a sense of self worth or usefulness. If you have been unfortunate enough to experience the devastation of communities without jobs, you know how important this contribution is to society. Sadly, it is only one of the many challenges to society that are upon us: feeding the billions of people that will join us on the planet is just a few short years; finding ways to create enough energy to economically supply the world with the modern lifestyle we are accustomed to…just to name a few. We need innovators to create solutions to these grand challenges. You are the job creator; the innovator.

As you start your entrepreneurial journey, you should **begin with the end in mind**. Imagine to yourself what your new venture should look like when it becomes the success you have planned. Would you like to sell your venture to a strategic buyer? Do you want to have an Initial Public Offering (IPO) like Google or AveXis? (I've mentioned one company that is quite famous and one not so well known to remind you that many IPOs go unnoticed by the average person.) Or is your idea of a successful venture one that you can use to provide a more than adequate income for you and your family and jobs for many others for years to come? Once you are clear on what you'd like your outcome to be, you can find other companies or founders who have built something similar and use those as your model. But like my grandmother use to say, you will take what you can use from them and disregard the rest.

You've probably heard many times over, how this journey of entrepreneurship will not be easy and how you'll have many challenges and problems to solve along the way. If I consider my own path of building a retail company especially while trying to maintain a service-based venture, I would certainly agree with this age-old assessment. But there are **some things that will make your path much smoother**. Above all, you should understand why you have chosen this path or as some may say, why this path has chosen you. Your why helps you establish the fortitude needed to persevere when seemingly insurmountable challenges arise. Don't pursue the journey alone, but rather surround yourself with networks of like-minded entrepreneurs and those that support entrepreneurs. Good networks will help you remember, you are not the only one experiencing challenges and they may even help you find the resources that become the solutions to some of your biggest problems. Finally, make sure you have a business plan of some sort – not necessarily the 25 page document you hear about (or the one you created in your business class) – but even a one to two pager that gives you some indication of major milestones (steps that make up the pathway to your larger goal) and metrics (how you will know when your goals are met). Milestones and metrics keep you accountable to growing & developing (e.g. staying in business!). When you are not consistently hitting your metrics, that is an indication of a pivot opportunity.

Famous last words: don't be afraid to pivot. Pivot is not failure or defeat but an opportunity to put your business on a trajectory that will yield a more positive outcome. It's also a backup plan for the unexpected.

Thank you for taking the leap of faith that is often required to make such a contribution to our society, our country, our world.

All the Best on Your Journey……. *Nicole W.*   CEO/Founder

Real Estate Investment Start-up

Shawn Way is a 2012 California State University Fullerton alumnus. He majored in Psychology and minored in Entrepreneurship. He has been the co-owner and property manager for Way Properties since 2006. To supplement his income while in college, Shawn set up an LLC to day trade in futures' markets.

Shawn won the first CSUF Business Plan Competition in 2012 with his business Tank Skinz. Unfortunately a bad deal with an investor caused Tank Skinz to go into too much debt and Shawn was forced to close it down. He signed on as an Executive Licensed Lending Officer with the Loan Depot. Shawn began searching for his next venture.

Soon, Shawn co-founded B&W Investment Group, LLC with another CSUF graduate Todd Bruno. B&W is a real estate investment company designed to acquire single family and multi-family rental properties in California & Arizona. It purchases homes that need a little TLC, (some need a lot of TLC). The cofounders then renovate the properties themselves and rent them out.

It all started with their first investment property in Arizona which they purchased in December of 2013 in a foreclosure auction. They did not have the funds to buy the home and did not qualify for a conventional loan. Still, they knew that somehow they would buy this house. They scraped together every penny they had (approximately $5,000 combined) to come up with a down payment and made an offer on the house. Shawn recalls, "Miraculously they accepted our offer, we then asked every person we knew for a loan. Almost 100 people turned us down." Finally, days before closing they got a hard money loan at a high interest rate from a friend to purchase the home.

About ten months later another auction came up with another deal that was too good to pass up. The cofounders did not have the money to buy it. However, Shawn did not want to lose the deal so he put the down payment on his personal credit card. The cofounders then had 30 days to figure out how to get a loan so Shawn would not lose the $5,000 down payment. They made a deal with a friend/investor who gave some money and co-signed on the mortgage. Once they completed renovations, they refinanced and pulled cash out to pay off the investor.

Their third property was purchased using the remaining cash they had left over from refinancing the second house. At this point a local bank deemed them established enough to qualify for a loan. Currently B&W owns a five-unit apartment building in California with long-term rentals and three single family homes in Arizona which are short-term vacation rentals. The cofounders are currently looking for more investment properties.

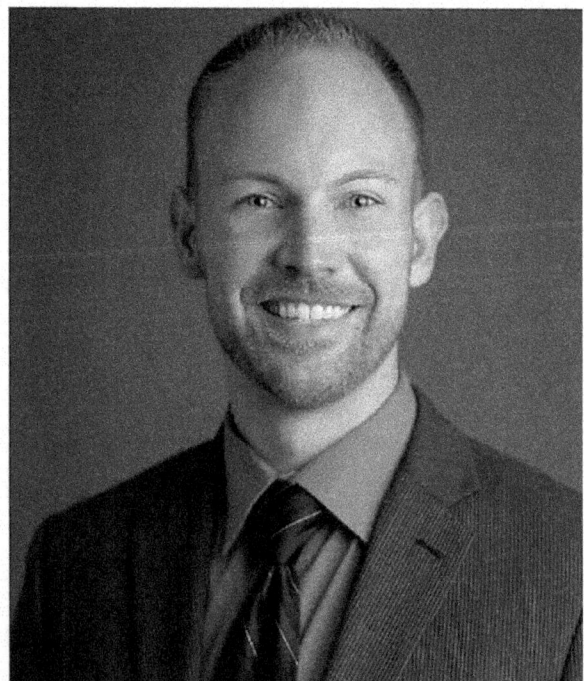

Shawn Way
San Juan Capistrano

Dear Founder,

Get it in writing

My two largest business mistakes were because I did not "get it in writing." The first was right out of college after I won CSUF's 1ˢᵗ Annual Business Plan Competition for my business, Tank Skinz. I was introduced to an investor out of Las Vegas, NV. He agreed to invest $100,000 to get my business up and running and I thought I hit the jack pot! He flew me out to Vegas and we made an agreement, I quit my job, I was going to move out there and set up shop in some office space that he owned. Long story short, I did not get this "agreement" in writing and I ended with no job, no investor and tons of debt.

The second time was with my real estate business, B&W Investment Group, LLC. My business partner & I needed additional financing to purchase another property and reached out to a friend of ours who had the money. We made an "agreement" to add him on title and when we could pay him back we would give him a percentage of the profits and he would be removed from title. I figured since it was a friend I didn't need any official documentation and a hand shake would be good enough. Boy was I wrong! Long story short he ended up gouging us for double the percentage we initially agreed to and we are no longer friends.

ALWAYS set goals and reward yourself for setting that goal

It is extremely important that you set benchmarks and goals along the way and it is equally important that you reward yourself when achieving those goals. The reward can be anything, go out to a fancy dinner at Ruth's Chris Steak House, buy yourself a new watch, or new rims for your car, etc. I really started achieving huge success when I put tangible goals in front of myself and rewarded myself with something that I really wanted. Make sure the goal is good enough that you will put the extra effort in and work +13 hour days to receive the reward.

Define your "why"

When starting a business and setting goals make sure you have an underlying reason why you're doing it and why you want to succeed. What is your purpose? What is the underlying purpose of what you're doing? Just a pointer, "to make a lot of money" or "to be rich" is not a "why." If you are unsure of your "why" do yourself a favor and think about it deep and hard. If you still do not understand exactly what a "why" even is, Google it. Once you have defined your "why," you will see your business grow much larger than you could have imagined.

Don't get distracted along the way with new ideas that do not benefit your main goal

This is a piece of advice I got from reading some of Robert Kiyosaki's books. I have been temped many times along the way by friends or fellow entrepreneurs who have come up with new business ideas and want me to be a part of it. In the beginning I was like a dog seeing a squirrel and running in any direction that would get me rich quicker, or at least what appeared to get me rich quick. These new business ideas just ended up distracting me and taking away from my primary business. If these new ideas do not directly benefit your main business goals than just let it go. Don't get caught up in it, there's always going to be the next greatest idea. Focus on your business and your goals and always remember WHY you're doing it.

Sincerely,

Shawn Way

Stellar Engineering

Bruce Welch is President of Stellar Engineering (SE). He founded the company in 1985. SE is a full service computer numerical control ("CNC") machine shop in Anaheim, California. It specializes in precision CNC machining for the aerospace, oil and automotive aftermarket industries.

SE has full conventional capabilities, a modern tool room and dedicated area to store materials. Its full service engineering staff is experienced and ready to handle clients' R & D challenges, and all facets of CNC machining, milling and turning. SE routinely routes work through logical work cells in order to "synchronize multiple operations," maintaining a competitive edge in the industry. The result is lower cost without compromising quality. SE's professional machinists are accustomed to working with exotic metals i.e. titanium, inconel, composites, plastic, ferrous and non-ferrous metals as well as castings and forgings.

Bruce has been a Small Business Institute student consulting client and is a friend of CSUF Entrepreneurship. He is a native Californian that has lived in Orange County since he was four years old. Bruce attended Fullerton College and California State University Fullerton but left before finishing his business degree to go to work in the family business.

Bruce is an avid fisherman. He also enjoys horseback riding and rooting for the Lakers NBA basketball team.

STELLAR ENGINEERING

Dear Founder,

Starting a business is easy. Fill out a few forms, pay a few fees and you're in business. Create a viable, profitable, growing business? Not so easy. Many obstacles and mistakes can plague the process. I will point out a few areas that I know you should address. First, cash is king. Nothing kills a business quicker than insufficient cashflow. Second, develop relationships with customers, employees and suppliers, they are your lifeblood. Third, there will be tough days, tough weeks, tough months and maybe even tough years. Don't be discouraged easily.

Cash is King. It is the fuel that drives the engine of your business. Plan carefully to make sure that your business is funded properly. Count on rainy days. Reinvest in the business to make it grow. However, plan the expenditures carefully so that your plans for growth don't end up stunting your operation. New equipment, people or inventory are nice but make sure that the cash is there to fund the growth while the new assets pick up steam and pay for themselves. Also, make sure that you have enough market visibility and confidence to know that the growth is warranted.

Develop Relationships with People. Do so whether they are customers (most important), employees or suppliers. The late author and motivational speaker Zig Zigler said, "You can have everything in life you want if you will just help enough other people get what they want". Our largest customer today came to us because of us doing a small favor for a friend of mine. He was an engineer at this particular large aerospace firm. From a sales standpoint the favor was small. But we got him out of a jam and he told other engineers about us. We did work for them and today that initial small relationship has turned in to a huge part of our current sales and future growth potential. The same goes for suppliers and employees. You need people on your side. Treat them well because they are important. Value them. More times than not they will reciprocate. Anybody with a fist full of dollars can buy equipment, inventory and raw materials. It's the people who make it happen on all levels.

Don't be Discouraged Easily. In the words of Winston Churchill, "Never, never, never give up." Common sense needs to come in to play here but the message is, never let the bastards get you down. There will be days you will be discouraged and want to throw in the towel. Don't make decisions based upon emotion. Thomas Edison said "Our greatest weakness lies in giving up. The most certain way to succeed is always to try just one more time". I have been through some tough times in my business life and I always believed tomorrow would be a better day. It's what gets you up the next morning.

Remember, cash is king. Develop relationships with customers, employees and suppliers. Don't be discouraged easily. I hope you find my thoughts useful. They are based upon my beliefs and my experiences. Others may have different viewpoints. Good luck in all your future endeavors.

Bruce Welch

President
Stellar Engineering

Brand Builder

Per Welinder is a legend in the skateboard world. Swedish born, He is a professional skateboarder and two-time World Champion Freestyle Skateboarder in the 1980s. Per co-founded some of the most successful brands in the industry.

After managing his own professional career, he went on to co-found Birdhouse Skateboards with fellow skate pro superstar Tony Hawk. The brand later spawned Blitz Distribution (BD). BD is a company that designs, markets and distributes proprietary and licensed lifestyle brands. , BD's primary focus is on North American, European and select Asian markets.

Over his extensive business career, Per co-founded some of the world's most recognized skateboard and lifestyle apparel brands. They include Flip, Baker, Hook-Ups, Howe Denim and JSLV clothing.

Per is an author, industry leader, board member, sneaker and CEO. He has a Bachelor's Degree in business from CSU Long Beach and he earned his Executive MBA at the UCLA Anderson School of Management.

Per is a long time member of the Board of Directors for the International Association of Skateboard Companies (IASC). IASC is a nonprofit trade organization that represents the united voice of the skateboard industry. Its goals are to promote skateboarding, increase participation, and push skateboarding forward globally.

As an internationally known entrepreneur in the action sports industry, Per is regularly engaged to speak on the topics of brand building and startups. He has great stories to tell about what it takes to make it internationally.

In 2011, Per teamed up with longtime skateboard advocate Peter Whitley to author Mastering Skateboarding. It features high-quality full-color photo sequences of all the biggest tricks while spanning techniques and equipment for riders of every level.

Today, Per is the Managing Partner of his namesake firm Welinder. Ut is an advisor and angel investor firm with a focus on the action sports and outdoors industries. Per is based in Huntington Beach, California.

Welinder

Dear Founder,

There is no way to plan for everything that will come up on your business and career paths. Surprises will happen, some good some challenging. Looking back there's one quality that has consistently helped me to work more effectively with the success and adversity that comes with being an entrepreneur...The idea of invest in myself. Weather the wind is in your sails or you are sitting in the doldrums, take time to sharpen your skills. I don't just mean your business skills alone, I mean invest in the whole person. What's worked for me is to break this into three categories: Health, Wealth and Friendship.

HEALTH
Cardio is Food for your Brain.
Taking part in any cardio exercise is like adding energy to your inner drive. It promotes building an edge physically, mentally and emotionally. I learned early on that in order for me to be a good partner to my wife, a good father to my sons and a strong leader in business, good physical health was an essential foundation. Now, cardio can take many different forms; I have always favored the free kind. In my 20's that involved hours on end of skateboarding at ungodly hours in empty parking lots. These days I mix it up a little and include running, walking, Pilates, and my most recent favorite, the 11-minute Royal Canadian Air Force workout-it's important to have fun with it. Maintaining a simple and engaging routine has helped me to keep my body and mind sharp, resilient and better able to handle the long hours, travel and the ups and downs. Stay fit.

WEALTH
Leadership is the Super Skill.
I've found it to be the most important tool for building wealth and enriching the quality of life. What it takes to be a good leader is constantly changing so it's important to continue to develop leadership skills throughout your career. This can be as involved as getting your Master's, if you haven't already, or as simple as (re) reading a book like 7 Habits by Stephen Covey, or join Toastmasters to improve your confidence in public speaking. A big part of my effectiveness as a leader over the years has come from the ability speak with conviction and enthusiasm. Stay hungry to improve.

FRIENDSHIPS
Genuine connections are priceless.
One of my greatest joys in business has been the relationships I have made and kept over the years. It comes naturally for me to take a real interest in the people I meet. I enjoy hearing about their life, what interest them and what makes them tick. At times, I may spontaneously ping someone with an interesting story, a bit of news, or perhaps an opportunity that I see as being a good fit for them – with no expectation of getting anything in return except perhaps a "thanks for thinking of me!" The world is smaller than you think. Don't hesitate to reach out.

There is no planning for all of the things that will come up on your career path but by keeping up your health, honing your leadership skills, and maintaining a great network you can effectively handle almost anything. Investing in yourself is a lifelong journey so stay engaged, be genuine and have fun with it.

All the Best,

Per Welinder

Mixing Entrepreneurship and Sales

Michael Wilkerson, eager to make some money, started his business career at fifteen years old. He worked on a student work permit and walked to work after school. Before attending college, he worked as a Records Manager for Oneil Storage a position he kept until college graduation. Today, Michael has an exciting career with Avitus Group where he advises his clients in the areas of Accounting, Payroll, Marketing, Recruiting, Information Technology, Human Resources, Safety and Risk Management, and more.

Born and raised in Orange County California Michael studied Business at California State University Fullerton. He graduated in 2011 with a BA degree in Business -- Entrepreneurship. At CSUF Michael participated in student consulting projects that he feels prepared him for a successful career with a company like Avitus Group.

However, before connecting with Avitus Group Michael went to work in sales. During College he started work as a personal banker for Wells Fargo. After graduation he joined Carmenita Truck Center as a Commercial Account Manager. Michael learned that he was passionate about sales. His experience combined with his college consulting experience to make him an attactive candidate for his present position as a business development specialist at Avitus Group.

Founded in 1996, Avitus Group has grown from a handful of employees in a cramped office to over 300 employees across the United States and overseas. The success of Avitus Group can be attributed to the employees that work there and the value they bring to their clients as a one stop shop for all business services. The company mission, to strengthen and grow companies with a comprehensive menu of business offerings designed to simplify the complex nature of business ownership while creating a meaningful and long-lasting relationship.

Michael is passionate about business and enjoys connecting with people that share in that passion. As a CSUF Entrepreneurship Alumni, he volunteers his time as a student mentor in Entrepreneurship classes.

Michael invites anyone reading this to connect with him. You can email him at mtwilks1@gmail.com or find him on LinkedIn.

306

AVITUS GROUP

Dear Founder,

As I write to you now, I try to imagine my mindset when I was a college student. With a lack of real world business experience, it was often difficult to truly understand some of the concepts taught in the classroom. What I didn't know was that there would be many failures, life changing decisions, and personal growth opportunities that would shape my career. The advice I would like to share with you comes from personal experiences as well as those from the founders I have worked with.

Plan for some failures. Failure can be your best teacher and create a new perspective. By understanding that a failure will present itself at some point, you can eliminate your fear of it and gain a level of confidence necessary to become a successful founder. Have you ever noticed that many great quotes about failure have come from successful founders? I am not saying to pursue failures or take uncalculated risks. I challenge you to look at failure as being one step closer to success. I have failed many times, and each one of those times I learned something, grew from it, and got better. One of my greatest failures was taking a job I hated because it paid well. At that point in my life I allowed money to be my only motivation. I lost a couple years doing something I had no passion for and I struggled to find motivation every day. I eventually left that job but it wasn't until later that I realized how much I had learned from that experience. My next move was to do something I have a passion for and not only am I much happier, I am more successful. Sometimes a failed attempt at something means you are on the right path. If it was easy, everyone would be doing it. Sometimes it's a wakeup call and a sign to change direction. You will have failures in your new venture, look at them all as learning opportunities.

Find your passion. If you are starting your new venture because you want financial freedom that's great but you will never make it past all your failures if you are not passionate about what you are doing. Starting a new business is one of the most difficult things a person can take on. When you have a passion for what you are doing it brings purpose into your business and when you hire people with that same passion, you will create a powerful culture.

A successful founder knows what they are good at and hires good people or rents the expertise to fill the gaps. If you're bootstrapping your business, you may be able to get away with wearing many hats at first. However, as your business grows, so will the need to delegate the non-productive administrative obligations required to run your business.

I have the privilege of advising business owners, all from different industries with different stories and paths to their success. I have never met a business owner that didn't have a few failures and I have never met a **successful** business owner that wasn't passionate about what they do. If you take anything from this letter I hope that you have a new confidence to go out there and fail as many times as it takes to achieve your success and that your courage to fail allows you to follow your passion.

May your failures be your best teacher and your passion become your purpose.

Good Luck,

Business Development - Avitus Group

307

High Tech Entrepreneur

Tony Wong started out his life in the ultimate startup — as an immigrant. Tony's parents emigrated from Macau, China to San Francisco's Chinatown with less than $200 in their pockets and towing Tony and his two younger brothers.

His parents did not know English. The family survived but was not able to give Tony help. Tony put himself through college by working at a variety of jobs including inventory clerk, retail janitor, and as an usher at the Santa Clara fairgrounds. He was the first person in his family tree to graduate from college earning a BS Degree in Marketing at Cal State Univ. East Bay and an MBA in Finance from San Jose State Univ.

When Tony graduated from college there were no jobs in the early '80s. Luckily NCR was hiring sales people through the college placement center. He applied and was offered a job... in sales of all careers; not exactly what Asian parents dream for their kids.

Tony eventually crossed over into Marketing at Hewlett-Packard and two years later was wooed by Apple. Firms on Tony's employment journey have included other Fortune 150 Companies and a startup -- Sun Microsystems, Printrak/Motorola, Gateway Computer, Black & Decker, 3M, and Firmgreen. Most of the job moves were achieved through networking.

Early in his professional career progression, Tony followed the advice received from his SJSU Real Estate Professor. He invested in real estate. Real estate investments coupled with good, practical stock market investment practices allowed Tony to retire at the age of 47.

Shortly after retiring, Tony self-published a career advice book for young professionals. He has given talks at many colleges and companies. Tony is a friend of CSUF Entrepreneurship. He has been a speaker at the CSUF Start-up Incubator and is a donor.

In 2012 , Tony co-founded BADU Networks (BADU), a software startup in Irvine. He has two partners, Dennis Vadura and Kevin Tsai. Vadura serves as CEO, Tsai as Chief Scientist and Tony as VP of Marketing. BADU is marketing a technology that accelerates wireless networks — it increases cellular and Wi-Fi speed by two to three times. BADU provides innovative software and appliance solutions that speed up network connection, reduce web page load times, optimize enterprise applications and optimize user traffic across the Internet.

August 18, 2017

Dear Founder,

I have three items to share from my run as a high tech entrepreneur — one is a must-have, one is a should-have, and one is a total mystery most entrepreneur can't help to have.

First item - get a partner or two. Why not more? You can but the logistics become burdensome so I'm suggesting just one or two. They could be co founders but don't have to be. They don't have to be with you for the entire journey. I think a must-have is to have a partner or two from the very beginning. Your significant other does not count. If you could choose the partner attributes, your partners must have money or connection to money and at least one should be technical. If that partner is a computer pro grammer you scored major bonus points. It's a long, lonely journey that requires way more skills, abili ties, tasks, and emotional support than anyone can imagine — and last bit about emotional support answers the question in your head, "why not go solo?".

Second item - you should prepare to network and sell like you've never networked and sold before. You or one of your partners better enjoy networking and selling. That's what you'll be doing for years start ing with day minus one. I've never seen an environment where the adage, "it's not <u>what</u> you know, but <u>who</u> you know" aids in success and reduces the odds of failure more. Networking is closely related to selling. Guess what fundraising is? It's a little of both on steroids.

Last item - recognizing a pivot moment and what to do about it. All I can do is describe the most anx ious, frustrating part about entrepreneurship — that fine line between being fixated on not deviating and when to pivot. I know all about the studies and advice about how startups must focus and be per sistence. I've heard and understood all about the process — to create an MVP (minimum viable prod uct), get feedback, make adjustments, do it again and again, and so on. Good process, I think this works but for a very narrow product/service. I don't think it works so cleanly for products/services we all dream of that is going to disrupt a market and change the world. To change the world, it's just NOT that easy, low cost, and quick. There are no clear signals as to when that line is reached and must be crossed. It's al ways easy looking back. Numerous successful and failed entrepreneurs tell stories about how clear the fork on the road was when looking back. They all agree IT ISN'T THAT OBVIOUS WHEN YOU'RE IN THE MIDDLE OF THE JOURNEY. There are so many competing and compelling forces. Even if you see a need to pivot, there's no obvious answer to "what to pivot to". My only advice is to get opinions and obser vation from lots of people and be open minded.

Good luck, enjoy the ride. Don't hold grudges against those who did NOT invest. And give back after you reach the top of the mountain.

Sincerely,

Tony Wong

Aidtree, Inc.

Benjamin Yip founded Aidtree, Inc. in 2012. He spent four years developing a philanthropic website platform/app. It enables coupon buyers to use their smart phones to purchase coupons, like they might do on Groupon. However, at Aidtree 70-90% of the coupon purchase price goes to the buyer's charitable cause and only the remainder goes to Aidtree.

Before founding Aidtree, Ben was an investment banker. He worked at a firm that was in the business primarily of raising capital for companies, governments and other entities.

In 2016 Ben came to the CSUF Start-up Incubator looking for help with Aidtree. He wished to turn his website and smart phone app into a viable business.

When Ben brought Aidtree to the CSUF Startup Incubator, it was in the minimum viable product (MVP) stage of development. (Similar to the alpha version of an inventor's product or service) He was trying to evolve his MVP to satisfy the early users of Aidtree. He knew the company was not at a stage where he could bring it to the investment banking community. The Incubator helped him to develop his MVP into a more functional offering. Ben recalls, "The Incubator helped me transition my [MVP] into an actual business with implementation guidance and positive support from my advisors. They were unlike a lot of other venture firms. They asked, 'how can we help?' That was very refreshing."

Once Ben joined the CSUF Startup Incubator, his advisors helped him put his efforts into overdrive. The Incubator experience helped Ben in six major ways: working with Ben to understand his market, conducting a top down review of his website, helping him with writing a business plan, conducting long interviews with potential users of his platform, creating a business model canvas and helping Ben form strategic partnerships on campus.

A key partnership is with the CSUF Philanthropic Foundation. The Foundation automatically deposits funds from Aidtree for a CSUF club or charity into the cause's account. This means no checks or tracking for cause leaders. This also allows CSUF causes to continuously raise funds in between their usual events.

As of this writing, Aidtree has successfully launched a soft rollout in the Fullerton area. The company is working on adding more businesses, causes and users to the site.

Ben has been a student consulting project sponsor, He has utilized several interns from CSUF and Troy High School. He also has personally donated time and money to CSUF causes.

SAVE MONEY. SUCCEED LOCALLY.

Dear Founder,

When doing a start-up venture there are many thoughts you'll have to consider. These thought processes range from the theoretical to functional. The points I've enclosed are to address what you, the reader, should consider today. This takes in account you are at the foundation considering your start-up or you have been working on your business and are not past the point of no return financially.

1.Know your business vertical - If you wish to create any type of business, make sure you know all the small nuances regarding this process. If you don't you will make mistakes that will be time consuming and expensive. Knowing the sector of your business focus will streamline creating your business model and bringing your idea to market.

2. The speed of your success may be a reflection of the pedigree of your team - Work with people that have a history of success in the business sectors related. These individuals should leverage your strengths and fill in the gaps of your weaknesses.

3. Early movers get the worm - If you pick a business sector for your start-up that has zero or low market penetration your idea will become the de facto standard. The key factor to that is to be nimble and move quickly.

When I started Aidtree (in essence a coupon platform for donations) I called upon my previous career in investment banking (how general internet businesses were modeled). Then I leveraged my experience with non-profits and my children's school to learn philanthropic funding practices. Finally, networking with people in the technology industry gave me the ability to believe in my idea. All of this was instrumental in creating the Aidtree platform.

I hope this helps with a slight insight on the basic steps for creating your future success.

Best Regards,

Benjamin Yip
Head Nut, Aidtree.com

Serial Student Consulting Client

Woody Young has had interests in over 15 companies that improve people's lives. The companies are diverse. They range from organic biofertilizers and server hardware to improved NASA technologies used in the tallest building in the world, hospitals and five star resorts. Woody's companies have been CSUF Student Consulting clients seven times.

Woody was already a highly successful entrepreneur by the time he graduated from The Ohio State University in the 1960s. IBM recruited him for its Young Executive Program straight out of college, followed by time at Kidder Peabody on Wall Street.

After moving to California, Woody started Young's Evergreen Nursery Company in 1976. He revolutionized how the landscaping industry met the needs of high end hotels and movie sets.

In 1982 Woody took over the California Clock Company, home to the iconic 1930s Kit Cat Klock®, the bestselling clock in US history. Since Woody has been president, Kit-Cat has been seen billions of times on TV, movies, and in music videos. Woody was featured on a float in the 2012 Pasadena Rose Parade® to celebrate Kit-Cat's 80th anniversary.

In 2004 Woody started Street Surfing®. He brought the globally popular "Wave Board" to market for the first time selling millions of caster boards worldwide.

Around the same time, Woody invested in Air Oasis® LLC becoming the Chairman of the Board. He led the company to become the global leader in air sanitization technology.

Woody has authored or co-authored over 30 published books. He was the executive producer for the movie Dog Jack.

Woody has received many awards over the years. They include the National Publisher of the Year, the California Nurseryman of the Year and the Golden Microphone.

Woody has served as a Promise Keepers Ambassador for over twenty years. The Promise Keepers Ambassador program is for serious men who want to make a big difference. He is a long time member of Mariners Church in Newport Beach, California.

Dear Founder,

After 5 decades of starting and growing companies I've learned more than a few things along the way. However, I can honestly say that nothing has been more important to my success than **integrity of character**.

"Trust is like the air we breathe. When it's present, nobody notices. But when it's absent, everybody notices."

--Warren Buffett

Since people trust me, they want to do business with me. It's the Speed of Trust. My strategic partners are eager to work with me. My vendors give me extended credit terms and service because they know I'm going to pay and follow through on commitments. My employees are willing to follow my leadership on big visions. You're fooling yourself if you don't work with integrity. Your reputation will catch up with you - for better or worse.

Three other qualities come to mind that have had a great impact on my success:

1. **The curiosity of a 5 year old.** It's paramount that you're constantly curious about discovering new things and how you can improve. Let your curiosity guide you to think differently and explore solutions that no one else has ever considered. This leads to innovative cutting edge companies. Curiosity is also why I'm still doing what I'm doing today and enjoying it. Curiosity goes hand and hand with continuous Self-Education. As an entrepreneur, whatever industry you go into, find the 10 best books on that industry and read them cover to cover. Really study it yourself. Become an expert by learning all you can from the existing industry experts. If you're really serious about what you're doing, you have to study your field seriously.

2. **People first mindset.** You can't continue to help other people without eventually being helped yourself. If you're genuinely seeking to help your customers, employees, vendors, and partners it's going to benefit you in the long run. But this mindset is not limited to business. In all aspects of your life think how you can serve and improve your community, activity groups, church, town, etc. This is the true spirit of entrepreneurship and it's this "people first mindset" which has led me to build many successful ventures.

3. **Basic business principals.** Many business principals transcend industry and technology. Some of my greatest successes have been built by sticking to rudimentary accounting, management and marketing principals. In contrast, I've seen thriving companies, that I had vested interest in, collapse from cash flow issues, incorrect margins, or poor legal agreements. Pitfalls which could have been avoided by staying true to solid principals. You're only creating headaches for yourself if you ignore them.

As a final note, one of the biggest mistakes that entrepreneurs make, myself included, is that we underestimate the cost and time it takes to achieve a vision. In my experience, "it" usually takes a lot longer than I expect. There will always be bumps in the road.

Perseverance, resiliency, and adaptability will be essential to your long-term success.

Kind regards,

Woody Young
Managing Partner, the Young Trust

Success Is Your Choice

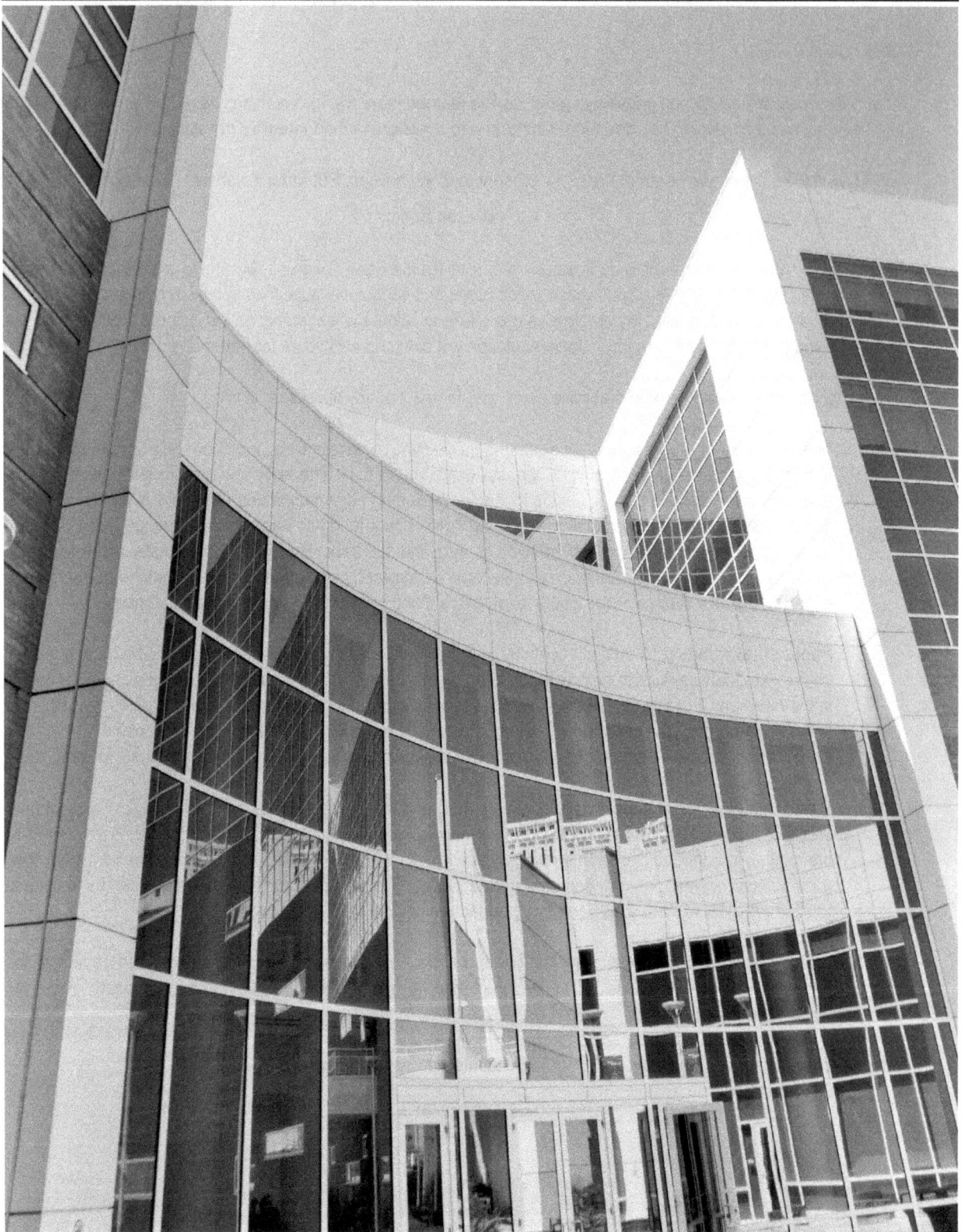

www.ingramcontent.com/pod-product-compliance
Lightning Source LLC
Chambersburg PA
CBHW051115200326
41518CB00016B/2510